WORD PROCESSING
WITH YOUR MICROCOMPUTER

No. 1478
$19.95

WORD PROCESSING
WITH YOUR MICROCOMPUTER

BY L. R. SCHMELTZ

TAB BOOKS Inc.

BLUE RIDGE SUMMIT, PA. 17214

FIRST EDITION

FIRST PRINTING

Library of Congress Cataloging in Publication Data

Schmeltz, L. R.
  Word processing with your microcomputer.

  Includes index.
  1. Word processing (Office practice) 2. Micro-
computers.   I. Title.
HF5548.115.S35   1982   652   82-5906
ISBN 0-8306-2478-3   AACR2
ISBN 0-8306-1478-8 (pbk.)

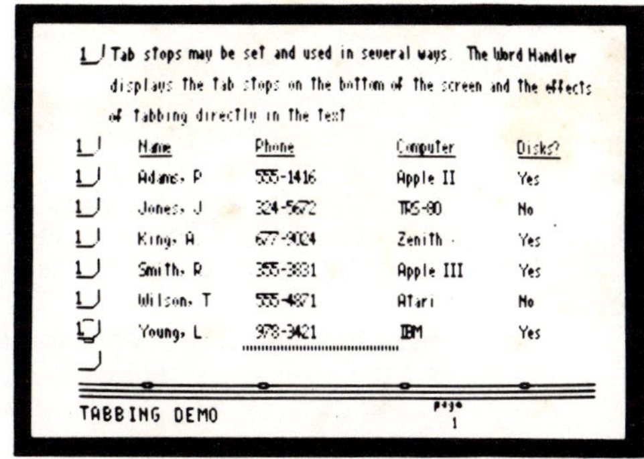

Contents

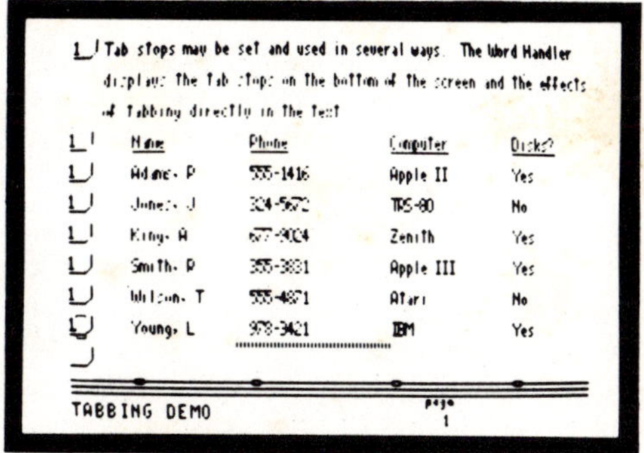

Preface

Word processing is a "hot topic" in microcomputing circles. Computer manufacturers and program suppliers devote a lot of advertising space and dollars to promoting this application for small computers. Computer-oriented publications are loaded with program reviews, hardware evaluations, and application ideas. Computer store shelves are crammed with programs, each promising greater sophistication than the others.

"What, write a whole book about word processing with microcomputers?" was my reaction when the idea was first mentioned to me. I couldn't imagine an entire book devoted to a topic I felt was really rather cut and dried. After all, hadn't I been using a word-processing program with my own computer for some time? How could anybody not know about this marvelous new application for personal computers?

After some thought, it occurred to me that not everyone is willing to buy a program for experimental purposes. The field of microcomputing has grown considerably since I made my first investment in a word-processing program for my then new personal computer. Although I have progressed through several more word-processing programs, each more sophisticated than the last, I never cease to marvel at the versatility afforded by relatively inexpensive programs.

Even after I decided to write this book, some practical problems remained. How do you explain a topic that encompasses so many features and capabilities? Isn't sitting at a computer and trying a program the best way to learn about it? How can you recreate in print the dynamic experience of actually using a program? Is anyone really interested in taking the time necessary to learn about word processing?

Many of my questions have been answered in contacts with other computer owners. I find the level of interest in word-processing applications exceedingly high and the level of confusion equally high. With all the claims and counterclaims permeating the marketplace, how does one make a rational decision?

What evolved from these discussions and questions follows. I have made a real effort to give you an honest feel for the field of word processing with microcomputers. My extensive use of photographs should serve as a substitute for sitting at a computer and trying each program. A lot of the advertising "hype" has been eliminated, and serious questions are posed for you to answer. I hope you find the answers to your questions about word processing within these pages.

Producing a book like this is by no means a one-man effort. In spite of the fact that my name appears as the author, many people were involved in the actual nitty-gritty groundwork necessary to assemble it. At the risk of leaving someone out, I would like to offer my heartfelt thanks to the people and companies involved.

The program suppliers mentioned throughout the book have been most generous in providing copies of programs, documentation, and information for presentation here. In every instance, I have received their complete cooperation and support for these efforts. Suppliers of printers, peripherals, and accessories have been equally generous in providing timely information regarding their products. Although photographs and materials are acknowledged at various places in the text, another hearty "thank you" must be given to those who offered their complete cooperation to this effort.

Memory Bank (Bettendorf, Iowa) rescued me from a chronic printer failure, repaired my computer with unprecedented haste, and provided a level of support that is unheard of in this age of indifference. My thanks, and most of my funds for buying computer supplies, go to them at every opportunity.

Finally, I would like to thank my family for their understanding and support when I disappeared downstairs to work on "the book" every evening.

I hope you enjoy reading this book as much as I enjoyed writing it. Experimenting with many new programs and looking at some of the old ones that were new to me was a very interesting experience. If you reach the end of the book with some definite ideas in mind, both our efforts will have been adequately rewarded!

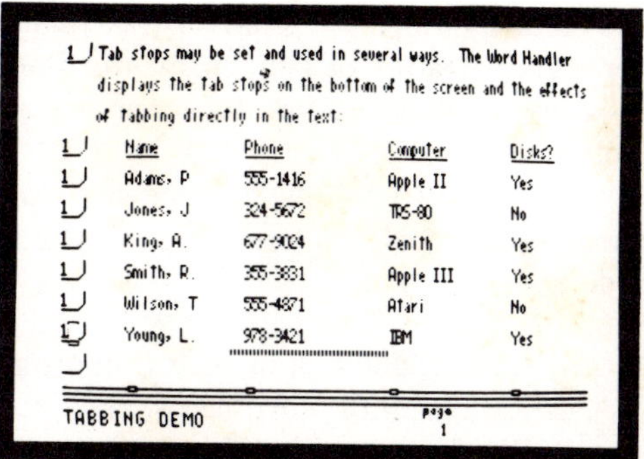

Tab stops may be set and used in several ways. The Word Handler displays the tab stops on the bottom of the screen and the effects of tabbing directly in the text:

Name	Phone	Computer	Disks?
Adams, P	555-1416	Apple II	Yes
Jones, J	324-5672	TRS-80	No
King, A.	677-9024	Zenith	Yes
Smith, R.	355-3831	Apple III	Yes
Wilson, T	555-4871	Atari	No
Young, L.	978-3421	IBM	Yes

TABBING DEMO   page 1

Introduction

Contrary to popular opinion, you do not need to be a computer expert to intelligently select and efficiently use a word-processing system. Many publications are available for those who are willing and able to consider an elaborate word-processing system. My efforts here are directed toward defining the role of microcomputer-based word processing for small business, personal, and professional applications.

This book looks at word processing primarily from the user's point of view. It emphasizes potential applications you may have for a word-processing system and attempts to integrate the equipment and programs in that context. In keeping with this emphasis, technical jargon and buzzwords are kept to an absolute minimum. Where it is necessary to use specific terms, plain English definitions are provided in the text. The illustrations help to clear up any points of confusion. Throughout this guide I call upon my own experience to help you understand areas that you may find confusing.

Prior to acquiring an Apple II microcomputer more than three years ago, my primary exposure to word processing was watching in wonder as specially trained operators used dedicated systems and mainframe computer programs to handle many of the same chores my Apple now does with ease. Shortly after buying the computer, I invested in a word-processing program primarily on the recommendation of another Apple owner. Although I can attribute the choice primarily to the fact that the program I purchased was the only one offered at the local computer emporium, it was a good program. I have used it (and others) steadily since that time.

My primary applications for word processing are correspondence, magazine articles, and (as you may have guessed) book manuscripts. Since I use several Apple II word-processing programs, my biases most certainly are reflected in what is to follow. Wherever possible, my opinions are clearly labeled as such. Ideally, you will be able to draw your own conclusions on the basis of the information presented.

Lest you think this guide is only for owners of Apple computers, rest assured I discuss others as well. Much of the information contained here pertains to microcomputers as a group. Even the program descriptions concentrate on characteristics and features which are relatively machine independent. As a matter of fact, many word-processing programs are offered for more than one variety of microcomputer.

In order to follow a somewhat logical sequence, this guide covers topics in the following order:

1. Background and historical information
2. Rationale for word processing
3. Word processing in a global sense
4. Explanation and illustration of common features included in most word-processing systems
5. Microcomputer-based word-processing programs as a group
6. In-depth user evaluations of several programs available for the Apple II, ranging from inexpensive to very expensive
7. Illustration of small business, office, and home applications using the various programs discussed
8. Guidelines for deciding which, if any, system is suitable for your applications
9. Hardware and accessories used primarily in word-processing applications with special emphasis on printers

The illustrated Glossary provides you with a handy reference to computer and word-processing terminology. Some sources of more information will be found in Sources of Information. Some of the word-processing programs available for the more popular microcomputers are listed in the Appendix.

## Chapter 1

The Computer Revolution

The last twenty years or so have seen tremendous strides toward automating traditional office functions, and great advancements have been made in many areas. The process of committing thoughts to paper has been a difficult one to automate, however, since the variables involved are numerous and diverse.

Ever-increasing personnel costs and correspondence demands have forced businesses to look for more efficient ways to handle paperwork. Recent studies have shown the cost of a simple business letter totals nearly $6.50. Anyone who has typed a series of rough drafts, revised an entire letter for one minor change, or sent essentially the same letter to several people can see the virtue in some sort of automation. One of the by-products of the search for efficiency was the form letter. Still used to some extent, the form letter was created to eliminate the need for repetitive typing. More sophisticated versions of the form letter allowed room for the recipient's name and address to be typed in at the appropriate places.

Typewriter manufacturers responded by producing units that could type repetitive documents from paper tape or magnetic cards designed for that purpose. Sophisticated versions of the tape and magnetic card units are still found on the market today. One fatal flaw of this approach is it doesn't offer you much assistance in the initial creation of a document. Although numerous letter-perfect copies can be printed once the document is set up, any minor change can be a real problem to handle.

One major computer and office equipment manufacturer tackled the concept of automated typing and coined the phrase *word processing* that has become the standard name for an entirely new approach to the problem. Originally applied to one particular line of equipment, the term became widely used to refer to any form of automated typing. Recently, the term word processing has been used to describe a variety of equipment and computer programs intended to make the transition from thoughts to paper as efficient as possible. Early efforts at creating such a system were the province of major business equipment and computer manufacturers. First and second generation word-processing systems required extensive operator training, infinite patience, and large amounts of computer overhead to operate efficiently.

Today's programs and systems are a far cry from the early versions. Great emphasis has been placed on ease of use, efficient memory utilization, and expanded features. Small computers have taken to word-processing applications in a very big way, as you can see by looking through the advertisements in any business or computer-oriented publication. Some of the more progressive suppliers are advertising on radio and television.

If we are to believe the advertising copy, word-processing programs and small computers are absolute necessities for anyone who still uses a typewriter. Claims of greater efficiency, user friendliness, extra features, and lower cost are part of virtually every advertisement. To quote an over-used Madison Avenue phrase, "new and improved" word-processing programs are being introduced into the marketplace almost daily. Hardware, particularly printers, is in much the same situation. The variety of programs and systems available can create a maze of decisions for anyone considering some form of electronic typing assistance using a microcomputer.

THE ELECTRONIC OFFICE

Not very many years ago, most small offices consisted of a few desks, chairs, filing cabinets, typewriters, and telephones. Financial matters were handled by ledger books and adding machines, or more recently, bookkeeping monstrosities. Larger offices required more desks, more chairs, more telephones, more filing cabinets, and more typewriters. Aside from a few unique items, one office tended to look pretty much like any other.

Office personnel requirements could be determined by surveying the number of typewriters, adding machines, and telephones to be staffed. Jobs tended to take on a routine sameness regardless of the name of the company. Managers managed, secretaries took dictation and typed, bookkeepers literally kept the books, and switchboard operators handled the phones.

With the advent of the computer, many accounting functions were relegated to the data-processing department. As equipment capabilities and user experience increased, other office functions were taken over by computers. Inventory control, production scheduling, shipping, and management of personnel records rapidly became accepted functions of every sizeable company's data-processing equipment. Computer manufacturers competed viciously to produce the biggest and best hardware, much to the delight of the many who viewed their computers as status symbols of the highest order.

The computer revolution in big business resulted in some profound changes in the office structure. People with strange titles like systems analyst, programmer, operator, and key punch operator were suddenly in great demand. Equipment with multitudes of lights, keys, dials, and whirring tapes was installed in air-conditioned seclusion behind glass walls. Closed doors protected this delicate electronic behemoth from all but the select few allowed to enter its domain.

Computer operations were separated, for the most part, from the more traditional parts of the office where the desks, chairs, typewriters, and telephones still were in ample evidence. The typewriters by now were electric, and the old telephone switchboard had given way to more advanced methods of routing calls.

The last few years have seen many changes. Everybody who's anybody in the company has a terminal, application software has become considerably more user oriented, and the company computer is doing scores of chores at any one time. Today's electronic office is a far cry from those seen a decade ago. An office worker returning after several years' absence would find it hard to even identify some of the new gadgetry, much less know how to use it.

NEW BUZZWORDS

With advancing technology has come a whole new and specialized vocabulary. Of course, some old terms are still heard, but they often mean something different than they did "way back when." For example, desks are now reserved for upper management; others are placed at work stations. Hardware refers to computer equipment, not what you pick up at the store for home projects. Time sharing means something other than taking a group coffee break. In-house refers to doing something on your own computer.

Paper shufflers no longer shuffle papers; they now manage information on VDTs (video display terminals) or hard copy (a fancy term for paper). Financial modeling, once frowned on if you displayed the bare facts, projects the course of the company fiscal operations. Thimbles, fanfold, floppies, and decollators are some other terms used to describe computer-related operations.

I could continue poking fun at the new buzzwords used today. The point of this frivolity is that one must speak the language in order to understand the natives. As I delve further into the topic, which necessarily involves the use of some terminology, you will find yourself becoming more comfortable with the language of word processing.

COMPUTER SIZE

As computers have become a way of life for business and industry, more and more applications have been heaped on already overburdened hardware. The fact that most computer hardware was obsolete by the time it reached the user didn't help a lot either! For a time, the solution to this problem was simply to purchase newer, larger, and more capable computers. To some extent, this is the best solution even today.

An alternative has been provided by the small computer. Many data-processing applications are better served by several small or medium sized computers rather than one giant unit. In response to this realization, manufacturers have devoted a great deal of research and development funding to the advancement of small computer technology. The end result of these efforts can be seen in the exploding microcomputer market we have today (Fig. 1-1).

Once thought to be the exclusive province of big business, the computer has suddenly become affordable for the masses. For little more than the

Fig. 1-1. An Apple II microcomputer, two disk drives, and a video monitor are used not only for word processing but also many other applications.

price of a major appliance, you can purchase a computer with more capability than the large units of just a few years ago. Add-on peripherals can be purchased to make tiny computers perform some of the same functions (and a raft of new ones) as their gigantic ancestors (Fig. 1-2).

Application programs for business, professional, and personal uses are sold across the counter in stores that could not have existed until recently. Users are writing some of their own programs, by choice or because they are unable to locate just what they have in mind.

Microcomputers are capable of handling many diverse functions, among them word processing. In the group referred to generically as microcomputers, some are considerably more versatile than others.

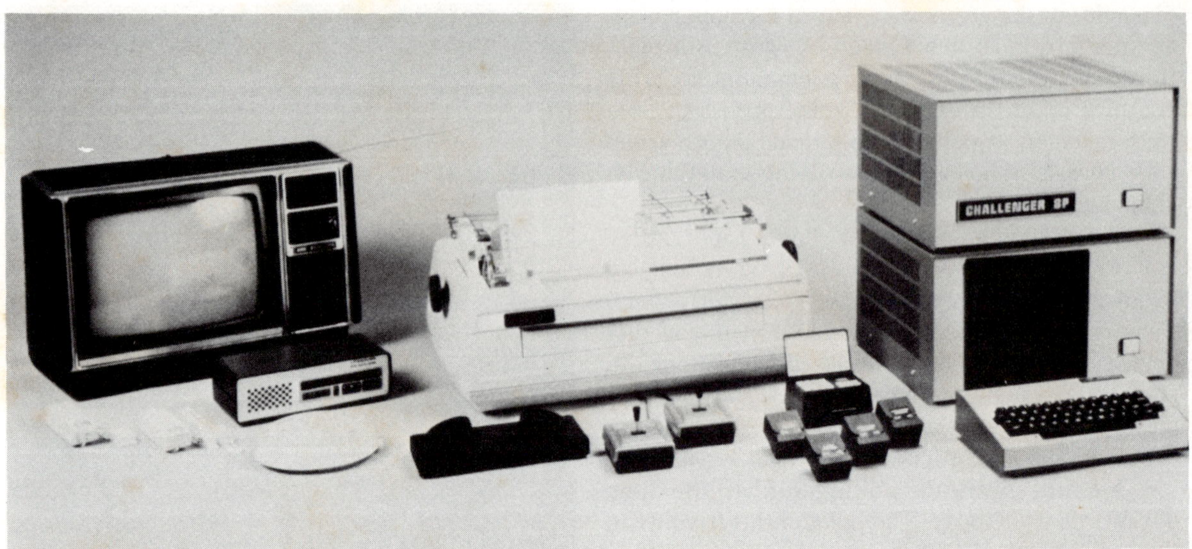

Fig. 1-2. Most microcomputers are supported by a host of available peripherals which greatly expand the computer's operational capabilities. (Courtesy of Ohio Scientific, Inc.)

WORD PROCESSING

Perhaps you have noticed that I have not yet fully defined the term word processing. It would be interesting if I could ask you what the term conjures up in your mind. As a matter of fact, every person I have asked offers a slightly different definition. This may be due to the fact that equipment and programs designated as word processors tend to vary widely in their construction and use.

Dedicated word-processing equipment is designed for only one purpose and, as such, offers the widest range of features. Programs for large mainframe computers have their distinct advantages, particularly where multiple users are involved. Microcomputer word processing presents probably the widest range of capabilities due, in large part, to the burgeoning number of programs available.

An all-encompassing definition, under these circumstances, has to be vague enough to cover all the contingencies. Although some may view word processing as simply adding intelligence to typewriters, there are many other considerations that need to be included. Perhaps the safest definition would be to say, "word processing is a computerized approach to putting words on paper in a more efficient and accurate fashion."

INFORMATION MANAGEMENT

The amount of data necessary to conduct the day-to-day operation of any business is staggering. Major corporations, particularly, have long realized the value of accurate and up-to-date information. Prior to the "computer revolution," business information tended to be very departmentalized. Each department kept the records necessary to conduct its part of the operations and reported to management on a regular basis.

The problems of departmentalized data management were readily recognized by anyone trying to obtain comprehensive current information. Just checking the status of an order or account could turn into a major project. The ever-increasing burden of paperwork decreed that a better solution be found. Inevitably, information was overlooked and not efficiently utilized in the departmentalized approach. Unless some elaborate system of filing and follow-up was developed, much of the peripheral information simply died outdated in somebody's files.

Of course, the computer has changed all that. Comprehensive and more importantly, current, information regarding any phase of the company's operations can be retrieved from the corporate computer at will. While the need for back-up paper records has not been eliminated entirely, the science of information management has made great strides in that direction.

Words are an important part of the information to be managed. Letters, reports, mailing lists, forms, and memos all find their way into the computer at some time or other. The value of efficiently handling written communication has long been recognized by any successful business.

The sum and substance of information managed by business is referred to as a *data base*, and the programs to accomplish this are referred to as *data base management systems*. The term *information management* came along later and is used to designate the total approach rather than a specific program.

Computer Networking. In the beginning of the computer revolution, each unit was pretty well self contained. Although remote terminals linked by telephone lines were utilized, the concept of one computer talking to another was still in the development stages. Part of the problem revolved around nonstandardization of operating procedures.

Early successful networking efforts revolved around the sharing of expensive peripheral equipment by more than one computer at a single location. This progressed to linking similar computers at various corporate locations by "hard wiring" dedicated telephone lines between them. The ability to share data, distribute processing chores among several computers, and use the same peripherals prompted further development of computer networks.

With the advent of standardized communication procedures, computer networks grew at a rapid pace. Incompatibility between different units and geographic distance were no longer limitations. Computer networking, like information management, has become an elaborate science providing direct benefits to the users of microcomputers. In an age when peripherals such as hard disks and elaborate printers can cost as much as several microcomputers, networking has many potential applications.

Electronic Mail. Since computers are able to "talk" with each other, it seems logical that correspondence and reports developed in one can be transmitted to and printed by another. As a matter of practical application, this substitute for mailing hard copy (printed) material is becoming very popular. In addition to eliminating the delay and potential for loss in the regular mail, this form of written communication can significantly lower the costs involved in a large volume of material.

Some computer networks are being developed just to handle electronic mail. The U.S. Postal Service is trying to get authorization to begin an electronic mail service of its own. Although the postal proposal will offer electronic mail services only between major cities, a combination of electronic and traditional mailing services has been suggested as a way of considerably speeding up the normal delivery process. Electronic mail represents a wave of the immediate future that should prove most interesting to watch.

MICROCOMPUTERS IN BUSINESS

Early users of microcomputers were quite properly branded as hobbyists, since much of the hardware and most of the programs were developed by users. Microcomputer hardware has advanced and developed at an astounding rate. Today's small computers are rapidly threatening to take over the functions of medium to large computers of a few years ago.

The development of programs (software) has had real problems keeping pace with the advancements in hardware technology. Software has changed radically in the last couple of years due, in no small part, to the demands of small business, professional, and personal users who would like some of the same data-processing capabilities that big business has enjoyed for some time. The research and development that led large business computers to handle information management, networking, electronic mail, and countless other chores has had a direct benefit for the microcomputer user, because the process of developing programs to accomplish similar functions on a microcomputer is considerably simplified.

The area of data base management, for example, has been well adapted for microcomputer use. Very capable data management programs have been written for several of the more popular microcomputers. First and second generation programs were hindered by memory and mass storage limitations. Recently, small computers with memory capacities of 256,000 bytes and sophisticated disk storage systems have been introduced. Almost immediately, data base programs to take advantage of the new memory capacity were on the market.

Other areas of computer use have shown similar developmental profiles. Surprisingly sophisticated programs for small computers offer accounting, inventory control, word processing, and numerous other capabilities.

The Future of Micros

We are in the middle of the second computer revolution—that of microcomputers. New hardware, accessories, and programs are introduced almost daily. What's state of the art today may not be tomorrow, will probably not be in six months, and most certainly will be outmoded within a couple of years. Some of the "old familiar" names are no longer in the forefront, and keeping track of new companies can be a full-time job. A whole army of second source suppliers, software houses, and support organizations have sprung up around the computer manufacturers themselves. "Old timers" in the microcomputer business have generally been around less than five years!

It is foolhardy to try to predict future developments in microcomputers. When you consider the fact that micrcomputers have been on the open market for less than 10 years, it is safe to predict that more changes will occur in the next decade. We can assume more and better hardware will be developed, as well as software to take advantage of any new capabilities introduced. Programs and systems will fall by the wayside as they become outmoded unless a conscientious effort is made to keep them current.

One of the real advantages to the use of a microcomputer is the relatively low cost of software. As new and better programs come along, upgrading your capabilities will generally not be prohibitively expensive. As you read through the sections on word-processing programs, notice the cost. Most of the programs mentioned sell for less than three hundred dollars, and even the most expensive is less than six hundred (Fig. 1-3). Sales demand for new programs and intense competition for market volume will allow, if not demand, that software suppliers keep the costs reasonable.

Management Versus Manipulation of Information

Information can be a valuable asset to any business. Similarly, applications other than business have very definite needs for information. Professional writers, educators, physicians, musicians, and others must manage significant amounts of information. Even the "hobby" computer user can locate and identify a large body of data pertaining to numerous fields of interest. We will refer primarily to business applications in this section, but keep in mind that whatever pertains to business relates equally well to other fields.

To be of significant value, information must be managed so that it will yield meaningful results. It would not be particularly useful to have a report of account aging data produced every 90 days, for instance, if your business was geared to a 30-day billing cycle. Using the same example, it would be overkill to have aging status printed daily before the 30-day cycle has expired. Optimum management in this case would be to have aging information produced along with the billing on a 30-day cycle.

Information encompasses not only data, but also numerous forms of written and verbal material. The spiraling cost and complexity of information management techniques have led to the search for more efficient (and less costly) methods. The computer has proven to be ideally suited for many information management applications. While significantly reducing the cost per unit, data-processing techniques have also opened a Pandora's box of procedures that are at best marginally useful and productive.

In any application, the amount of information management must be carefully viewed in terms of cost efficiency and final profitability. Profit, of course, can come in the form of time saved or additional dollars generated. As a rule of thumb, excessive information management becomes useless manipulation, and efficient management becomes additional profit.

While it may seem this topic is unrelated to word processing, nothing could be further from the truth. Data base management and word processing both deal with information as a primary raw material. Both require operator interaction, specialized programming, and computer overhead to run. Both can be horrendously unprofitable if used inefficiently, inappropriately, or infrequently.

WHY PROCESS WORDS?

In a field of young, dynamic, and potentially profitable as word processing, it is difficult to separate the objective rationale for its use from the subjective desire to just keep up with advancing technology. If microcomputer-based word-processing programs are to justify their existence and pay their own way, some measure of applicability to your situation must be used.

Slick television commercials, glossy magazine advertisements, and program data sheets offer a multitude of reasons why you shouldn't go another day without adding word-processing capabilities to your microcomputer. Computer store shelves are laden with the latest offerings from software houses, each proclaiming to be bigger and better than all the others. Of the reasons offered for you to buy, three of the most frequently used are:

1. Increased productivity
2. Reduced cost
3. Efficient storage

Fig. 1-3. A few of the many word-processing programs presently available for the Apple II. Programs for other popular microcomputers are readily available.

The promised increases in productivity are oriented toward the operator who will be able to eliminate repetitive typing through the use of standardized text, use preconstructed files, easily revise any document, and effortlessly correct typographical errors. Many of the skills formerly required to accomplish special applications are incorporated into the program itself. Reducing the cost per unit is promised by allowing fewer people to produce more output. Efficient storage and retrieval of documents in machine-readable form can also justify the elimination of paper draft copies by working directly from the computer display for revision, checking, typesetting, and so on. While each of these may be a valid reason for buying a word-processing program for your microcomputer, cast a jaundiced eye on the total group, because more than a few factors have been overlooked.

WHO DOES THE PROCESSING?

To paraphrase a line from some of the old comedians, wherever there is a processor there must be a processee! As I describe programs and systems, you must make many decisions based on your own situation. The first of these is "who does the processing?" Are you looking at word processing for your own use, for your secretary, or will you be hiring someone just for that purpose? Will there be multiple users involved? How often will the system be used?

Typing skills and computer sophistication are variables which must be considered before going any further with word-processing considerations. If you were to rate skills in a continuum, the top of the skill scale would be occupied by a specially trained word-processing typist who has had extensive experience with microcomputer hardware. The other end of the scale would be occupied by the new computer owner, hunt-and-peck typist who has no idea how the finished product should look.

Most of us fall somewhere between the two extremes in the skill scale. At the time I acquired my first word-processing program, I had owned my Apple II for several months and possessed slightly above average typing skills. Still, the transition was an interesting learning experience. If you have yet to learn about your computer, possess marginal (if any) typing skills, or don't really know what you will do with a word-processing program, plan on a lengthy transition period before the letter-perfect documents promised in the advertisements come spewing forth.

To repeat: Look carefully at your own skill levels if you plan to use the word-processing program yourself. If someone else will be the primary user of the program, it would be prudent to get them involved in the initial selection process.

If you plan to be the primary user of a word-processing program, another variable must be considered. The value of your time must be included in the projected operating costs of a system. Could you spend your time more efficiently (and profitably) in other pursuits and leave the word processing to someone else? It hardly makes sense for the owner of a small business to put more emphasis on typing letters than dealing with customers. A lawyer can make more money by seeing new clients than producing contract copies. Word processing can be efficient and extremely useful, but not if you are being "penny wise and pound foolish" and trying to economize by saving the few bucks it would cost to have some things typed. If, on the other hand, you can demonstrate efficient use of your time, by all means proceed with your plans.

In my case, I find that my word-processing system allows me to be more creative and flexible in my writing activities. Composing rough drafts has never been a favorite activity with me, so doing it on the computer has eliminated many steps leading to the production of a final copy. This has enabled me to save a great deal time and effort. A profitable use of my time? Definitely!

The Idealized Picture of Word Processing

Advertisements for word-processing systems or programs tend to present an idealized picture of what is actually happening. I am constantly amused by the 8-by-10-inch glossy ads that feature an impeccably attired young lady effortlessly pulling text from here, there, and everywhere and producing a veritable flood of flawlessly printed copies simply by pushing one little button (Fig. 1-4). There's not a

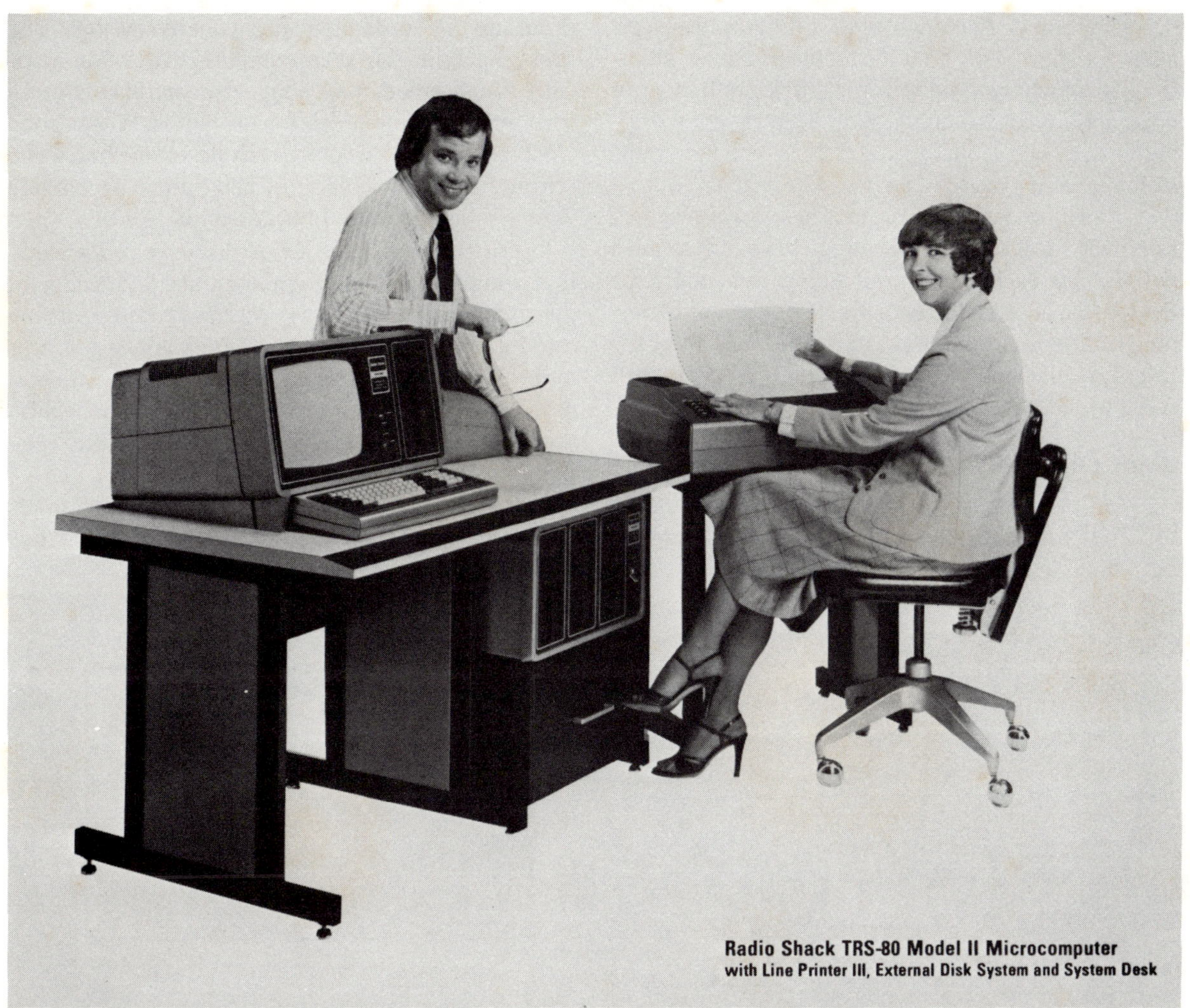

Fig. 1-4. Microcomputer systems used for word processing are rarely found in this ideal environment. The system pictured here however, is a very capable one for word processing applications. (Courtesy of Radio Shack, a division of Tandy Corp.)

speck of clutter anywhere. No worn out ribbons, stacks of overdue papers, floppy disk storage cases, boxes of paper—nothing! The implication must be that the computer, in it's uncluttered fashion, needs only the slightest twinge of attention from its fashion-plate operator.

The grim reality of the situation is this: Word-processing programs and systems are tools! Sure, the hard work of producing documents is made easier with the proper tools but it is still w-o-r-k. If you view your microcomputer and word-processing programs as a means to an end, rather than the end

itself, your perception will be far more accurate than what is shown in 8-by-10 glossy.

Are Typewriters Obsolete?

Numerous magazine articles and word-processing program advertisements imply that you can now throw away your typewriter and jump into the word-processing revolution without so much as a backward glance. Speaking strictly from personal experience, I have found that it often takes longer to set up the word-processing system than it does to just go ahead and type a short, simple letter. Addressing one or two envelopes, filling in forms, or adding a short reply to a letter received are situations in which the typewriter is still king. If most of your applications involve short letters, a few envelopes, or occasional typing chores, you may want to leave your typewriter right where it is.

Word-processing programs are to typewriters as power saws are to hand saws. There is a definite purpose for each, and you need the right tools for the job. To answer the question posed at the beginning of this section, typewriters are far from obsolete. It is also possible to use a single unit for both word processing and low-volume typing.

WHAT DOES THE PROCESSING?

"Microcomputer-based word-processing system" is an elaborate name for a single-purpose program that is loaded into your computer. The basic capabilities of your computer are not dramatically transformed into a magical means of solving all your written communication problems. What a good word-processing program will do is maximize the strengths of your computer and find an acceptable way to minimize any limitations.

For the purposes of this discussion, I assume that you have at least a rudimentary knowledge of microcomputers and are interested in learning more about word-processing applications for your unit. If you are just starting to look into the field of personal computers, you should read one of the many excellent references now available (see Sources of Information for a few ideas).

If you have a microcomputer that is functional for more than the demonstration programs fur-

Fig. 1-5. To convert a basic Apple II into a capable word-processing system, some additional hardware is needed. A printer is, of course, the most obvious necessity.

nished with it, chances are you won't need much more hardware for successful word-processing program use (Fig. 1-5). The information sections describing the various programs outline additional hardware requirements for each. The last chapter of this book will discuss in some detail additional hardware you may want to consider if yours is a "bare bones" computer.

As you read the following, keep in mind that word processing is only one of many possible applications for your microcomputer. Although this may sound strange in a book devoted to the topic, you'll be surprised at all the other functions your computer is capable of handling if you give it a chance.

I will discuss word processing from several perspectives and recommend different selection approaches based on the amount of time and energy you are willing to spend. Hopefully, by the time you finish this book you will be able to select and effectively use a word-processing system that fits your potential applications while allowing room for future expansion.

You may wish to look over the information in the next couple of chapters and then skip to the section on applications. If you can find several of your projected applications described and illustrated, one type of program may be of greater interest to you than the others. Keep in mind that the programs described are presently available for the Apple II (and, in many cases, other computers), but specific details are presented primarily to help you sort out the features that may be of interest to you in considering word processing for your own situation. Since this is a user-oriented approach to word processing, feel free to accept those ideas pertinent to you and discard others which may not be of help.

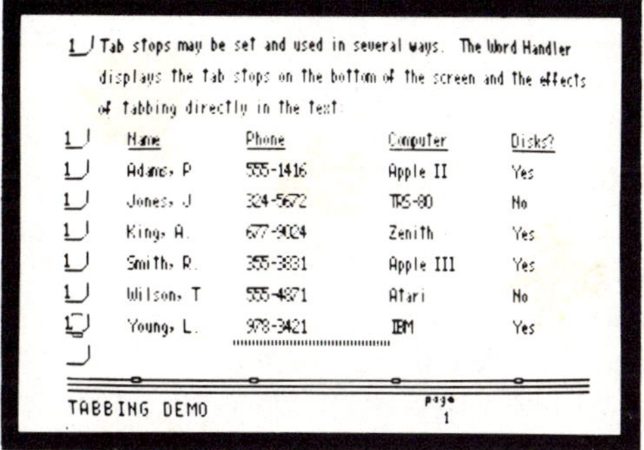

## Chapter 2

What Is Word Processing?

The definition for word processing offered in Chapter 1 ("a computerized approach to putting words on paper in a more efficient and accurate fashion") doesn't really tell you what word processing does. If the traditional process of typing is viewed as one of the pressing keys and seeing the results immediately on paper, then word processing adds an intelligent interface between the input device (keyboard, in this case) and output device (printer). Just how intelligently that interface operates depends on many of the factors discussed in this chapter.

Microcomputer word processing involves four major components: an input device, the computer itself, one or more mass storage units, and an output system. In some cases, two or more of the components may be combined in a single unit. The Apple II, for example, combines an input device (keyboard) with the computer board (containing CPU and associated chips) and peripheral control cards into a single cabinet about the size of an office typewriter. Another popular microcomputer, the TRS-80 Model III, combines a keyboard and video display with two floppy disk drives, memory, power supply, peripheral controllers, and assorted other features into a single molded cabinet about the size of an average television set.

No matter how your computer is configured, the basic operation of word-processing programs follows essentially the same pattern. First, the computer must be prepared to execute the necessary commands by loading a word-processing program into its memory. In most cases, the program is contained on a floppy disk or tape cassette which the computer reads on a command from the user. Any other hardware (printer, disk drives, video display, or special attachments) that is needed during program execution should be ready for operation at this time.

Once a word-processing program is loaded into the computer's memory, the system is prepared to handle the functions specified by commands contained in the program. Text (the term used to designate words or other groups of characters) is entered from the keyboard or other input device, manipulated by the computer, and sent to storage or output devices connected to the computer. Simple? In theory, word processing is a remarkably simple operation. In fact, however, the manipulation and storage steps can range from relatively crude to surprisingly sophisticated.

PROGRAM STRUCTURE

Let's consider the nature of word processing by first examining the organizational structure common to most microcomputer-based programs and then describing some of the features they are most likely to contain. Once loaded into your computer and operating, a typical word-processing program contains five distinct capabilities—input, storage, output, editing, and special features.

Input, in it's simplest form, consists of characters typed in from the keyboard. Adding some sophistication to this process often takes the form of controlling program functions with a single keystroke, defining short keystroke sequences to serve as abbreviations for frequently used words or phrases, or adding special characters for desired output operations. Text contained in storage devices must also be accessible to the user. Special commands allow intermingling of text from storage with freshly typed material.

Storage for text previously entered from the keyboard (or other device) is provided on tape cassettes, floppy disks, or hard disks. Although the specific format for text storage varies from one program to another, the computer's operating system and hardware capability are used to keep text in some sort of file for later retrieval or manipulation by the user. Provisions to make additional (back-up) copies of text files for the inevitable time that a disk fails or a tape breaks are usually included in the program.

Output takes place in two forms for most microcomputer word-processing systems. Immediate output of text being typed, retrieved from storage, or edited takes place on the video display. Whether the display device is external (such as a television set or monitor) or a built-in video tube, programs handle text in much the same way a typewriter immediately displays its output on paper. The impression you get is that of typing directly on the video screen. The second form of output consists of text sent to the printer by the program. In some cases, this output may be shown on the video display as it is printed. Other programs provide status information (like the name of the file being printed), while some simply blank the screen when the printer is in operation. Very few programs provide an additional feature called *print spooling*, which allows you to continue with other word-processing operations on the video display while a text file is being printed. Some programs contain a "typewriter mode" which causes the text to be sent directly to the printer as it is typed without program interference.

Editing provides the means to correct, modify, or otherwise alter text previously entered. Some editing functions, like backspacing and typing directly over errors, are intended for use during the input operation. Others, like insertion and deletion of text, block operations, and reformatting, are used primarily for editing text already contained in storage files. Microcomputer word-processing programs, as a group, have a wide range of effective editing features. Differences among programs are primarily reflected in the user friendliness, accuracy, and convenience of editing features.

Special features show the widest range of variation among programs. Some of the word-processing programs I use, for instance, are capable of generating individualized form letters from a mailing list, editing text files created by other programs, printing "mirror image" (alternating) margins, checking text files for spelling errors, or creating an electronic filing system. I could go on for pages describing the enhancements available for word processing with microcomputers. "New and improved" versions will undoubtedly be offered by the time you read this.

The list of special features available is a good clue to the general level of sophistication of a particular program if all the basics are included and well implemented. Often, but not always, the price of the program also reflects the number of special features included. As you examine the individual program descriptions, pay attention to the special features included in each. The programs selected

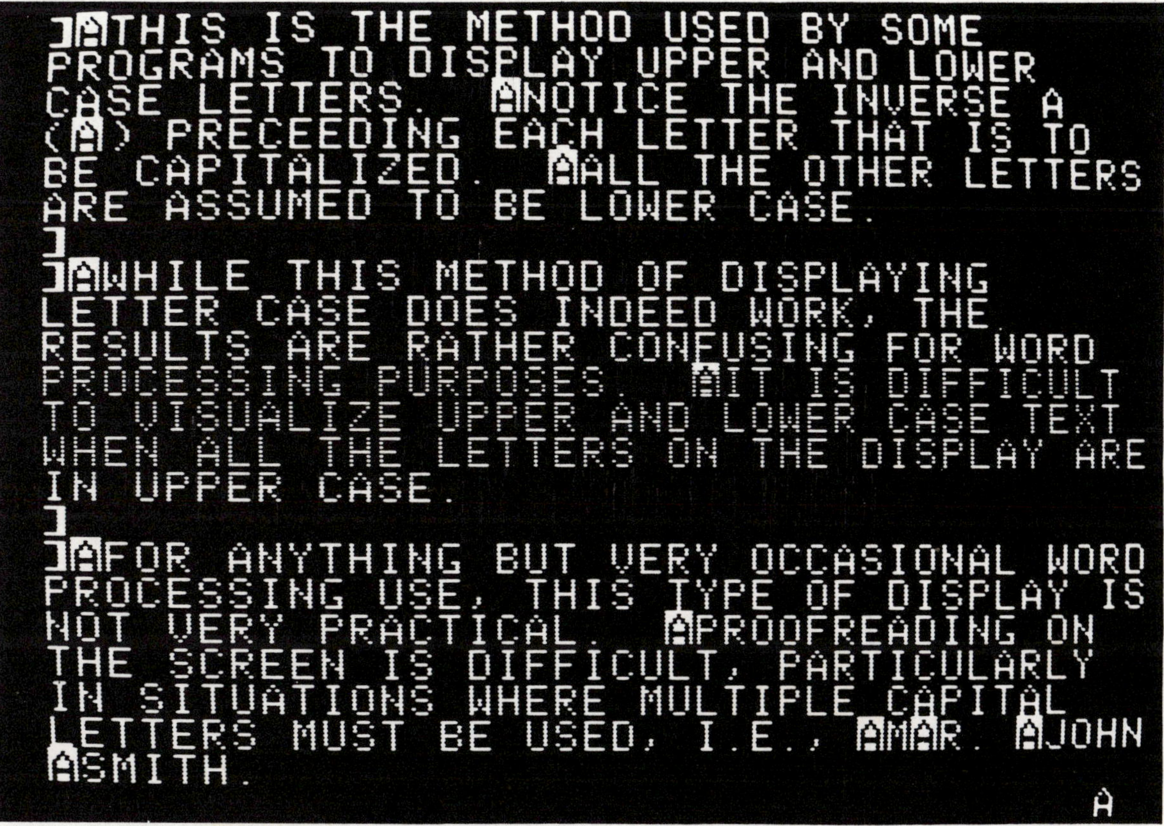

Fig. 2-1. Upper- and lowercase character display: characters to be printed in uppercase are preceded by an inverse A.

for detailed description in this book are representative of the level of sophistication available in their particular price range.

COMMON PROGRAM FEATURES

In order to understand the actual construction and operation of word-processing programs as a group, I will begin with general descriptions of the features that are included in virtually all of them. In looking at these features, I will use parts of several programs to be described in more detail later. Where it might be helpful (and possible without a computer at hand) for you to actually see the feature being described, a photograph of the video display on my Apple II is included. When you look at the figures showing the screen displays, notice the program that created it is sometimes identified in either the text or caption. The purpose in identifying the program is *not* to imply the particular feature is exclusive or even unique to that program. I selected the displays only to illustrate the feature being discussed.

Input Features

Character Display. Although it is not as common today as in the past, some computers (Apple II among them) are capable of displaying only uppercase (capital) letters without hardware or program modifications. All-capital letters may be suitable for some computer applications, but word processing is definitely not one of them. If your computer contains both upper- and lowercase display capabilities, chances are the word-processing programs will pass them through unaltered. To get around the uppercase only limitation, particularly in the Apple, one of three methods is commonly employed: distinctive display of only those characters intended to be printed in uppercase (Fig. 2-1), an additional hardware adapter to generate both cases (Fig. 2-2), or character fonts contained within the program itself (Fig. 2-3). All computers are able to output the appropriate ASCII codes for both upper- and lowercase letters to be printed. Very few, if any, printers sold today are limited only to uppercase. Once the computer outputs the proper codes, most printers will automatically shift case as needed.

Case Shifting. On a typewriter, uppercase letters are produced by pressing the shift or shift lock keys. Some computers function in exactly the same fashion. Others use the shift key to produce another character from a specific key. For example, SHIFT-P on the Apple produces @, and SHIFT-G sounds a bell. Various combinations of keystrokes have been used to shift from one case to the other. A simple hardware modification, which involves soldering one end of a wire to one of the keyboard contacts and placing the other in the game paddle socket, has been developed for the Apple II. Recent word-processing programs use this modification for activating the shift key and requiring several keystrokes to produce the alternate character on the key.

Line Width. The "big computer" standard for video display line width is 80 characters. Some computers (the Apple, for example) are not capable of displaying that many characters on a standard video display line. The unmodified Apple II will display 40 characters per horizontal line (Fig. 2-4). As you may have guessed, there are methods of circumventing that limitation. One of the more popular methods has been provided by the add-on 80-column display board (Fig. 2-5). Some recent word-processing programs have adopted an alter-

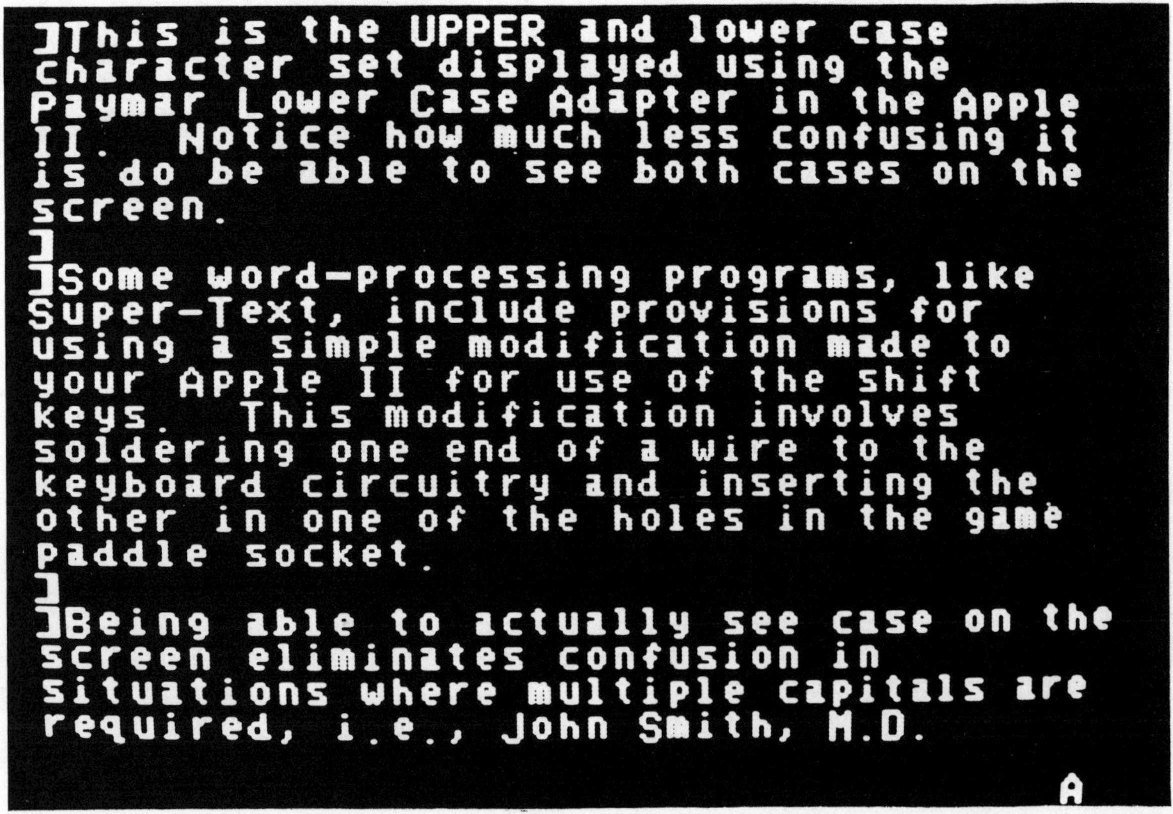

Fig. 2-2. A hardware adapter is used here to modify the Apple II for on-screen display of both upper- and lowercase letters.

Fig. 2-3. A software upper- and lowercase character set as generated by The Word Handler word-processing program.

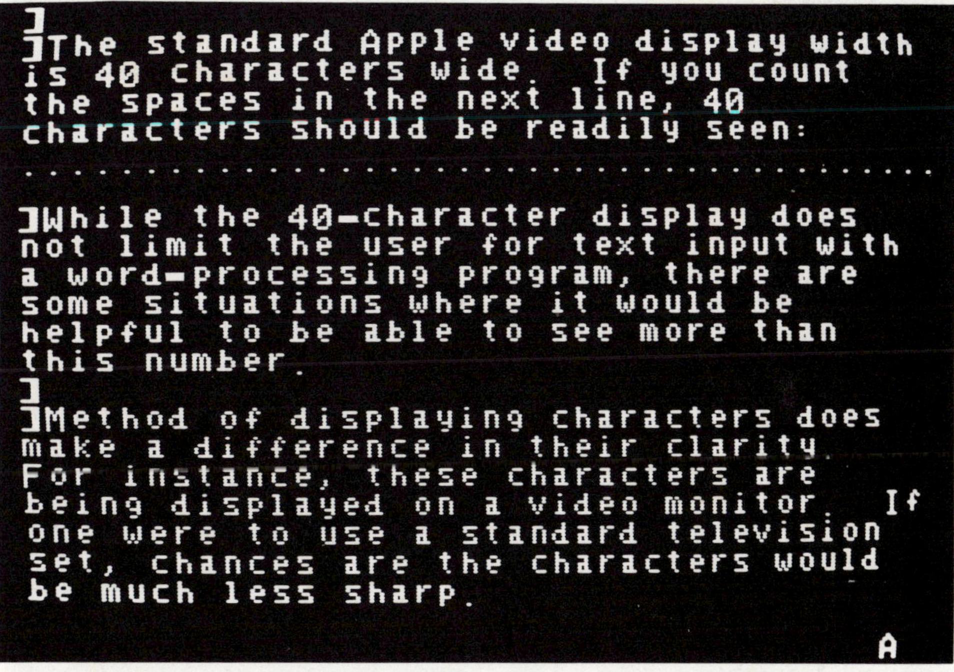

Fig. 2-4. This 40-character video display line width is characteristic of the unmodified Apple II computer. Other popular microcomputers offer line widths ranging from 32 to 80 characters.

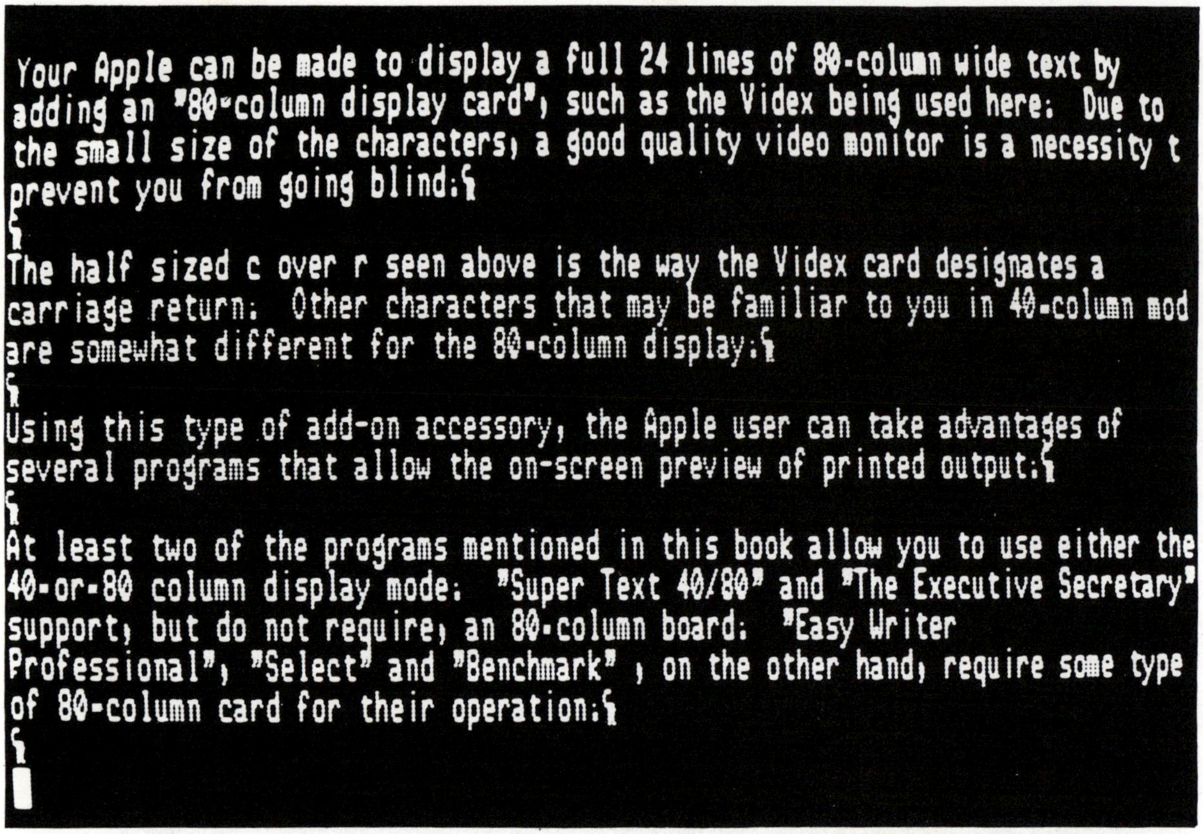

Your Apple can be made to display a full 24 lines of 80-column wide text by adding an "80-column display card", such as the Videx being used here: Due to the small size of the characters, a good quality video monitor is a necessity t prevent you from going blind;

The half sized c over r seen above is the way the Videx card designates a carriage return: Other characters that may be familiar to you in 40-column mod are somewhat different for the 80-column display;

Using this type of add-on accessory, the Apple user can take advantages of several programs that allow the on-screen preview of printed output;

At least two of the programs mentioned in this book allow you to use either the 40-or-80 column display mode: "Super Text 40/80" and "The Executive Secretary" support, but do not require, an 80-column board: "Easy Writer Professional", "Select" and "Benchmark" , on the other hand, require some type of 80-column card for their operation;

Fig. 2-5. The Apple II can be modified to display full 80-column lines through the use of an add-on 80-column display board.

native (and much less expensive) solution using software character sets that can display lines wider than 40 characters (Fig. 2-6).

Word Formatting. Most word-processing programs feature a capability that senses when a word will exceed the allowable length of the line on which it is being typed (Fig. 2-7). When this happens, all characters back to the preceding word space are automatically shifted to the next line (Fig. 2-8). This feature, known as word wraparound or automatic return, allows you to type without regard for line length. Press the return key when you want to start typing on an entirely new line or to defeat the automatic return for some specific purpose (Fig. 2-9).

Tabbing and Indentation. Like a typewriter, most word-processing programs offer some method of designating stops across the page for specific applications such as tables, columns, etc. These are referred to as tab stops. Spaces left at the beginning or end of a line are known as indentation, the most common form of which is employed to designate the start of a new paragraph. Two methods are commonly employed to indicate the effects of tabbing and paragraph indentation: a distinctive character (Fig. 2-10) or actual on-screen shift (Fig. 2-11). Many programs allow you to define paragraph indentation in terms of spaces from the left margin and preserve that relationship regardless of the setting of the margin.

Justification and centering. Most word-processing programs will print text with a flush left margin. Most will also print text flush with the right margin by adding extra spaces between words in the line. This method of justification is called *word*

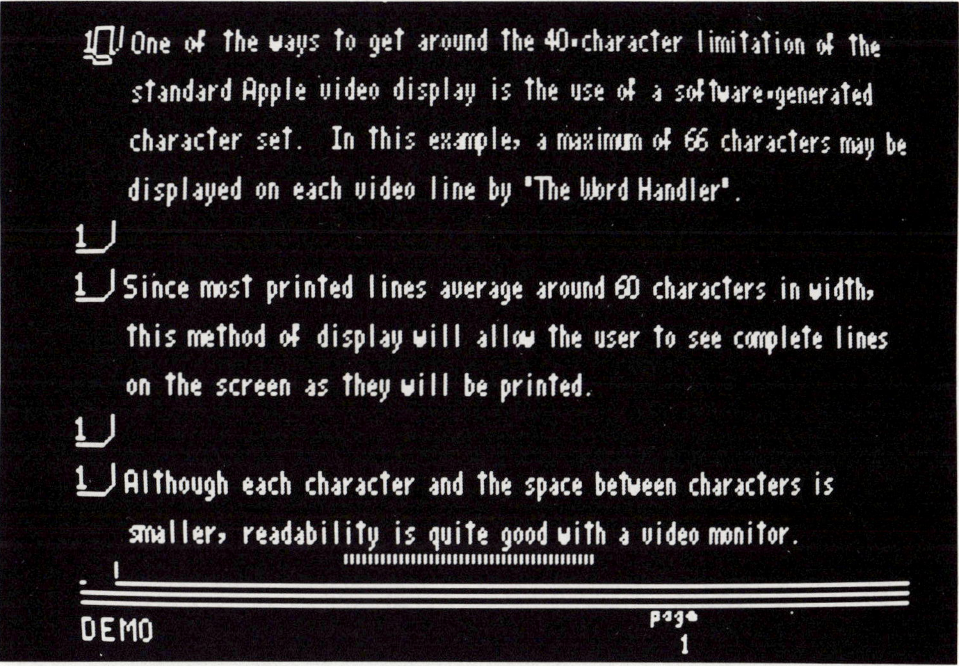

Fig. 2-6. The 66-column software-generated character set of The Word Handler offers a practical solution to the 40-column limitation of the Apple II.

Fig. 2-7. Words too long for one line are automatically shifted to the next. This is a standard feature of word-processing programs.

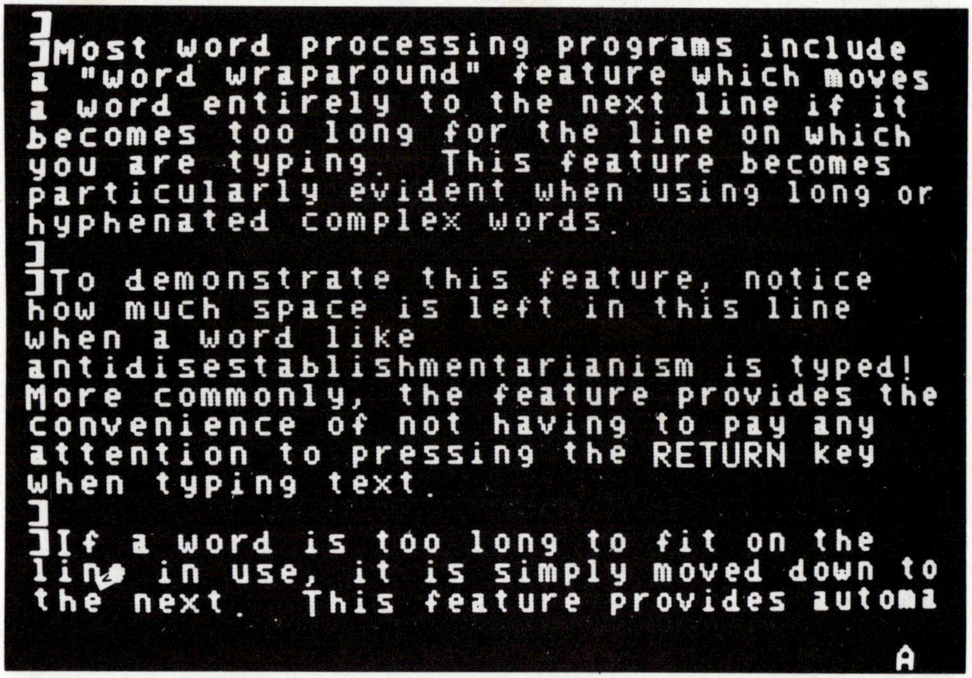

]
]Most word processing programs include
a "word wraparound" feature which moves
a word entirely to the next line if it
becomes too long for the line on which
you are typing. This feature becomes
particularly evident when using long or
hyphenated complex words.
]
]To demonstrate this feature, notice
how much space is left in this line
when a word like
antidisestablishmentarianism is typed!
More commonly, the feature provides the
convenience of not having to pay any
attention to pressing the RETURN key
when typing text.
]
]If a word is too long to fit on the
line in use, it is simply moved down to
the next. This feature provides automa
A

Fig. 2-8. Notice how the word "automatic" has been shifted to the bottom line by the word wraparound capability of this program.

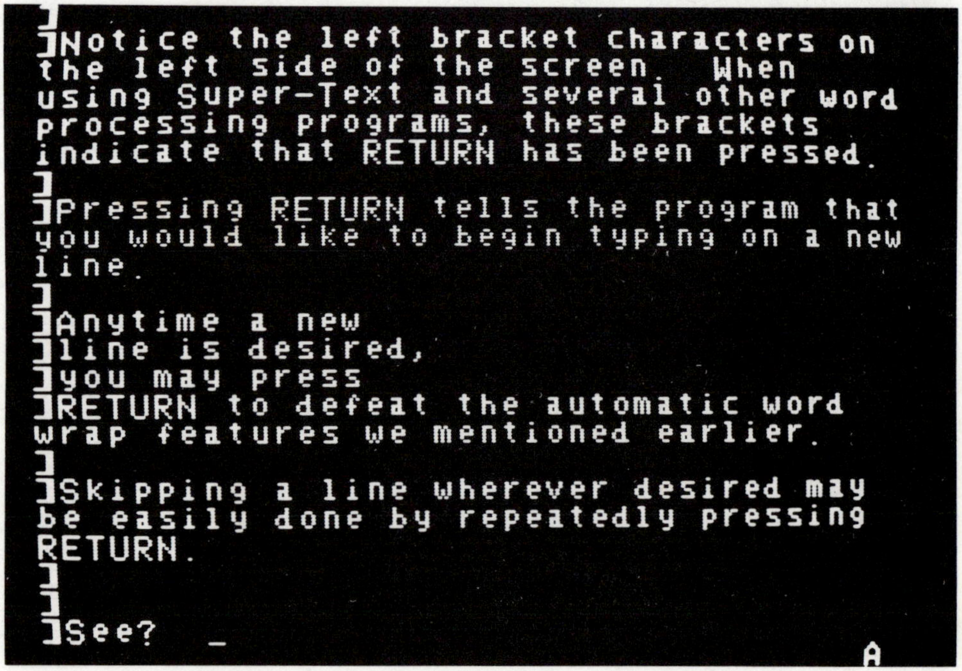

]
]Notice the left bracket characters on
the left side of the screen. When
using Super-Text and several other word
processing programs, these brackets
indicate that RETURN has been pressed.
]
]Pressing RETURN tells the program that
you would like to begin typing on a new
line.
]
]Anytime a new
]line is desired,
]you may press
]RETURN to defeat the automatic word
wrap features we mentioned earlier.
]
]Skipping a line wherever desired may
be easily done by repeatedly pressing
RETURN.
]
]See? _
A

Fig. 2-9. The return key is pressed, in most word-processing programs, when you want to type on a new line. Most programs provide no other means of defeating the automatic return feature.

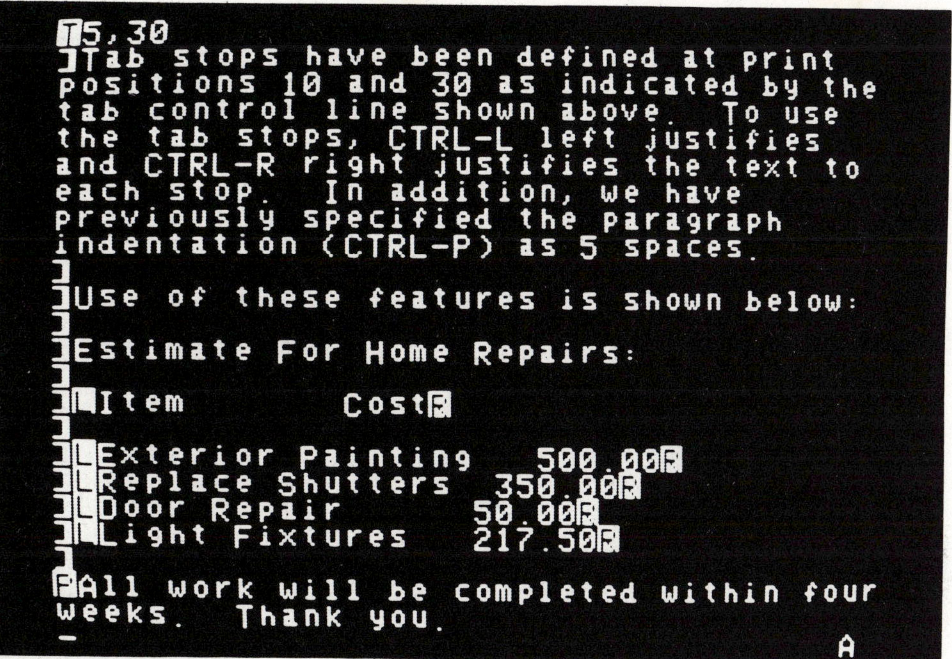

Fig. 2-10. The system of tab stops and paragraph indentation shown here uses control (inverse video) characters to indicate the presence of commands in the text.

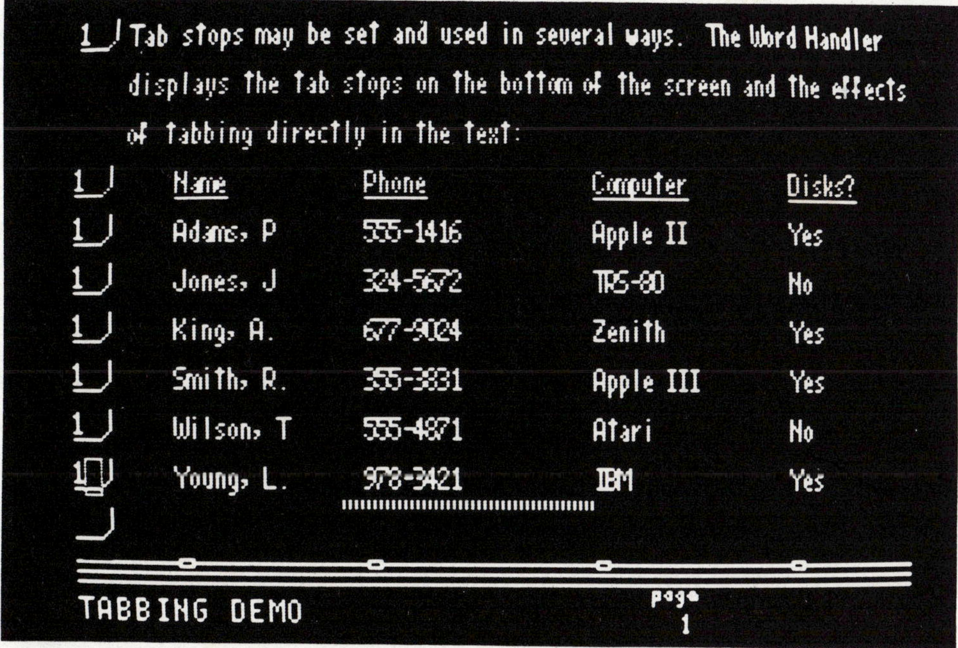

Fig. 2-11. Tab stop locations are indicated by the rectangular boxes on the first status line. The effects of tabbing are actually seen, rather than simply indicated, in the body of the text.

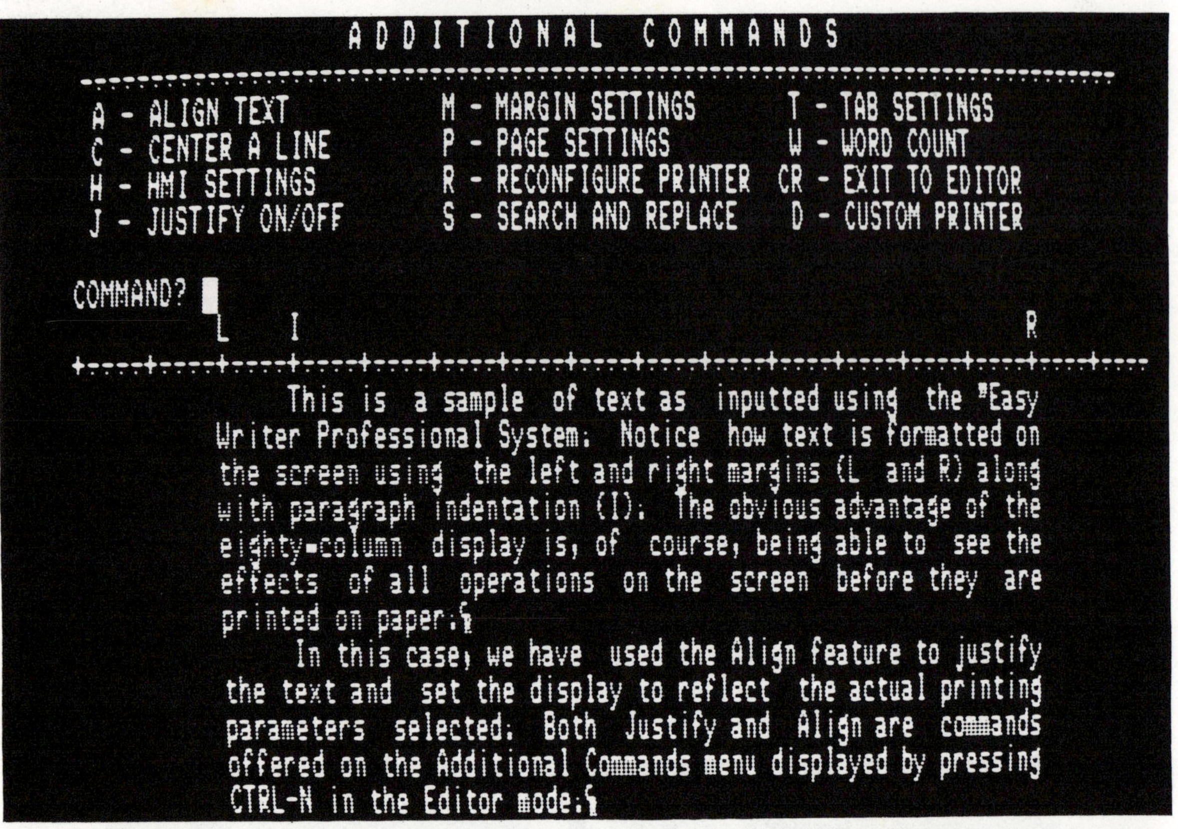

Fig. 2-12. The text shown below the page width scale has been justified left and right on the video display by EasyWriter Professional System. Notice the extra spaces between some of the words used to achieve the flush margins.

spacing and is the most common (Fig. 2-12). Using word spacing, most programs will also print lines centered between the margins. A few programs will justify text either to the right or left of tab stops. Some printers are capable of printing characters with spacing that varies according to the width of each character (*proportional spacing*) or infinitely varying the space between each character (*letter spacing*). Justification under these circumstances is much more sophisticated and not readily found in microcomputer word-processing programs, although some do offer this capability. Commonly available in the output (printing) phase, some programs also offer a video preview so you can study the final effect of justification commands prior to finalizing them in print.

Status Display. Most programs will show the operating mode being used and current cursor position (Fig. 2-13). Some also continuously display tab stops, margins, page breaks, space remaining for new text, or other operating conditions that may be of concern during the input phase of word-processing operations. Programs that do not routinely display status during input operations often include a command which provides for a status display on demand (Fig. 2-14).

Specification Adjustment. Most programs allow you to temporarily (or permanently) alter selected portions of the output format during text entry operations. Super-Text's format line (Fig. 2-15) provides adjustments for left and right margin, paragraph indentation, top and bottom margin, text length per page, line numbering selection and position, spacing, justification, etc.

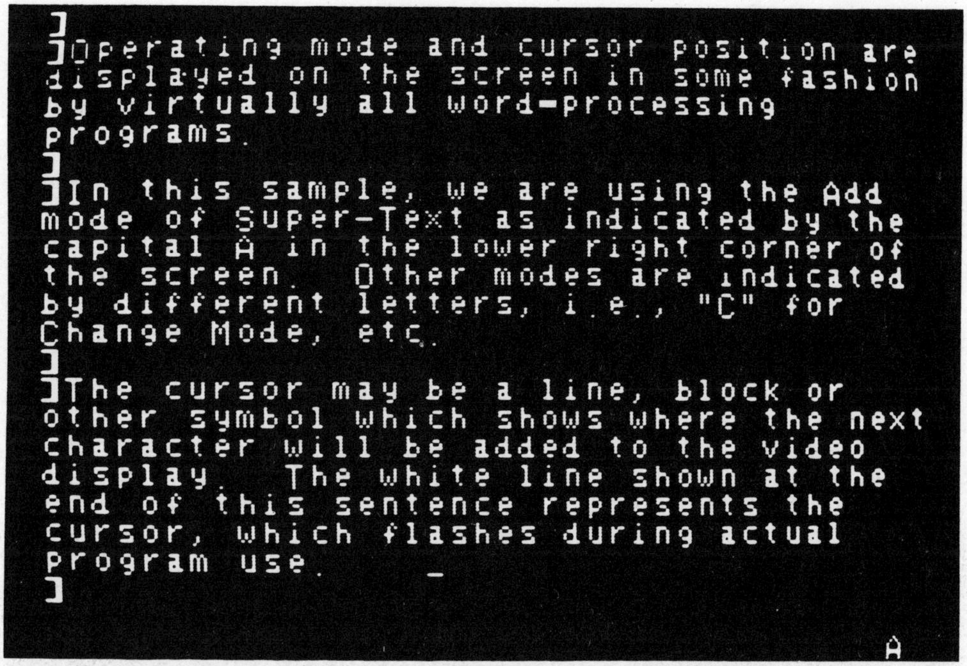

Fig. 2-13. The simplest status display during input operations includes operating mode and current cursor position.

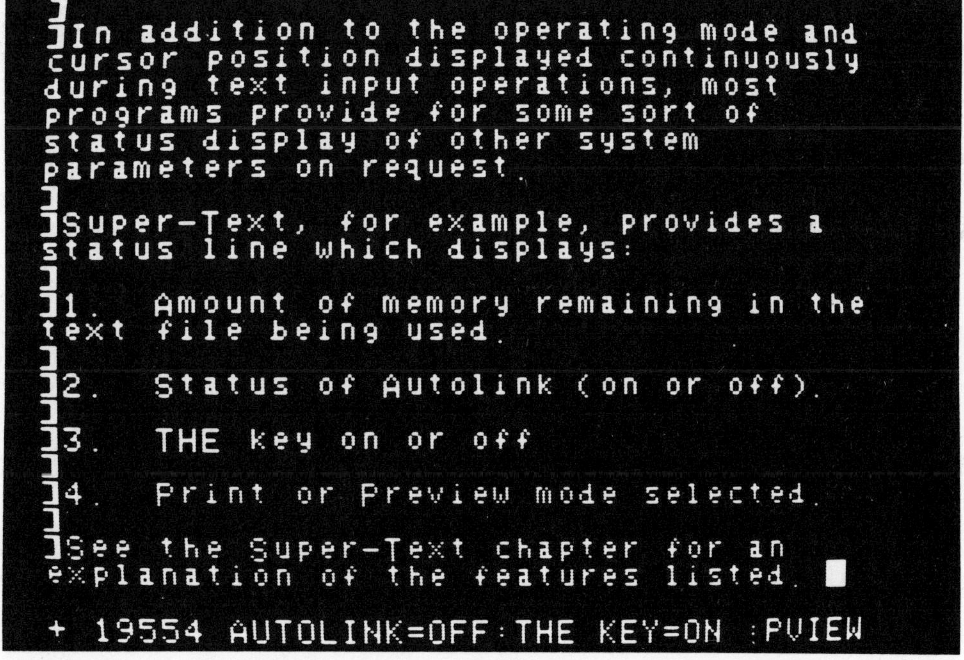

Fig. 2-14. A more elaborate status line, shown by user request, is seen at the bottom of this video display.

```
F10,70,4,6,54,6,3,39,SJ

Although output formats are almost
always defined separately, the ability
to alter them during text input
operations represents a considerable
convenience for many applications.

A "format line" is used by Super-Text
for alteration of output specifications
during text input.  For instance, the
line below (preceded by an inverse F)
resets the left and right margins
previously set by the format line above:

F15,65

Format lines may be inserted as often
as desired.  Most programs include
similar capabilities to alter margins,
line spacing, justification mode, page
length, etc.
```

Fig. 2-15. Output format adjustments are made during text entry operations using a format line, embedded commands, or other specification system.

Storage Capabilities

Text File Length. Some programs limit text file length to the memory remaining after the program is loaded. In this situation, when memory is full, the file must be saved on the mass storage medium before further input is allowed. Retrieving this type of file dictates that the one currently in memory be deleted. Some programs provide for automatic text file manipulation by the program, with the user specifying only the name of the group. These types of programs use the disk, in effect, as a virtually unlimited memory for text-handling operations.

File Name. The program usually limits the file name to a specified number of characters, and, quite often, files are assigned numbers which may be used as a sort of shorthand during disk operations (Fig. 2-16). Some programs allow comments or other identifying data to be added to a file name. These are used strictly for informational purposes.

Multiple Disk Drive Access. The exact operational details may vary, but almost all word-processing programs can use more than a single disk drive for text storage and retrieval operations. The most obvious benefit of this is reduced "disk shuffling" with relatively lengthy text files.

Disk Status Display. Some programs consistently show you how much storage space is remaining on a particular disk (Fig. 2-17). This information is important for judging when to change data disks. Programs which do not display space remaining often wait until the disk is full before displaying an error message.

Disk Utilities. In many cases, programs to initialize new data disks or make copies of those currently in use are provided (Fig. 2-18). Other

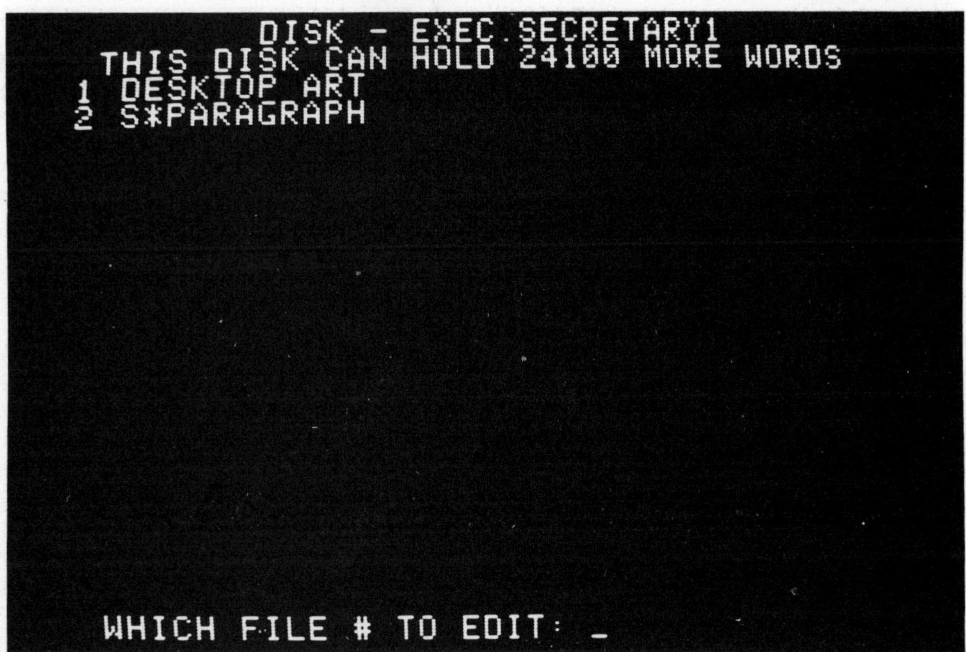

Fig. 2-16. Once files have been assigned names and numbers, The Executive Secretary requires that you type only the file number for some operations.

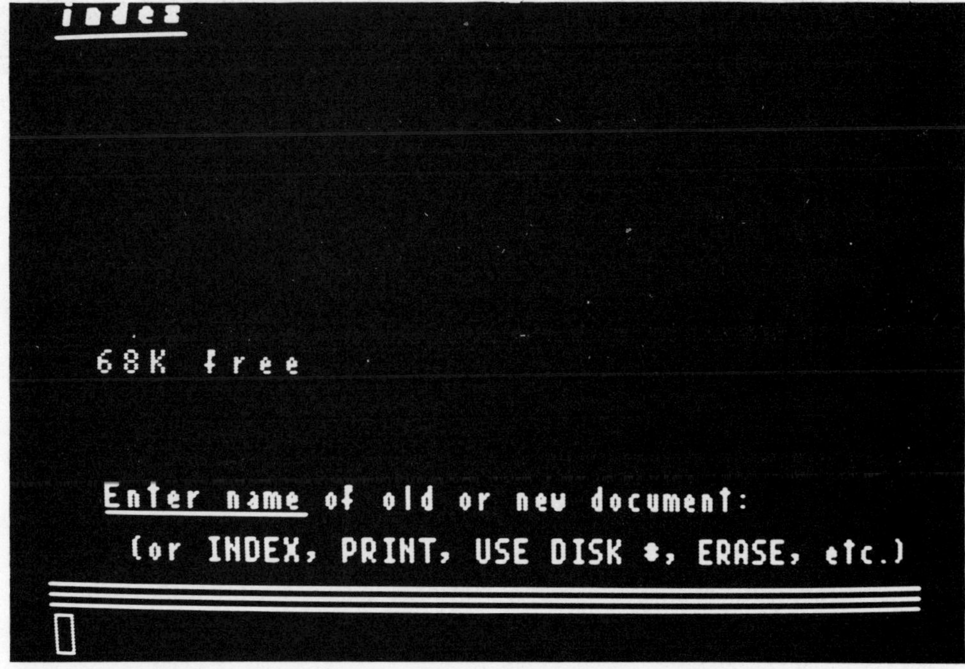

Fig. 2-17. The amount of unused space remaining on each disk is an important part of any disk status display.

Fig. 2-18. Utilities to initialize new data disks or make copies of those presently in use can be selected from this Super-Text II menu.

utilities may be included, but the two mentioned above seem to be the most regularly needed.

Compatibility. Some word-processing programs allow you to use text files in common with other utility programs. Write-On! provides a translation routine for converting "foreign files" (Fig. 2-19). Common text files, where offered, are frequently used in conjunction with form letter generators, mailing lists, or data base management programs.

Output Capabilities

Printer Configuration. Although all word-processing programs require at least minimal printer connection and operation information, some are more convenient to use than others. One of the easiest ways to provide this information is to simply identify your printer from a list of options displayed by a program (Fig. 2-20).

Special Feature Utilization. To be truly effective, a program should allow you to take advantage of any special features included in your printer. Many printers provide such features as adjustable line or character spacing, forms control, and different character fonts. Some programs provide, either automatically or by specific control codes, capabilities to use these special features (Figs. 2-21 and 2-22).

Page Identification. Most programs allow, at minimum, consecutive numbering of the pages printed in a document. You can usually specify the position on the page for the number to be printed. Some word-processing programs provide for elaborate chapter-relative numbering, headers or running heads (phrases printed at the top of a page),

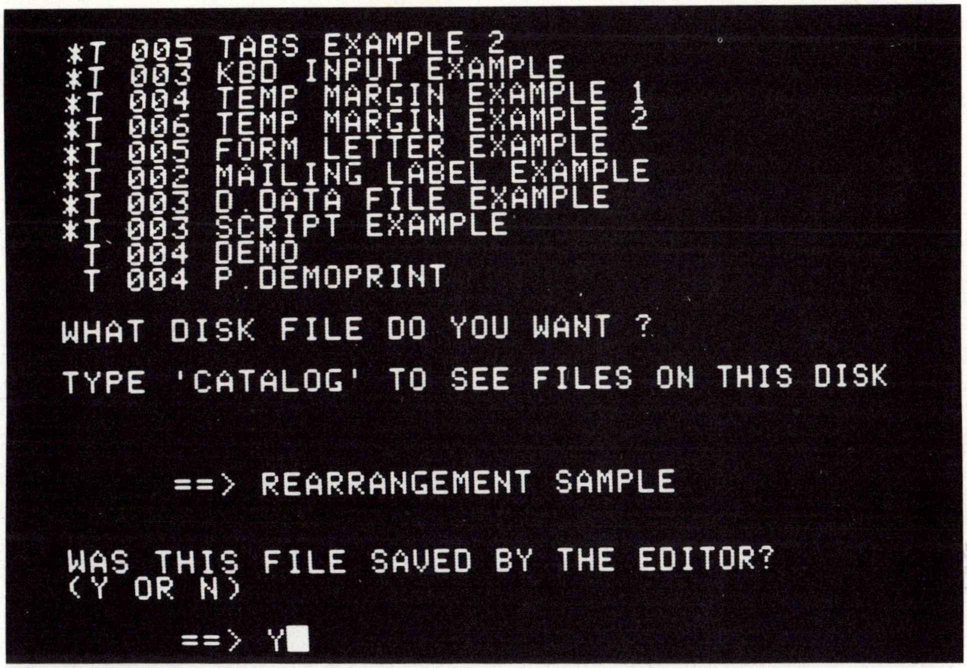

Fig. 2-19. Files not saved by the Write-On! editor may be used by responding N to the screen prompt shown.

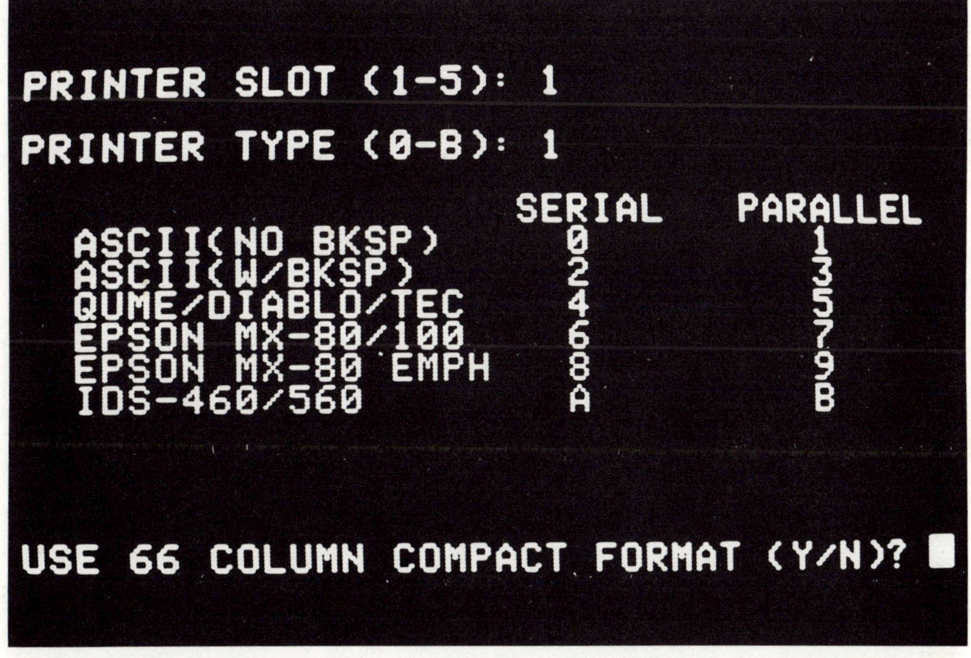

Fig. 2-20. Providing printer information to The Word Handler is simply a matter of selecting your unit from the list presented.

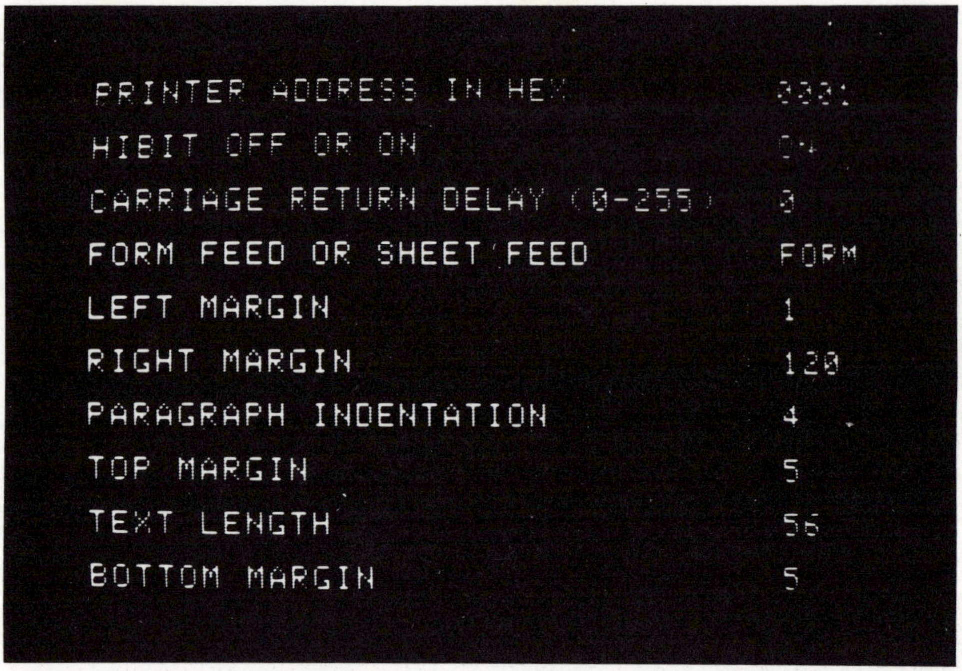

Fig. 2-21. Special printer features can be specified and default page format parameters defined in Super-Text II.

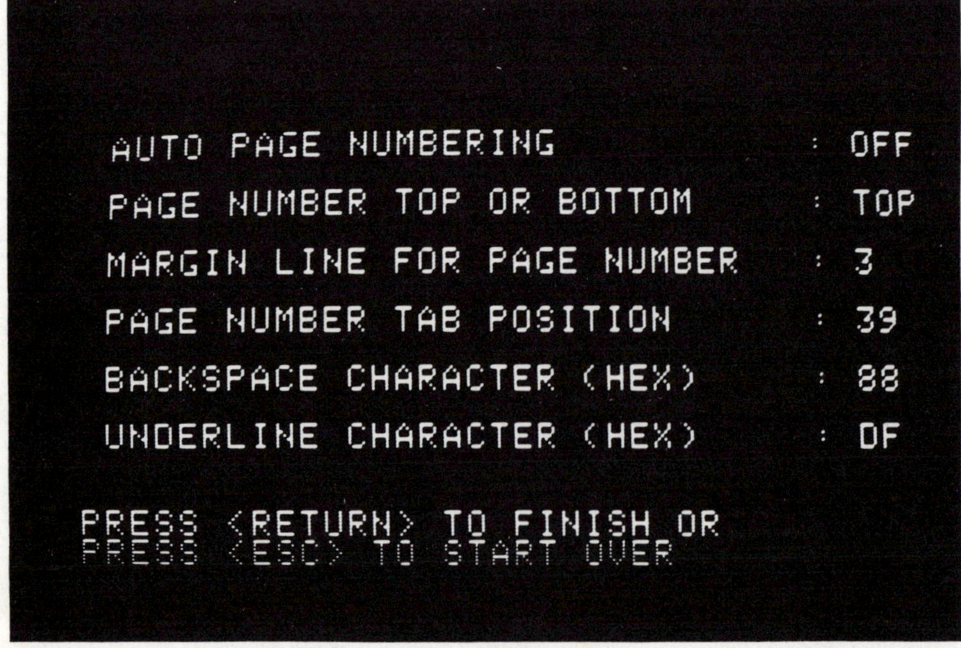

Fig. 2-22. Special features that can be specified in Super-Text II.

footers or running feet (phrases printed at the bottom), alternating number positions, and so on. (Figs. 2-23 and 2-24.)

Multiple Copies or Files. Programs regularly allow the printing of a specified number of copies of a single file or a single copy of multiple files on a disk. The exact procedure for invoking this function varies, but the capability is quite common (Fig. 2-25).

Screen Preview of Printed Document. If not provided for during the input phase, many programs allow you to preview the printed output on the video display. Some programs display 40 specified characters of each line, while others show the lines in their entirety.

Response to Printer Problems. Many, if not most, printers will generate specific status signals to indicate problems such as out of paper, ribbon empty, or paper jam. If the word-processing program is geared to handle these signals (most of the programs presently offered are not), output will automatically cease until the error condition is remedied. In most cases, you are required to manually stop the printing operation or forced to start the whole print cycle again once the printer problem has been corrected.

Editing Capabilities

Cursor Control. You should be able to move the cursor (a square, line, or other character indicating the current screen position for editing) around the screen with ease. Some computer keyboards contain special cursor keys which control the direction of movement. Those that do not must depend on the program to provide more than

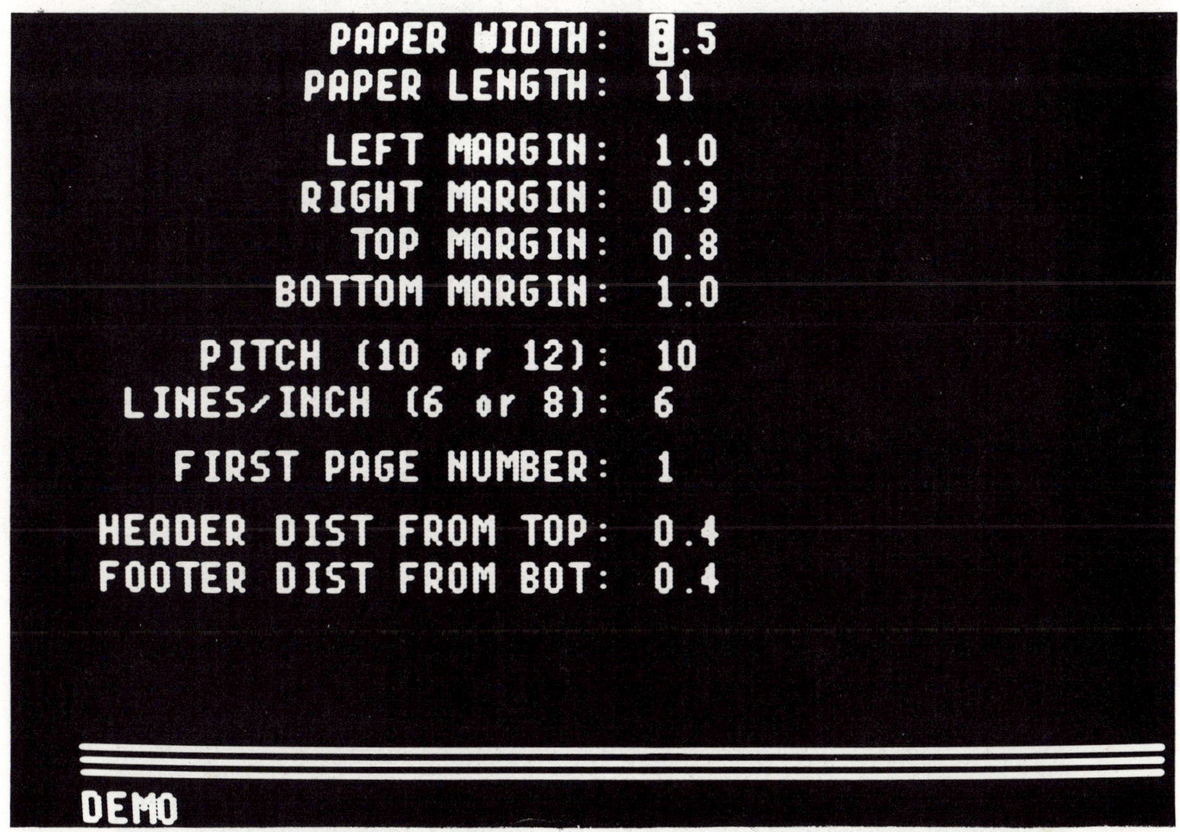

Fig. 2-23. Page format specifications and an elaborate system of printing headers, footers, and page numbers can be selected with The Word Handler.

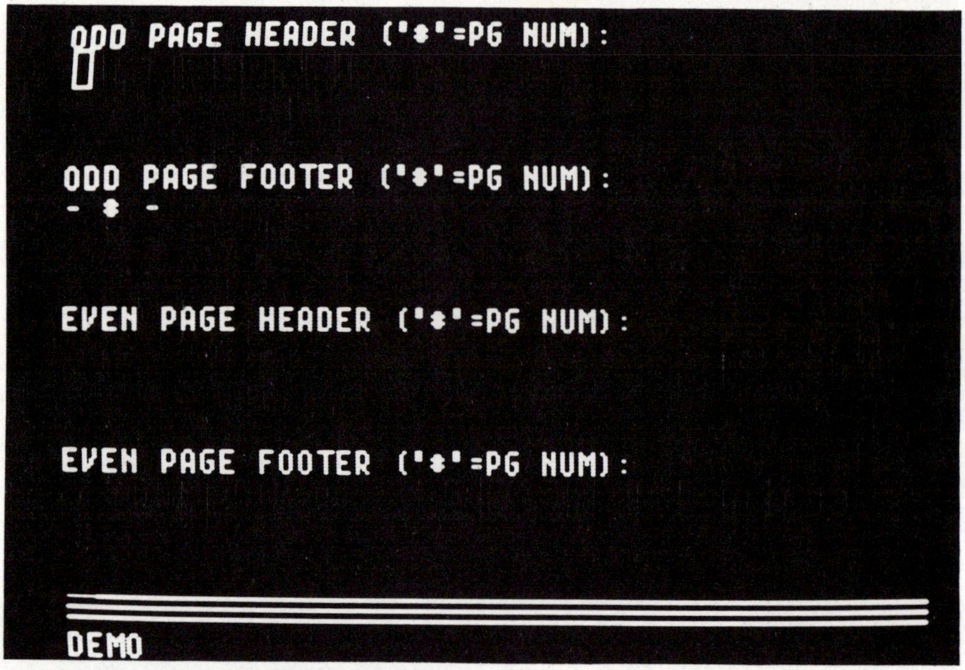

ODD PAGE HEADER ('#'=PG NUM):

ODD PAGE FOOTER ('#'=PG NUM):
- # -

EVEN PAGE HEADER ('#'=PG NUM):

EVEN PAGE FOOTER ('#'=PG NUM):

DEMO

Fig. 2-24. Both headers and footers can be selected with The Word Handler.

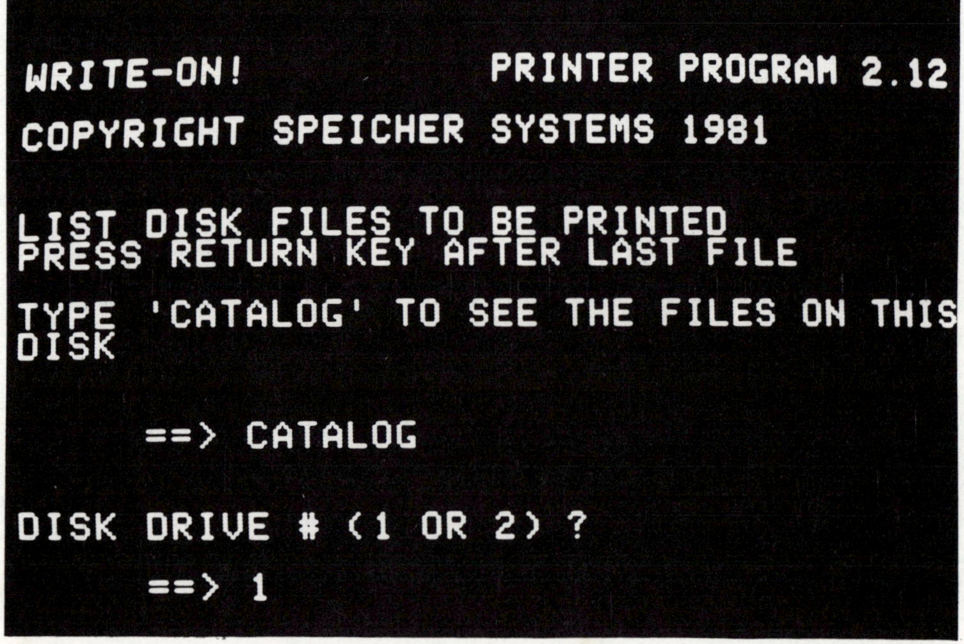

Fig. 2-25. Multiple files can be printed by listing them in the desired order when using Write-On!

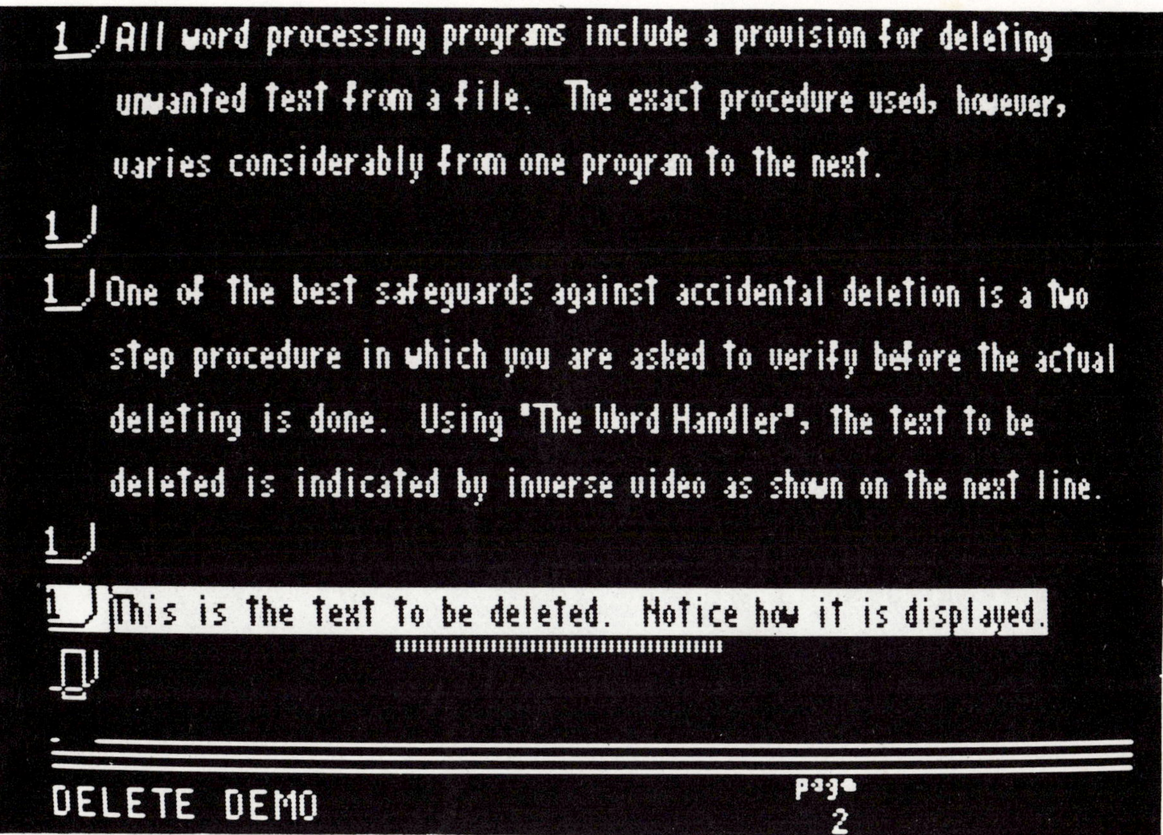

Fig. 2-26. A two-step delete procedure is used by The Word Handler to prevent the accidental loss of desired information.

very limited cursor control. Word-processing programs frequently provide rather sophisticated commands to move the cursor a specified number of spaces, characters, words, or lines.

Text Insertion. A commonly used editing feature is the ability to insert additional text at any point on the screen. The text to be inserted can come from the keyboard or a file contained on your mass storage device. Some programs indicate text insertion by actually moving all the characters ahead of those being inserted across and down the screen while others blank the screen ahead of the text being inserted.

Text Deletion. A convenient means of deleting unwanted text from a file must be provided. Most programs provide for deletion of single characters, words, screen lines, specified blocks, or entire files of text. A few programs provide a two-

step procedure designed to avoid accidentally deleting text (Fig. 2-26). In most programs, the remaining text on the video display is automatically adjusted to reflect any deletion made.

Search. One of the more versatile features found in almost all word-processing programs is the ability to locate a specified character or group of characters within a text file. This capability, commonly known as search or find allows you to quickly locate desired words and phrases for editing purposes (Fig. 2-27). In some cases, this capability is expanded to allow you to choose all occurrences or the one specific occurrence of the character group.

Find and Replace. The search capability mentioned above is almost always combined with a replace command, so you can specify text for both location and replacement. For example, if the word "their" was consistently spelled as "thier" in a par-

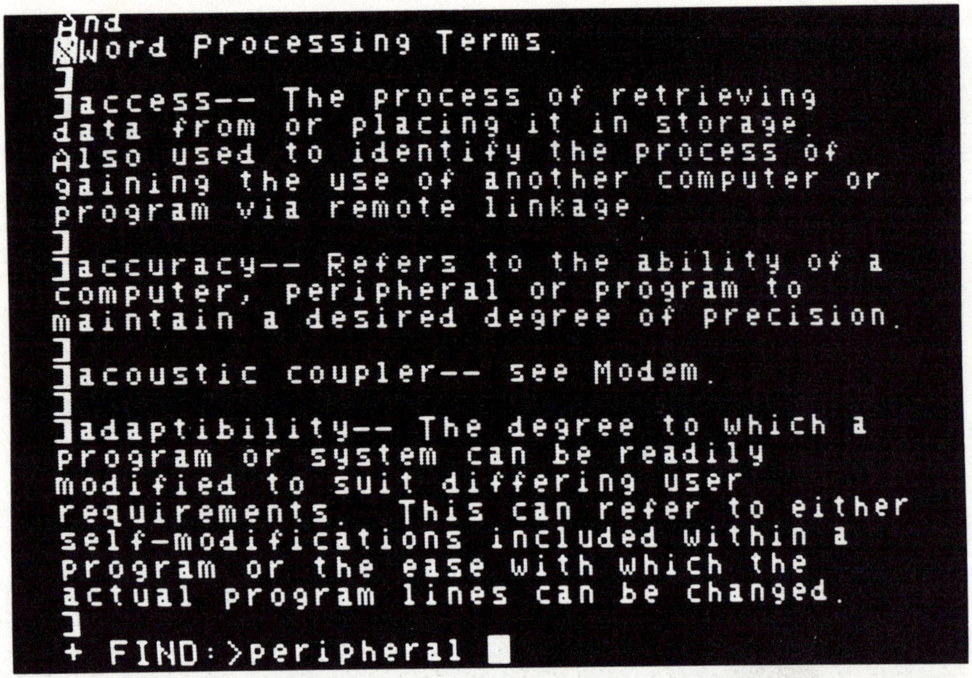

Fig. 2-27. Search or find capabilities allow you to quickly locate a desired word or phrase in the text.

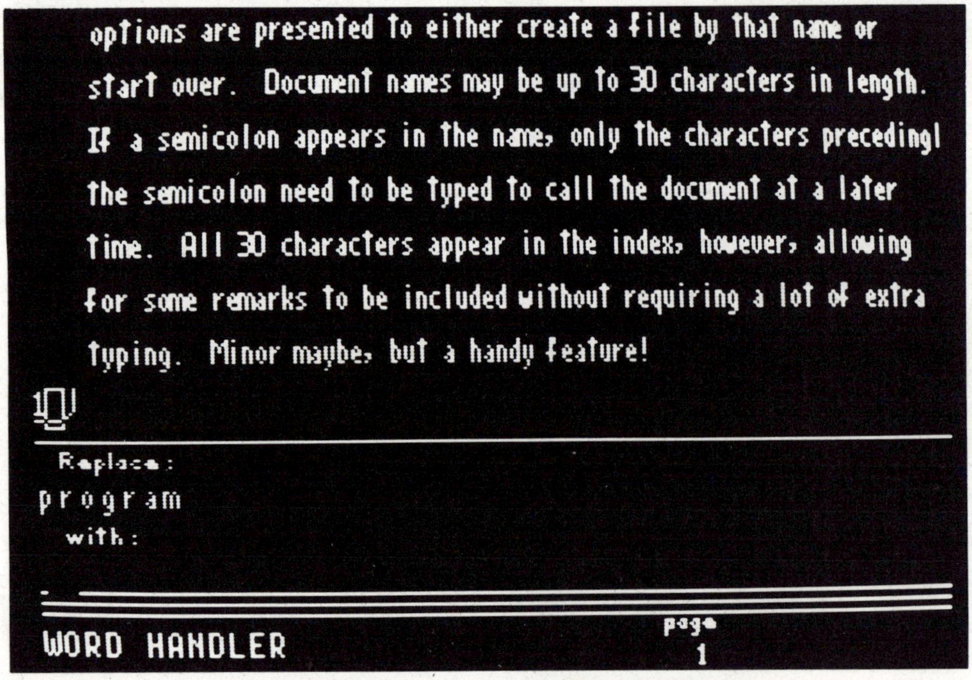

Fig. 2-28. Initiating a find and replace operation using The Word Handler.

ticular file, find and replace could be used to correct every occurrence of the misspelling. Provisions for approving each occurrence or automatic replacement of all are usually included in word-processing programs (Fig. 2-28). Some new programs allow for simultaneous search and/or replace operations involving multiple words or phrases.

Block Operation. This form of text manipulation provides the means for marking a portion of text for movement, copying at some other location, saving in a separate file, deleting from the present location, or insertion into another file (Fig. 2-29). A few programs allow marking more than one block of text for later manipulation.

Special Features

Special features are those which show the widest variations among programs. Just a few of the most commonly included features are outlined here. They will be covered in greater detail in the individual program descriptions.

Program Control by Menu. Most programs provide you with multiple-choice lists, known as menus, to access various features in the program (Fig. 2-30). Menus are designed to make the program easier to use, because necessary decisions can be made with a minimum of fuss.

Logical Commands. Early word-processing programs had intricate systems of commands which were difficult to use without a great deal of training. The present generation word-processing programs have simplified command structures that are easily understood by even the most inexperienced user. In many programs, a command can be invoked by typ-

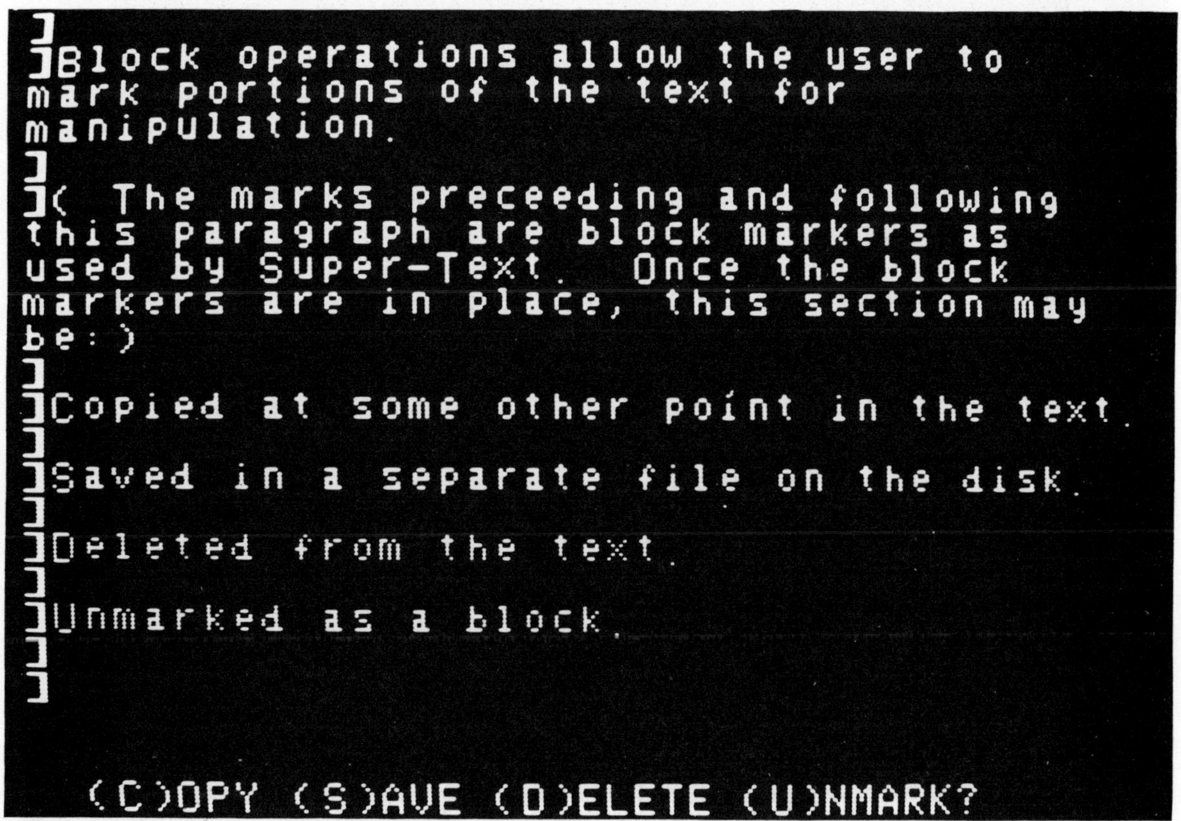

Fig. 2-29. The text enclosed by parentheses has been marked as a block and is manipulated using the options presented on the bottom of the screen.

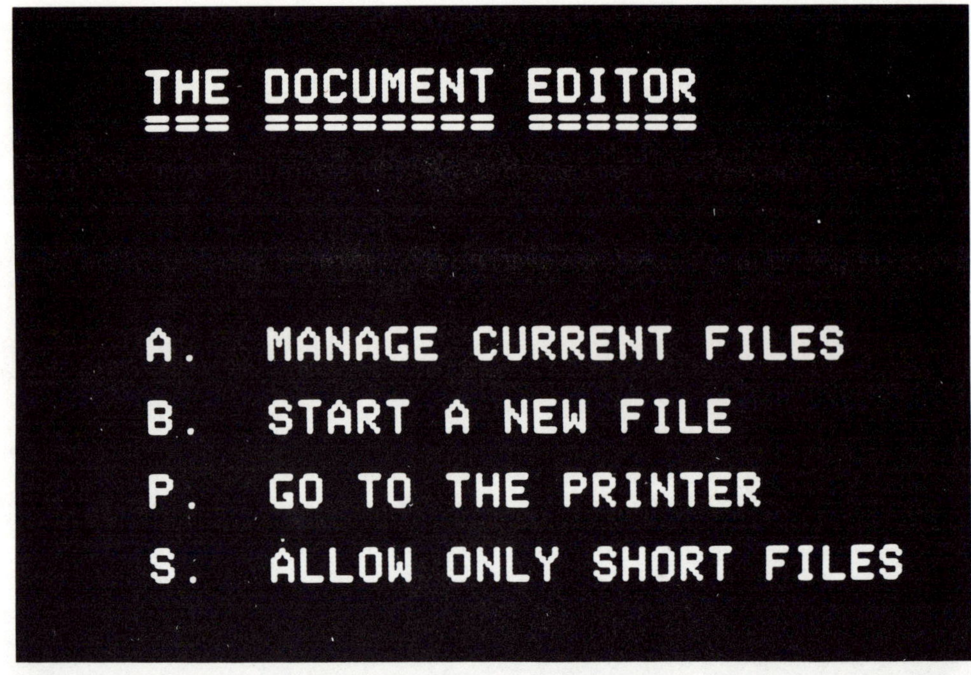

Fig. 2-30. One of the menus used for control of program operations by The Executive Secretary.

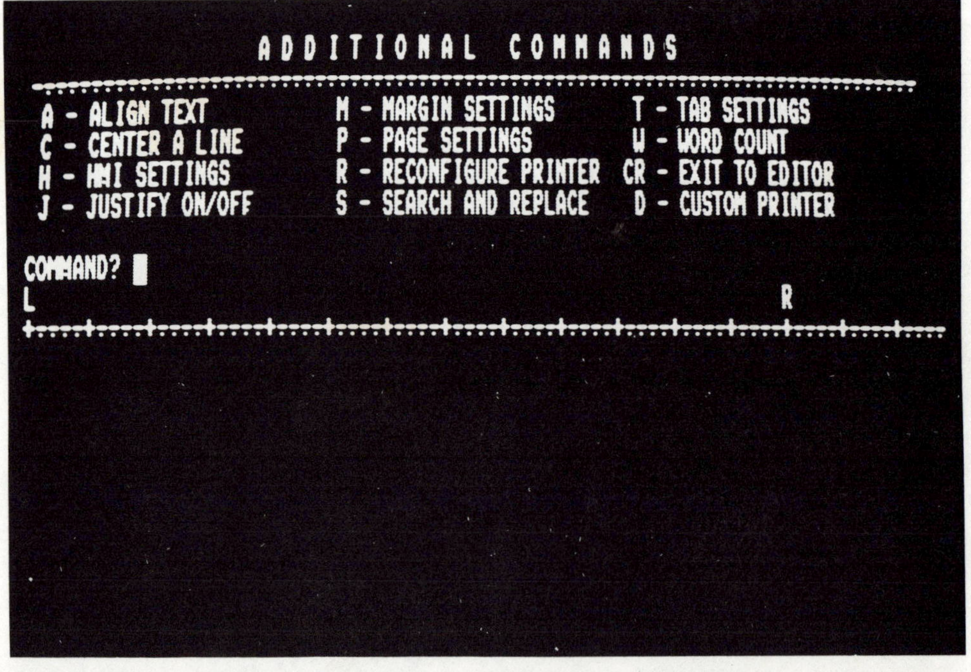

Fig. 2-31. Most of the commands available to the user of EasyWriter Professional System are displayed in one of the several menus which may be requested at any time during program use.

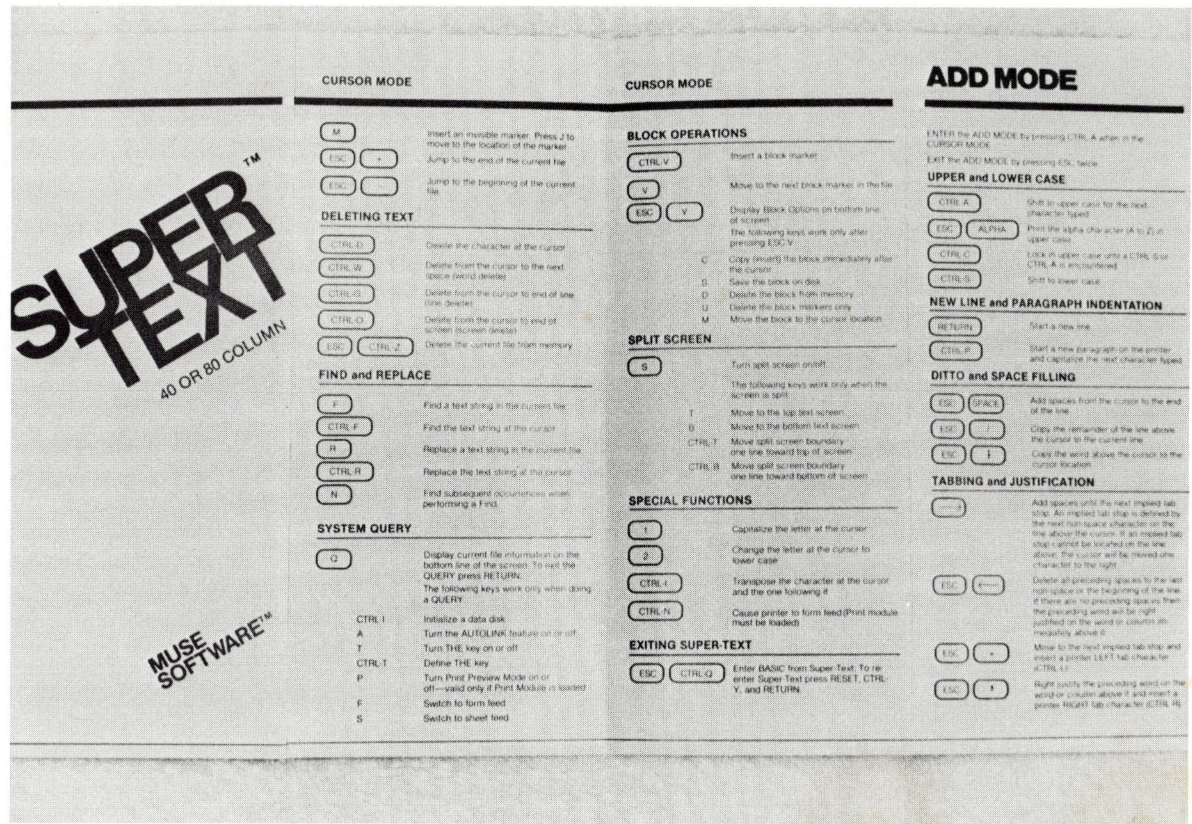

Fig. 2-32. A reference card is provided with most word-processing programs outlining the commands available.

ing the first letter of its name or selecting it from a menu displayed by the program (Fig. 2-31).

Tutorial Documentation. Program manuals teach you how to take advantage of all the capabilities included in a word-processing program. Often, an on-screen tutorial system to demonstrate functions discussed in the manual and a "help file" for quick tips during use are included on the program disk(s). Most word-processing packages include a reference card which outlines most of the commands available (Fig. 2-32).

Obviously, I have not covered every feature found in word-processing programs. By now, however, you should have an idea of the basic features found in virtually all microcomputer-based word-processing programs on the market. Take a few minutes to review any of the features that may be unclear, since I will not discuss them in general terms past this point. The individual program descriptions concentrate on the details of how these common features are implemented and the capabilities that make each program unique.

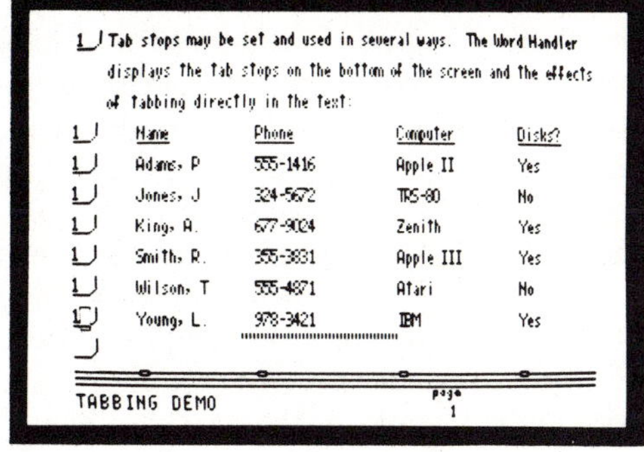

## Chapter 3

Word-Processing Programs

There are literally hundreds of word-processing programs offered for microcomputers. A few of the programs are described in the Appendix. Computer stores usually offer several different programs for the more popular personal computers. Business, educational, and computer-oriented publications carry page after page of word-processing program advertisements, announcements, and reviews. Program packages are being marketed to appeal to a diverse group of computer owners, from raw beginners to those familiar with every aspect of word processing.

Is it any wonder the average computer owner or prospective buyer approaches the word-processing program market with apprehension? Learning enough about word processing to intelligently select a program suitable for your applications is difficult without actually having a program at hand to try on your computer. If you select a program because you want to learn about word processing, it will probably not be your final choice. The more you learn about and actually use word processing, the more special features you will want in your next program. If I can do no more than save you the cost of one or two intermediate learning programs in this book, our time and your money will have been well spent.

The potential market for word-processing (and numerous other) programs for microcomputers is exploding. Personal and small business computers are selling at a rate never envisioned by even the most optimistic market forecasters. New computers and more sophisticated hardware are being introduced at a frenzied pace. Every computer sold creates additional demand for application software. Traditionally, software development has been unable to keep pace with hardware advances. Computer manufacturers are aware of this problem and placing a greater emphasis on programs availability, however, most programs on the market are offered by software suppliers not associated with computer manufacturers.

Anyone with a computer and some programming knowledge has the potential to become a software supplier, and many of the major software houses started in just such a fashion. Some of the best application programs on the market were developed by outside programmers who either used them to form the basis of a new business or sold distribution rights to an existing firm. Professionals in many fields are learning about programming in order to develop software that is pertinent to their requirements. Other professionals in the same field learn about the programs and want copies, and another software supplier enters the marketplace.

Intense competition for software sales dollars has benefitted the user in several significant ways. First, totally inadequate or obsolete products are eventually forced off the market. Second, good programs can be expected to sell enough copies so the amount of development cost that must be recovered per unit can be held to a minimum. Third, the profit potential offered by successful products attracts the best programmers. Finally, prices must be structured to keep programs with similar capabilities attractive to potential buyers.

As software customers become more discriminating, the ratio of price to program features becomes an important yardstick in determining the marketing success of any program. Word-processing programs are a good example of this phenomenon. Early word-processing programs for microcomputers offered a standard list of features, largely determined by the software designer. As the number of available programs expanded, buyers tended to gravitate toward those with additional desirable features. The most successful of the new programs are those that incorporate features of interest and utility to the relatively sophisticated user or combine an adequate word-processing system with an easy method of operation for the first-time user.

Program suppliers have learned that word processing is not a single-interest application. This is reflected in the diversity of features in today's word-processing programs. Software designers concentrate on providing programs that give the end user a reasonable range of features for the price. Limited-feature programs usually sell for a lower price than those with extensive special features. For some applications, the inexpensive program may be entirely adequate. Others may require, and be willing to spend the money for, pro-grams with strengths in a particular area of interest.

The entire microcomputer word-processing market has matured tremendously over the last couple of years. There are still inexpensive, limited capacity word-processing programs offered (and selling rather well, I might add!). Recently some word-processing programs with vast arrays of special features have been introduced. These "high end" programs appeal to an entirely different segment of the word-processing market and are also selling quite well. Some companies offer software in several price and feature categories, allowing you to upgrade your system as your needs change.

The frontiers of microcomputer-based word processing have been pushed back much faster and further than were those of the old west. Standard program features have been around for a relatively long time. Such features were originally found in large computer word-processing programs and have been adapted for use in micros. Over the past few years, programs for microcomputers have become increasingly versatile. Exciting new capabilities are usually introduced in one or two programs and adopted by a number of others. Mailing list and form letter merging were among the first features added, allowing personalized letters to be printed automatically (Fig. 3-1). Other features of note include spelling and grammar checking, transmission of files by modem, print spooling, intermingling of text and graphics in print files, and voice input. While not all of these capabilities are available in all programs, they will very likely be common in the near future.

MEETING HARDWARE DEMANDS

Word-processing program suppliers, as a group, have been quick to respond to the increased potential of more sophisticated hardware. As newer and better computers are introduced, word-processing programs are generally among the first available for them. I began seeing advertisements for a word-processing program for the Apple III long before I saw the computer itself.

Effective use of new peripherals has also been characteristic of word-processing programs. Presently there are several hard disk and memory-type

Fig. 3-1. The Super-Text word-processing system offers an add-on module for customizing form letters and documents using mailing list data supplied by The Address Book.

disk emulator systems on the market. Some programs have already made provision for this technology, and others are sure to follow.

Printer technology has advanced by leaps and bounds over the past couple of years. Programs to take advantage of such recent printer capabilities as multiple print font selection, graphics printing, proportional spacing, and overstriking were released soon after the hardware was introduced. Several new printers capable of multicolor printing have just been released, and programs to take advantage of this exciting new feature will probably be readily available by the time you read this.

COMPUTER STORE DEMONSTRATIONS

One way to learn about word-processing programs is to visit your local computer store. In addition to providing literature, most stores have demonstration copies of the more popular programs available. While the store demonstration is, in theory, a good idea, circumstances often make it a less than ideal setting in which to make a decision.

With the tremendous growth experienced by computer retailers in the last couple of years, recruiting qualified sales personnel is an almost impossible task. Those who are knowledgeable about computers may have little insight into the subtle differences between word-processing programs. In defense of the sales personnel, it is difficult to gain an extensive background in all the available microcomputer applications.

Even the most competent sales person in a computer store feels the pressures of time and machine availability. While it would be ideal to be able to spend the two or three hours it takes to adequately educate a potential user about word processing, most stores do not have enough sales people or machines to allow it.

Computer stores that specialize in software (programs) can now be found in some areas of the country. Although I have not had the opportunity to visit one, the idea appeals to me. This type of store offers programs to try, sales people who are not trying to sell you the higher ticket hardware items, documentation to read, computers for demonstrations, and plenty of time to make an intelligent decision! What luxury!

Perhaps I have been unnecessarily harsh on computer retailers. If your favorite computer store is able to provide you with all the information and support you need, count yourself among the fortunate and patronize it at every opportunity.

CAN YOU BELIEVE ADVERTISEMENTS?

Advertising found in computer and business-oriented periodicals is another source of information regarding word processing and other types of programs. Most advertising is accurate, as far as it goes. The supplier usually provides a way for you to obtain further information on the product. The data received in reply to an inquiry to the supplier is generally more detailed. The strong points of the program are emphasized in both advertisements and data sheets. Rarely are limitations mentioned in any great detail, yet they may be of critical importance to your intended application.

Some progressive software suppliers offer the program manuals and documentation separately, usually at a reduced price. This is an excellent way to get better acquainted with a program that you may want to purchase. User manuals are almost always the best way to accurately assess the actual capabilities (and limitations) of a program. Most expensive programs I have purchased have been the direct result of my being able to study the documentation before I made a decision. If the supplier does not offer separate documentation prices, perhaps you could talk your local dealer into letting you borrow a copy of the manual for a day or so. If not, you may be able to purchase the package with the understanding that it can be returned within a few days (disks unopened, of course) for credit if it fails to meet your needs.

REVIEWS AND ARTICLES IN PERIODICALS

There are numerous magazine articles and books being published about word processing. Many computer-oriented magazines have printed in-depth comparisons and reviews of nearly all the word-processing programs on the market. In any given month, some type of article about word processing appears in almost every small computer magazine.

Are these articles helpful? Indeed yes, particularly if you have some background knowledge of word-processing programs. Most articles and program reviews presume at least a cursory knowledge of word processing. Publishers are reluctant to publish beginning level tutorials very often. It really doesn't do much good for you to spend time reading in-depth comparisons of word-processing programs if you don't have the faintest idea of what they are talking about.

CHOOSING A WORD-PROCESSING PROGRAM

The best way to get acquainted with a word-processing program is to sit down at you computer and use it. If you own a computer with enough hardware for any word-processing chore and have enough money to buy every program offered for your computer, the final decision is easy. Just use all the programs, and discard those you don't like!

There is a better, and far less expensive, way to decide which program (if any) is suitable for your intended applications. Hopefully, the method I am using will apply just as well a few years from now as it does today. Instead of telling you which program I like best for this or that application, I will concentrate on giving you a way to make your own decision about any program offered for your computer.

You will be provided with the next best alternative to actually sitting down at a computer with several programs. I have selected several word-processing and utility programs for the Apple II computer that represent a wide range of capabilities and special features (Fig. 3-2). I have chosen these programs because the range of features they offer is representative of other programs in their price range.

PROGRAM EXPLANATION

Each of the programs selected for detailed

examination in the next few chapters represents a unique combination of features and limitations. In order to provide a structure for each description, I used roughly the following outline.

Initial Requirements

1. Apple system required—RAM, number of disks, etc.

2. Other modifications required—CP/M, 80-column display board, lowercase adapter, shift key modification, etc.

3. Cost of the program.

Text Input Features

1. Upper- and lowercase display, shift key, method.

2. Line width displayed, method.

3. Automatic word formatting—moves word to next line if too long to fit on the one in use?

4. Paragraph indentation—auto or manual, how set and used.

5. Hyphenation—prompt, user approve, automatic, or not available.

6. Tabbing—available? If so, how are the tab stops set and their effects displayed on the screen?

7. Justification—available? Which—left, right, center, decimal point. Method used, how selected.

8. Status display during text input? If so, what is displayed—operating mode, tab stops, margins, space remaining for new text, page number, line spacing, etc.

9. Can you reset page specifications in the text?

Fig. 3-2. Some examples of word-processing programs for the Apple II.

10. Accepts files from other programs?

11. Accepts text from an external device?

12. Automatic checking for spelling?

13. Formatting for text output—centering, underlining, bold printing, super- and subscript, two-pass printing, character size selection, etc.

14. Maximum text length per file.

15. Maximum speed accepted for text input.

Editing Features

1. Cursor positioning, how? Express moves provided for. If so, which?

2. Scrolling—backward/forward through the text.

3. Change a few characters—how?

4. Insert text at the cursor position—how?

5. Delete text from cursor—how?

6. Block functions—copy, move, save, delete, markers.

7. Search—first occurrence, all occurrences, Nth occurrence.

8. Search and replace—first, all, or Nth occurrence. Action completed automatically? User prompts? Manual override?

9. Operates on multiple file document?

10. Mathematical or columnar functions included?

11. Miscellaneous editing features.

Text Storage and Retrieval

1. DOS used. Program backup possible or supplied? Is program user modifiable? If so, to what extent? Method of multiple drive access.

2. Text file backup—procedure. Automatic, prompted, or user initiated. Disk copy utilities included? Other disk utilities included?

3. Text file creation and documentation. Length and type of title allowed. Can descriptive phrases be added? Dating included? Maximum size document allowed?

4. Amount of text actively in memory.

5. Displays amount of space remaining on disk?

6. Merging text from other documents—how?

7. Files compatible with other programs?

Output Operations

1. Printer configuration—how set up and changed.

2. Initiating printing—how?

3. Printer control—spacing, top of form, tabbing, changing fonts or character size.

4. Justification—word spacing, letter spacing, or full proportional spacing supported?

5. Forms control—continuous, single sheet, variable.

6. Page numbering, headers, footers—how done and which are available?

7. Does system respond to printer problems?

8. Text insertion during printing—if so, how?

9. Print mode description—pause, control, abort, etc. Does this mode fit your needs?

10. Screen preview of document? If provided, how is this accomplished?

11. Can you print multiple copies, multiple files?

Special Features

Here we will consider such things as extensive temporary margins, capability to input variable values during printing, interface to other programs, communications capability, etc.

Human Engineering

1. How is the program booted? What method of selecting desired operations is used?

2. Logical, easy to use commands?

3. Are there provisions for verification of potentially dangerous commands (delete, for example)?

4. Error recovery, emergency procedures?

5. Is there a HELP file on line?

Documentation

1. Do you need a tutorial?

2. What structure and form is used?

3. Are reference cards, charts, etc. included?

Support

1. Who supports the program—dealer, supplier, author, all of these?

2. Is an extra copy readily available?

3. What is the warranty? Read the fine print.

For each of the programs, I start with installation and proceed through modes of operation, features, special capabilities, likes, dislikes, and overall impressions. Wherever possible, I use screen photographs to illustrate the point being discussed. Following the detailed description chapters, one chapter is devoted to a brief discussion of several programs that offer special capabilities in exchange for some rather expensive hardware requirements.

MAKING YOUR SHOPPING LIST

My intention is to help you become acquainted with features offered in each program, not to provide a review. If you find a specific program of interest and decide to buy it, I'm sure the supplier will be happy to accommodate you. I hope that you will look at each of the features and think about just what your program should (or should not) include.

You may decide, for instance, that the method of screen display in one program is great. The block operations from another may appeal to you. Special capabilities from several programs might be required for your specific applications. As you read through the description chapters to follow, try to come up with a "shopping list" of features that should be included in any program you consider for your own situation. Just as important will be a second list of features that you really can't think of a use for or wouldn't be willing to pay extra money to obtain.

Chapter 10, which deals with small business and home applications, may cause you to review your lists. Spend enough time to come up with lists that reflect your best judgment of both types of features; it will save you a lot of money and grief in the long run.

By learning about programs presently on the market, you can find out how they work without having to bear the cost. Literally hundreds of dollars worth of programs are represented in the next few chapters. Although none of the programs may interest you at this time, the price ranges represented will give you an idea of what you can expect to spend for a program that meets your needs.

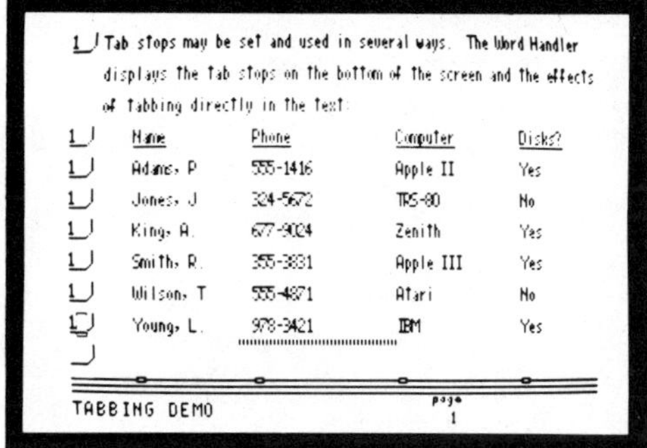

Name	Phone	Computer	Disks?
Adams, P	555-1416	Apple II	Yes
Jones, J	324-5672	TRS-80	No
King, A.	677-9024	Zenith	Yes
Smith, R.	555-3831	Apple III	Yes
Wilson, T	555-4871	Atari	No
Young, L.	978-3421	IBM	Yes

Write-On!

Publisher: Datamost, 9748 Cozycroft Avenue, Northridge, CA 91326
Hardware Required: Apple II Plus or Apple II with Applesoft ROM card, 48K, Disk II, and printer
Price: $129.95

Write-On! is a surprisingly capable wordprocessing program for the Apple II. Many of the program's features are unique in its price class.

TEXT INPUT FEATURES

Selecting Text Input Mode. From the Editor program. Text input is selected from a menu. You are asked to designate whether text will be coming from the keyboard or a disk file (Fig. 4-1).

Upper- and Lowercase Display. Display of upper- and lowercase characters requires one of the many lowercase adapters available for the Apple II. Instructions for completing the relatively simple modification to allow use of the shift keys are included. If no modification is done, ESC is used as a shift key and ESC-ESC for shift lock.

Video Display. The standard Apple II 40-character lines are displayed on the screen. During text input, the cursor remains in the center line of the video display and 10 lines of text are displayed at a time. As new lines are entered, the top line scrolls vertically off the screen (Fig. 4-2).

Word Formatting. As is usual in most word-processing programs, words too long to fit on the current screen line are automatically moved in their entirety to the next line. A space is considered the separator between words, and no provisions are included to set "unbreakable" spaces.

Paragraph indentation, selected by pressing CTRL-P, is user defined. A command in the form of \ PIn \, where n is the number of spaces to be indented from the left margin, sets the value. The program is supplied with a default indentation of 0 spaces for printing block-style paragraphs.

Tabbing. Up to nine horizontal tabs may be defined using the tab set command. The format of this command is \ TSnp \—tab set, number (1-9), position relative to the left margin. Once tabs have been set, each may be used pressing CTRL-T followed by the tab number. The screen then displays \ Tn \ at the appropriate spot in the text (Fig. 4-3).

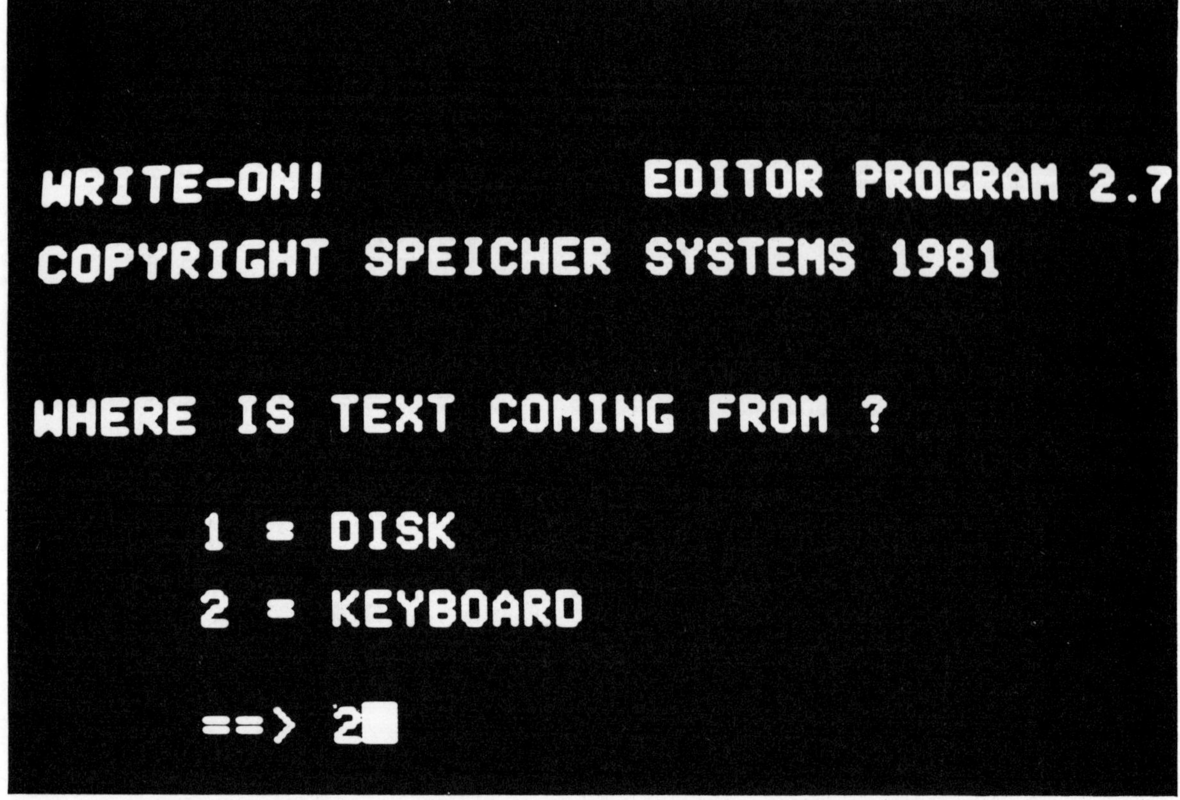

Fig. 4-1. In the editor mode, text may be typed from the keyboard or retrieved from a disk file.

Effects of tabbing are not shown directly on the screen.

Tab stops may be cleared globally or selectivity. The command \ TCO \ clears all tabs,   TCn \ clears only the n numbered tab. Tabs may be set or cleared in the process of text entry, so the nine available positions may be used and reused as necessary within a document.

Justification. Text with flush left and right margins, using word spacing, can be created by selecting the \ JY \ (justify yes) or \ JN \ (justify no) printer command embedded in the text. If no justification command is present, the program automatically prints in the justified mode.

By embedding the commands in the text, you can select to print some portions of your text with a ragged right margin and justify the rest. No provision for displaying the effects of justification on the video screen is included.

Status Display during Text Input. During the process of text input, status is displayed across the top of the screen by a line which reads "TYPE INSERTED TEXT   CTRL-E TO END." Ten lines of inserted text are displayed, along with the status line, at a time. Scrolling of text lines does not affect the status display.

Page Specification Change. Resetting page specifications involves the use of either printing format commands or line commands. The manual differentiates between the two types by saying that printing format commands affect all of the text which follows them and line commands affect printing of text only at the point where they occur. In this section, I will discuss only the line commands. A little later, the printing format commands will be covered in some detail. Either type of command may be embedded in the body of the text.

Some of the line commands available include

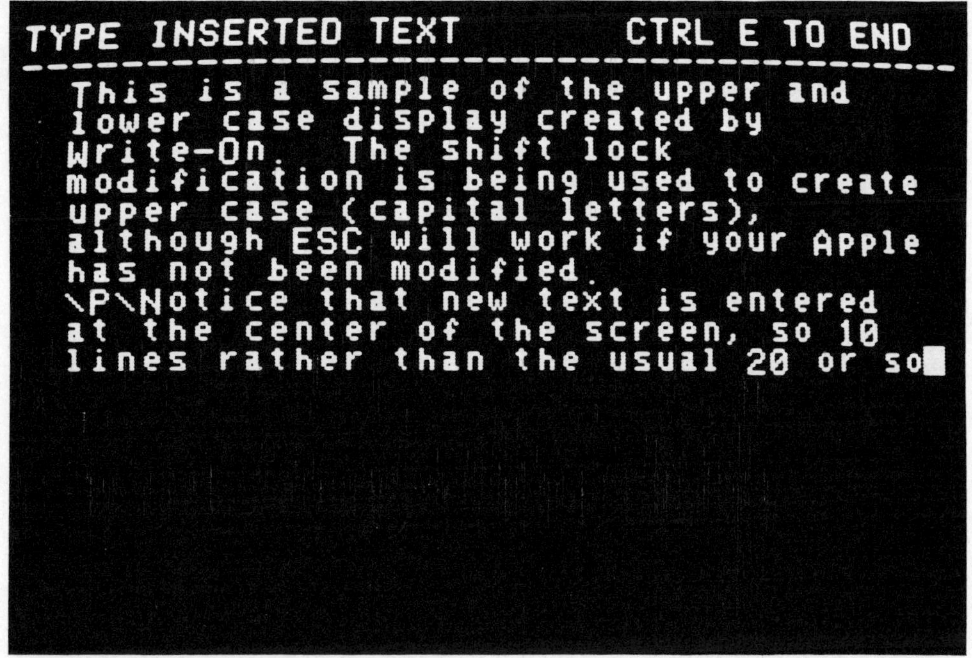

Fig. 4-2. As text is typed, it is shown at the center of the screen. Filled lines scroll toward the top, so a total of 10 lines may be displayed at one time.

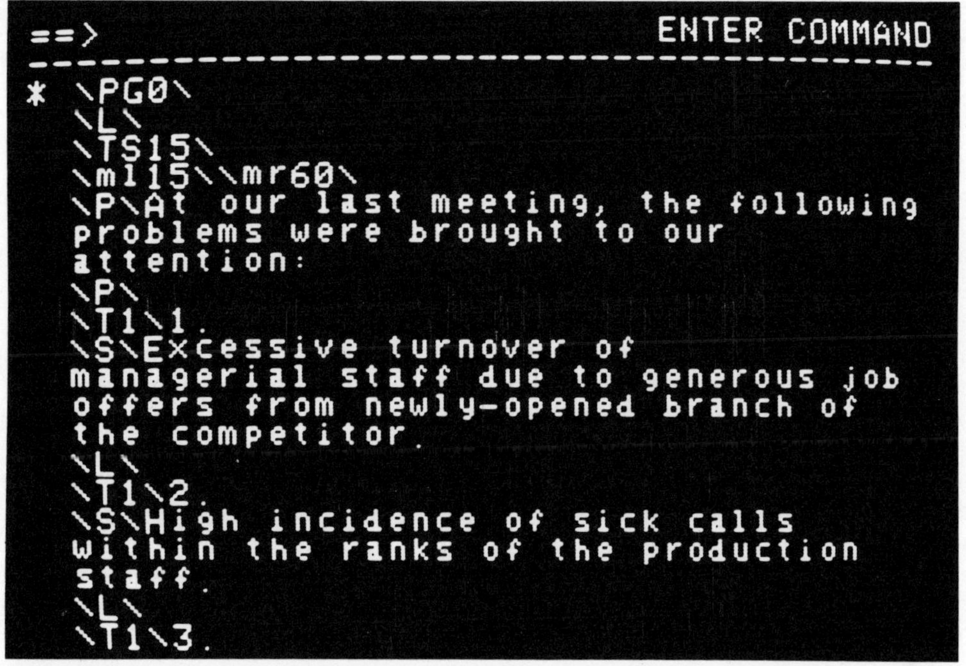

Fig. 4-3. Tab stops are designated using the tab set command and used by pressing CTRL-T and the tab number.

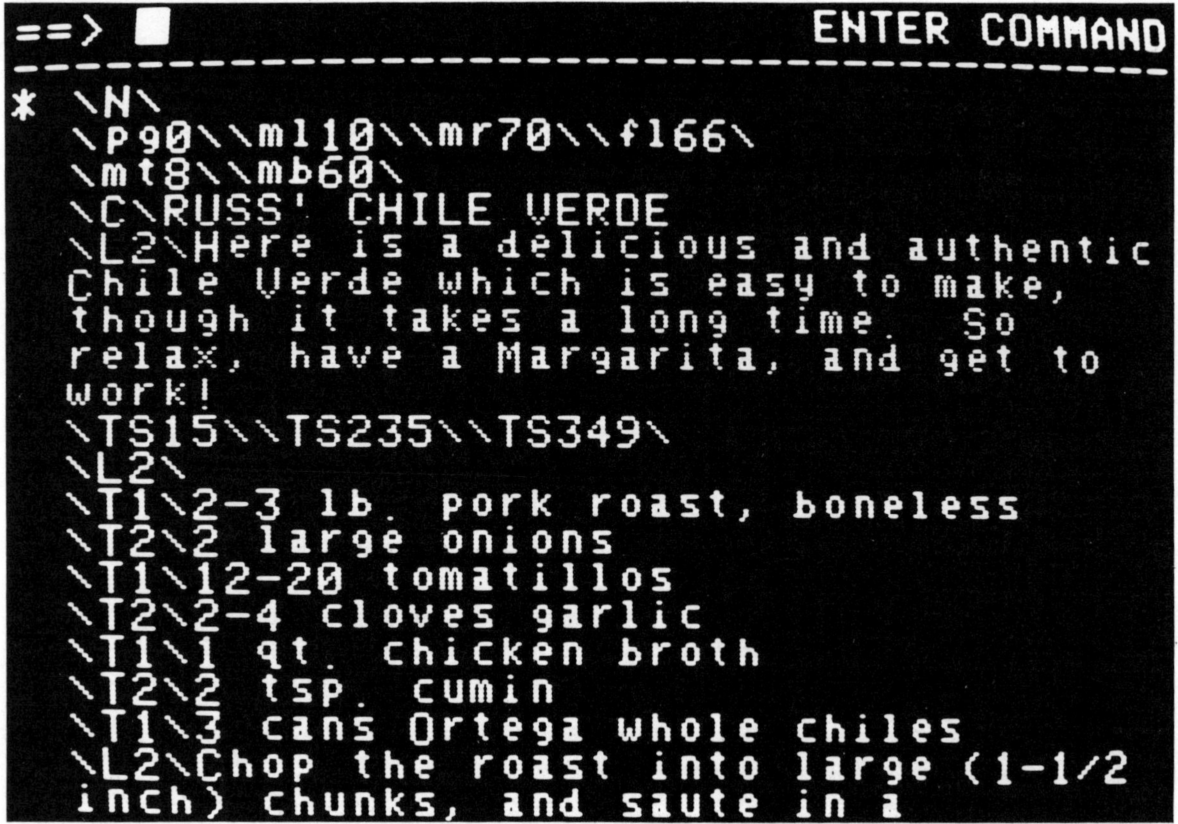

Fig. 4-4. Line commands used to format text output may be inserted directly into the text.

\P\ (new paragraph and indent, if indentation has been previously defined), \ L \ (start a new line), \ In \ (indent n spaces),\ R (align text with right margin), and \ N \ (start printing on a new page). Page numbering can also be temporarily or permanently altered with the text (Fig. 4-4).

Temporary margins (up to 10 levels) may be set using the \ S\ command. This program contains extensive temporary margin features which will be discussed under the special features heading of this chapter.

Text Files from Other Programs. Data files may be converted from another program's format for use with Write-On! through the use of the file conversion routine included with the program. Again, we will discuss this in the special features section.

Formatting for Text Output. Text to be centered on the printed page must be preceded by \ C \ (created by pressing CTRL-C) and followed by another line command such as \ L \ or \ P \. Selected text may also be aligned with the right margin by using the \ R \ command preceding and another line command following.

If your printer is capable of backspacing, underlining or triple overstriking to produce a boldface effect can be used to highlight parts of the text. Text to be underlined is preceded by \ U \ (CTRL-U) and followed by another line command. Similarly, text for overstriking is indicated by \ O \- (CTRL-O) and followed by a line command. A combination of centering or aligning with the right margin and underlining or using boldface may be done by using a combination of the two commands. In this case, the underline or overstrike command must immediately precede any \ C\ or \ R| selected.

No provisions for selecting variable print sizes, superscripts, or other special printer features are included.

Maximum Text Length per File. Maximum file length is determined by available RAM. In a 48K Apple, this is about 10 typewritten pages. The program issues warning messages when you get to within 25 lines of capacity. Error trapping is included to protect you from trying to repeat a line or block or merge in a disk file when memory capacity will be exceeded.

Typing Speed. During normal text entry operations, this program can keep up with a fairly fast typist. During the "housecleaning"periods, data entry may be interrupted, and characters dropped.

EDITING FEATURES

Current Line Pointer. The current line pointer (CLP) is used to direct text insertion, deletion, movement, and other editing functions. Indicated by an asterisk at the left margin, the CLP may be moved up or down. Express functions are provided for multiple-line moves. U or D followed by a number moves the CLP the specified number of lines in the desired direction (Figs. 4-5 and 4-6). UP or DP moves the CLP up or down a page. To go directly to the "top" or "bottom" of the text, simply type T or B. For most editing functions, there is no cursor as such. The combination of the current line pointer and editing commands allow you to do without a cursor.

Scrolling. Text is not actually scrolled on-screen during most of the editing functions. The effect is one of refreshing the screen, because the desired line of text appears after a "blink" of the display. When you insert text, a cursor appears at

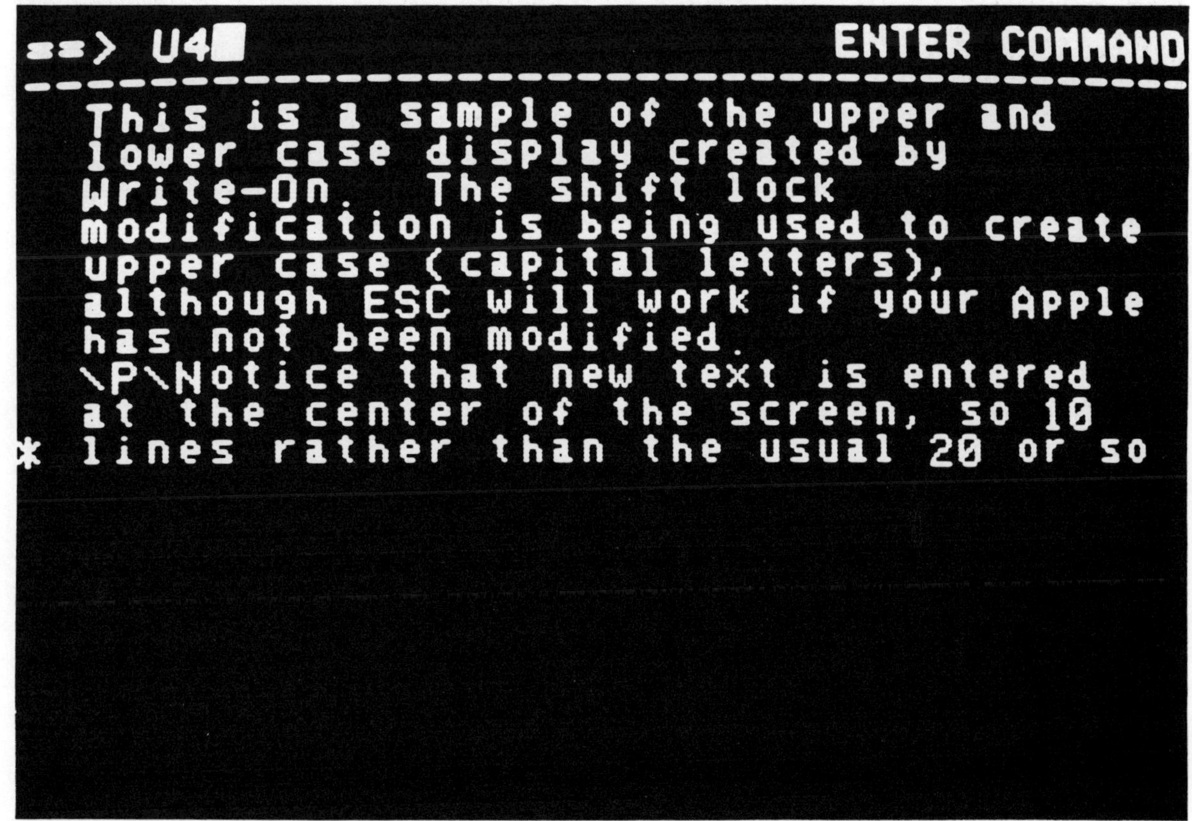

Fig. 4-5. The current line pointer (*) will be moved up four lines by the U4 command shown.

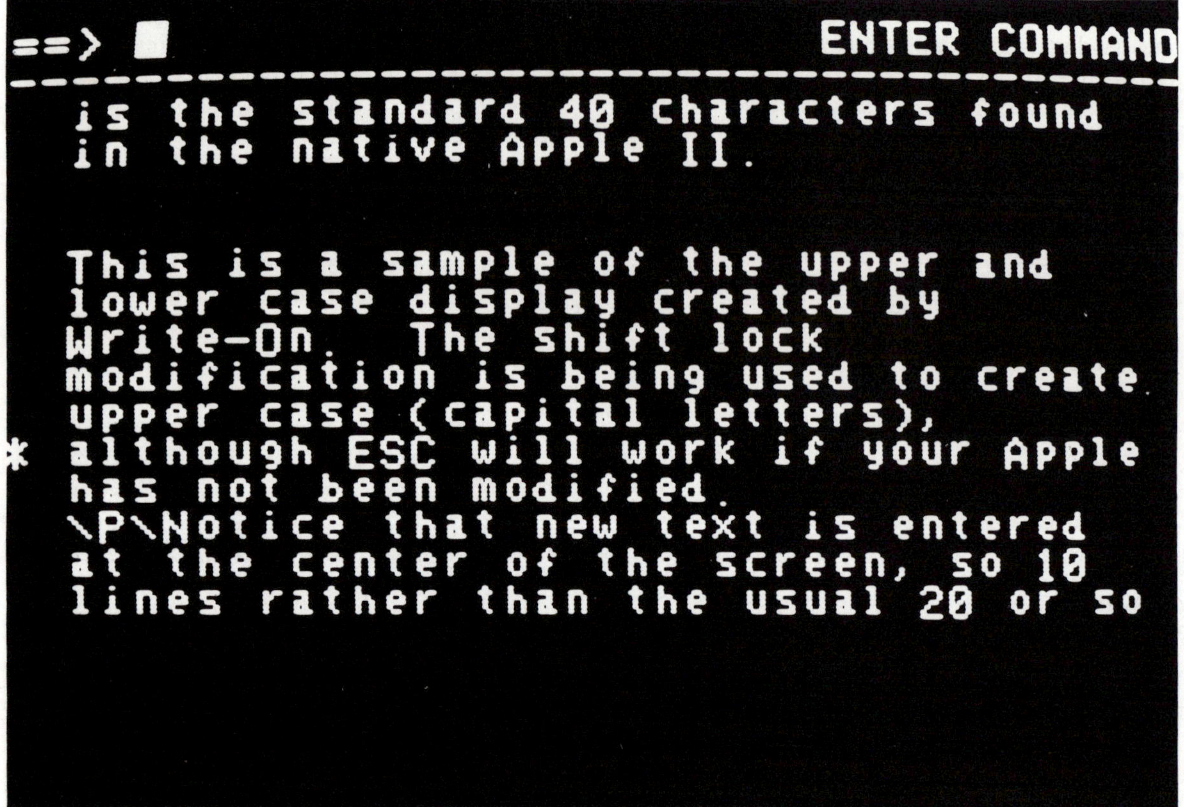

Fig. 4-6. After the U4 command is executed, the current line pointer is shifted to the designated line.

center screen, and lines of inserted text scroll toward the top of the screen.

Changing a Few Characters. The C (change) command is used to change a few characters in the line indicated by the CLP. After selecting C, you are asked to specify string #1, which should contain the characters as they are found in the line. String #2 is requested next and should contain the characters to be substituted for string #1 (Fig. 4-7). Although this may seem like an awkward procedure at first, it works quite efficiently to make the desired changes.

Inserting Text. Text insertion is selected from the command mode by pressing I. By positioning the current line pointer you determine where text is to be inserted. If new text is to be inserted at the end of a document, pressing B locates the CLP, and I enables the insert mode. An

express command, IT, allows simultaneous movement of the CLP to the beginning of text and entry into the insertion mode. For entering text somewhere in the middle of a document, the CLP is positioned to the line above where the new text is to be inserted before selecting the insert mode.

What about entering text in the middle of a line? The program provides the SP (split line) command, which divides the line for insertion purposes. Type SP, and you are asked to enter string #1. After this string has been entered, the line will be split at the first space following that string. The insert mode may then be selected for text insertion at that point.

Text insertion takes place at the center of the screen. The lines being entered scroll toward the top of the screen, while those following the insertion point are constantly displayed toward the bottom.

50

Deleting Text. In general, the X (cross-out) command is used to delete lines and blocks of text. Merely pressing X will delete the line indicated by the current line pointer. If you would like to delete only a portion of a line, use the SP command prior to using the X command. The combination XB will delete an entire block of text. Use of blocks is discussed later in this section.

Copying and Moving Text. Lines of text may be moved by first specifying a location and designating that location as the LD (line destination). Next, the CLP is moved to the desired line and ML (move line) is typed. The line at the CLP is then automatically moved to the destination previously specified. To move a line to the middle of an existing line, the SP command is used first and then the destination specified. The RL (repeat line) command allows you to command repeat lines of text. A number may be typed after the command to indicate the number of repetitions desired (Fig. 4-8).

Blocks of text may be defined by locating the CLP at the first line desired and pressing BF (block first), then moving the CLP to the end of the block and pressing BL (block last). Once a block has been marked, it may be moved to a specific location in the text by specifying BD (block destination) and pressing MB (move block). Repeating a block involves specifying the destination and entering RB (repeat block). If desired, a number may be typed following the RB command, and the block will be repeated the specified number of times. XB will cause a marked block to be deleted from the text.

Also included are commands for printing a marked block (PB) or saving it to disk (SB). The block commands included are quite versatile and

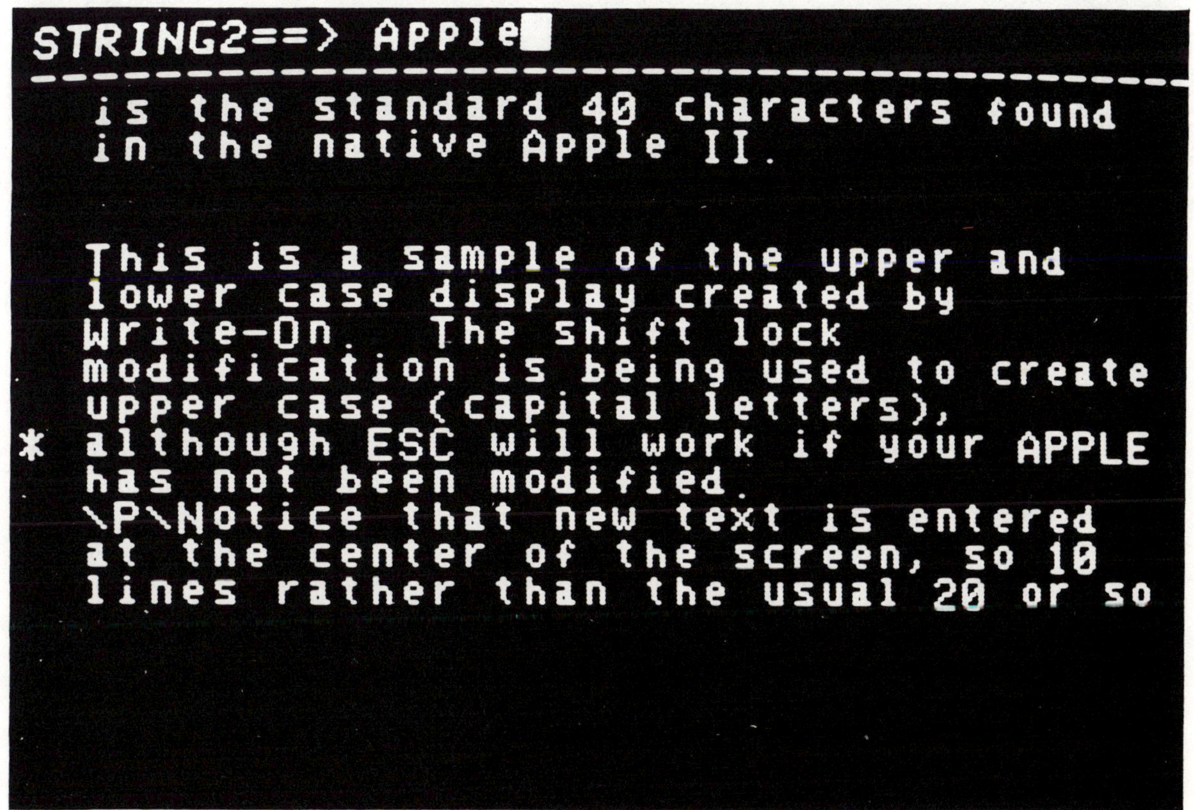

Fig. 4-7. The C (change) command is used to change a few characters in the text. In this example, APPLE will be changed to Apple.

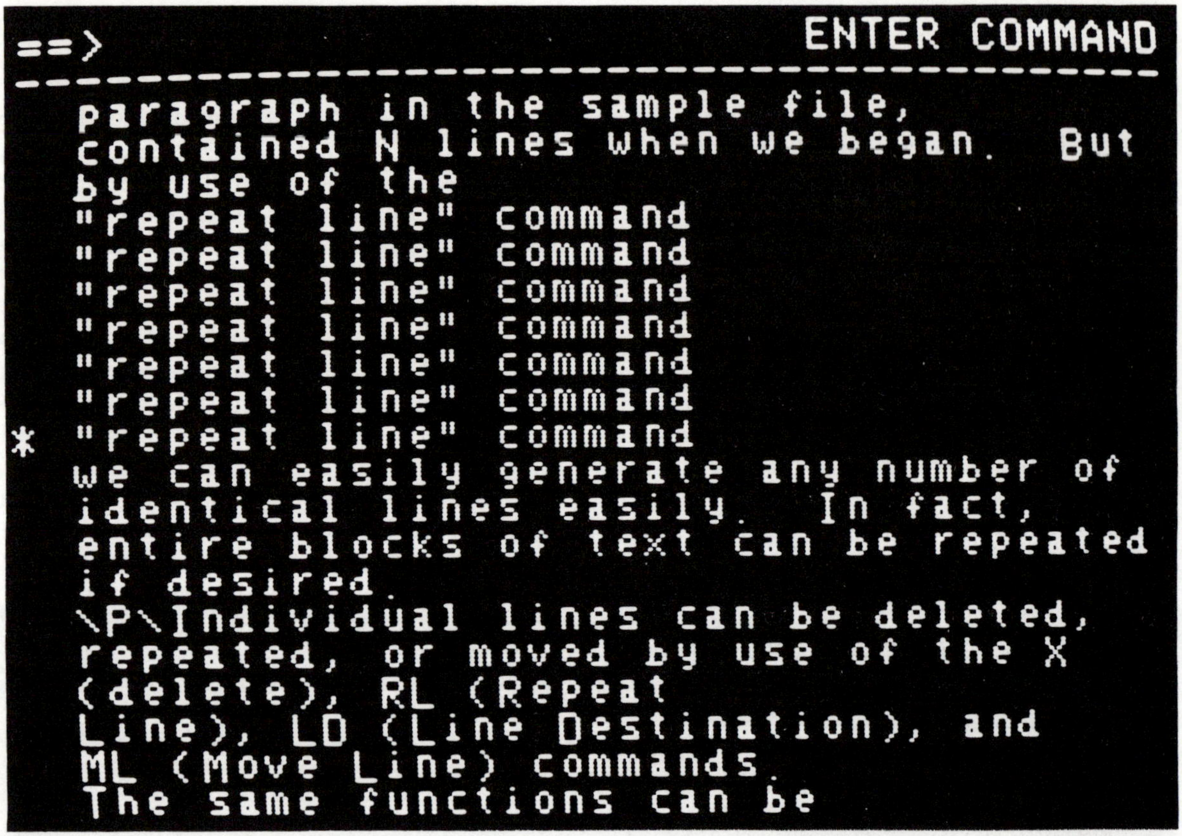

Fig. 4-8. The RL (repeat line) command may be used to duplicate any number of text lines.

easy to use. Just be sure to specify both the beginning (BF) and end (BL) of the block before attempting any of the commands provided for block operations.

Inserting text from another disk file (merging) is also provided. Position the CLP at the line above the point where text from the desired disk file is to be inserted and type M (merge). Once you supply the information requested, the disk file text will be inserted into the one in memory at the time.

Search and Replace. Commonly thought of as CLP-positioning commands, the program includes both F (find) and RF (repeat find) capabilities. Pressing F in the command mode brings a SEARCH STRING prompt to the screen. Once the string has been typed, the program scans from the CLP forward until the desired string is located (Fig. 4-9). Pressing RF at that point locates the next occurrence of the same string.

The C (change) command to change just a few characters at the CLP was discussed earlier. If the same series of characters is to be changed in another line, type RC (repeat change) after locating the string with RF (repeat find).

A CA (change all) provision allows for global change of a specified string. Typing CA, the string to be located, and its desired replacement causes the editor to search and change all occurrences of the string in the file. A word of caution—leading and following spaces must be specified in order to replace whole words. One of the uses for the CA command suggested by the manual involves construction abbreviations for frequently typed words or phrases during text entry and using the change all command later to replace them with the entire word or phrase. Clever!

DOS Used. The program is supplied in Apple DOS 3.2. Instructions are included for creating back-up copies of the program disk in either DOS 3.2, or the more recent DOS 3.3. You can create multiple copies of the program. In fact, you can put the system on every one of your data disks! This is system backup of the highest order and should only be used as such.

Text File Backup. Standard DOS is also used to create data disks, so making back-up copies of text files is a simple matter of using any one of the many disk copy programs available. No disk copy routines are included on the Write-On disk.

Multiple Disk Drive Access. The initial configuration routine asks whether your system has one drive or two. If you have two drives, you are asked to designate which drive you want to use for both storage and retrieval operations on each file.

Text File Creation and Documentation.

Text file length is limited to the amount of memory remaining in your computer after the program is loaded. Once memory is filled, the file must be saved on a disk before any additional text may be entered. CATALOG is used by the program, as well as the standard Apple DOS, to display the names of files on a disk.

Creating a text file is initiated by pressing S from the command mode. You are then asked to supply a name for the file and designate on which drive the file is to be saved (Fig. 4-10). Once the file is saved, the program automatically returns to the command mode.

Neither the length of each file nor space remaining on the disk are directly displayed by this program. As we will see in the special features section, both data files and print-image files may also be created and manipulated by the program.

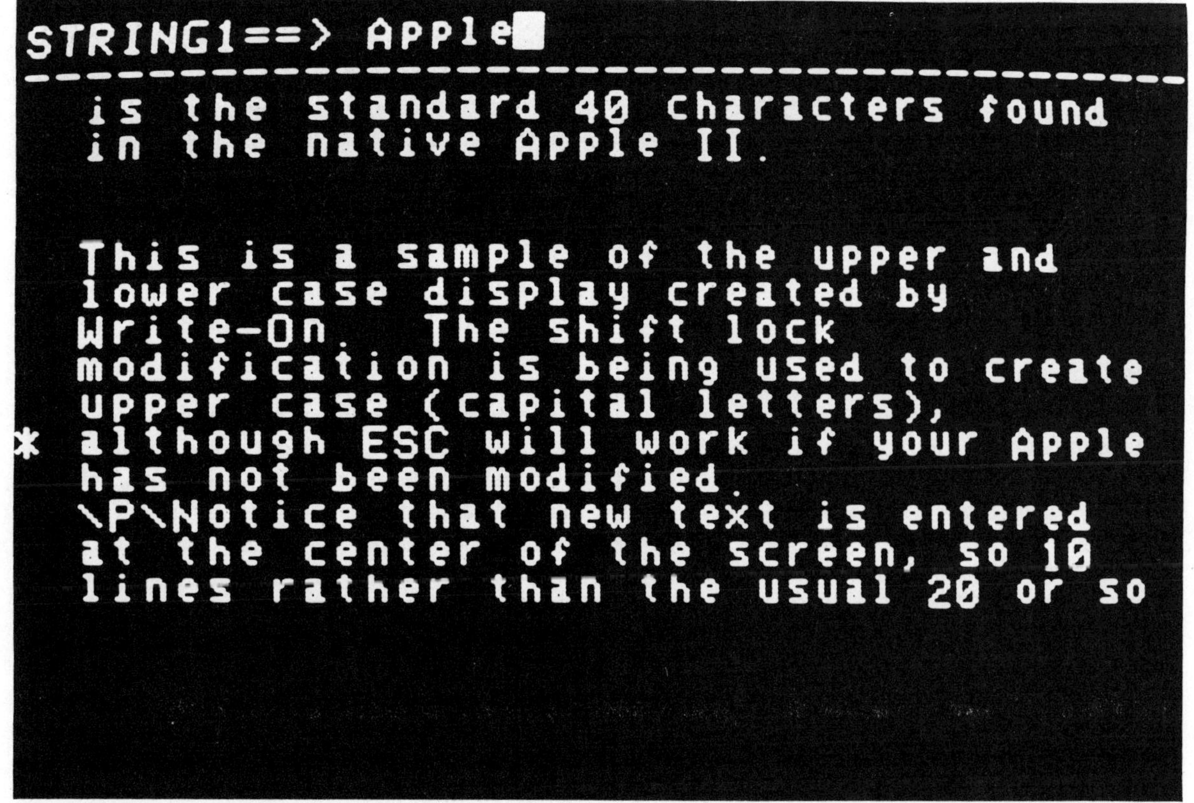

Fig. 4-9. F (find) is used to locate a word or phrase within the text. The operation may be repeated by pressing RF (repeat find).

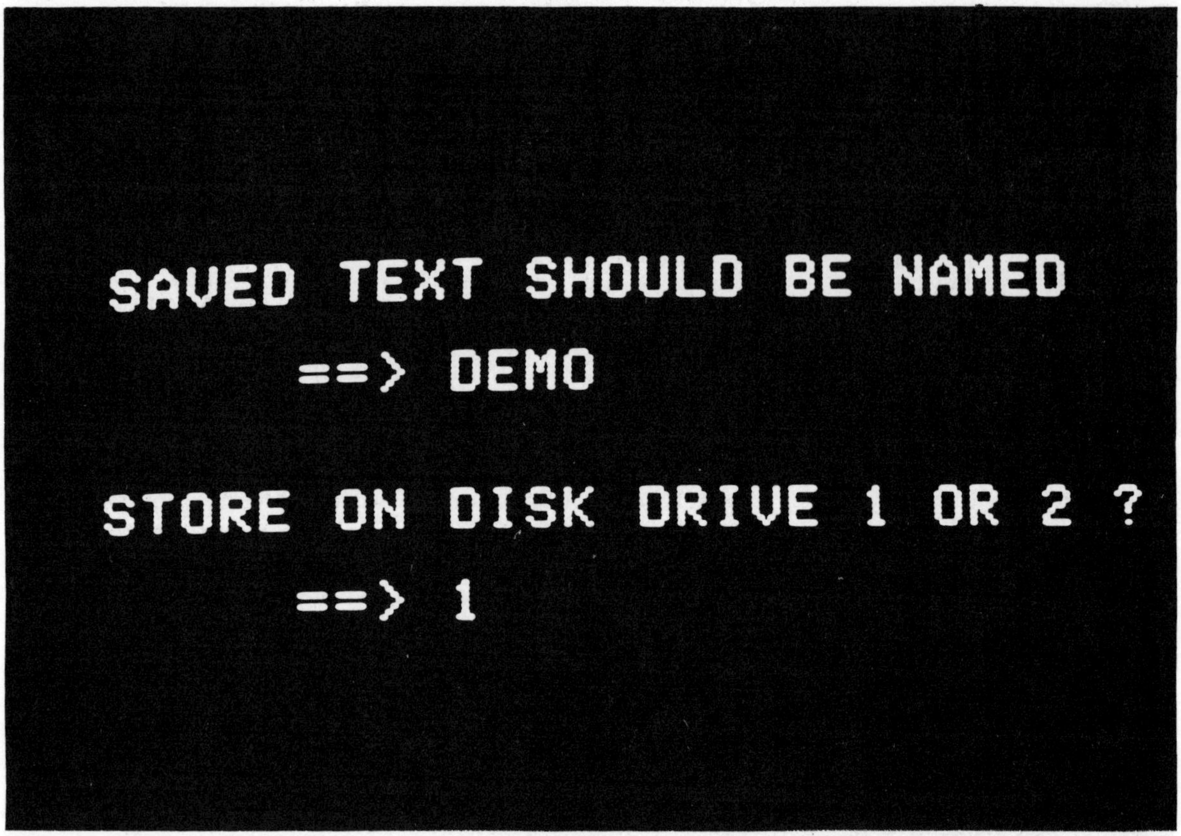

Fig. 4-10. Disk files may be created and saved on either disk drive, as shown by this menu.

Provisions to use files created by other programs are included.

OUTPUT

Printer Configuration. Initial designation of printer and other hardware is done by selecting the "INSTALL NEW SYSTEM" option from the first program menu (Fig. 4-11). Arranged in a series of questions, this routine asks whether or not you have a lowercase adapter, if you have two disk drives, which slot the printer occupies, any special characters required to start your printer, and whether or not the printer requires a separate line feed at the end of a line. After all the questions have been answered, your responses are reviewed, and you are given an opportunity to correct erroneous entries (Fig. 4-12). The installation routine may be rerun whenever changes are made in your system.

Printer Control. This program controls spacing, top of form, tabbing, margins, and other standard printer functions. The default printing format parameters are set to accommodate standard 8½-by-11 inch sheets with minimal margins on the top, bottom, left, and right sides. Single spacing, block paragraph indentation, justification, and page numbers centered in the bottom margin are also specified in the default printer format. You may designate whether or not you want to use continuous forms (default specifies yes), a convenience if you have a tractor fed printer. Special features found in some printers are not directly supported by Write-On! The program author notes, "Since the program is 99% listable, modifiable BASIC, many Write-On! users have modified the program to use special printer drivers and software selectable printer features."

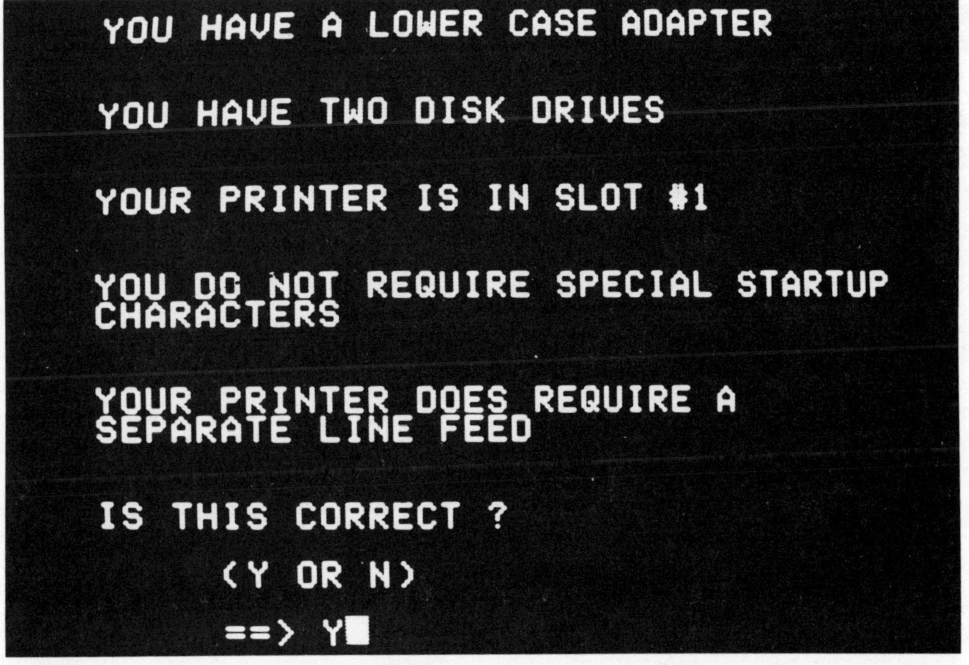

Fig. 4-11. The installation program lets you designate the printer and other hardware in your system.

Fig. 4-12. Your responses to the configuration parameters are reviewed before the installation process is finalized.

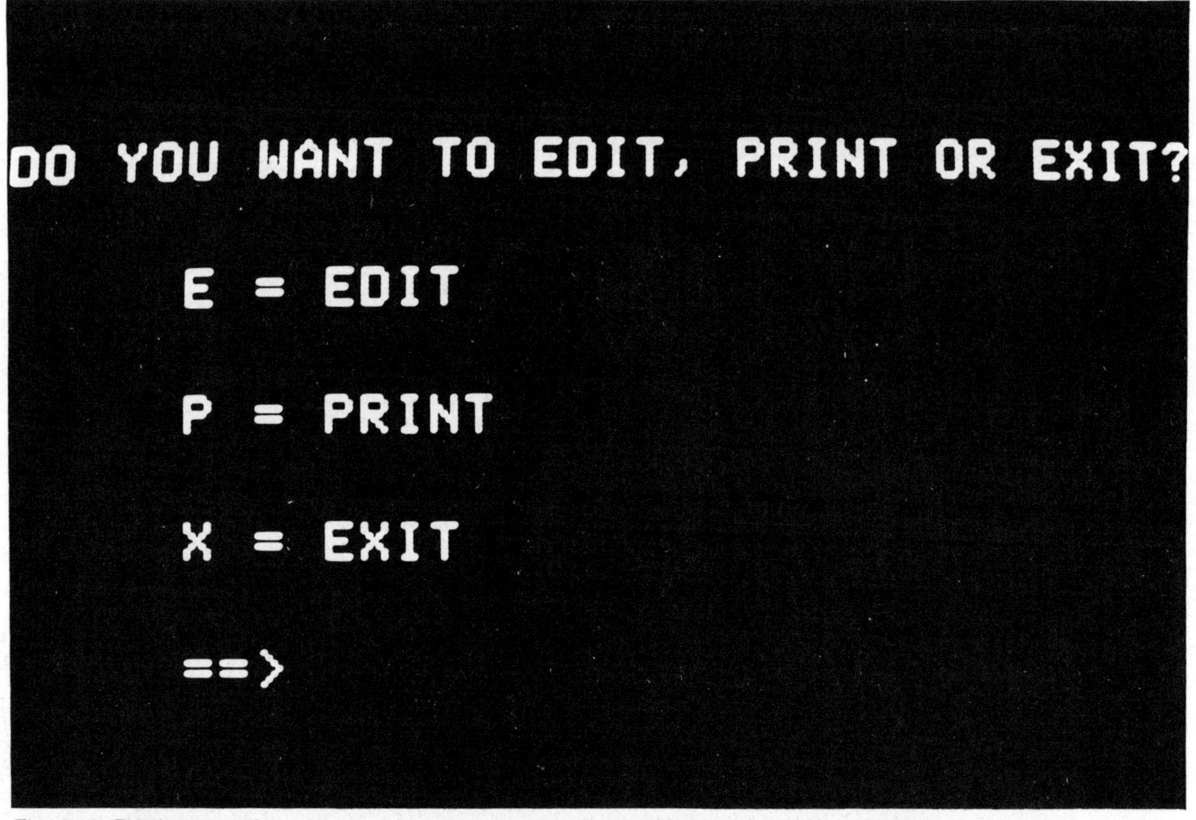

Fig. 4-13. Printing operations may be initiated by pressing P when the main menu is displayed.

Initiating Printing. Print operations are controlled, logically, by the Printer program. There are several ways to call this program. You can select it from the main menu or after editing by typing P (Fig. 4-13). If DOS is booted, you may also type RUN PRINTER. Once the Printer program is running, you are asked to enter the names of files to be printed, and the program checks that the files are present on the data disk in the drives (Fig. 4-14). Next, you are asked to designate the destination, either a printer or a print-image file. If you have requested output to the printer, pressing RETURN after aligning the paper will start printing.

Justification. Since proportional spacing is not supported, this program (like most others) adds extra spaces between words to achieve flush margins or both the right and left sides of the printed page. Justification may be used intermittently during the process of text entry. Unless specified to the contrary, justification is used for all printing.

Headers, Footers, and Page Numbers. Up to 20 headings can be specified using the \ HDn \ command. The headings are centered and printed at the top of each new page. Clearing a heading within the text is done by typing \ HDn \, where n is the number of the heading to be cleared, followed by another printer command. \ HDO \ clears all the headings. There is no provision for printing footers.

Page numbers, by default, are centered at the bottom. Combinations of letters and numbers may be printed by specifying what is to appear to the left and right of the page number. For example, printing page numbers with a dash and space preceding and following (—3—) would be done by specifying the dash-space sequence on both the left and right using \ PL— \\ PR — \. This feature may be used to create chapter-relative page numbers, if desired.

The position of the number on the printed page

is specified using the \ PPx \ (page position) command, where x can be T (top), B (bottom), R (right), L (left), C (center), A (alternating), or S (suppress). Although most of the options are self-explanatory, A (alternating) puts even numbers on the left side of the page and odd numbers on the right side of the page. The effect achieved is that of always having the number on the "outside" of the page. S (suppress) is used to identify those pages you do not wish to be numbered.

Printer Problems. I could find no reference in the documentation to suggest that the program will respond to error indications generated by certain printers. The most common of these problems are out of paper and ribbon jam.

Text Insertion during Printing. During the process of text entry, a keyboard input printer command, \ K \, may be inserted into the text at any point. This command is used in either of two ways: to type in additional text or to stop the printing process for some other reason.

A prompting word or phrase may be added to the command between the K and right backslash, such as \ KCURRENT DATE \. Before printing a line containing a keyboard input command, the computer will pause and prompt you to ENTER CURRENT DATE or whatever prompt is contained in the command. The keyboard input text will then be printed in the proper place. Any number of keyboard input commands can be contained in a text file. Using the \ K \ command in this fashion allows form letters or other documents to be personalized to fit the situation (Fig. 4-15).

The keyboard input command can also be used to program a pause in the process of printing for other purposes, such as changing paper or a typewheel. You can even add a prompt to remind you of what is to be done at that point. The proper

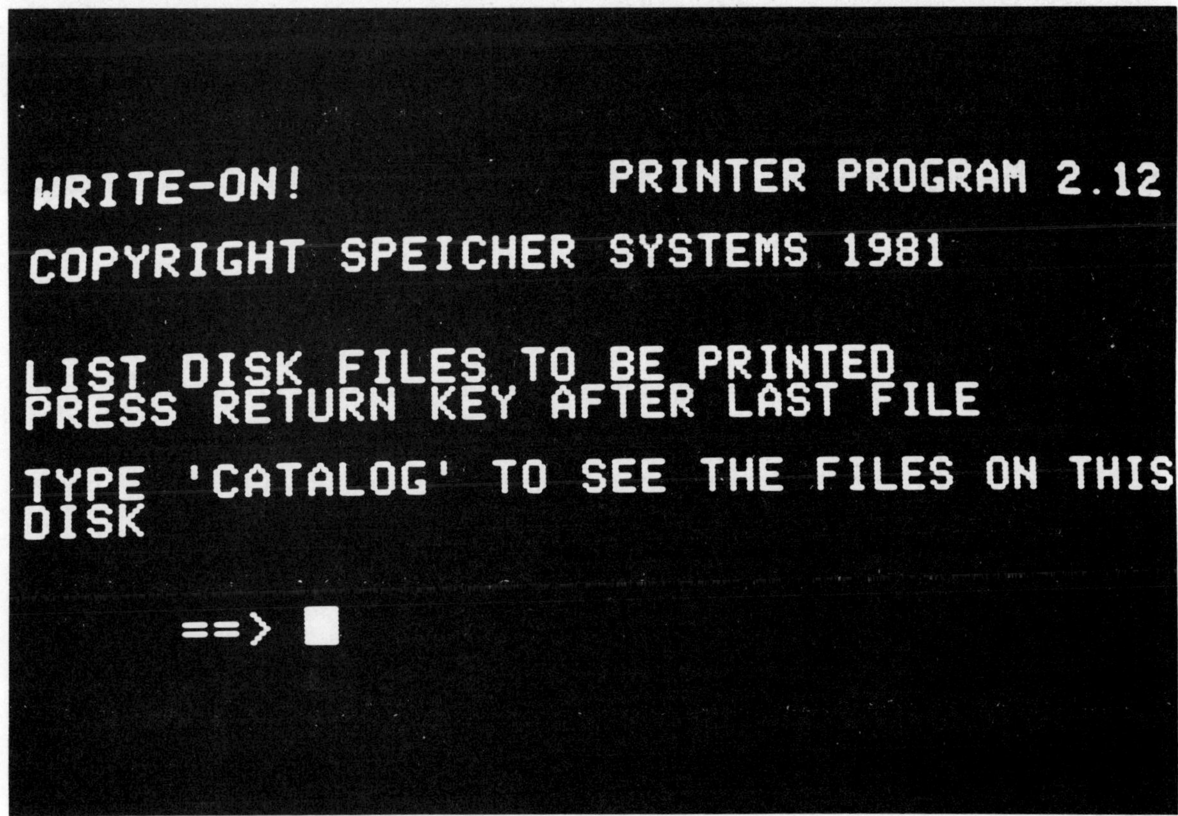

Fig. 4-14. Multiple files may be printed by listing them in the desired order when using the Printer program.

```
==>  ▮                              ENTER COMMAND
------------------------------------------------------
* \N\
  \P90\\ml10\\mr70\\f166\
  \mt8\\mb60\
  \L5\Dear
  \KName\,
  \P\Thank you very much for your
recent inquiry regarding
  \KProduct\.  You will find enclosed a
brochure with a complete description.
  We feel that our price of
  \KPrice\ is very competitive, and we
look forward to receiving your order.
  \L5\
  \I30\Sincerely,
  \L3\
  \I30\Irving Moss
  \I30\Sales Manager
```

Fig. 4-15. The keyboard input command is used to insert text from the keyboard into a document prior to printing.

response to this type of input prompt is just a RE-TURN, at which point normal printing will continue.

Print Mode Display. Text is displayed on the screen as it is printed, although the screen is unable to display the full page printing width. A double space between identifies where the actual printed lines will end (Fig. 4-16).

Screen Preview of Document. No provision is included for previewing the final format of documents to be printed.

Print-Image Files. In normal operation, the program formats each line of text as it is printed. It is possible to create a print-image file to speed up this process considerably. A print-image file is one which contains text already formatted and ready to print. The Printer program includes provisions for designating a print-image file rather than the printer as the destination for formatted text output (Fig. 4-17).

Using a print-image file to store formatted text has distinct advantages. No matter how many disk files or input operations were used to create it, once a document is set into a print-image file it can be reprinted any number of times with a minimum of fuss.

Print-image file names begin with a P. (letter P and a period) to identify them in the disk catalog. As you can see in Fig. 4-18, error trapping is included to remind you of this requirement if P. does not precede your file name. Any test can be made into a print-image file with the exception headings.

Printing Multiple Files or Copies. The Printer program allows you to specify up to 100 files for printing in sequence. Unformatted and print-image files may be mixed on the list, as may files on

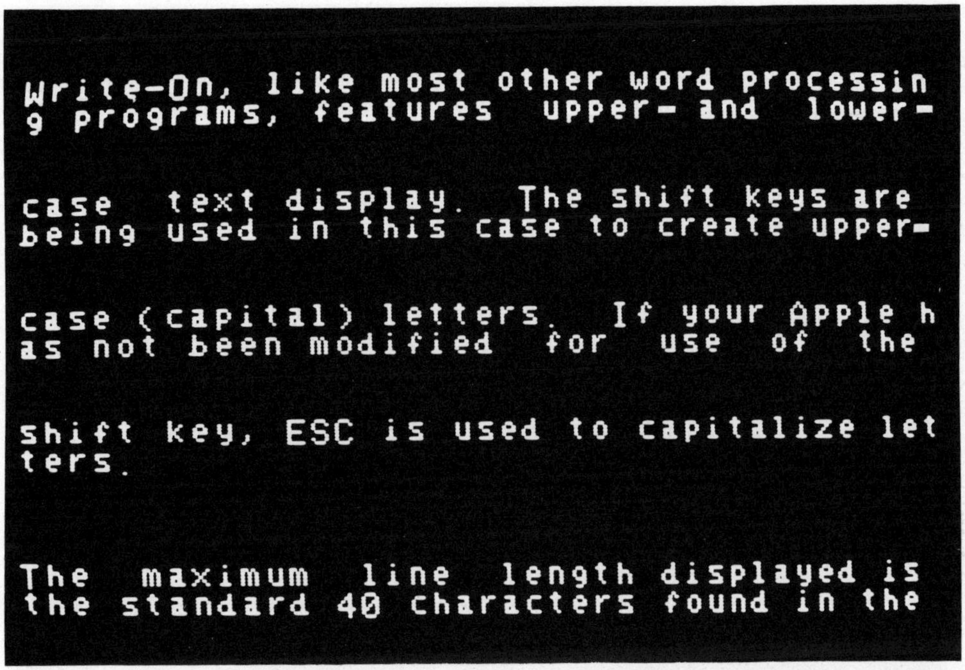

Write-On, like most other word processin
g programs, features upper- and lower-

case text display. The shift keys are
being used in this case to create upper-

case (capital) letters. If your Apple h
as not been modified for use of the

shift key, ESC is used to capitalize let
ters.

The maximum line length displayed is
the standard 40 characters found in the

Fig. 4-16. During printing operations, double spaces identify breaks between lines as they are actually printed.

WHERE WILL THE OUTPUT GO?
     1 = PRINTER
     2 = PRINT-IMAGE DISK FILE

     ==> 2

PRINT-IMAGE DISK FILE SHOULD BE NAMED

     ==> DEMOPRINT

PREFORMATTED FILE WILL BE STORED ON
DRIVE # (1 OR 2) ?

     ==> 1

Fig. 4-17. Text formatted in final output form may be saved in a print-image file on a data disk.

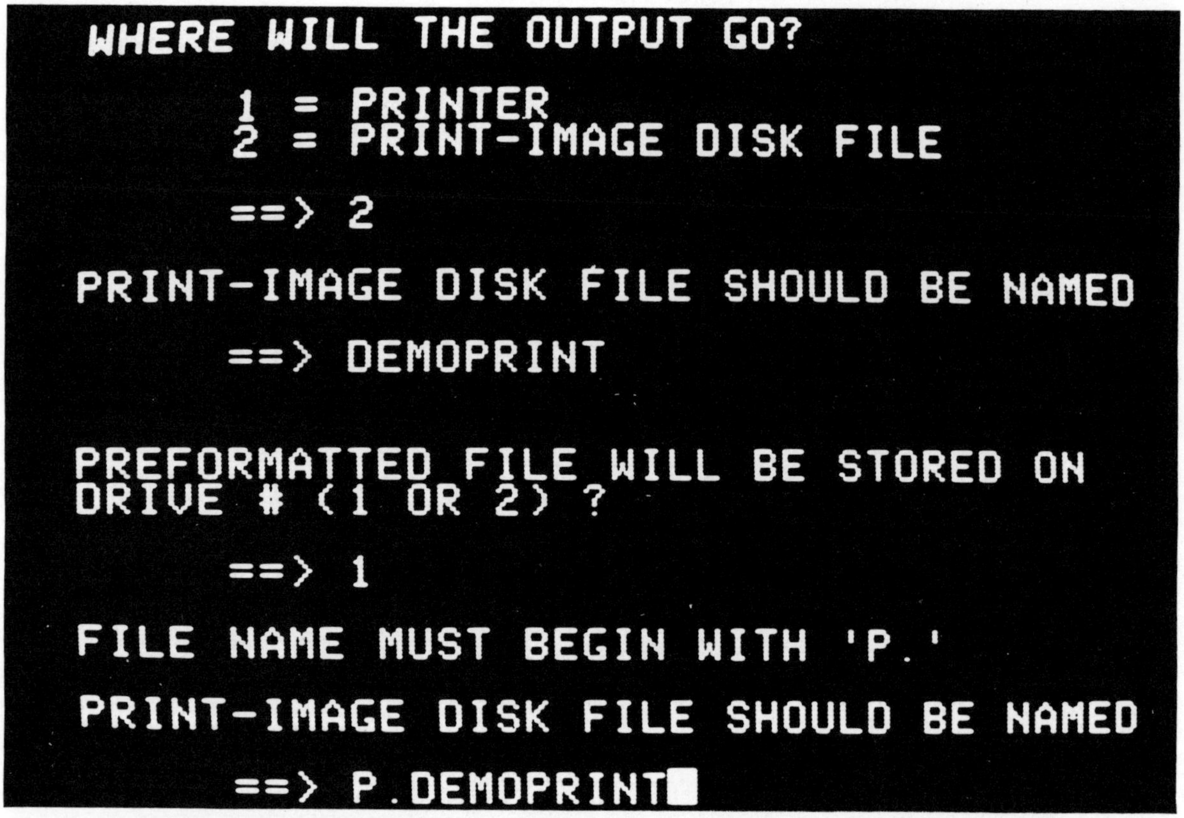

Fig. 4-18. Gentle chiding by the program's error trapping reminds you that P. must precede a print-image file name.

either disk drive 1 or 2. This feature is helpful for assembling printed documents from several files and printing those too long to be contained in one file.

No provision is included for printing multiple copies of a document. Each copy must be individually specified in the print routine.

SPECIAL FEATURES

Alternate (Script) Margins. Three levels of alternate margins have been predefined in Write-On! The documentation notes that these were originally designed for use by playwrights and screenwriters. The definitions offered in the manual reinforce this concept. Margin A (\ A \ ) is called stage directions; B (\ B \ ), character names, and D (\ D \ ), dialog (Fig. 4-19). In word-processing terms, the effect of using these commands is as follows:

\ A   skips two lines and resets the left margin to 10 and the right to 70.

B \ skips two lines and resets the left margin to 30 and the right to 79.

\ D \ starts a new line and sets the left margin to 20 and the right to 60.

You can redefine the three alternate margin settings for any purpose. Resetting these margins uses commands such as \ MARn \.

Data Files. Data files may be created to hold information which will be inserted into designated places of text as it is printed. The most obvious use for these types of files is mailing list information, but many other applications are possible. Names of data files begin with a D. (letter D and a period). Each record in a data file may contain up to nine fields of up to 256 characters in length.

Data files are created by deciding what information is to be contained in each data field and keeping a separate record of the order (no prompts are included in the program). Select the Editor program, and answer Y when it asks if you want to create a data file (Fig. 4-20). Enter the fields in sequence, pressing RETURN at the end of each. CTRL-R is used at the end of each complete record and a record separator, consisting of three asterisks, is shown on the screen (Fig. 4-21). Less than and greater than (< >) symbols are used to identify lines longer than the 38 characters capable of being displayed on a single video line.

Editing data files is made considerably easier by a special set of commands providing for complete record manipulation. For instance, the CLP may be moved up or down through the file, a record at a time, using URn or DRn.

Using data files in printing applications is a relatively simple process. During the process of text entry, the \ Fn \ command is used to identify the location where a specific field of information is to be printed (Fig. 4-22). When the text file is to be printed, both its name and the name of the data file must be specified. The number of copies of the completed document is equal to the number of complete records in the data file. Of course, multiple text and data files may be specified for printing. The only requirement is that all the text files must be specified before the data files.

Data files created by other systems can be converted for use with Write-On!. Specific instructions contained in the program manual outline the necessary procedures.

HUMAN ENGINEERING

Logical, Easy to Use Commands. The process of booting the program should be familiar to every Apple II owner. Since standard DOS is used, the process is much the same as running any other

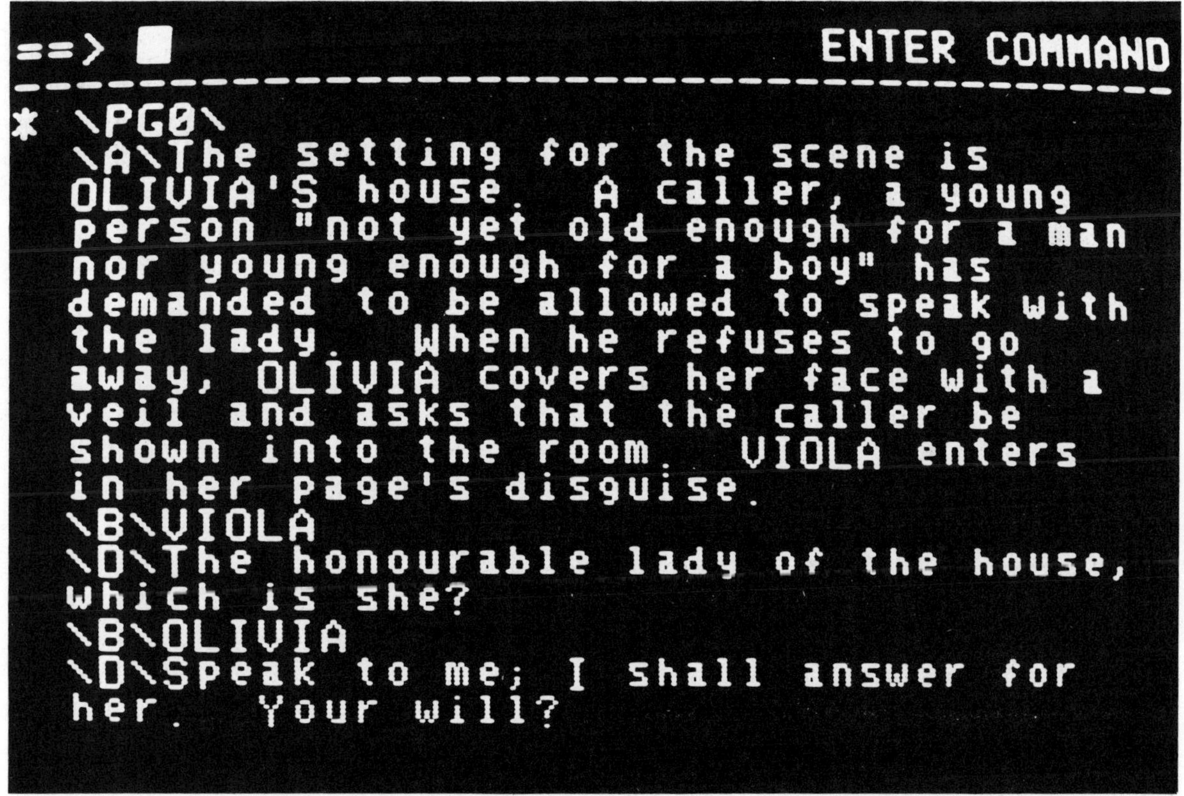

Fig. 4-19. Three levels of margins are provided in Write-On! These may be used as set or redefined as desired by the user.

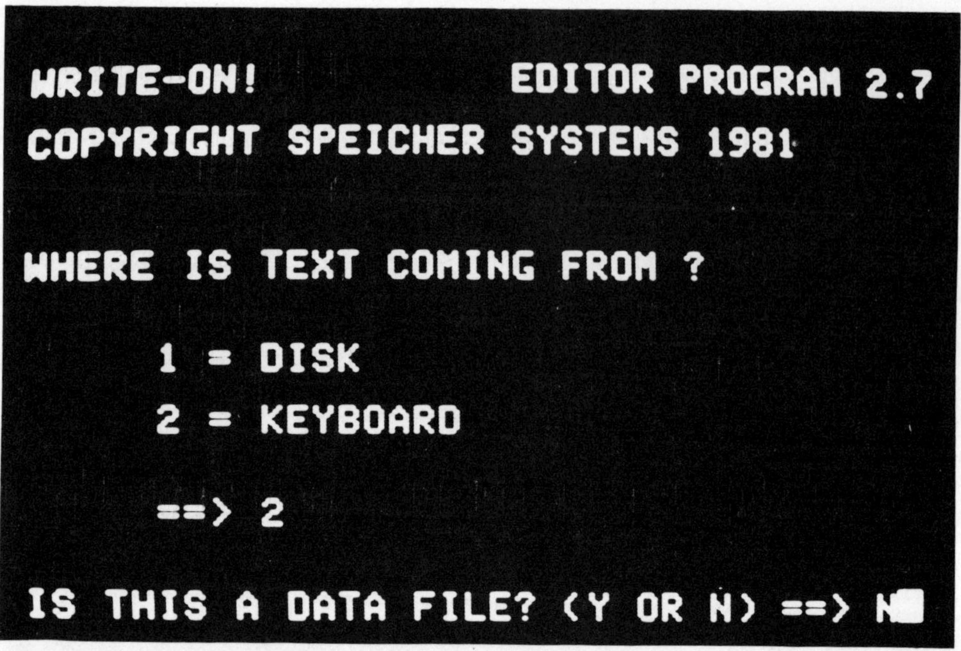

Fig. 4-20. Data files, such as mailing list information, may be created to hold information which will be inserted into designated locations in text to be printed.

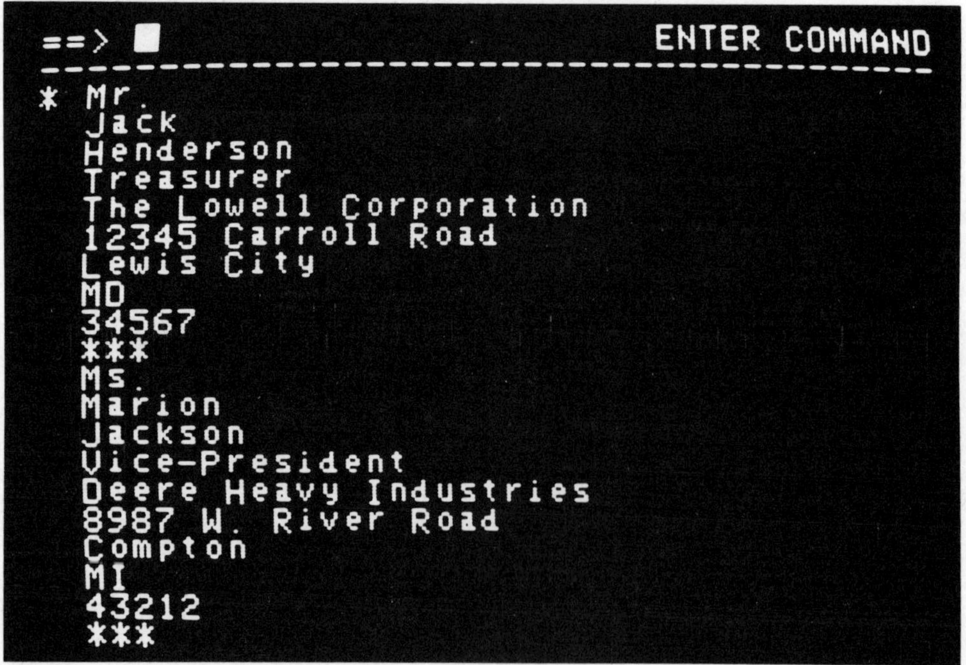

Fig. 4-21. Mailing list information as contained in a data file. Three asterisks are used as a record separator.

Applesoft program. Once started, the program leads you through the initial steps using a logical series of menus. Prompts for important operations are quite clear and easy to understand (Fig. 4-23).

The command structure may seem somewhat confusing to the beginner, but it is easily learned. A command usually begins with the first letter of its name, so remembering the commands is not difficult.

Verification of Potentially Dangerous Commands. Except for asking if you would like to save the text in memory before exiting the program, no other verification is necessary before commands are executed.

Error Recovery and Emergency Procedures. The program prints error messages for many of the conditions that are due to operator error. A section of the manual is devoted to explaining both both the probable cause and correction for each error. Another section of the manual outlines some of the problems and solutions that have been encountered by users of the program.

On-Line Help. Most of the information included on the program disk is in the form of examples. These are extremely helpful in illustrating how to handle specific application problems.

DOCUMENTATION

User's Manual. The manual (Fig. 4-24) supplied with Write-On! is organized in a semitutorial fashion. Instructions for installing the program and initial use are clearly stated in a step-by-step fashion. Descriptions of other program capabilities are intermingled with examples of various applications. Finally, troubleshooting and error recovery

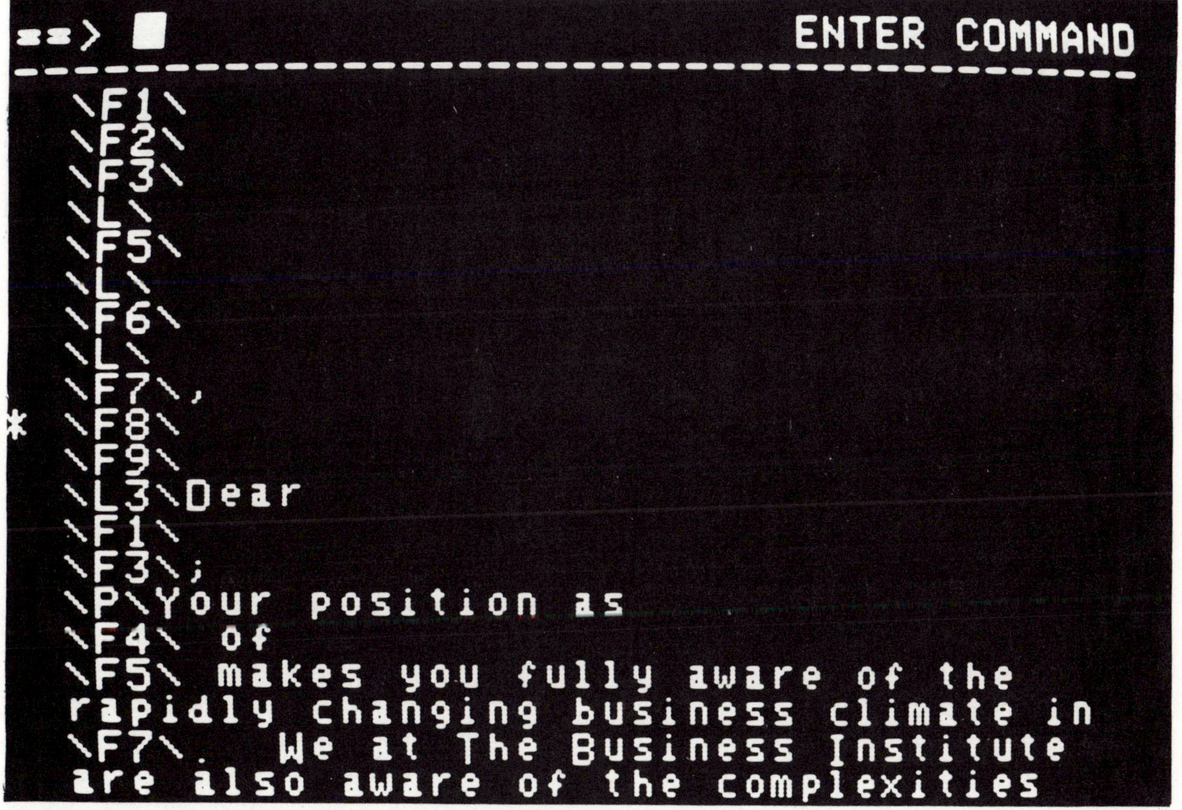

Fig. 4-22. The F (field number) command is used to designate the location where information from a data file is to be inserted into the printed text.

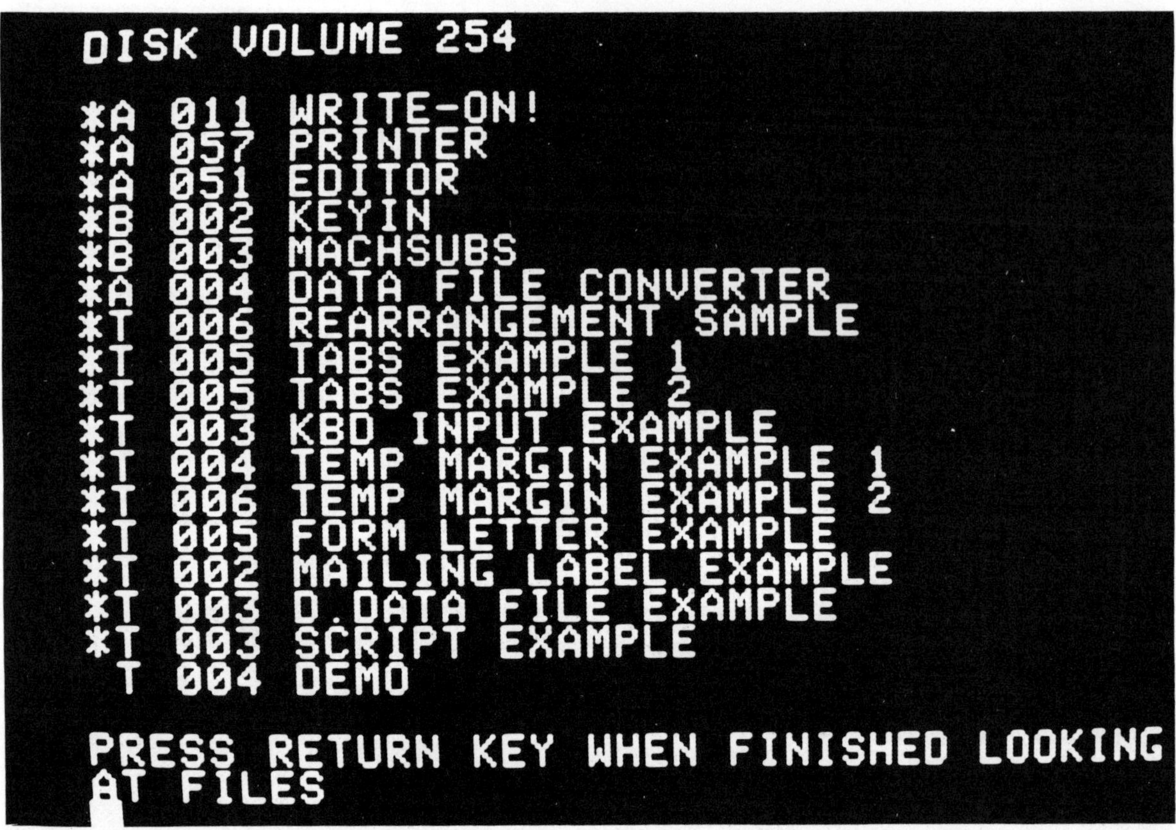

Fig. 4-23. Most of the commands and prompts used by Write-On! are easy to understand. The prompt shown here removes the disk catalog from the screen.

procedures are outlined. Plain, understandable English is used throughout the manual. A rank beginner should have little difficulty learning how to use the program in a relatively short time.

Reference Material. A comprehensive reference card is included in the program packet. In addition to listing all the commands used, default parameters and short explanations of the command functions can be found on the card. Experienced word-processing users could skip most of the material in the manual and go directly to the card for most of the program's uses.

Steps necessary to accomplish the shift key modification on the Apple II are included in the program manual.

SUPPORT

Only one copy of the program disk is included in the program package. Since the DOS used is standard Apple 3.2, making back-up copies is possible, and the publisher encourages it. If the disk fails to boot on your system, you could probably obtain a replacement with no difficulty.

The last page of the program manual contains a reader service card which may be used for descriptions of program errors, corrections to the user's manual, requests for information, or suggestions for additional features. You are encouraged to include samples of problem text and output.

IMPRESSIONS

The documentation included with this program is extremely helpful without being wordy. The examples included on the program disk help to reinforce the concepts presented in the manual without undue duplication. The diverse group of

A computer without a **word processing program** is only being half-utilized. And the unused half is the most important, because we all have reams of letters to write, scripts to type, text to edit, files to keep and data to record.

Write-On! was developed to solve all these problems, and more, for you...easily, quickly, and effortlessly. Have we succeeded? In the June 81 issue of Byte magazine, they reviewed Write-On! against the competition. And here are just some of the nice things they had to say.

"Write-On! is **amazingly error-free** and it ran the first time we put it on the computer. One of us thinks it's his **choice of all** the word processors that we reviewed." "Write-On! is a super word processor....touch typists can enter text quickly and easily....performs its editing chores with ease and speed ...even provides for form letters using data files. This is a **tremendously powerful** and useful feature (especially for the price)."

To continue with words from Byte, "Along with excellent human engineering, Write-On! provides **superlative documentation**....leads the user by the hand...explanations are **clear** and concise..." And... "...undoubtedly the most powerful features found in a microcomputer-based word processor."

Our users have been saying the same kind of things about Write-On! The reason, we believe, is because of all the word-processors available, this one was designed to be **user-oriented** ...to be easy for non-computer types to get professional results with. Whether used for business, professional, home or school ...Write-On! is the right one because it is right-on.

Fig. 4-24. The Write-On! user's manual.

examples should help you find what you need for most applications.

Looking over the documentation prior to actually booting the program, my first reaction was one of severe cursor withdrawal symptoms. Most of the word-processing programs I have used are geared entirely to operations at the position of the cursor. After using the program, I became very comfortable with the line orientation of Write-On! Surprisingly rapid moves are possible when you divorce yourself from that little blinking square!

Write-On! contains a range of features which is unusual for a program in this price category. I particularly like being able to design and redesign the final format of printed output during text input operations.

Datamost is to be applauded for supplying a program that can be copied at will by the user. Supplying two copies of the program disk, as is the standard practice for uncopyable programs, is nowhere near as comforting as being able to put a copy of the program on each of your data disks. I always get a little nervous when a disk goes "dump in the night," and I am down to only one copy of a program I use a lot. Although software piracy may be a problem, I am inclined to think that most purchasers of this type of program are most interested in uninterrupted operation than in making extra money running off copies for their friends and neighbors.

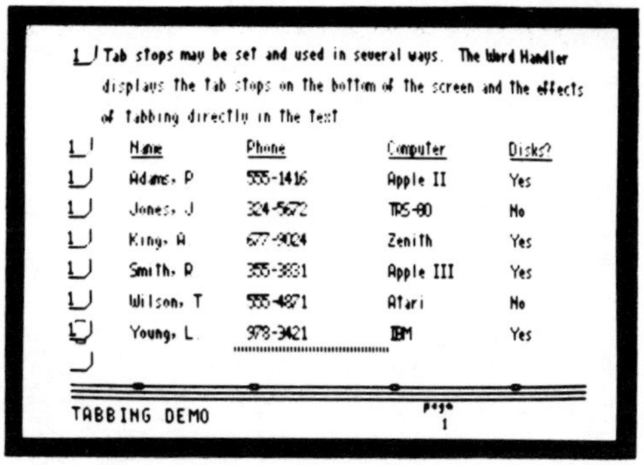

## Chapter 5

The Word Handler

Publisher: Silicon Valley Systems, 1625 El Camino Real, Suite #4, Belmont, CA 94002
Hardware Required: Apple II or Apple II Plus, 48K, Disk II, and printer
Price: $249.00

The Word Handler (Fig. 5-1) is one of the new generation word-processing programs that does not require a large investment in additional hardware modifications for the Apple II. As you will note in this chapter, some rather interesting features are included.

TEXT INPUT FEATURES

Upper- and Lowercase Display. This program will automatically display upper- and lowercase letters without any hardware modification to the native uppercase Apple (Fig. 5-2). ESC is used for shifting case; CTRL-K, as a shift lock. There are several simple modifications which enable the Apple's shift keys to operate for case shift. The program promises to recognize any of these modifications, and it does indeed operate with the single-

wire modification I installed on my own machine. The cursor is displayed in the form of a one-character-wide rectangle.

Video Display. Text is displayed on the video screen in either of two character formats, intended to accurately represent what the text will look like when printed. The standard 40-character display is similar to that seen in many other programs. A 66-column compact video display (Fig. 5-3), using a software-generated character set, is also offered. For lines longer than 66 characters, it is best to use the 40-column display; in this case, lines are broken up into two or three parts on the screen, so all the text is visible. Distinctive spacing and slight character shift are used to distinguish multiple parts of the same line from other lines on screen. You can select either display format by answering the "USE 66 COLUMN COMPACT FORMAT? (Y/N)" question posed when starting the program.

Word Formatting. Like most other word-processing programs, words too long to fit on one line will automatically be shifted to the next line by

Fig. 5-1. The initial logo displayed by The Word Handler.

The Word Handler. Normally, a space is interpreted by the program to be the separator between words. A provision to set an "unbreakable" space between words for special situations is included.

Tabbing. Horizontal tabs are set at the desired positions by CTRL-Q. Each tab stop is displayed, along with the current cursor position, on the bottom of the screen. Pressing ESC (or ESC-ESC if no shift key modification is being used) advances the cursor to the next tab stop. The effects of tabbing are immediately shown on the video display (Fig. 5-4). Predefined tabbing for paragraph indentation capability is not included in this program, although a tab stop may be set for that purpose as described above.

Justification. Text justification, in the form of word spacing, is selected during text entry by pressing CTRL-J. Another CTRL-J switches the justification feature off. Centering a line of text is done by pressing CTRL-X; this functions only if the line begins and ends with a RETURN character. The program justifies text to create flush left and right margins only. In addition to displaying the results of justification on screen, the selection is indicated at the bottom of the screen. Justification may be selected (or deselected) at each RETURN character, allowing considerable flexibility for final text format (Fig. 5-5).

Line Spacing. At each RETURN character in the text, line spacing is displayed and may be modified. By pressing CTRL-V, you can designate single, one-and-a-half, double, or two-and-a-half spacing. An extra half space between two lines may be added by pressing CTRL-L (Fig. 5-6).

Status Display during Text Input. Operating mode, strictly speaking, is not displayed as

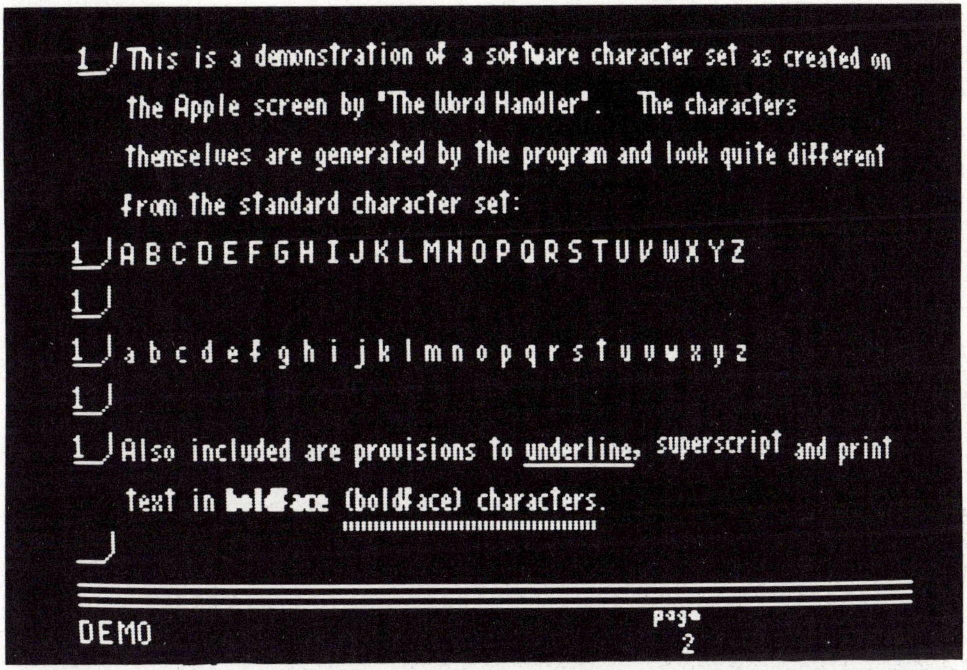

Fig. 5-2. No additional hardware is needed to generate upper- and lowercase characters on the video display.

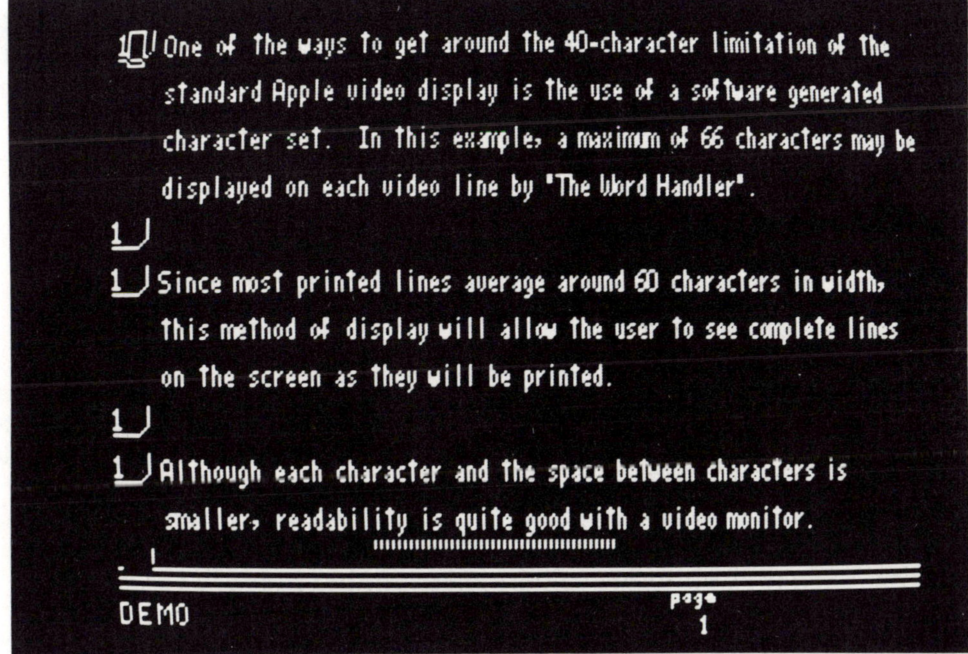

Fig. 5-3. Using characters contained in software, a maximum line width of 66 characters is featured by The Word Handler.

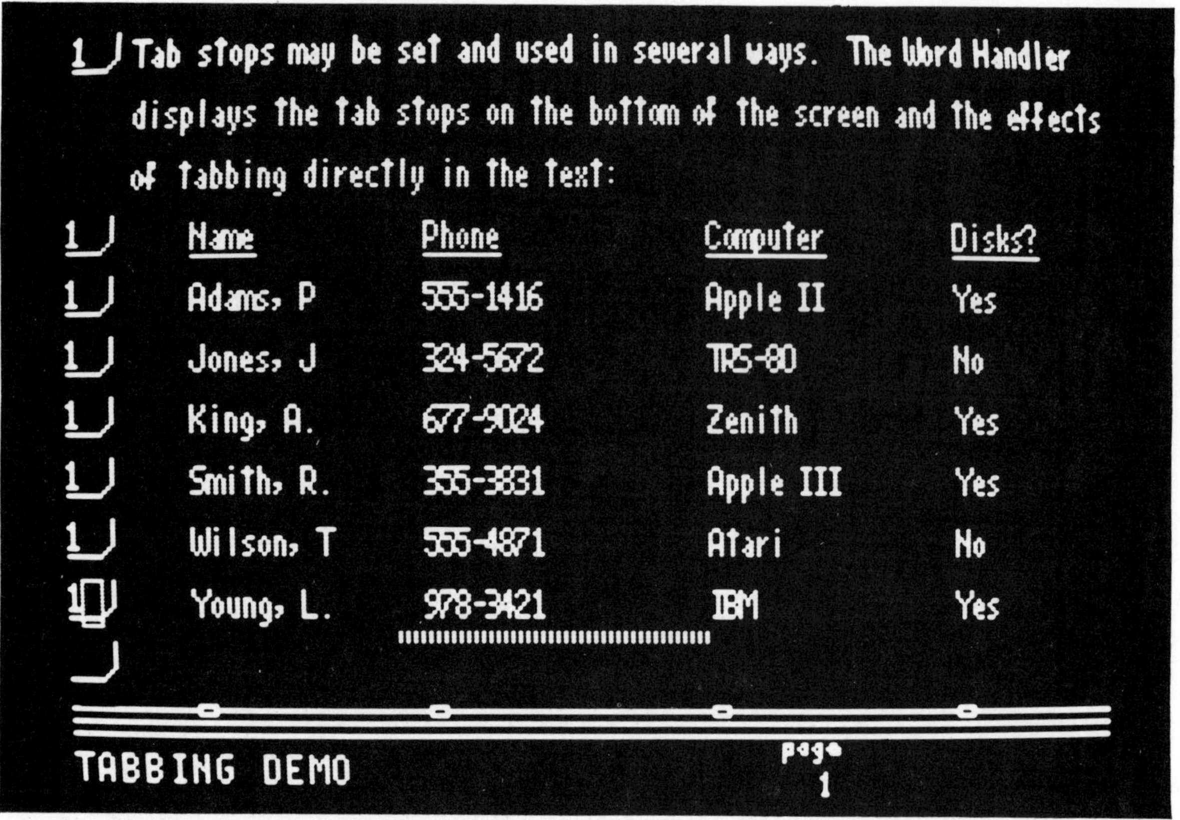

Fig. 5-4. Horizontal tab positions are shown as rectangular boxes along the status line at the bottom of the display. The effects of tabbing are shown directly in the text.

such. If special features are selected, such as justification or print features, these are shown. Tab stops and margins are indicated, along with current cursor position, in the status line shown at the bottom of the screen. Space remaining for new text is not displayed during entry. The status area does include the name of the current file and page number.

Page Specification Change. During text input operation, page breaks may be forced by pressing CTRL-P. A page break is indicated by an empty RETURN character and the page break bar. Vertical spacing and justification can be set and reset. Tab stops can be set or changed during input. Other page specifications, such as margins or paper length, are not accessible individually. A page format setting procedure must be used to change them.

Text Files from Other Programs. No provisions to use files from other programs are included in this program.

Formatting for Text Output. Pressing CTRL-F displays the format file for the present document and allows you to change any items desired (Fig. 5-7). Paper width, length, margins, and distances for special features are specified in decimal inches, rather than the more commonly used number of characters. Headers, footers, page numbers, and other special features (to be described later) are also specified in the print format routine. The format (either the default or user selected) is saved along with the document in a text file on the disk.

Special printer features (underlining, boldface print, and superscripts) can be entered directly into the text and are shown on the video display. Each feature is selected with a CTRL- sequence and is

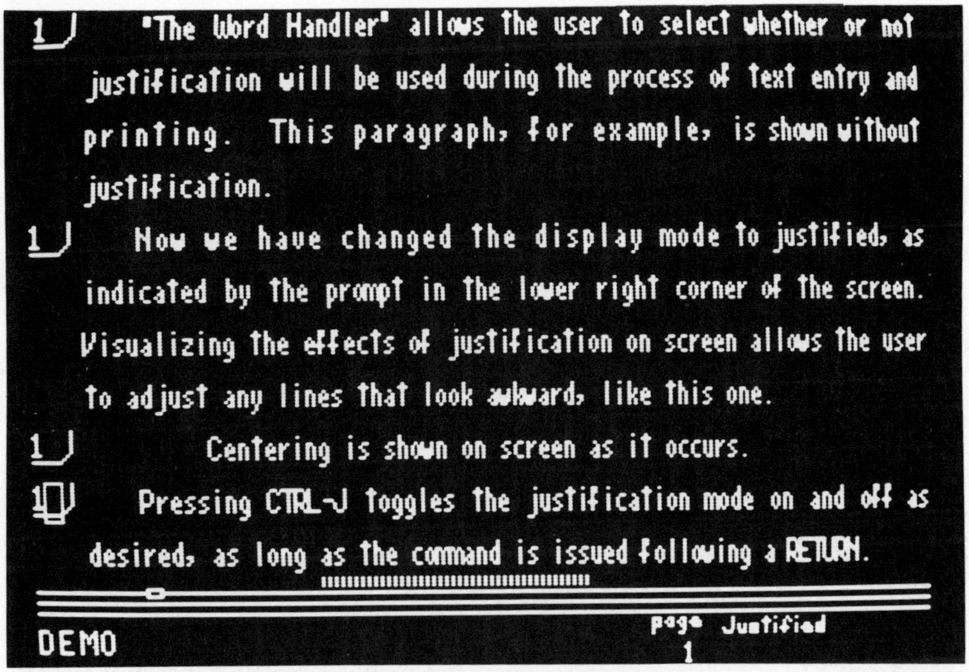

Fig. 5-5. The effects of justification are displayed as text is entered.

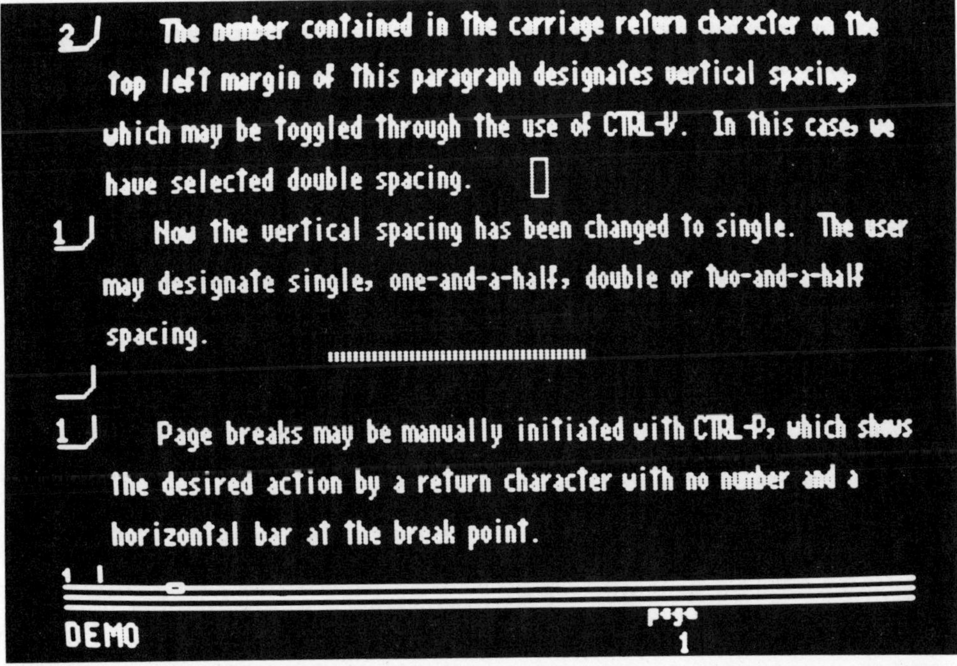

Fig. 5-6. Line spacing may be altered at any point during text entry by pressing CTRL-V.

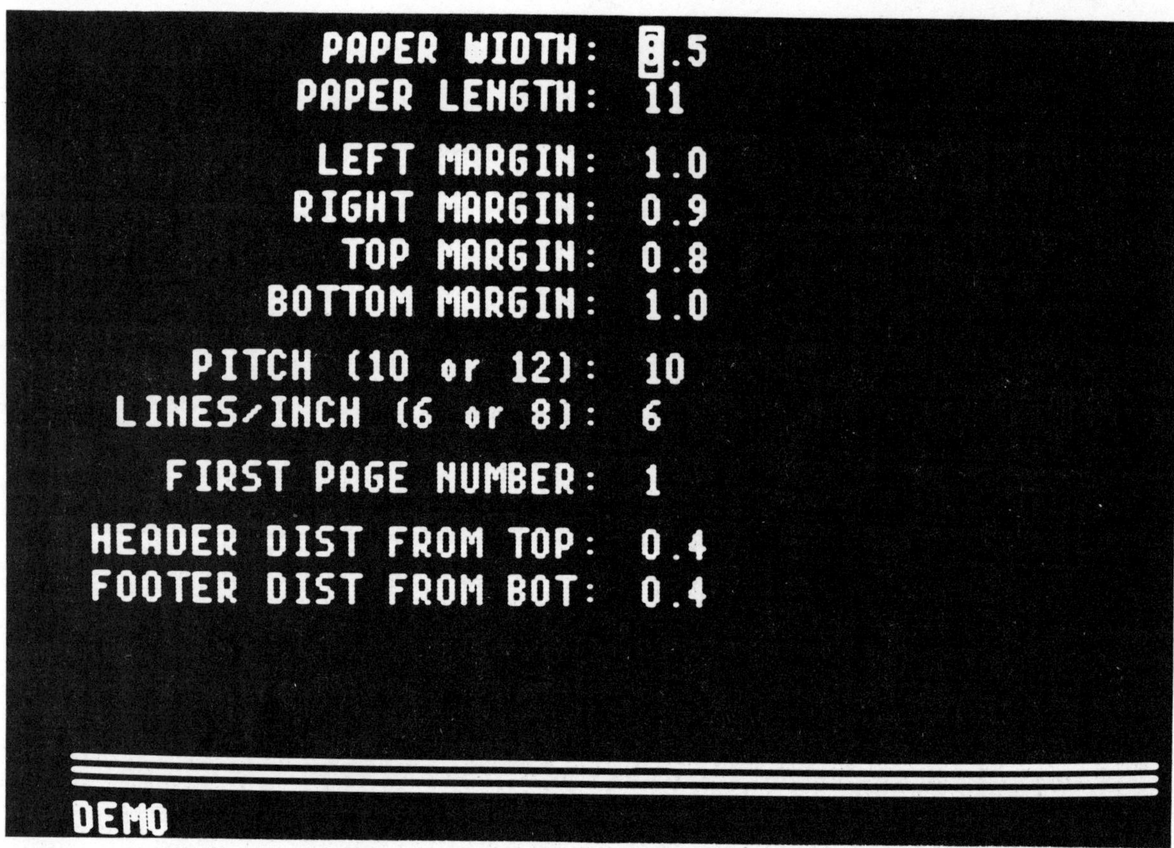

Fig. 5-7. The format for the final appearance of the printed document is saved with the text in a disk file.

displayed on the screen in its final printed form (assuming your printer has the capability to print them). The sequences provided are CTRL-Y (start underlining), CTRL-B (start boldface type), CTRL-S (start entry of text for superscripts), and CTRL-N (resume entry of normal text). See Fig. 5-8.

Maximum Text Length per File. File handling is a dynamic process, so one text file could take up the whole 120K-plus available on a disk. This would be equal to something over 100 typed pages and not much of a limitation for most purposes.

Typing Speed. I have not found any instances where the program could not keep up with a fairly fast typist during text input operations.

EDITING FEATURES

Cursor Positioning. The right and left arrows on the Apple keyboard are used to set the direction of cursor movement and to move the cursor a character at a time through the text. You can move the cursor a little faster by pressing the appropriate arrow and the repeat key. Express functions are included to move the cursor a word (CTRL-W), line (CTRL-L), or page (CTRL-P) at a time. RETURN is used to move the cursor forward to the next RETURN mark. Once the direction of movement is established, multiple moves may be handled by using the express functions repeatedly. For example, a two-word move would be CTRL-W CTRL-W.

Scrolling. Forward and reverse scrolling takes place in conjunction with the cursor-positioning commands mentioned above. No separate provision is included for scrolling through the text in either direction.

Changing a Few Characters. Once the cursor is positioned properly, the character under the cursor may be changed by simply typing over it. The screen display updates with each change, an action that takes a little getting used to. Multiple changes may cause the display to lag behind your typing, but the screen will eventually catch up.

Inserting Text. Adding text to an existing document is initiated by moving the cursor to the position where the new text is to begin and pressing CTRL-I. All text beyond that point is removed from the video display but not the file. Insertion operations may then proceed as described earlier. Completion of text insertion is signaled by pressing the right arrow, at which time the new text is merged into the existing material on the screen. All the commands discussed earlier for text insertion function exactly the same in this situation.

Deleting Text. In general, the CTRL-D sequence is used to signal a deletion. Once the cursor is positioned on the desired character, pressing CTRL-D causes the character to be displayed in inverse video. Deletion is finalized by pressing another control key (usually the right arrow or CTRL-I). Any other key unmarks the character. To delete words, lines, or pages, the CTRL-D sequence is followed by the appropriate length sequence. For instance, deleting a line would require CTRL-D CTRL-L. You are always required to finalize the delete command with a control character or cancel it by pressing any other key (Fig. 5-9). Remaining text is automatically adjusted to reflect any deletions which take place.

Copying Text. The control sequence CTRL-C initiates the copy function. When it is in operation, the copy mode looks very similar to the de-

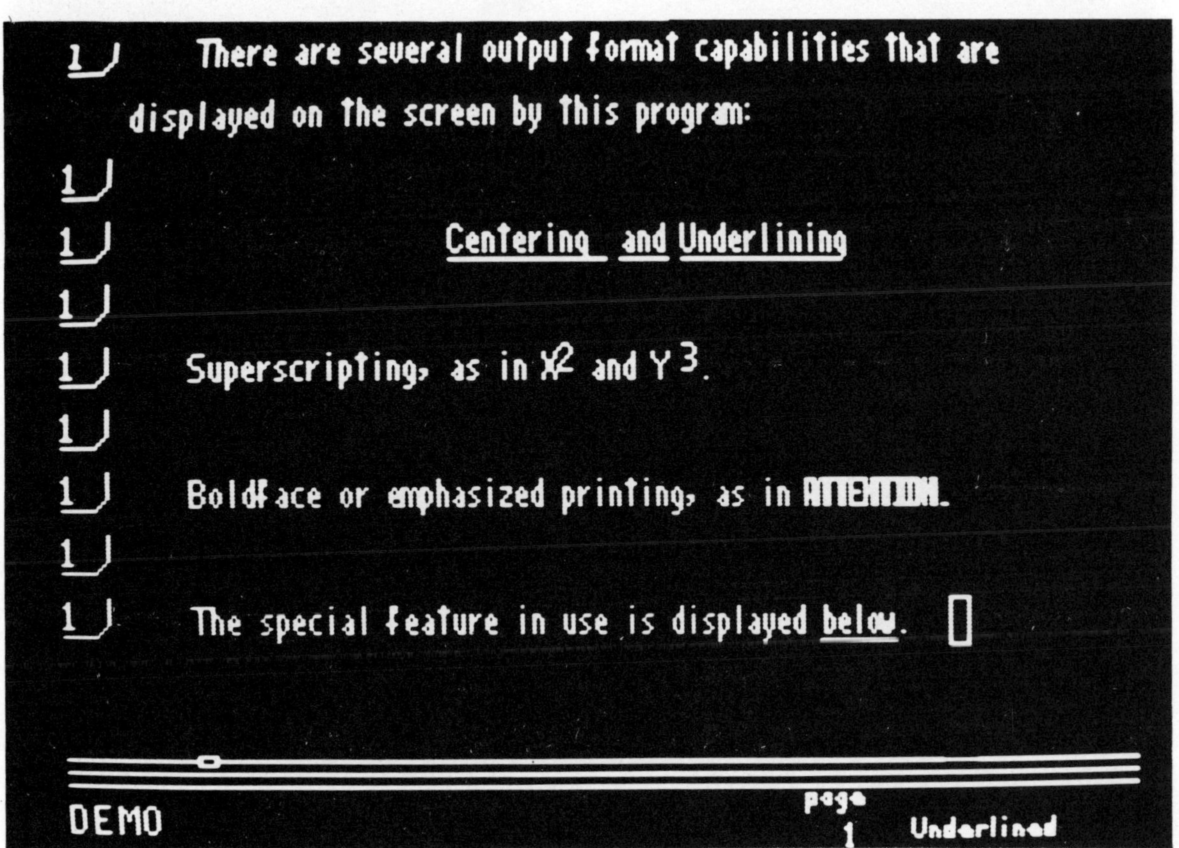

Fig. 5-8. Centering, superscripts, boldface print, and underlining are shown on the screen as they will appear when printed.

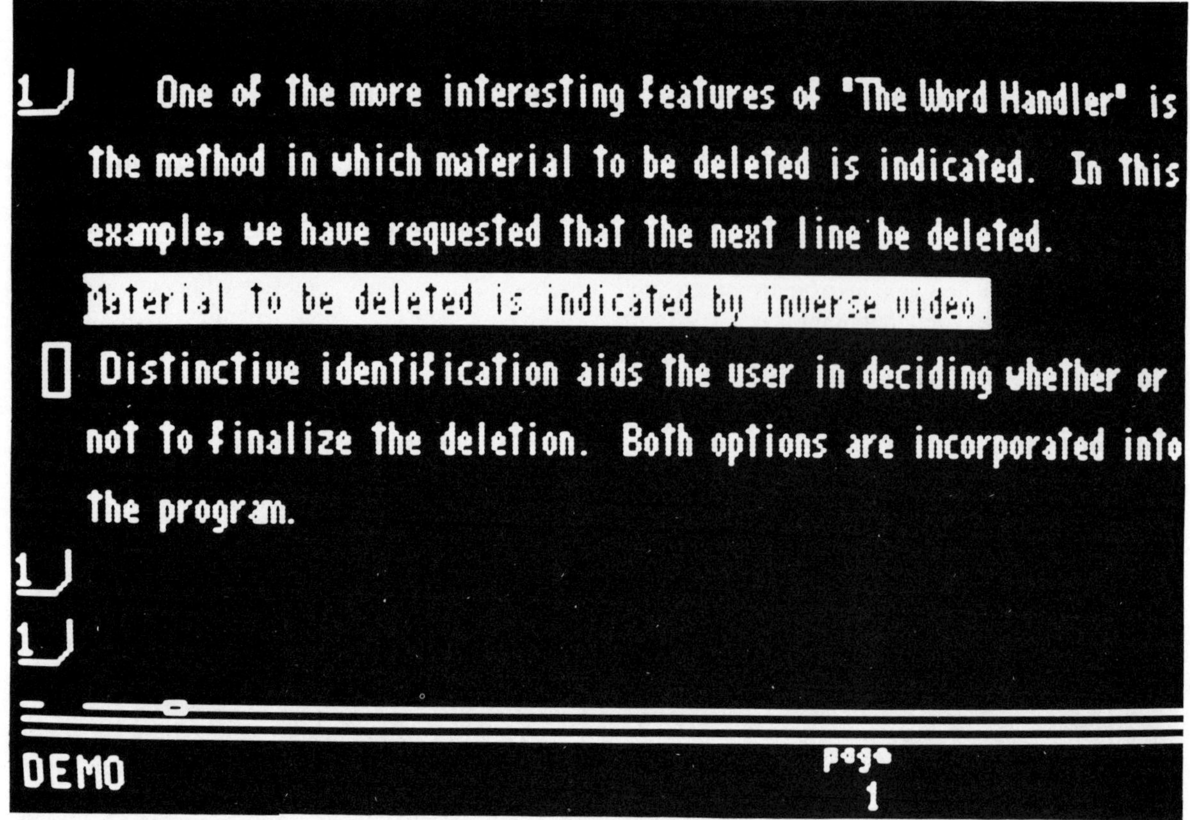

Fig. 5-9. Separate verification is required before the text marked for deletion is removed from the file.

lete mode, because the desired text is displayed in inverse video before finalizing. For instance, copying a page of text would be done by CTRL-C CTRL-P, followed by a control character. All text copied in this fashion is added to a temporary holding file on the disk. Each new addition to the holding file is simply added in a sequential fashion to whatever is there.

Copied text may be inserted at some point in a document by pressing CTRL-I (insert) CTRL-C (copy). Deleting text from the screen and adding it to the holding file is done by using a combination of the CTRL-C and CTRL-D commands, along with the length sequences (Fig. 5-10).

Selected text from other document files can be retrieved and merged using the CTRL-G command. After pressing CTRL-G, you are requested to enter a document name and list or range of line numbers separated by commas, for example, LETTER, 1, 23, 2-15, 16-22. Notice that the line numbers (or ranges) do not have to be in sequence, allowing text to be retrieved in a somewhat random fashion. The document name may be omitted; in that case, text is retrieved from the last document used. The named document is assumed to be on the secondary disk drive.

The use of line numbers in this operation may be somewhat confusing, since this is the only place in the program where they are mentioned. According to the documentation, lines are taken from the named file as it appeared when last edited. You are required to go through the document and actually count the lines; I could find no provision in the program for printing documents with their line numbers.

Search and Replace. A particular word or

phrase is located in the text by using the CTRL-T (for till) command. The direction of movement is established by the left or right arrow key. Pressing CTRL-T followed by the word (or phrase) desired and RETURN will cause the program to locate the specified word. After locating the first occurrence, pressing CTRL-T again will continue the search until another occurrence is located. The search is by word, so parts of words will not inadvertently be located. For instance, a search for the word "the" will not find "then," "there," "they," or "these."

Pressing CTRL-R selects the replace function in this program. First, the word or words to be replaced are requested. Then the replacement is entered. The program searches through the document in a forward direction only, starting at the cursor position and stopping at the first occurrence of the word(s) to be replaced. Pressing CTRL-R at that time replaces the word(s), and RETURN bypasses that occurrence and moves forward to locate the next. The replace function is terminated by pressing any key other than CTRL-R or RETURN (Fig. 5-11).

TEXT STORAGE AND RETRIEVAL

DOS Used. A nonstandard DOS is used on the program disks, preventing you from creating back-up copies or modifying the program. Two copies of the program disk are included in the package.

Text File Backup. Provisions are included for creating back-up copies of text files on either single or multiple disk drive systems. Either blank or initialized disks may be used for back-up or additional text files. ERASE allows deletion of un-

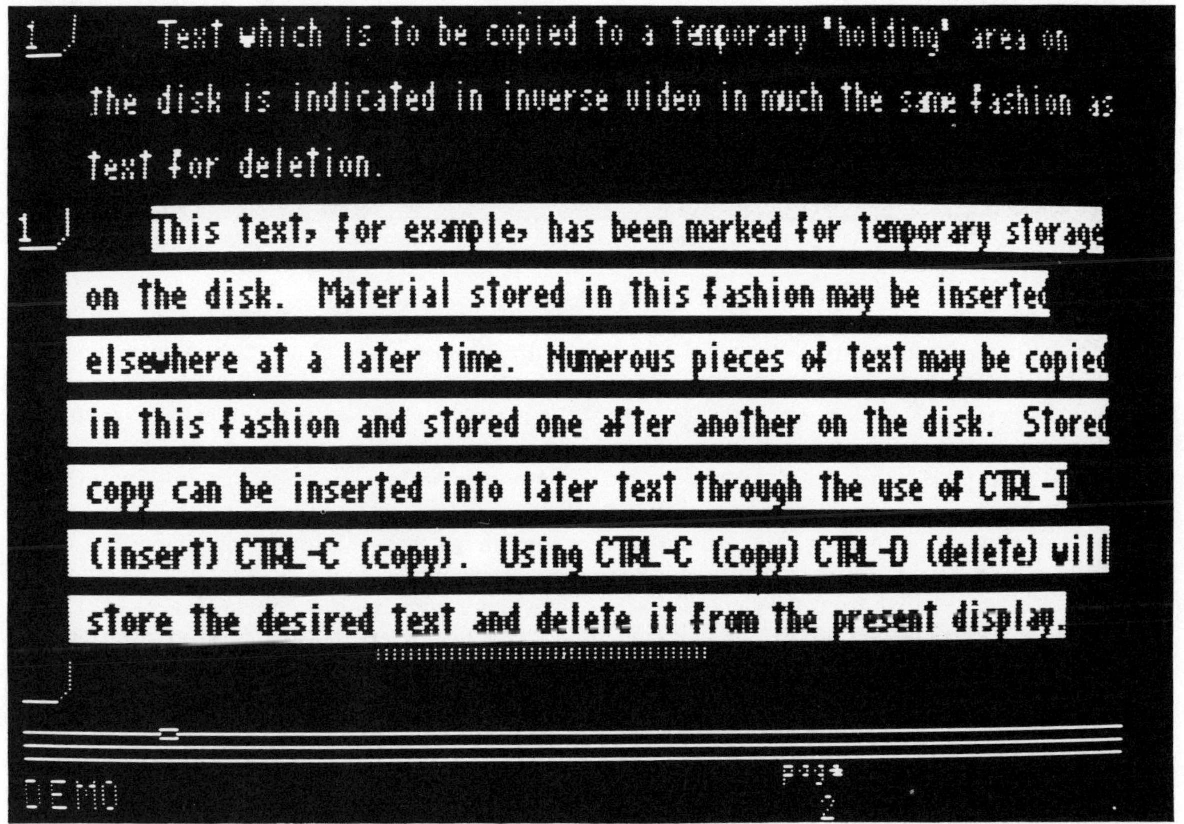

Fig. 5-10. Text marked for copying (block) operations is displayed in inverse ratio.

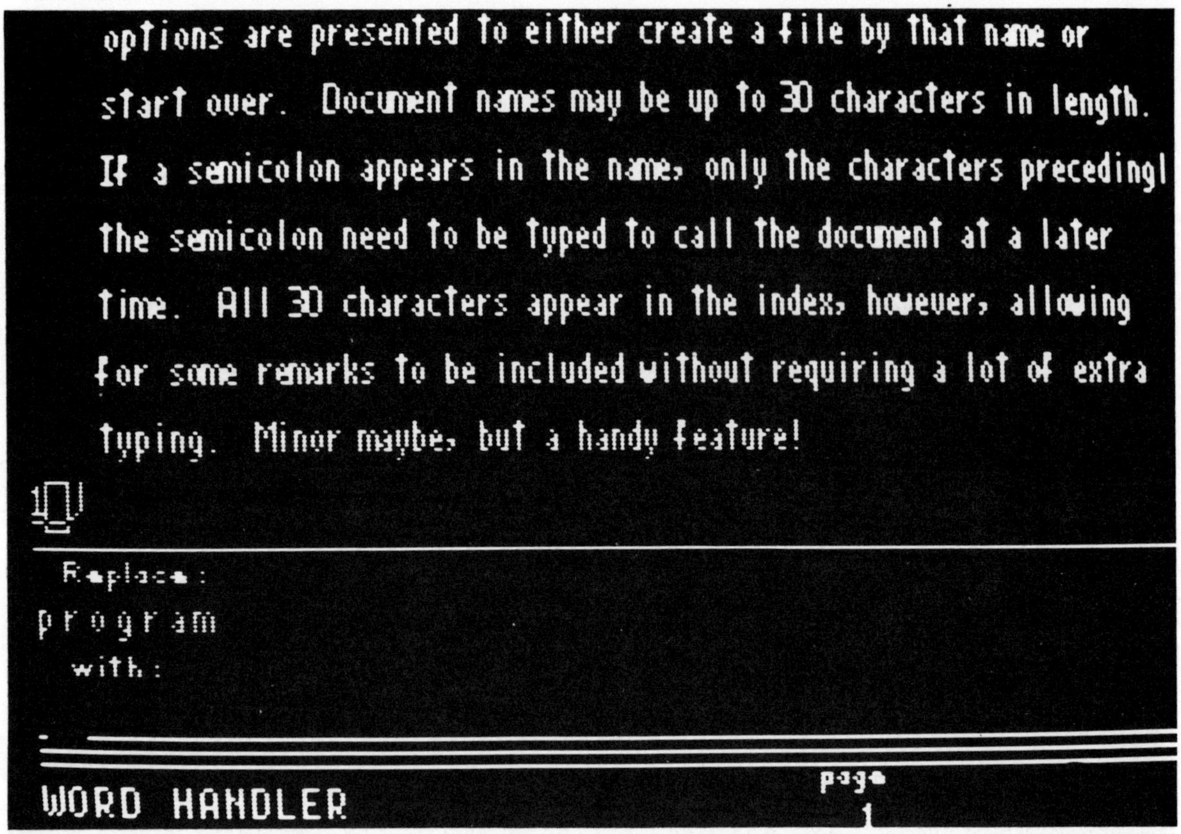

Fig. 5-11. Pressing CTRL-R selects the replace function. As each occurrence of the desired word or phrase is located, it may be either replaced or bypassed.

wanted files from a disk, and RENAME permits changing the name of any text file (Fig. 5-12).

Multiple Disk Drive Access. Unless specified otherwise, all disk operations are conducted on the same drive from which the program was booted. The USE DISK # command permits use of an alternate drive for all further operations and certain disk-to-disk functions. You are permitted to define a primary and secondary drive for use by the CTRL-G (get text from a selected document), FILL-IN (form fill-in), and BACK-UP commands (Fig. 5-13).

Text File Creation and Documentation. Text files are capable of holding over 120,000 characters, over 50 pages of single-spaced text. File names are displayed by using the INDEX command. New files are created by typing the name desired and pressing the space bar in response to the file not found prompt. File names may contain up to 30 characters. An interesting capability is provided when a semicolon is used in a file name; all the characters are displayed in the index, but only those preceding the semicolon need to be used in any command involving the file. In effect, this allows you to insert remarks into file names. The program has no provision for displaying the length of individual files on a disk, although the amount of free space remaining is shown (Fig. 5-14).

Text files created by this program are not compatible with other programs. No provision is included to use "foreign" text files in The Word Handler.

OUTPUT

Printer Configuration. The printer selection (configuration) routine is invoked by pressing

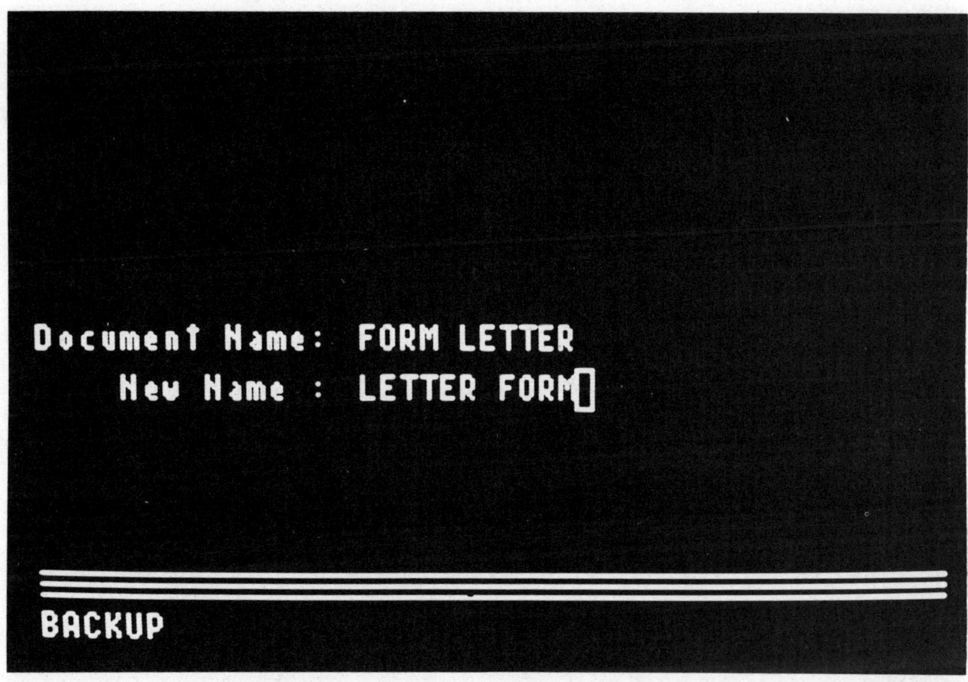

Fig. 5-12. Making back-up copies of text files is possible using either single or dual disk drives.

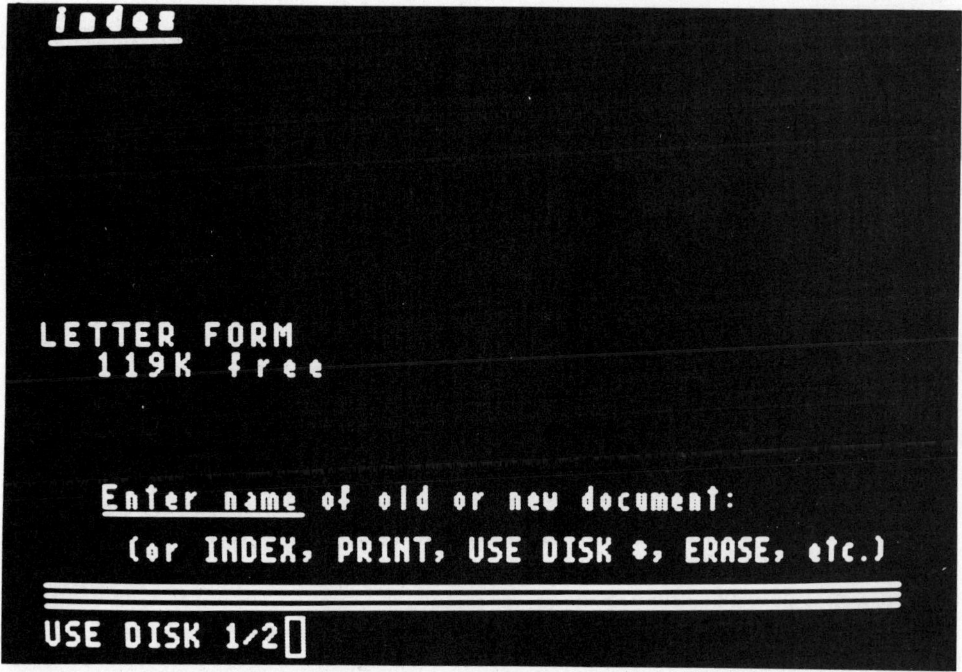

Fig. 5-13. Primary and secondary disk drives may be designated by the USE DISK # command.

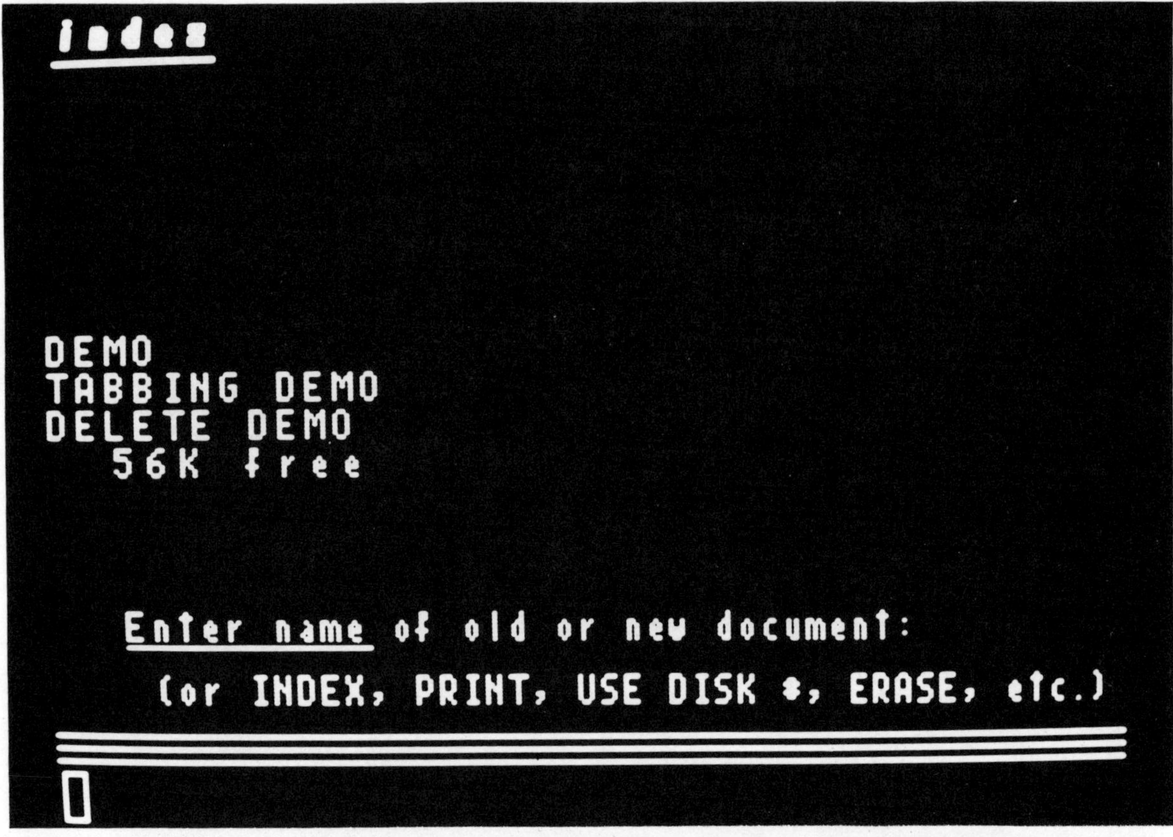

Fig. 5-14. The amount of unused space remaining on a disk is routinely displayed by The Word Handler.

the space bar while the program is booting. First, you are asked to designate the slot in which your printer interface card is located. Next, you are asked to type the number which corresponds to the type of printer and interface you will be using. Several of the more popular printers are named; others will fall into two general categories (ASCII without backspace or ASCII with backspace) with either serial or parallel interface cards. After the first two questions are answered, a default is established which needs to be redone only if the printer is changed. The final question asks whether or not you want to use the 66-column compact display format. If the space bar is not pressed during booting, the display question is the only one that needs to be answered (Fig. 5-15).

Printer Control. I have used the program with two different printers and found its operation to be adequate with both. Spacing, top of form, tabbing, margins, and other general functions worked perfectly on my first printer. The second printer, a Paper Tiger 560, capable of handling superscripts and boldface printing, also worked as advertised by simply choosing it from among the options presented in the selection routine. Some printer functions, such as the ability to change character size, are not supported.

Initiating Printing. From the program's idle state, typing PRINT results in a request for a document name and pages to be printed. A range of pages or particular page numbers may be specified. There is no provision for displaying the number of pages contained in a text file, so you must guess or review the file and make mental notes prior to requesting printing. For each page to be printed, the program instructs you to position paper and press the space bar (Fig. 5-16).

Justification. When justification is called for in the text, this program adds extra spaces between words to achieve flush margins. Proportional printing and infinite letter spacing are not supported, despite the fact they are presently available on many printers.

Headers, Footers, and Page Numbers. As part of the format entry, you may select from an impressive array of options. Page numbers may be specified as either headers, footers, centered, or at a designated number of spaces from the margin. Numbers can be inserted at any point in the header or footer text or used alone. Both headers and footers can be printed on the same page if desired. Header or footer text can be different for odd- and even-numbered pages. Once set in the format file, there is no provision for changing the text or num-

bers contained in the headers or footers during text input or editing operations (Fig. 5-17).

Forms Control. Form length and width are specified in the format file. Printing continuous forms (fanfold paper) is not supported. The space bar must be pressed to begin printing on each new page. This is a convenience if you use single sheets on your printer or in situations where the fanfold paper must be frequently adjusted. In most other situations, the effect is that of slowing down the printing process.

Printer Problems. No provisions are included for responding to error or problem indications from the printer. The single page printing limitation mentioned above can be an advantage in this situation, because the problem can be rectified before the next page is printed. Any page which does not print correctly can be reprinted by

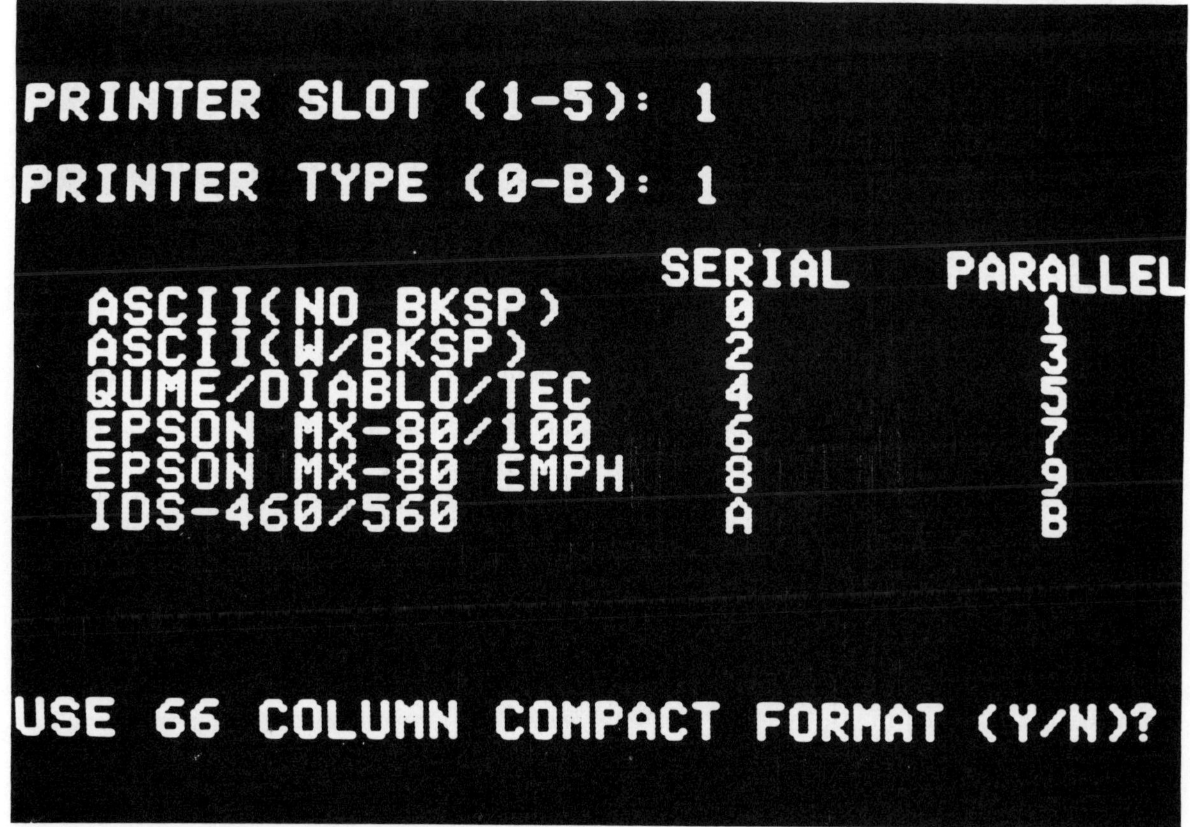

Fig. 5-15. The configuration routine allows easy input of printer and interface parameters.

Fig. 5-16. Pressing the space bar will print text a page at a time.

specifying only that page when initiating the print routine. Once begun, there is no way to stop the printing operations until all the pages have been completed.

Text Insertion during Printing. Once printing is requested, no provision for adding text is included.

Print Mode Display. Text is not displayed on the screen during printing operations. The document name and pages selected remain on the screen throughout the print cycle. Instructions to position paper and press the space bar reappears on the screen as needed.

Screen Preview of Document. Since The Word Handler is geared to display actual printed pages during input and editing operations, no separate provision is included (or really necessary) for separate previewing of the final format of the printed document.

Multiple Files or Copies. Each file and page range for printing must be specified when initiating the print routine. No provisions are included for printing multiple copies or text from multiple files.

SPECIAL FEATURES

Form Fill-in. Using the standard text entry and editing features, you can create a "form" document which uses variables that may be filled in for specific purposes. One such use might be a letter which is to be addressed to several people. Using variables, such items as the name, address, city, state, zip code, and so on, can be specified for each intended recipient. Variables are designated in the body of the form document through the use of less than and greater than symbols, as follows: < variable >. Capitalization of words used to fill the variables generally follows the same form in which the variables are specified in the form document.

For instance, < Name > will cause the actual name inserted there to be printed with the first letter uppercase, while < name > will give you a name printed in all lowercase. Spacing for variable values remains the same as that specified for the variable itself; that is, if a space precedes and follows the < variable >, the replacement will be printed with a space preceding and following (Fig. 5-18).

To use this capability, enter FILL-IN when the program asks for an old or new document name. You are then asked for the document name (form) and new name (the name of the document to be created). Each field to be replaced is displayed on the screen, and you are asked to supply the replacement (Fig. 5-19). At the conclusion of this process, the document created is displayed for your examination and any additional editing that may need to be done (Fig. 5-20).

Alternating Margins. For some printing applications, it is desirable to have wider margins at the binding side of the pages and narrower margins at the outside. This is particularly helpful for documents that are to be used in looseleaf or stapled bindings. The Word Handler will automatically print such margins if you include the letter A after either the left or right margin value when setting up the page format. For example: LEFT MARGIN 2A RIGHT MARGIN 0.5 will set a wider margin on the left side.

Folded Sheet Printing. Printing on folded sheets of paper is a virtually impossible task with many word-processing programs. The Word Handler includes a feature which allows you to do this with ease. Using this feature requires that you set the paper width in the format to the size of the half-sheet and include a D following the value. All

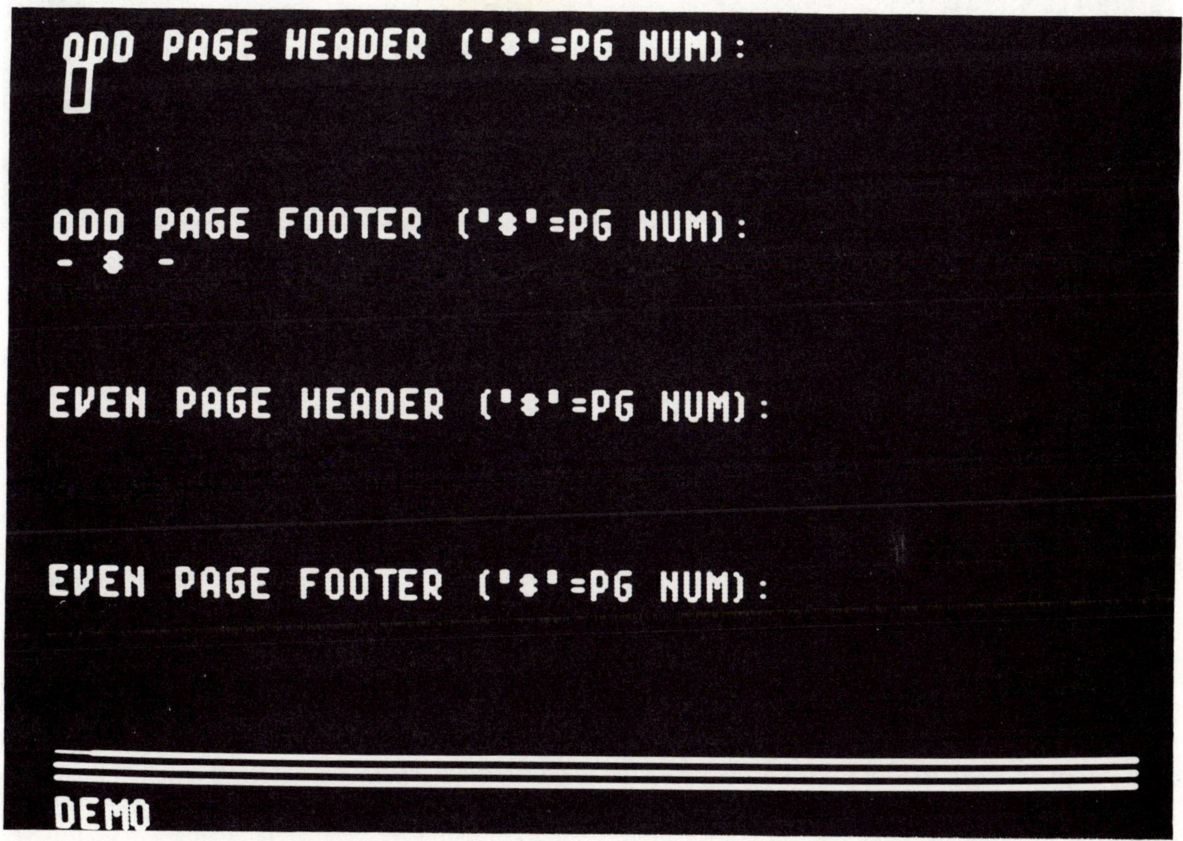

Fig. 5-17. Header and footer specifications are contained in the format saved with each text file on a disk.

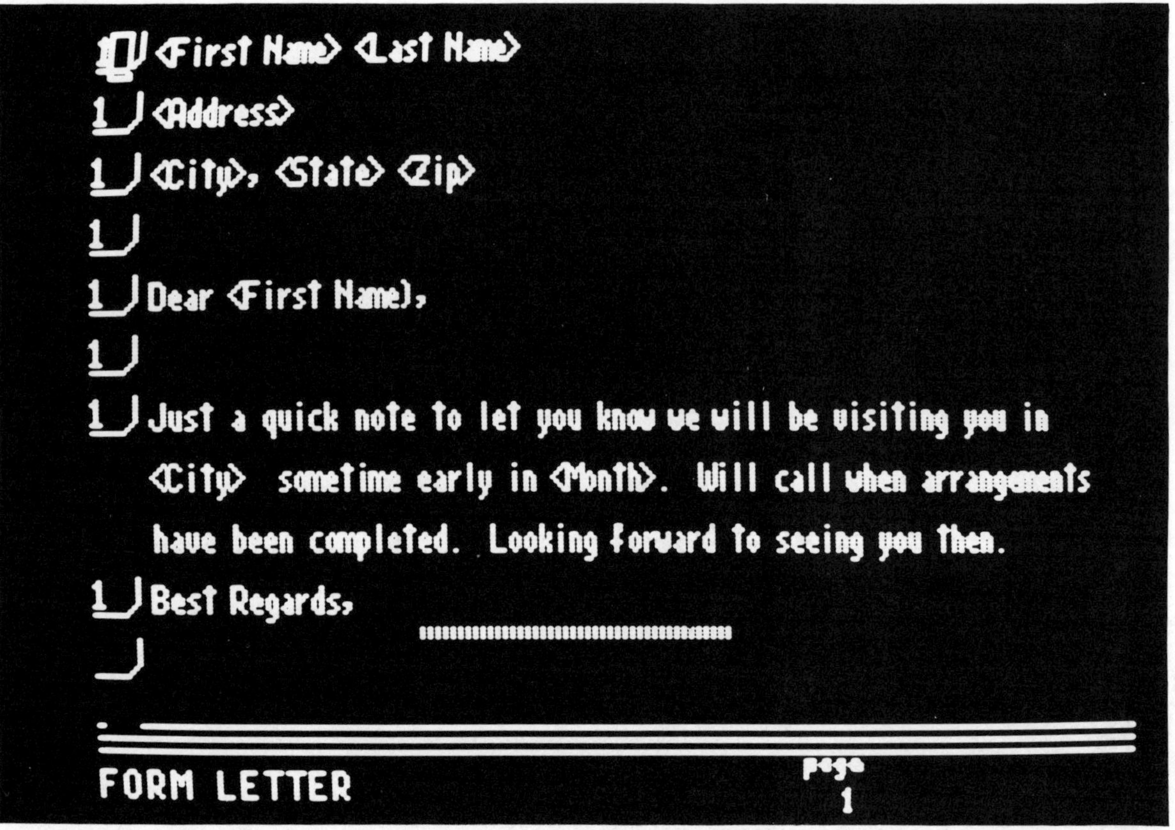

Fig. 5-18. Variables used by the form fill-in feature are preceded and followed by less than and greater than symbols in the text.

odd-numbered pages are then printed offset to the right, and the even-numbered pages are printed in the leftmost number of inches specified.

Each sheet of paper has to be printed more than once, so you must know how many sheets the final document will require and number the sheets appropriately. Although the process seems quite confusing at first glance, some experimentation will help you to better understand the process. Once you have printed one or two documents in this fashion, initial set-up requirements will seem very logical.

HUMAN ENGINEERING

Logical, Easy to Use Commands. Once the program has been booted, most of the commands available are displayed in the program's "idle" state. You are instructed to type the name of a new or old document, such as INDEX, PRINT, USE DISK #, or ERASE. At the termination of each operation, this display returns to the screen (Fig. 5-21). Most of the commands used by this program are logical, in that the CTRL-letter combination or word used represents the actual operation. Some commands, however, must be found in the documentation. One significant omission is a graceful way to exit the program; the only methods I have found are pressing RESET or turning the computer's power off.

Verification of Potentially Dangerous Commands. Most of the commands that could result in the loss or serious alteration of text must be verified separately before the actual operation takes place. Delete, for instance, requires the marking of text (which is displayed in inverse video) and verification by a control character.

82

Pressing any other key aborts the operation before significant damage can be done.

Error Recovery and Emergency Procedures. The documentation and the program make no reference of what to do if a problem is encountered. In my own experience, I encountered a problem with my printer. It was not functioning properly, evidently causing a signal to be sent to the interface card. Typing PRINT from the program's idle state caused the program to just "hang up," with no indication of what type of problem was evident. For those of us with older Apple IIs, recovery procedures from accidentally pressing RESET would also be most helpful.

On-line Help. No tutorial or documentation files are included on the program disk.

DOCUMENTATION

User's Manual. The manual (Fig. 5-22) included with this program is one of the briefest I have seen. It consists of 47 small pages (some blank) containing short descriptions and examples of program operations. Although most of the information you need is included, very few extra words are used. Early in the manual, you are encouraged to just experiment with the program to clear up any points of confusion.

Reference Material. Two copies of a comprehensive reference card are included in the program package. All commands and significant syntax requirements are outlined on the card.

SUPPORT

An extra copy of the program disk is included in the program package. Actually, the package itself is rather unique in that a stiff piece of plastic is used to prevent damage to the material included. If you've ever received a program packet with the

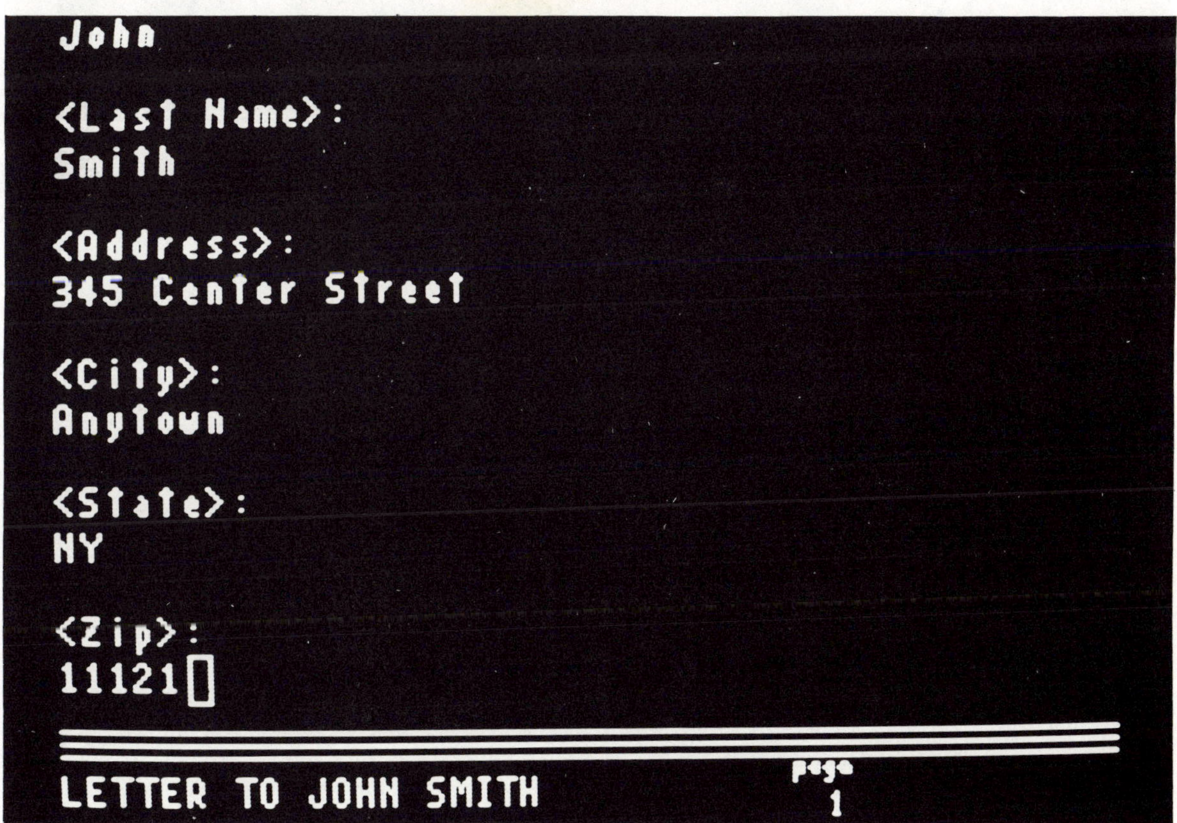

Fig. 5-19. Values for the variables are requested before the document is ready to be printed.

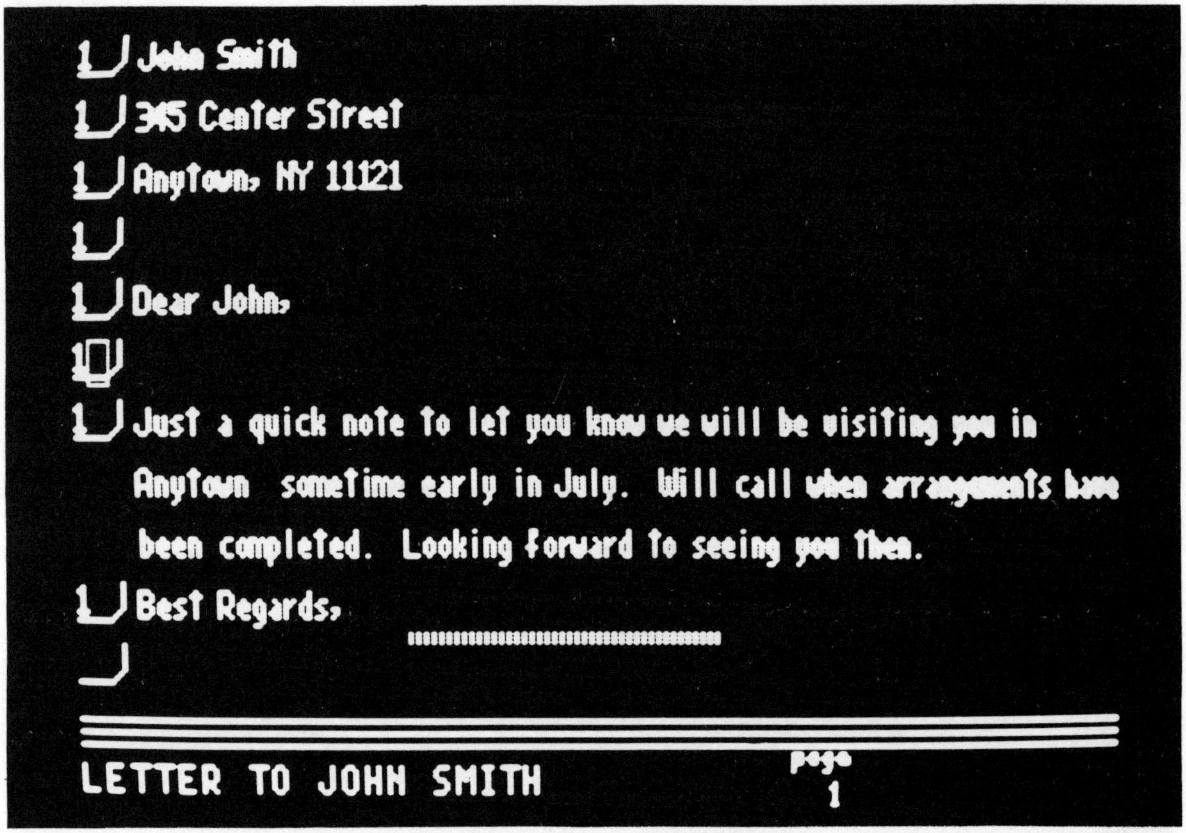

Fig. 5-20. The completed document with values inserted in place of the variables.

disk damaged, this feature may be of interest to you.

No warranty or disk replacement policy is indicated in either the manual or any other material included. You are encouraged to call Silicon Valley Systems if problems, including disk destruction, are encountered. I'm sure arrangements can be made to replace a disk under these circumstances.

IMPRESSIONS

The documentation included with the program is designed to convey a maximum amount of information in minimal space. This is a good idea, but if you have not used a word-processing system before, it is hardly a tutorial. Some of the most useful features may go unnoticed unless you study the manual very closely. You are encouraged to experiment with the program to resolve questions, and this process is very helpful. Excellent on-screen prompting and disaster safeguards do help allay any fears you may have about destroying the program disk. Personally, I would like to see the manual include some mention of error recovery procedures and disk replacement policy.

One of the best features, in my estimation, is the way in which the video display is handled. Aside from the status line at the bottom, everything that appears on the screen will appear in the printed document. Being able to see the effects of tabbing, using superscripts, boldface printing, underlining, margins, etc. makes word processing a lot easier. The compact display format and special characters (except boldface characters) are very readable on a video monitor, but you may have problems if you use a standard television set. Plan on using the

Fig. 5-21. The Word Handler's idle-state menu allows easy access to the other program commands.

Fig. 5-22. The Word Handler operator's manual.

noncompact format if your system does not include a video monitor.

Disk utilization is very convenient. Not having to worry about individual text file length and disk management during text entry is sheer luxury. The disk index feature shows the name of each file and space left on the disk, but number of pages included in each document is not indicated. Since the print routine requests page numbers, it would seem logical that the disk index should include them.

There are some other features that would be helpful for the user of this program. Provisions could be included for dynamic formatting within the text for such applications as outlining or printing long quotations. Changing justification and vertical spacing globally within a document would allow for printing the same document in several different forms. For instance, I often print one or two single-spaced versions of a manuscript before printing the final, double-spaced version for submission. Including provisions for printing a document with line numbers (used in the GET command) would certainly make using this feature more convenient.

Although the program package may seem a bit expensive for the features included, keep in mind that no additional hardware is required for using this program with an unmodified Apple II. The cost of lowercase adapters, 80-column display cards, and other hardware is considerably higher than the price of this program alone. Silicon Valley Systems plans to add many more features to future versions of The Word Handler, so you should check on the current version before making a definite decision.

## Chapter 6

Super-Text 40/80

Publisher: Muse Software, 347 N. Charles Street, Baltimore, MD 21201
Hardware Required: Apple II or Apple II Plus, 48K, Applesoft ROM, Disk II, printer with interface card, lowercase adapter or Videx 80-column board.
Price: $175.00

Super-Text 40/80 (Fig. 6-1) has just been introduced as an updated version of the very capable Super-Text II word-processing program from Muse Software. Although the changes are not dramatic in the new version, several interesting features have been added. My discussion will center around Super-Text 40/80, since that will be the standard version of Super-Text by the time you read this.

TEXT INPUT FEATURES

Text input from the keyboard is done in what Super-Text 40/80 calls the add mode, selected by pressing CTRL-A from the cursor mode. The cursor mode is the "idling" mode for this program and allows selection of all the other operating modes.

Upper- and Lowercase Display. "Super-Text 40/80" displays upper- and lowercase letters on the screen, using any of the popular lowercase adapters on the market. For those without a lowercase adapter, Muse offers a unit of their own. Instructions and a length of wire are included in the program package for completing the shift key modification on your Apple, although the program will work without the modification. The cursor in the add mode is a blinking underline character.

Video Display. Without the addition of a Videx 80-column board (discussed in the special features section), the video display consists of the standard Apple 40-character lines. Control characters, identified by inverse video, appear at various points throughout the text to denote special features selected.

Word Formatting. Words too long to fit on one line are automatically moved to the next without operator intervention. The space between words is used as a separator to determine points where words should be shifted. Although it is not included as a standard feature, instructions are provided for defining a control character to represent

Fig. 6-1. The Super-Text 40 /80 title screen and initial selection menu.

an "unbreakable" space in the text for special situations.

Paragraph indentation, indicated by an inverse P on the screen, can be specified in a format line or the default parameters file. Whenever CTRL-P appears in the text, the next line is automatically indented the specified number of spaces and the first character of the new line capitalized. To use block paragraphing, the indentation value may be set to zero. No provisions for hyphenation are included.

Tabbing. Horizontal tabs may be defined using a tab control line. Tabs are set according to printer positions and are not relative to the margins defined (or redefined) in the text. Pressing CTRL-T in the add mode starts a tab control line. The format for defining tab stops is T(position), (position), (position), up to a maximum of 15.

Using tab stops within the text is done by specifying either CTRL-L or CTRL-R. CTRL-L left justifies text at the next tab stop; CTRL-R right justifies it. During the process of text entry, CTRL-L and CTRL-R are shown in inverse video (Fig. 6-2). The actual effect of using tabs can be visualized on the screen using the print preview feature (see the output section for details).

Justification. Word-spacing justification is available during text entry by inserting a J in a format line. An R returns to ragged right margins. Justification creates even left and right margins by inserting spaces between words in the text. As mentioned earlier, both left and right justification are available for tabbing purposes. A system of implied tabs and justification is available to produce justified columns of words or numbers. Decimal point justification is also included for operations involving the math mode. See the editing section for details.

Line Spacing. Line spacing can be altered during the process of text input through the use of a format line. Inserting S selects single spacing; D designates double spacing. There are no provisions for other spacing combinations.

Status Display during Text Input. The word "Add" displayed in the lower right corner and the direction indicator (+ or −) in the lower left corner of the screen tells you that the add mode has been selected. No other information is routinely included on the screen display.

Page Specification Change. During add mode operations, page specifications may be altered with ease. Page breaks can be forced by inserting a CTRL-N. Margins, paper length, and most other page specifications can be adjusted at any point by inserting a format line, initiated by pressing CTRL-F.

Text Files from Other Programs. No provisions are included to accept text files from other programs. There are two related programs that interact with Super-Text 40/80: Address Book and Form Letter (see the special features section). Other programs, such as The Voice from Muse, can use text files created by Super-Text 40/80.

Formatting for Text Output. A format line may be inserted anywhere in the text, although it is common practice to put it at the beginning of a text file. Pressing CTRL-F initiates a format line which contains values for left and right margins, paragraph indentation, top and bottom margins, text length per page, a line for printing page numbers, the character position about which the line number will

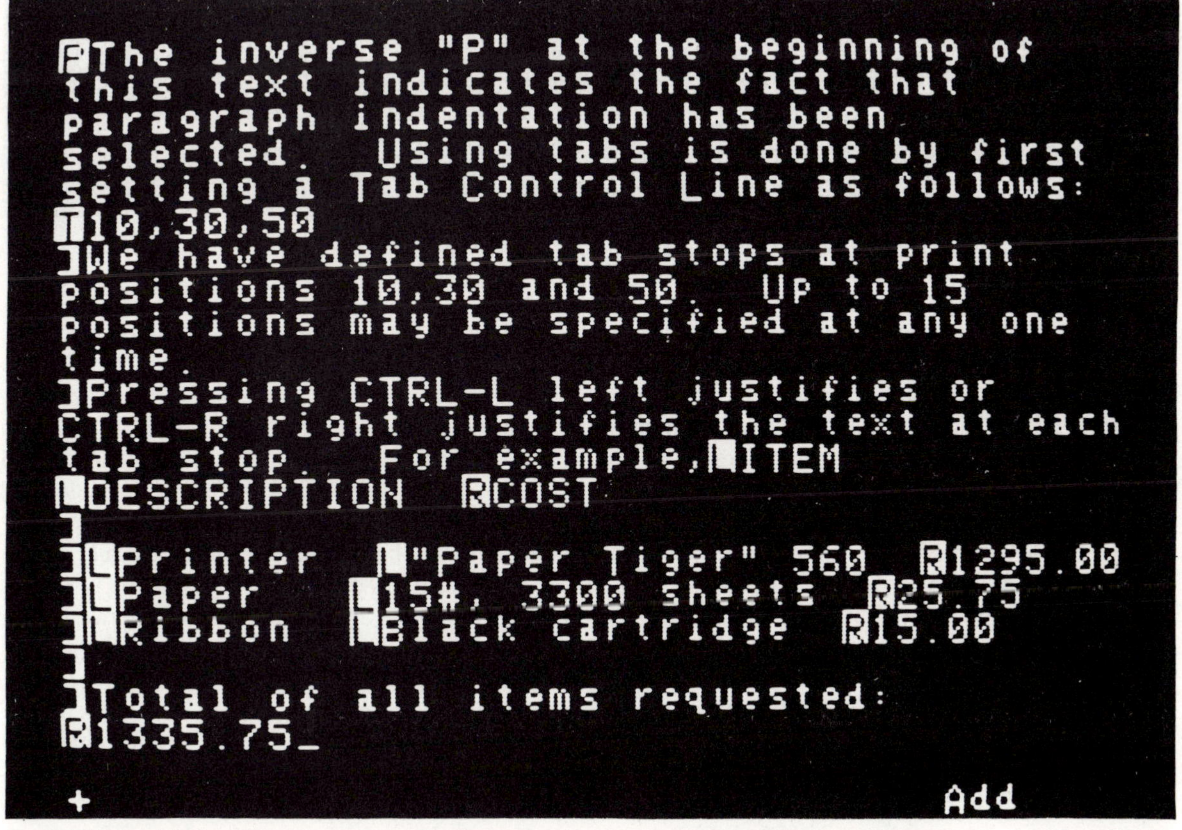

Fig. 6-2. Paragraph indentation and horizontal tabbing operations as seen on the video screen.

```
]
]A Format Line is used to set, or
alter, page specifications from within
the text.   Initiated by pressing
CTRL-F, the format line is shown on the
screen as follows:
]
F10,70,4,5,56,5,3,40,2
]
]In this case, we have set the left
margin (10), right margin (70),
paragraph indentation (4), top margin
(5), text length per page (56), bottom
margin (5), line number in margin for
page number (3), character position for
page number printing (40) and 2
overprints for boldfacing.
]
]Letters may be used to select single
or double spacing, top or bottom page
numbering and justified or ragged edges.
+                                    Add
```

Fig. 6-3. Format lines are used to specify text output parameters. If no format specifications are contained in a text file, the system default values are used.

be centered, and number of times to overprint for boldface type (Fig. 6-3). All values are stated in terms of character positions on the printed page. In addition, letters may be added to select page numbers in the top margin (T), page numbers in bottom margin (B), single spacing (S), double spacing (D), justified right margin (J), or ragged right margin (R). Provisions for printing special page numbers, headers, footers, and other special features accessed through a format line will be described later.

Format lines are saved along with the text in a file. If no format line is specified, default values entered into the system during initial configuration will automatically be used. When creating a format line, it is not necessary to redefine all the parameters each time. For instance, to select double-spaced justified copy you would type CTRL-F D, J.

Special printer features, such as underlining, selection of character size, emphasized printing, ribbon color selection, and backspacing, are provided for in two ways. Some of the more common capabilities are specified in the program and called by a CTRL-(key) sequence. Others may be defined by the user and called by other CTRL-(key) sequences. See the output section for details.

Maximum Text Length per File. Text files are limited to the amount of available memory after the program is loaded. The maximum file size is 14,094 characters.

Typing Speed. One of the limitations of earlier versions of Super-Text was a reduced character acceptance speed toward the top of the video display. Once text entry had progressed past the center of the screen, no problems were noted.

Super-Text 40/80 has solved this problem by incorporating a type ahead buffer which permits rapid entry of data at any point on the screen.

"The" Key. Earlier versions of Super-Text allowed you to select automatic printing of the word "the" by pressing the colon (:). This feature has been expanded, as you will see in the special features section.

EDITING FEATURES

Cursor Positioning. The cursor movement commands provided are left arrow (move one position to the left), right arrow (move one position to the right), RETURN (move up one line on the screen), and slash (/) (move down one line). Other cursor moves provided are space bar (move one character to the right), period (move to the center of the line), ESC-period (move to the center of the screen), ESC-RTN (move to the top of the screen), ESC-/ (move to the bottom of the screen), ESC-right arrow (move to the extreme right of the line), and ESC-left arrow (move to the extreme left of the line). In general, the cursor movement controls are logical and easy to use. No provisions are included for moving the cursor a word, sentence, or paragraph at a time.

Scrolling. Scrolling through the text by either a line at a time or page at a time is possible. First, the direction of scrolling is established by pressing either the plus (+) for forward movement toward the end of the file or minus (−) for reverse movement toward the beginning. Pressing L will move the text a single line; P, a video page in the selected direction. Repeated pressing of either key or holding down either key and REPEAT will cause multiple moves in the desired direction. Express scrolling is provided by ESC−, which displays the first page and moves the cursor to the beginning of a file, and ESC+, which displays the last page and moves the cursor to the last character in a file.

Changing a Few Characters. Characters may be changed using the change mode, entered by pressing CTRL-C from the program's idle, or cursor mode. A C in the lower right corner indicates the fact that the change mode has been selected. In the change mode, all the cursor movement commands mentioned earlier are still available. When the cursor is positioned at the desired character, it may be changed by simply typing over it. Each replacement takes place immediately on the screen and is accompanied by a short sound from the Apple's speaker for confirmation. The change mode may be exited by pressing ESC-ESC.

Inserting Text. New text may be added to a document presently displayed on the screen in either of two ways. First, the cursor is located at the position where text insertion is to begin. If the keyboard is to be used for insertion, pressing CTRL-A will call the add mode. Text is added on a dashed line which is placed between the original cursor position and the character following the position of the cursor when the add mode was selected (Fig. 6-4). All the commands discussed earlier under text input will function in exactly the same way in this situation. The add mode is exited by pressing ESC-ESC.

Text from a disk file can also be inserted at the cursor. From the cursor mode, pressing CTRL-L will initiate the necessary disk operations. See the text storage and retrieval section for details.

Deleting Text. In either the cursor or the change mode, text is deleted by pressing one of several command sequences available. Pressing CTRL-D deletes the character at the cursor, CTRL-W deletes from the cursor to the next space, CTRL-G deletes all characters from the cursor to the end of the line, and CTRL-O deletes from the cursor to the end of the screen. The effect of any deletion is shown, and remaining text is adjusted immediately. In addition, pressing ESC-CTRL-Z deletes the current file from memory. When using either CTRL-O or ESC-CTRL-Z, you are asked to finalize the delete by pressing the # (SHIFT-3) key, or any other key to cancel the delete command (Fig. 6-5). The other delete commands do not require confirmation before they proceed.

Block Operations. Super-Text 40/80 includes a set of commands which allow you to mark a portion of the text in memory and then manipulate the marked "block" in one of several ways (Fig. 6-6). To use these capabilities, it is necessary to first identify and mark the text desired. By the way,

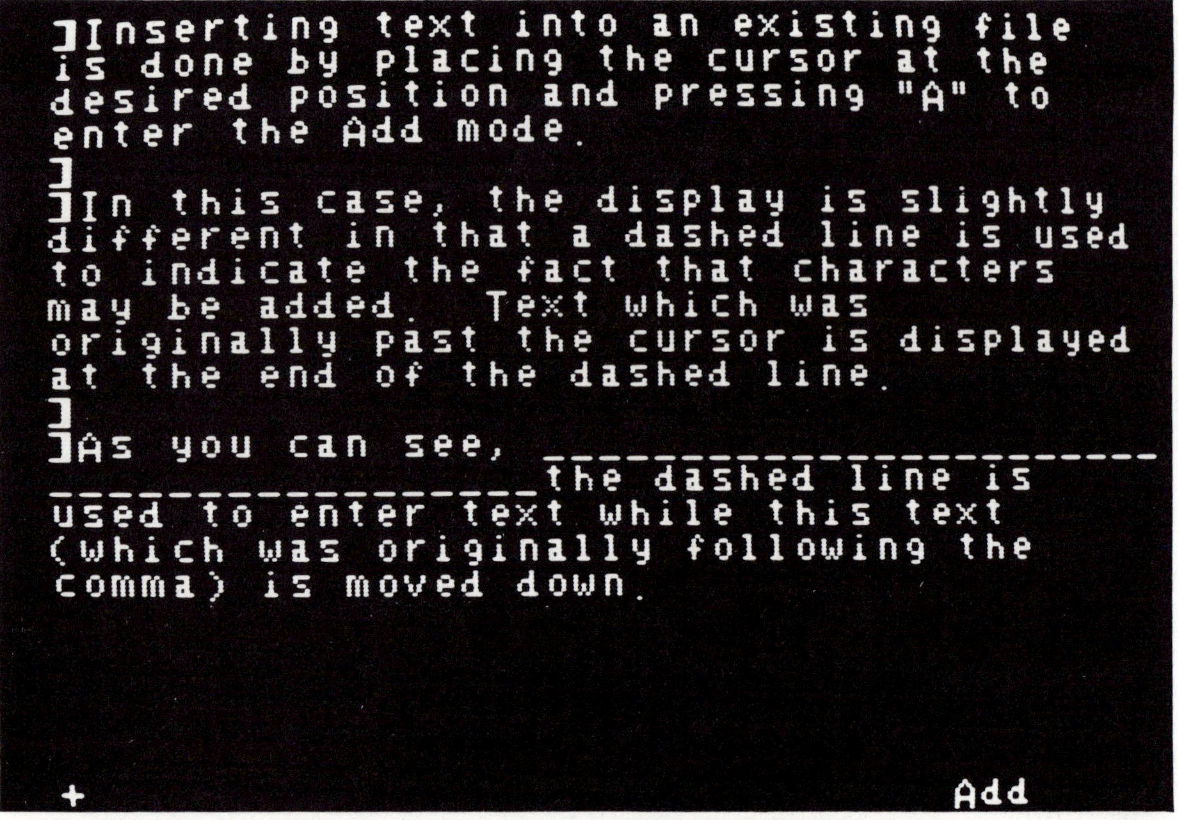

Fig. 6-4. Text inserted into an existing document is preceded by the dashed line shown. When the Add mode is exited, the extra dashes disappear and the new and old text are automatically merged.

a block may be as small or large as desired, but only one block can be marked at any time.

To initiate block operations, the following procedure is used. After the cursor is moved to the beginning of the block, press CTRL-V to insert a block marker (a flashing left parenthesis—( ). A second marker (a flashing right parenthesis—)) is inserted at the end of the text block by again pressing CTRL-V when the desired cursor position is reached. The position of block markers may be reviewed by pressing V: you will hear a beep when the end marker is indicated.

Once a block has been properly marked, several options are available that can be selected by pressing ESC-V. The block can be saved as a separate file or appended to an existing file on the disk by pressing S. Blocks saved in this fashion can be retrieved at any time using the text insertion procedure outlined earlier. To copy a block somewhere else in the text, move the cursor to the desired position, press ESC-V, and select C (copy). Multiple copies of the same block may be inserted in this fashion. Moving a block to another location and deleting it from the marked location is done by locating the cursor, pressing ESC-V, and selecting M (move).

Two of the block operation commands are relatively independent of the cursor position, although the cursor does not have to be located within the marked block when selecting them. Deleting the entire block and its markers from memory can be done by pressing ESC-V and selecting D (delete). Markers are removed by selecting U (unmark) after pressing ESC-V.

Find and Replace. Both the find and replace commands can handle strings of up to 30 characters

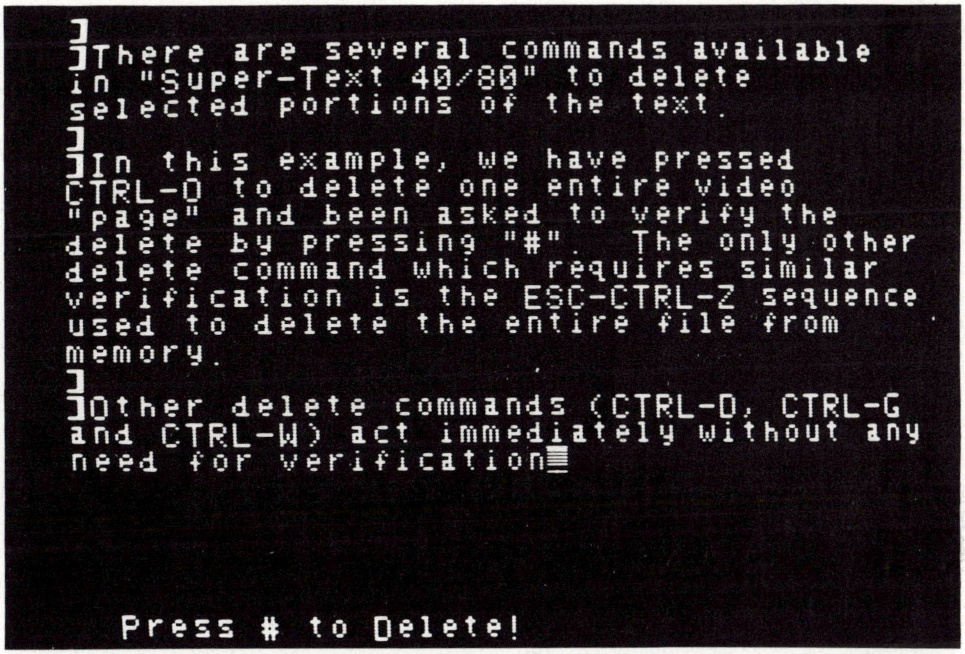

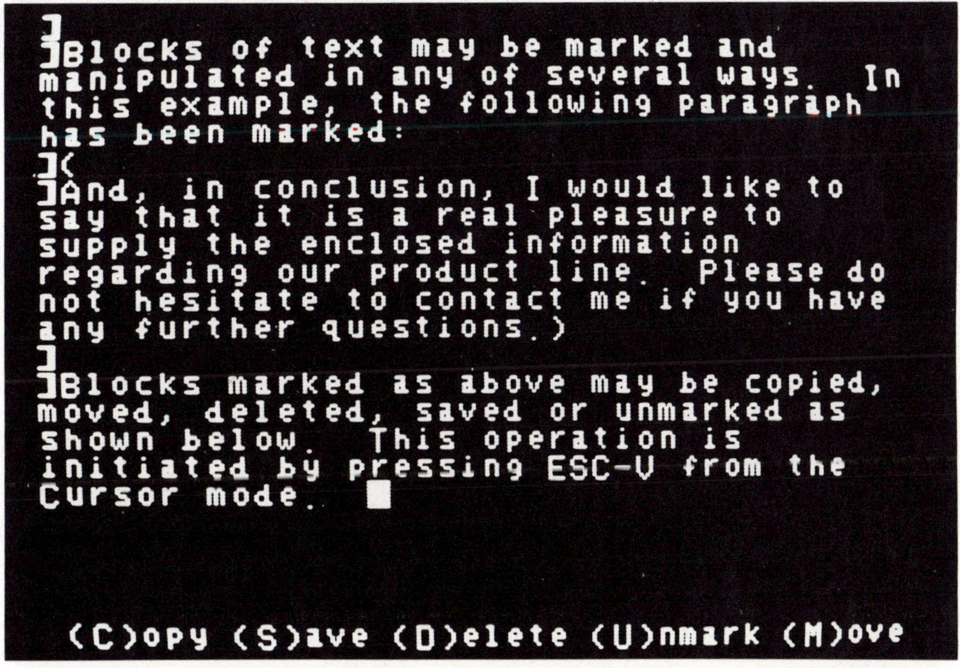

Fig. 6-5. Verification is requested before the program will delete one video page or the entire file in memory.

Fig. 6-6. The text enclosed by parentheses has been marked as a block and may be manipulated by using the commands listed at the bottom of the screen.

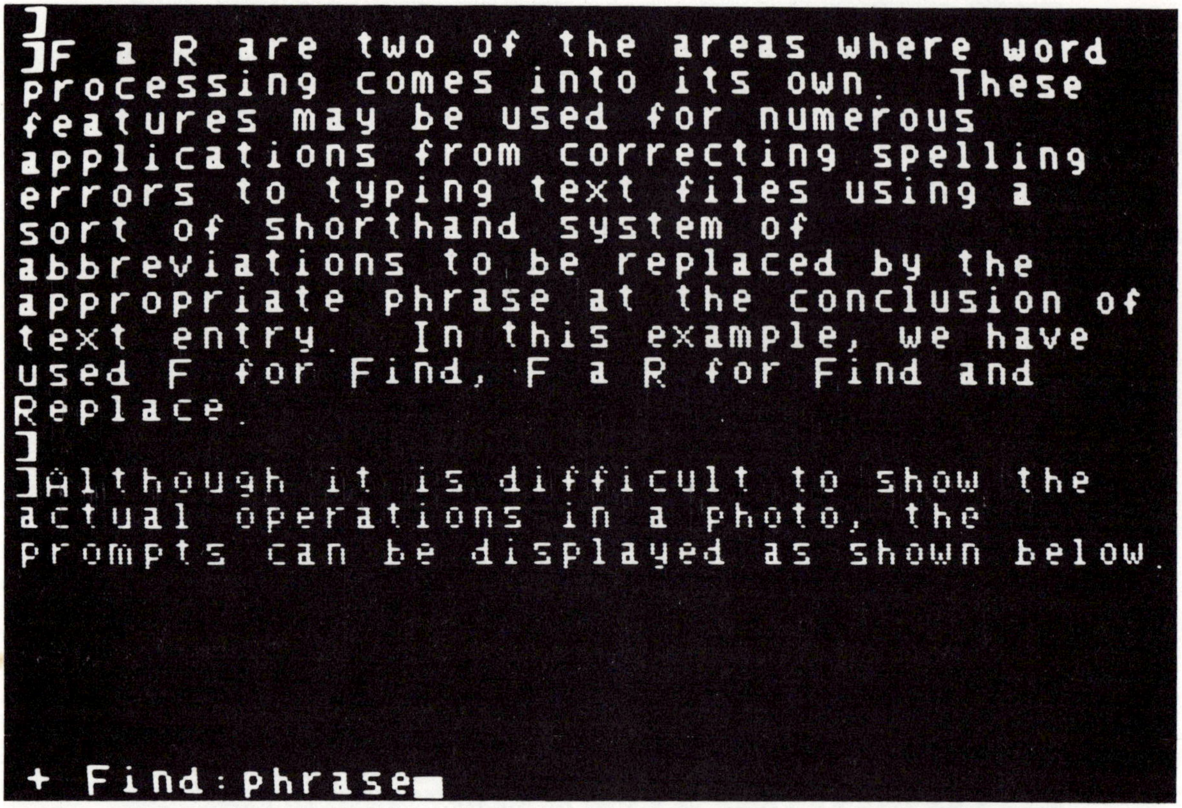

]
]F a R are two of the areas where word
processing comes into its own. These
features may be used for numerous
applications from correcting spelling
errors to typing text files using a
sort of shorthand system of
abbreviations to be replaced by the
appropriate phrase at the conclusion of
text entry.   In this example, we have
used F for Find, F a R for Find and
Replace.
]
]Although it is difficult to show the
actual operations in a photo, the
prompts can be displayed as shown below.

+ Find:phrase

Fig. 6-7. Find may be initiated by pressing F and typing the word or phrase desired. Pressing CTRL-F will automatically use the word at the cursor as that to be found.

in length. Both operations proceed from the current cursor position in the direction selected for text scrolling, as noted earlier. Two unusual features are included: multiple strings and special characters. The 30-character strings may consist of any number of words or phrases to be located or replaced, each separated by a comma. The & character will match on any number of spaces, and ! is used as a "wild card" which will match any character.

Initiating the find operation is done by pressing F and entering the desired word in response to the prompt or pressing CTL-F which enters the word at the cursor as that to be found (Fig. 6-7). As each occurrence is found, it will be displayed in the center of the screen. Press N to locate the next occurrence or RETURN to cancel the FIND. To search for several words at a time, press F and enter a comma, followed by the desired words, separated by commas. The operation will take place as noted earlier, except that every occurrence of each word specified will be displayed.

Using & in a find operation permits spaces to be ignored (Fig. 6-8). Substituting ! for any character will allow any other character in that position to cause a match. For instance, FIND: A!!le would return Apple, ample, or any other five-letter word beginning with a and ending with le.

Replace is quite similar in operation to find. Press R and enter the desired word, or press CTRL-R to replace the word at the cursor (Fig. 6-9). After the word is specified, you are asked whether or not you want to replace all occurrences. Responding Y automatically replaces all occurrences; N pauses at each occurrence and re-

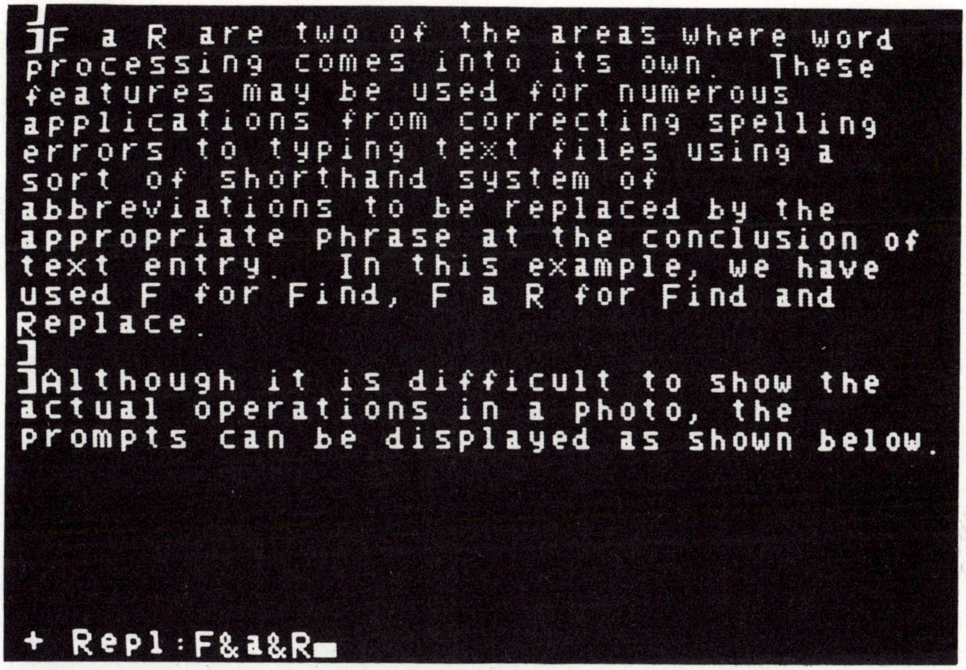

Fig. 6-8. In a find or replace operation, & permits spaces to be ignored, and ! is used as a "wild-card" character.

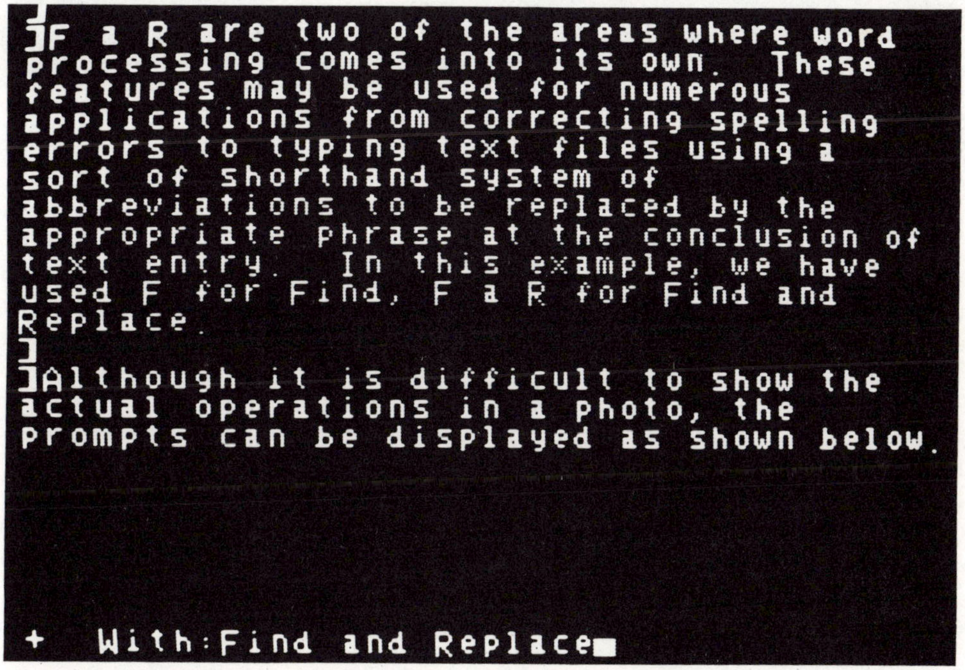

Fig. 6-9. The replacement word or phrase is typed in response to the WITH: prompt.

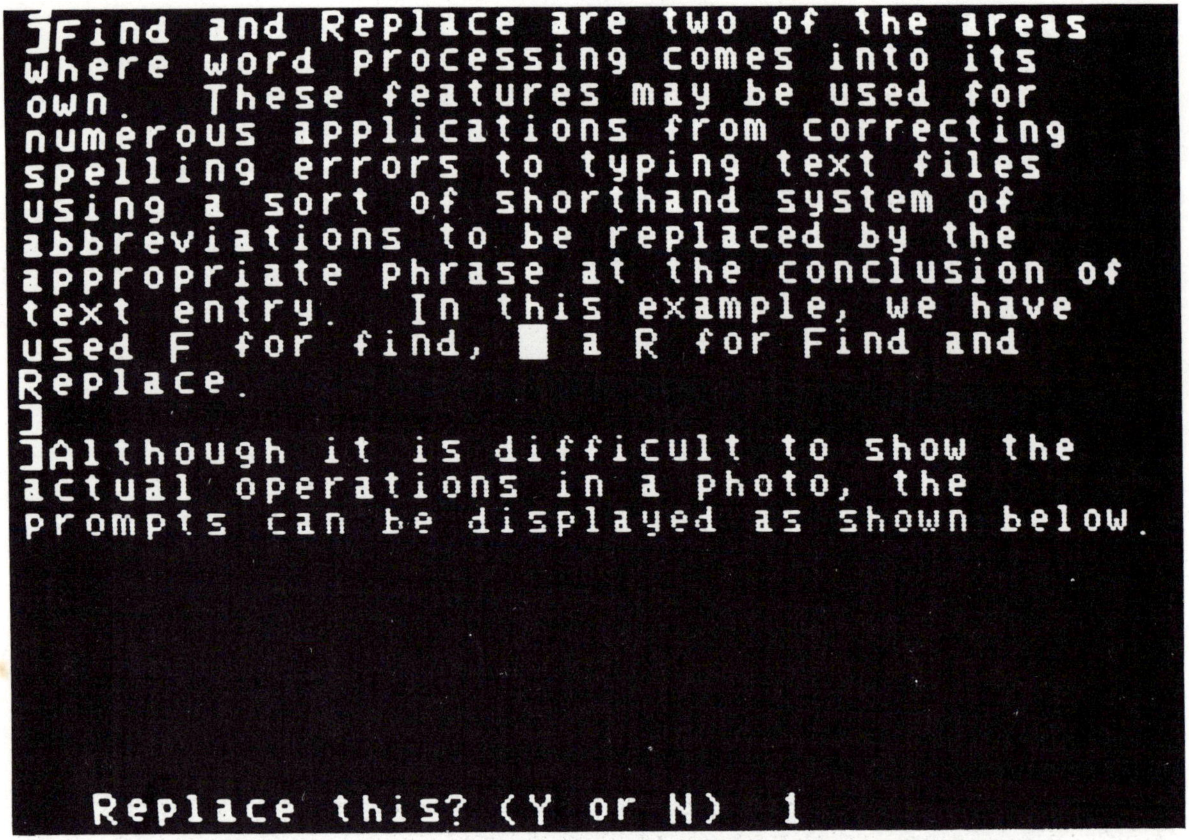

Fig. 6-10. Individual occurrence replacement approval is requested if manual replace has been specified.

quests approval (Fig. 6-10). After all the occurrences of the desired word or phrase have been replaced, the program tells you how many occurrences were replaced (Fig. 6-11). As in find operations, multiple words or phrases may be specified for replacement. Press R, enter a comma and the desired items, separated by commas. Each occurrence of every item will be replaced automatically if you responded Y to the ALL? (Y/N) prompt or presented for your approval if not.

Replace may also be used for two additional functions: counting occurrences of a specific word or phrase and estimating the approximate number of words in a file. To count the occurrences of a word, press R, and enter the word or phrase desired, in response to the REPL: prompt. Press RETURN in response to the WITH: prompt, and the screen will display the number of occurrences. The number of words in a file may be approximated by entering a space as the word to be replaced and pressing RETURN in response to the WITH: prompt. The number of spaces displayed in the line that gives the number of occurrences that were counted is roughly indicative of the total number of words in the file.

Both find and replace will operate on multiple files through the use of the Autolink featues described in the special features section.

Mathematical Functions Available. Super-Text 40/80 features a math mode which can be used as a direct 15-digit calculator or to perform calculations on numbers contained in a text file. The math mode is contained in a module which must be loaded from the disk when math functions are desired. The memory location for the math mode is the same as that used for the print mode (see the output section), so only one of the modules can be present in memory at any one time. Since math and print are not likely to be needed at the same time, there is no real conflict with this arrangement.

Once the math mode module is loaded from the disk, pressing either E or CTRL-E activates the math functions. The bottom of the screen contains a status line displaying the direction indicator, operand, accumulator, mode, and item counter (Fig. 6-12). The cursor movement, text scrolling, and text delete functions may be used in the math mode.

Direct entry calculation operations are enabled by pressing E or any number once the math mode has been activated. When using the calculator, Z acts as a clear entry command, and Z Z clears the operand, accumulator, and item counter. The calculator functions in much the same way as any of the self-contained units with which you are probably familiar. Enter an initial value and press +, A, or RETURN. The next and succeeding values can be entered and manipulated using the following commands: RETURN to add the operand to the value contained in the accumulator, A or + to add the operand to the accumulator, S or − to subtract the operand from the value contained in the accumulator, M or * to multiply the accumulator value by the operand, D or / to divide the accumulator by the operand, and ∧ to exponentiate (raise to the power indicated by the operand) the accumulator figure.

When you have finished your calculations, the result may be transferred from the accumulator into the file in memory (Fig. 6-13). Position the cursor at the desired point, and press R. The value contained in the accumulator will replace a number in the file, if the cursor is on a number. Pressing CTRL-R transfers the accumulator value to the text and right justifies it with the number or word on the line

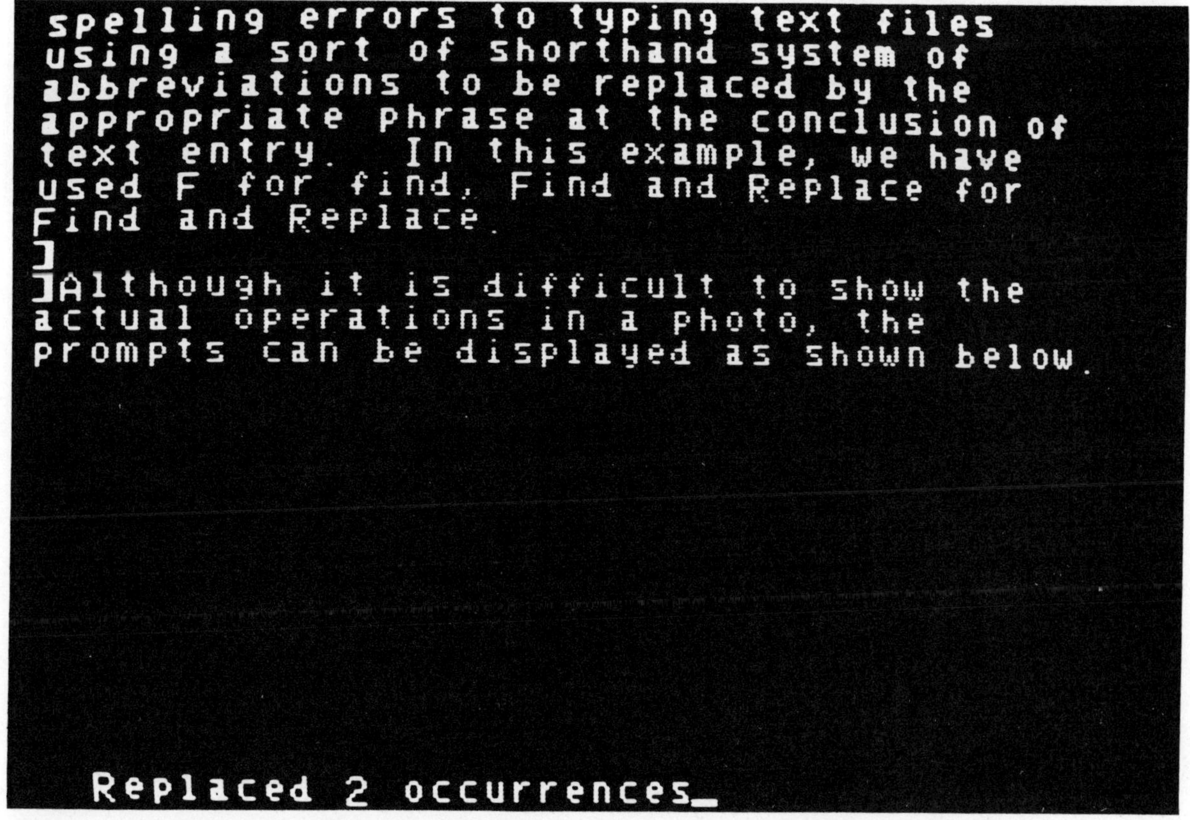

Fig. 6-11. Super-Text 40 /80 provides a total count of the number of occurrences replaced.

Fig. 6-12. The status line shown at the bottom of the screen indicates that the math mode has been selected.

above the cursor. ESC, pressed once, exits the direct calculation function and returns you to the math mode.

Arithmetic operations can also be performed on numerical data contained in text files. The process is quite similar to that used for direct calculations. After clearing the accumulator (Z Z), the cursor is positioned at a number. Pressing A places that number in the accumulator. Succeeding numbers are entered by placing the cursor on them, and pressing A to add, S to subtract, D to divide, or M to multiply. The total will be displayed in the accumulator and can be placed in the text using R or CTRL-R (Fig. 6-14).

A separate set of commands is used to perform columnar addition. The cursor must be placed at the bottom of the desired column. After clearing the accumulator, pressing C will add to the top of the screen or top of the column, whichever comes first (Fig. 6-15). CTRL-C allows addition of columns which extend beyond the top of the screen. In this case, the text is scrolled down until the top of the column is reached. As in other operations, the sum is displayed in the accumulator and may be placed at the cursor anywhere in the text (Fig. 6-6). Column alignment capabilities are also included.

The math mode also provides some special functions. Pressing the period (.) moves the cursor forward to the next number in the text; the comma (,) moves the cursor to the preceding number. The (SHIFT-3) key allows you to define the number of decimal positions the accumulator will display. As with the other modes in Super-Text 40/80, pressing ESC-ESC returns the program to the cursor mode.

Miscellaneous Editing Features. Super-Text 40/80 contains a split screen feature which allows you to examine one portion of a text file

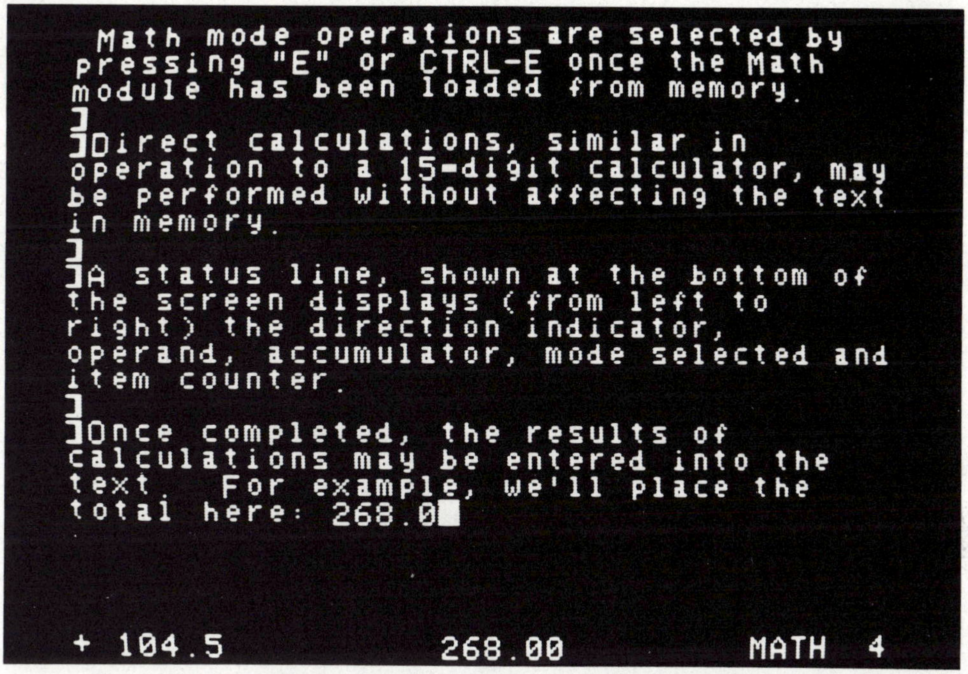

Math mode operations are selected by pressing "E" or CTRL-E once the Math module has been loaded from memory.

Direct calculations, similar in operation to a 15-digit calculator, may be performed without affecting the text in memory.

A status line, shown at the bottom of the screen displays (from left to right) the direction indicator, operand, accumulator, mode selected and item counter.

Once completed, the results of calculations may be entered into the text. For example, we'll place the total here: 268.0

```
+  104.5                 268.00               MATH   4
```

Fig. 6-13. The result of math mode calculations can be placed directly into the text file in memory.

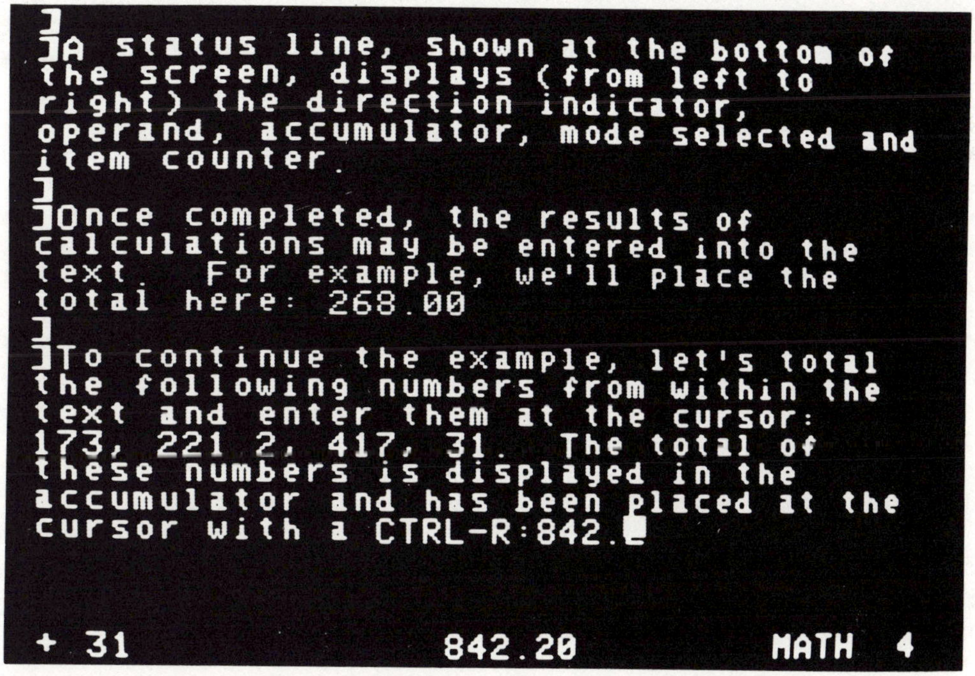

A status line, shown at the bottom of the screen, displays (from left to right) the direction indicator, operand, accumulator, mode selected and item counter.

Once completed, the results of calculations may be entered into the text. For example, we'll place the total here: 268.00

To continue the example, let's total the following numbers from within the text and enter them at the cursor: 173, 221 2, 417, 31. The total of these numbers is displayed in the accumulator and has been placed at the cursor with a CTRL-R:842.

```
+  31                    842.20               MATH   4
```

Fig. 6-14. The math mode permits mathematical operations on numbers contained in a text file.

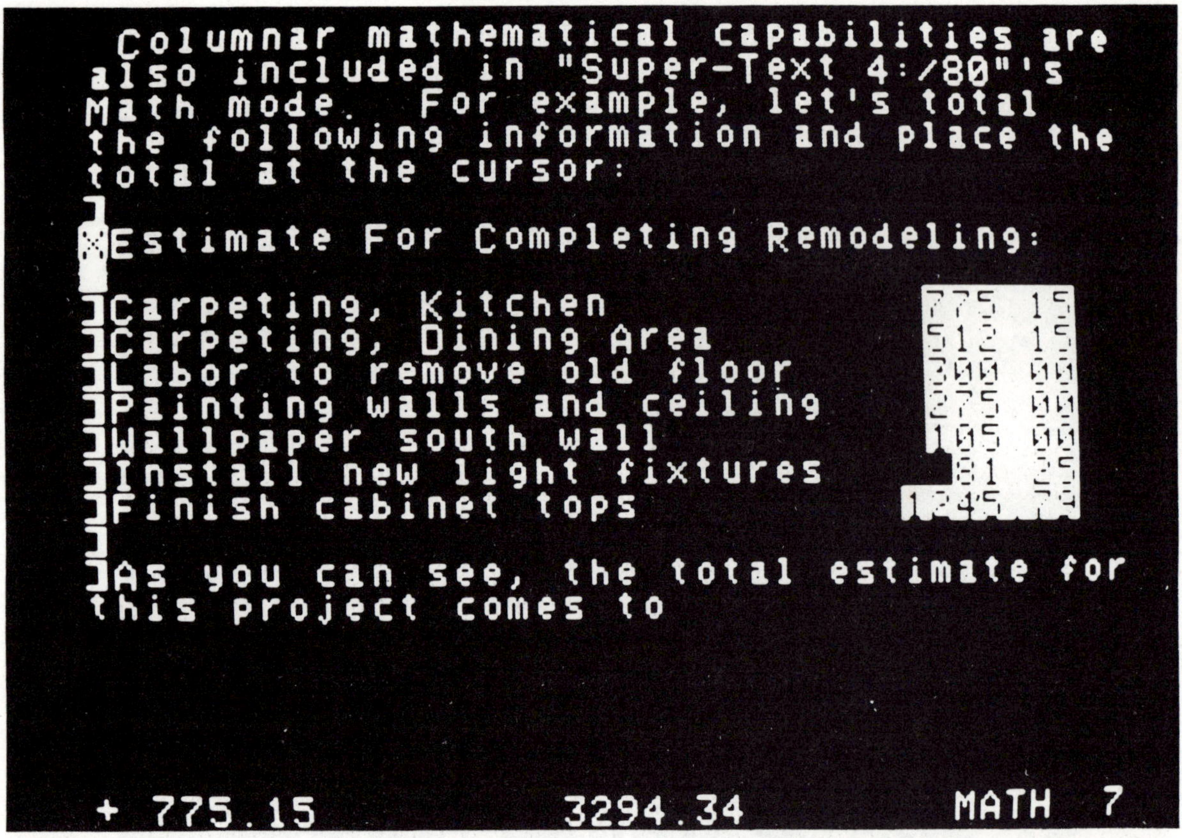

Fig. 6-15. Columnar addition can be performed automatically using commands provided in the math mode.

while editing or reviewing another. The portion of the screen in which the cursor is placed is active and will respond to all the normal editing commands, while the balance of the screen remains unchanged (Fig. 6-17). To split the screen, press S from the cursor mode. A copy of the current text page will be displayed on both the bottom and top halves of the screen. Pressing B positions the cursor in the bottom half; T moves it to the top. CTRL-B moves the screen boundary one line toward the bottom of the screen, and CTRL-T moves it one line toward the top. To return to full screen operation, press S again.

If you want to change markers, Super-Text 40/80 will position the cursor at the last change made to the file in memory by pressing J from the cursor mode. The last four changes are located by repeatedly pressing J. Four specific locations in the text can be marked and identified by the J function. Press M to place a marker in the text and J to locate the marker. The program does not differentiate between actual changes and locations marked by the M command. Markers are not retained when a file is saved on the disk.

The case of a character at the cursor may be changed by pressing 1 to shift from lower- to upper-case or 2 to change from upper- to lowercase. The position of two characters may be transposed by pressing CTRL-I.

TEXT STORAGE AND RETRIEVAL

DOS Used. A nonstandard DOS is used on the program disks, preventing you from creating back-up copies or modifying the program for a specific purpose. Two copies of the program disk are included, and Muse has a rather liberal disk replacement policy (more details on that later).

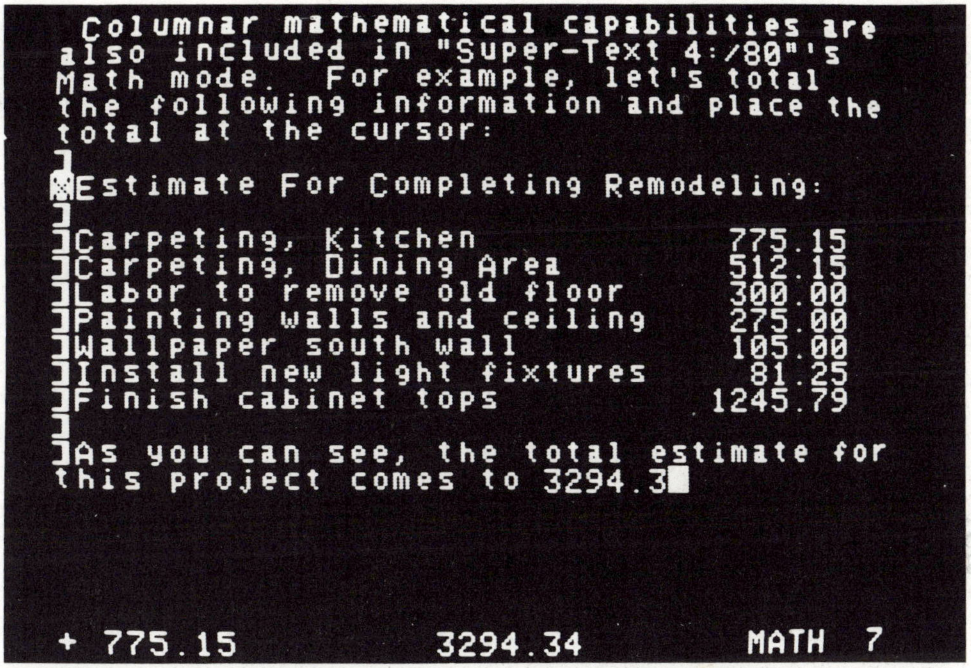

Columnar mathematical capabilities are
also included in "Super-Text 4:/80"'s
Math mode. For example, let's total
the following information and place the
total at the cursor:

Estimate For Completing Remodeling:

Carpeting, Kitchen   775.15
Carpeting, Dining Area   512.15
Labor to remove old floor   300.00
Painting walls and ceiling   275.00
Wallpaper south wall   105.00
Install new light fixtures   81.25
Finish cabinet tops   1245.79

As you can see, the total estimate for
this project comes to 3294.3

+ 775.15   3294.34   MATH 7

Fig. 6-16. The result of columnar addition may be placed anywhere in a text file.

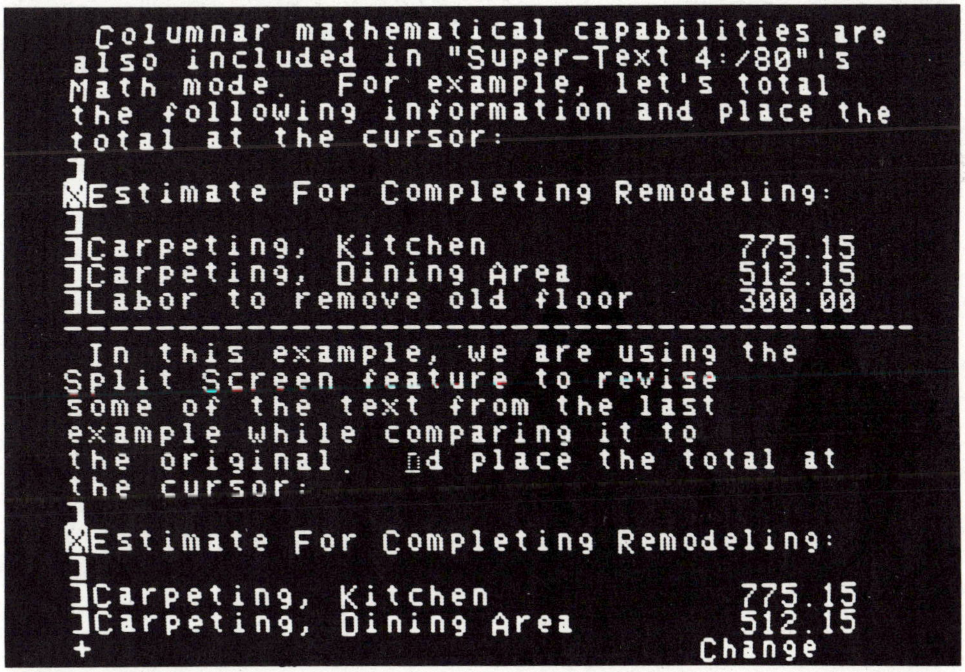

Columnar mathematical capabilities are
also included in "Super-Text 4:/80"'s
Math mode. For example, let's total
the following information and place the
total at the cursor:

Estimate For Completing Remodeling:

Carpeting, Kitchen   775.15
Carpeting, Dining Area   512.15
Labor to remove old floor   300.00

In this example, we are using the
Split Screen feature to revise
some of the text from the last
example while comparing it to
the original.   d place the total at
the cursor:

Estimate For Completing Remodeling:

Carpeting, Kitchen   775.15
Carpeting, Dining Area   512.15
+   Change

Fig. 6-17. Split screen capability allows you to examine one portion of a text file while editing or
reviewing another.

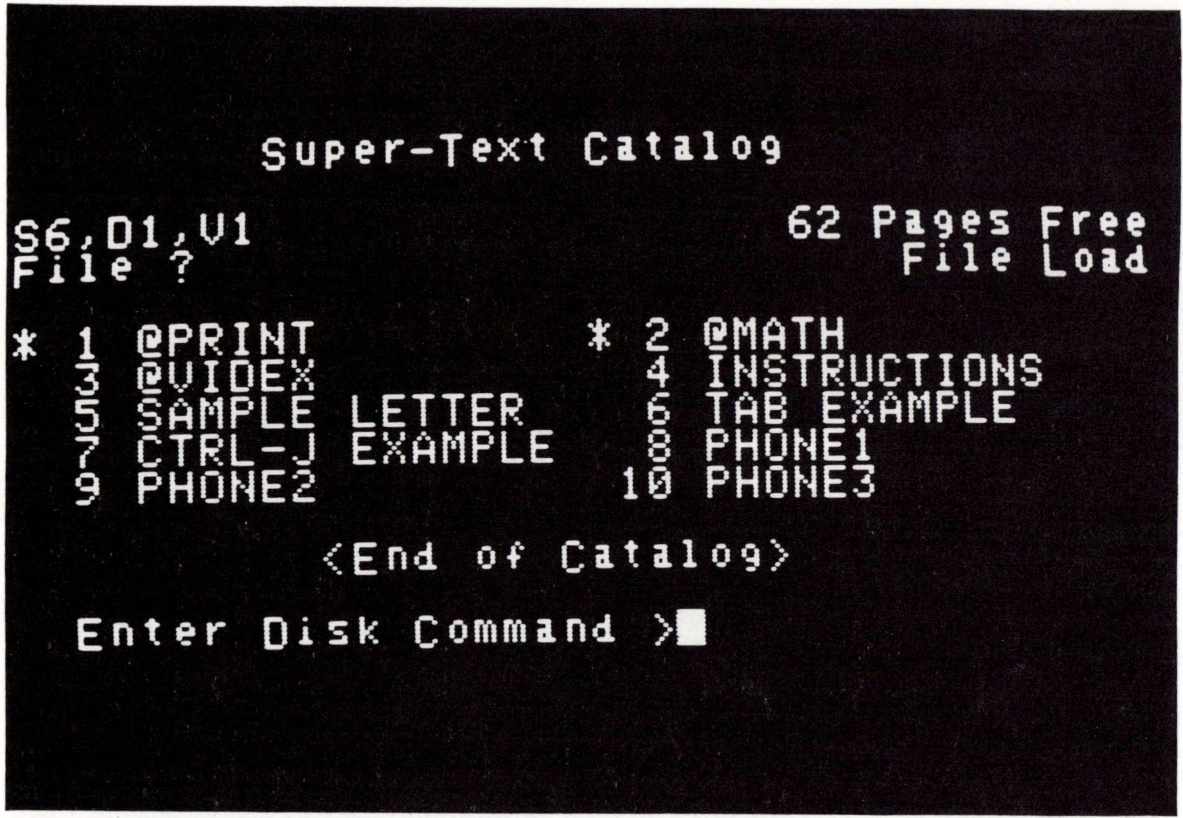

Fig. 6-18. Pressing CTRL-D when the catalog is displayed allows the use of the disk commands DELETE, RENAME, LOCK, and UNLOCK.

Text File Backup. For those with more than one disk drive, a copy program is included on the program disk. This program will initialize and copy the contents of an entire data disk onto a blank disk. Interestingly, the copy program includes capabilities to bypass defective sectors or tracks on the disk being copied: this is a real plus if you are trying to recover as much data as possible from a damaged disk.

Single drive users can make back-up copies the hard way, by loading each file contained on a disk into memory and saving it to another data disk.

The DOS commands DELETE, RENAME, LOCK, and UNLOCK are supported in Super-Text 40/80. The ability to LOCK and UNLOCK files provides security against unwanted alteration or deletion of their contents. To access the disk commands, press CTRL-D when the disk catalog is being displayed (Fig. 6-18).

Multiple Disk Drive Access. In order to use more than one drive, you must identify it from the disk catalog, accessed by pressing CTRL-L. When asked for a file name or number, type the slot number and drive number, and press RETURN (Fig. 6-19). A catalog showing the contents of the disk in the drive specified will be displayed, and the drive is on-line. When a particular file is requested and not found on the drive currently in use, all other drives will be searched to locate the file. The copy program uses a slightly different procedure by asking you to specify a master and slave drive for its operations.

Text File Creation and Documentation. Text files are limited to 14,094 characters and must be saved on data disks initialized by Super-Text 40/80. File names are limited to 15 characters and must begin with a letter. To create a text file, press CTRL-S from the cursor mode. A catalog of files already on the disk is displayed along with the number of pages free on the disk, the name (if any) of the current file in memory, and SAVE to indicate that a save operation has been requested.

When the catalog is displayed, several options are available. Typing a name and pressing RE-TURN will save the file in memory on the disk. If that name already exists in the catalog, the file in memory will replace it. If you are using a file that already exists in the disk catalog, you may save the contents of memory by entering its catalog number, or, if it was the last file accessed, pressing the period (.) key. To return to the cursor mode without saving the file, press RETURN. You may also enter slot and drive numbers to access another disk drive.

Loading files from a data disk is done by pressing CTRL-L from the cursor mode (Fig. 6-20).

Once the disk catalog is displayed, a file may be loaded by entering the file name or its number from the catalog. If the file name is not found on the disk drive currently in use, the other drives on-line will automatically be searched. If a file is not located, pressing R will cause the program to attempt to locate the file again.

Super-Text 40/80 does not include provisions for displaying the length of individual files on the disk, although the amount of remaining space on the disk is shown. Text files created by this program are compatible with several other programs offered by Muse.

OUTPUT

Printer Configuration. Super-Text 40/80 can be used with a wide variety of printers through a somewhat elaborate system of interface and control

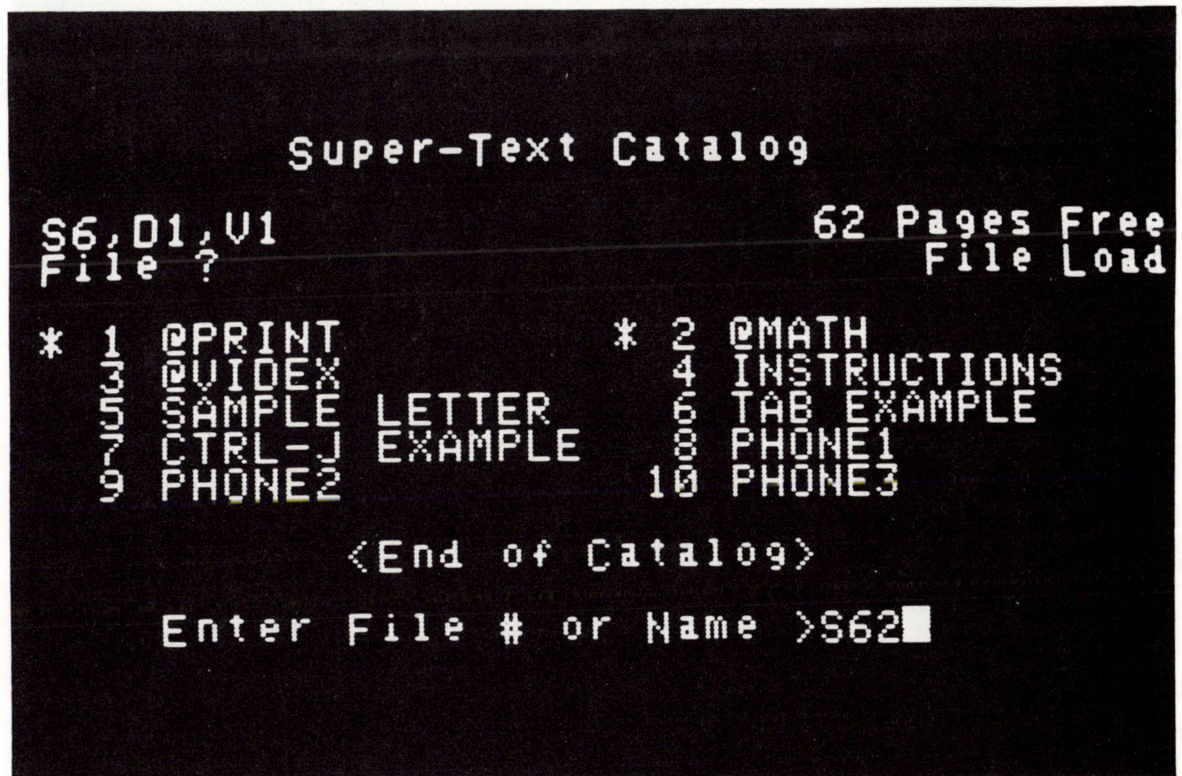

Fig. 6-19. Additional disk drives may be placed on-line by typing their slot and drive numbers in response to the file number or name prompt.

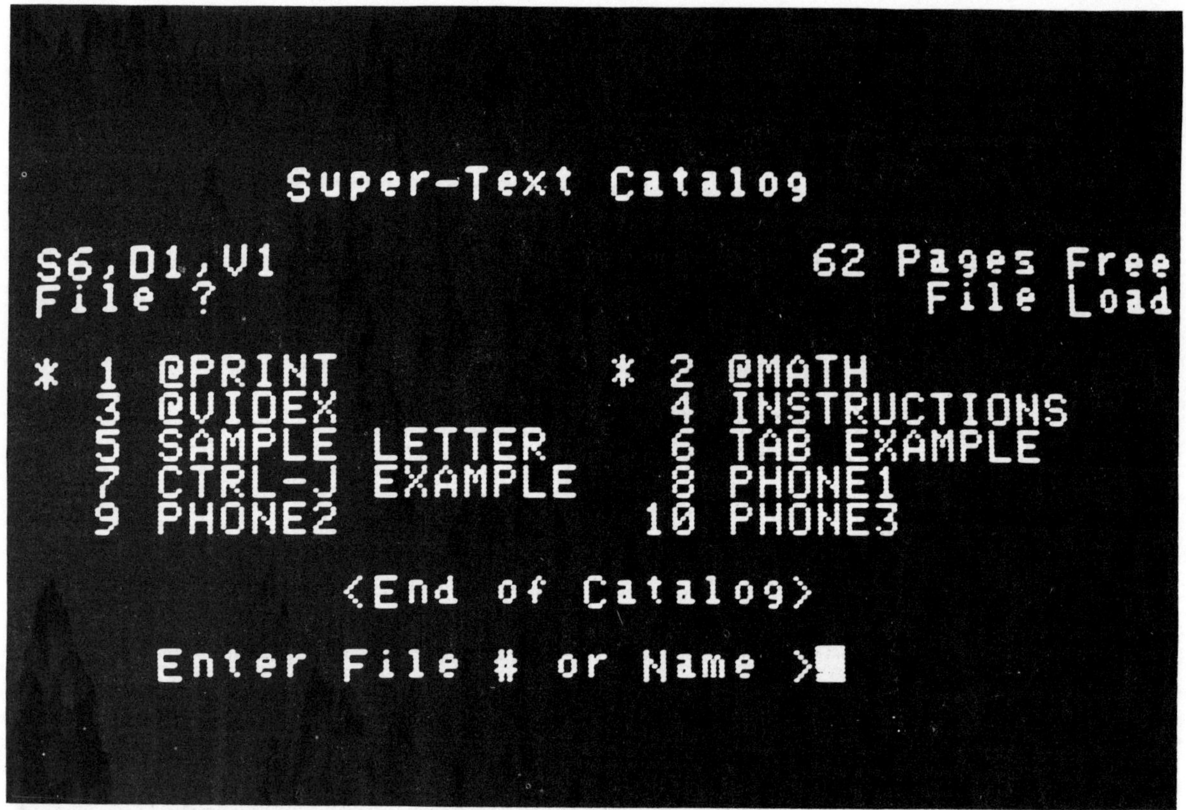

Fig. 6-20. Disk files are loaded into memory by typing either the name or catalog number.

sequence files. Earlier versions of the program provided much the same capabilities but required a great deal of programming sophistication on the part of the user to take advantage of them. One of the most valuable changes in the new version, in my opinion, is the simplification of this process.

To set or change printer configuration, select the Options program from the title page. After the Options program is loaded, the menu allows you to define printer interface parameters, default print format, page numbering, or special control sequences (Fig. 6-21). All of these values are contained in the $\wedge$ PARAMS files on the program disk.

Printer interface parameters (Fig. 6-22) are set according to the explicit directions in the program manual. Next, the default print format (used when no format is specified in a text file) is set. Default page numbering, used in printing text files without directions to the contrary, is set in a similar fashion. Finally, control key sequences can be defined to take advantage of special features offered by your printer (Fig. 6-23). Although this may seem to be a confusing process, the instructions provided in the program manual are very helpful. Using the documentation for your printer and these instructions, setting the control key sequences is a relatively simple matter (Fig. 6-24).

To save some time, $\wedge$ PARAMS files for Epson MX-80, Epson MX-80 with GRAFTRAX, Diablo compatible, Centronics, Anadex, Apple parallel card interfaced, NEC, and IDS printers are contained on the program disk and may be loaded according to the instructions provided. The control key sequences for each of these files are carefully explained in the documentation. You may change these sequences once the $\wedge$ PARAMS file has been selected.

Printer Control. I have used this program

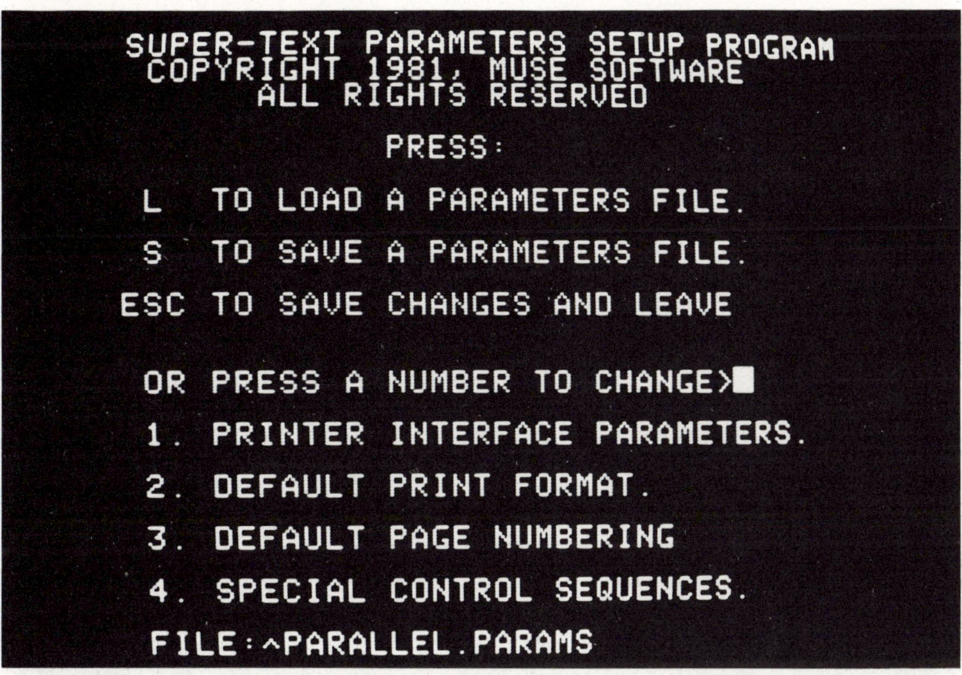

Fig. 6-21. The menu to set up parameters is displayed when Options is selected from the title page menu.

Fig. 6-22. Printer parameters are set by responding to the prompts provided.

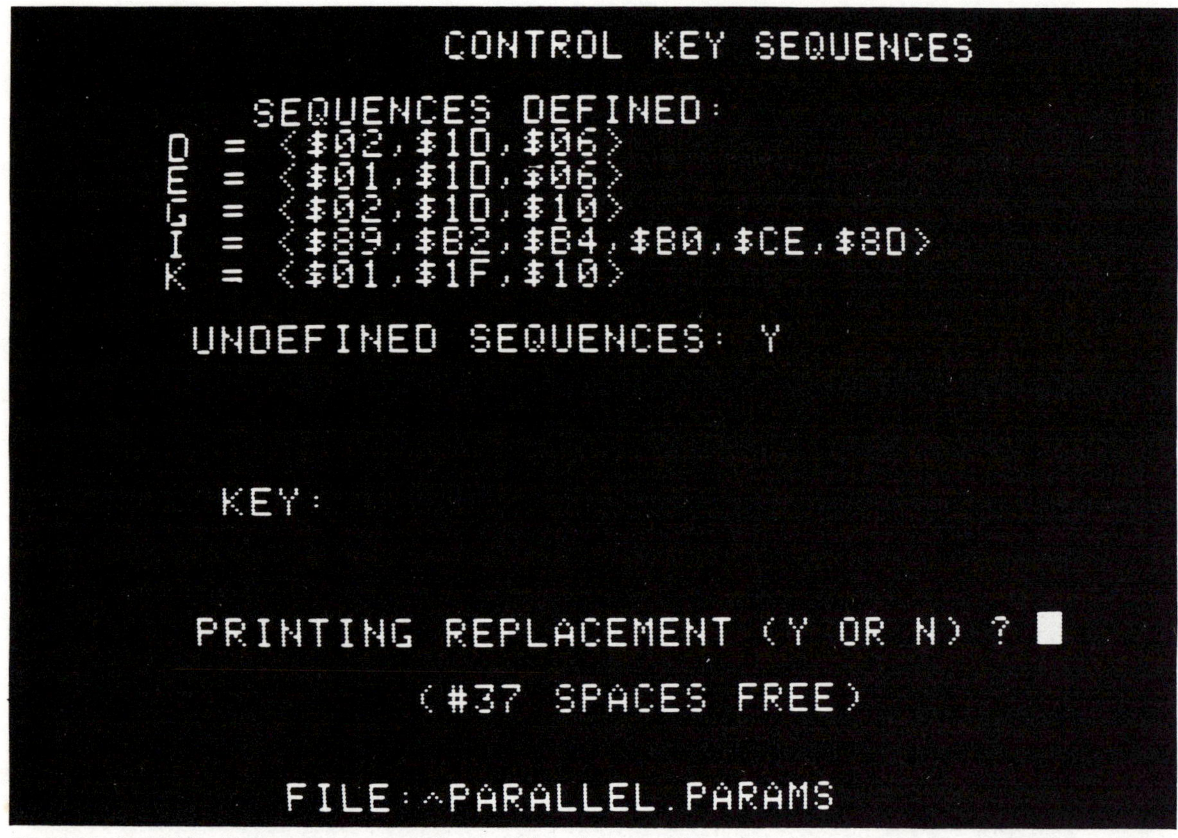

Fig. 6-23. Control key sequences can be defined to take advantage of special printer functions.

with two printers and found it to effectively control them both. My IDS 560 offers more features than may be selected by the number of control key sequences included, so I did change several of the sequences defined in the IDS ∧ PARAMS file. One of the beauties of this type of approach is that you are free to define, and redefine, features to be used.

Initiating Printing. Printing operations are initiated from the program's cursor mode by pressing X. The print module must be contained in memory and may be loaded by selecting the @PRINT file from the disk, if the math mode is still in memory. The module currently in memory is displayed in the status line shown by a system query (press Q). If everything is in order, pressing X will display the Number of Copies? prompt. Choosing a number between 1 and 255 will cause that many copies of the file in memory to be printed. To return to the cursor mode without printing anything, press 0 and RETURN. If you press RETURN, the disk catalog will be displayed and multiple file numbers (separated by commas) can be entered. The files selected will be printed in the order they were entered. Files can also be linked together for printing, as you will see in the description of Autolink in the special features section.

Justification. As used in the program, justification adds extra spaces between words to obtain flush right and flush left margins. Although you may select proportional spacing on your printer through the user-definable control key sequences, justification using proportional or infinite letter spacing is not supported.

Headers, Footers, and Page Numbers. The normal page numbering used in Super-Text 40/80 is defined in the default parameters file and is easily altered by a format line command inserted into the text. Numbers can be printed in any position on either the top or bottom page margin. Setting the page number character position to 0 will cause the page number to print on the right margin of odd-numbered pages and left margin of even-numbered pages.

Entering CTRL-N followed by a number turns the page numbering on and starts the numbering with the value specified. Chapter-relative numbers may be specified by pressing CTRL-N, followed by a chapter number, dash, and next page number. Page numbers will be incremented normally and printed following the chapter number and dash. CTRL-N 0 is used to turn the page numbering off.

Page headers or footers may be printed on any page, all pages, or on alternating pages. To set a header, press CTRL-T, enter a location symbol, and type the text of the header enclosed in quotation marks. Four location possibilities are defined by variations of the CTRL-T command: CTRL-T prints the header in the top margin of every page, CTRL-T+ puts the header in the bottom margin of all pages, CTRL-T2 prints the header in the top margin of even-numbered pages only, and CTRL-T2+ prints the header in the bottom margin of all even-numbered pages.

A combination of standard and even-numbered page headers are used to print alternating headers. Header text enclosed in double quotation marks is printed at the left margin of the page. To center this text, enclose it in single quotation marks. Horizontal positioning may also be altered by inserting spaces within the quotation marks. Vertical positioning normally locates the text in the first line of the margin but may be altered by preceding the text

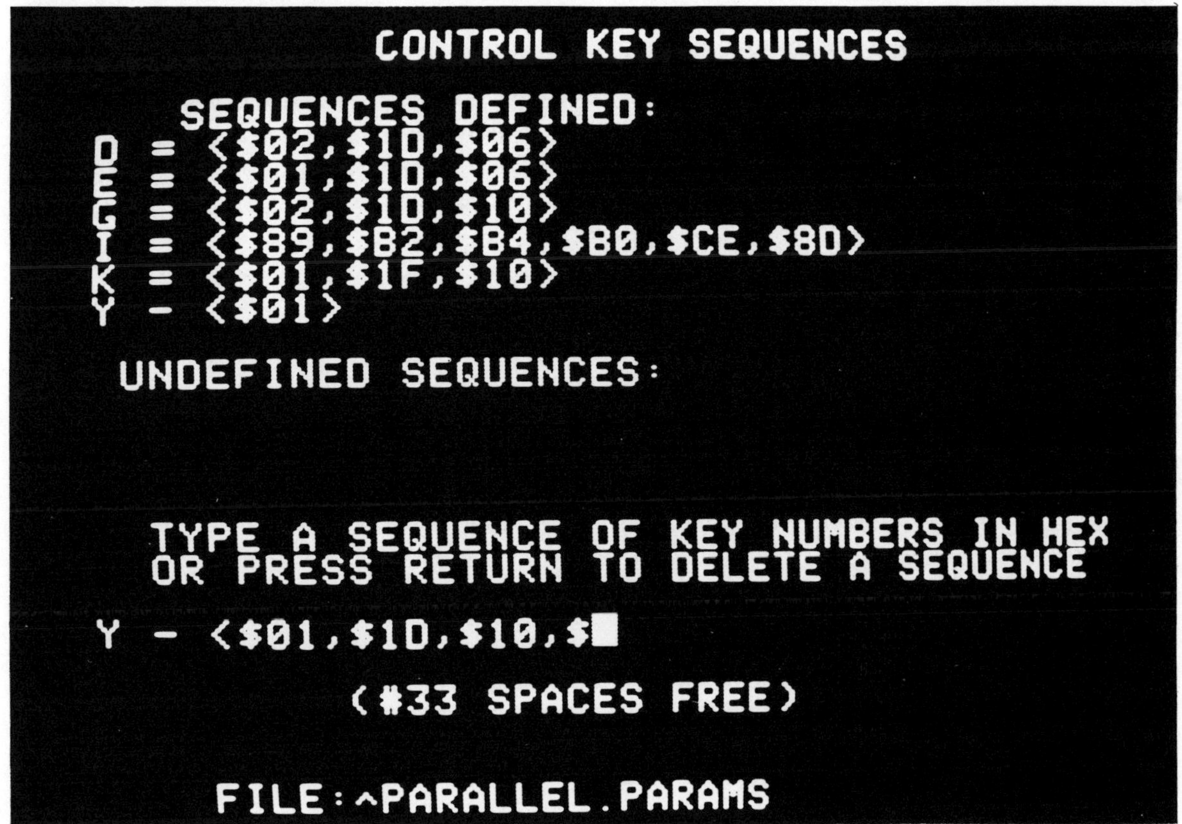

Fig. 6-24. Defining a control key sequence is simplified by the excellent prompts provided.

of the header with carriage return characters. It is also possible to combine headers with page numbers following the procedure outlined in the program manual.

Forms Control. Form parameters are specified in a format line, or you can use the system default parameters. Switching from form feed to single sheet feed is done through the system query status line display. Pressing F selects form feed; S designates single sheets. In the single sheet mode, the program will pause at the end of each printed page, beep twice, and prompt you to insert another sheet.

Printer Problems. No provisions are included for responding to problems signaled by the printer. When the program is being booted, the printer must be on and on-line. This is sensed by the program, and a prompt to TURN PRINTER ON is displayed if it is not configured properly. Some degree of response to printer problems is obtained manually by interrupting or terminating the print operation at any desired point.

Text Insertion during Printing. No provisions are included for adding text from the keyboard during printing operations.

Print Mode Control and Display. Text is not displayed on the screen during printing operations. The Number of Copies? prompt remains on an otherwise blank screen. The last file name accessed, when printing multiple files or Autolink printing, is displayed. While printing is in progress, you can press ESC to return immediately to the cursor mode. Press the space bar to interrupt printing after the current line. Once printing is interrupted, you may press ESC to terminate printing entirely, the space bar to print the next line and pause, or any other key to resume normal printing operation. When printing has been terminated, the screen will display the portion of the file being printed when termination was requested.

Screen Preview of Document. A preview mode, selected through the system query, is used to provide a video approximation of the printed document (Fig. 6-25). When using the standard display, a 40-column "window" can be set to view a selected portion of the printed text. Once preview has been selected in the system query mode, pressing X will start the preview operation. The left margin of the video display is set by pressing L. Press RETURN continues the preview at the new left margin.

Termination or interruption of document preview uses the same commands as the print mode. In addition, you can press N to back up the display one printed page. You can preview several pages more than once by repeatedly pressing N. If your Apple is equipped with the Videx 80-column display board, the window for previewing text is expanded proportionately. All the commands for preview function in exactly the same way.

Multiple Files or Copies. Printing a single copy of multiple files is done by listing the file numbers in response to the prompt issued after you press RETURN when setting up the print mode. Files may also be linked together using the Autolink feature.

Multiple copies are even easier. Just type the number of copies desired in response to the Number of Copies? prompt displayed when print is first requested.

SPECIAL FEATURES

System Query. From the cursor mode, a system query is initiated by pressing Q. A status line is used to monitor and control several program functions. The first status line displays the on-off state of Autolink and the "the" key, number of occurrences replaced in the last replace operation, and which module (math or print) and print option has been selected (Fig. 6-26). When the status line is being displayed, the following commands are available: CTRL-I initializes a blank disk to accept Super-Text 40/80 data. Disk are also initialized by selecting option 2 from the title page menu. A toggles the Autolink feature on and off. T toggles the "the" key on and off, and CTRL-T allows you to define the "the" key. P selects the print preview mode, providing the print module is presently in memory. F designates form feed for printing operations, and S switches to single sheet feed for print operations. Pressing any other key will display the file status line.

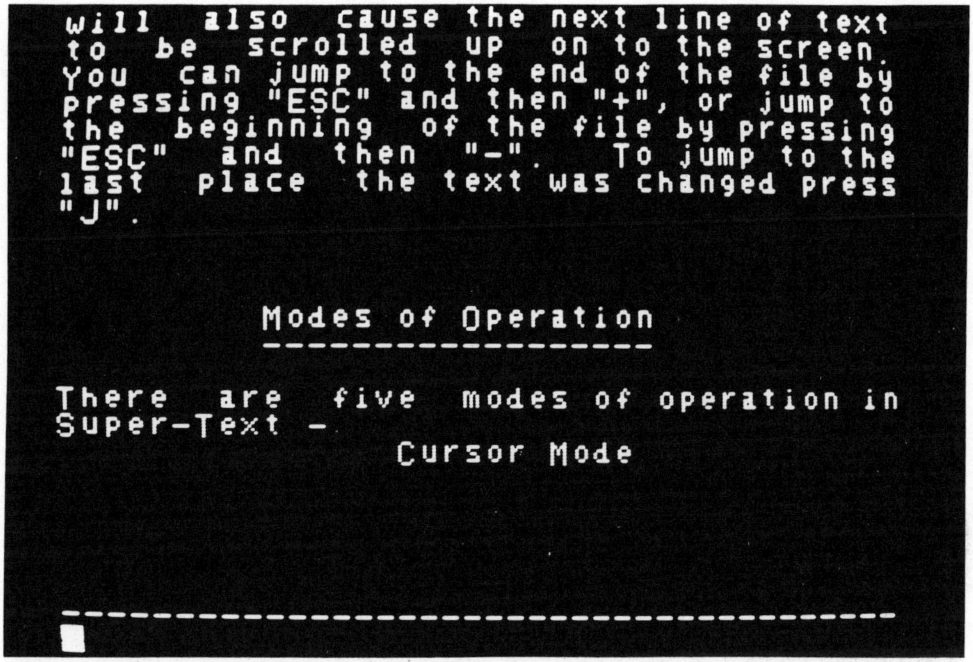

Fig. 6-25. The preview mode provides a video approximation of the final appearance of the printed document.

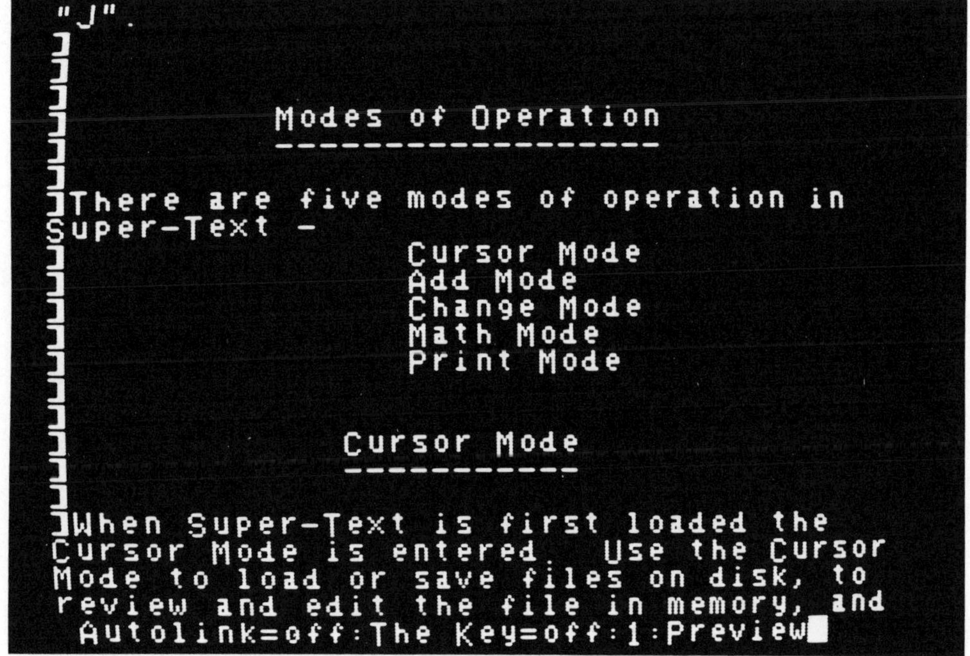

Fig. 6-26. The status line is displayed when a system query is requested by pressing Q in the cursor mode.

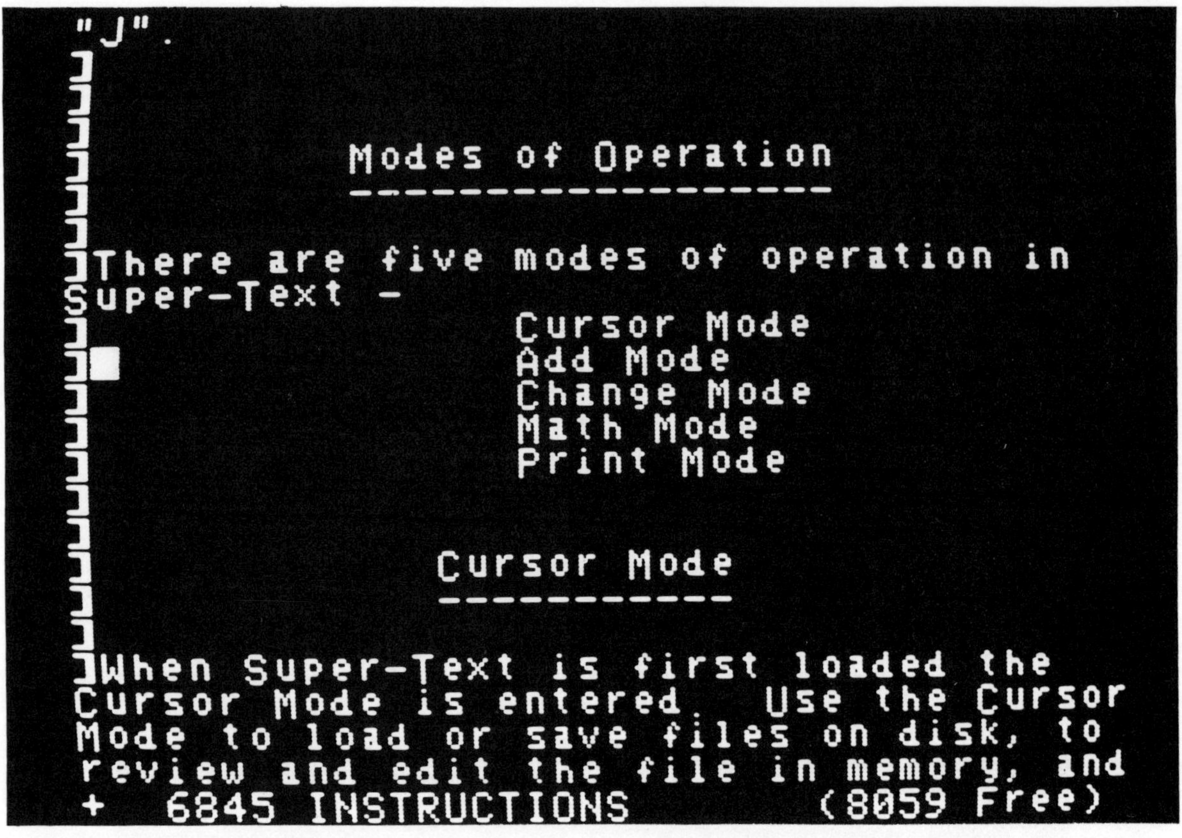

Fig. 6-27. File status is displayed before exiting the system query mode.

On exiting the system query, a file status line will be displayed (Fig. 6-27). This line contains the number of characters in the file presently in memory, the file name, and number of characters that may be added to the file. Pressing C clears the file status line from the screen.

"The" Key. Previous versions of Super-Text have contained a feature that printed "the" whenever the colon (:) was pressed. Super-Text 40/80 has expanded this feature and made it considerably more versatile. The capability to print "the" on pressing the colon is still present, but any word or phrase of up to 30 characters may be substituted. A character set may be defined by pressing CTRL-T from the system query, entering the desired characters in response to the prompt, and pressing RETURN twice to return to the cursor mode.

After a character set has been entered (or "the" used as a default), using the key is quite simple. Pressing T from the system query status line toggles the key on and off. In the add mode, pressing the colon (:) inserts the defined character set, in all lowercase letters, at the cursor. CTRL-: capitalizes the first character and inserts the character set. CTRL-C: shifts to uppercase and inserts the characters, CTRL-S: shifts back to lowercase and inserts the characters. Since the colon is being temporarily used for another purpose, pressing CTRL-K inserts the colon character at the cursor.

Autolink™. Super-Text 40/80 will process linked files for find, replace, and print operations with the Autolink feature. Files may be connected to each other by creating "links" at the very beginning or end of each one. Links are created in the add

110

mode by enclosing a file name between two colons. For instance, :NEXTFILE:. Links may be preceded by CTRL-Q (turn printer off) and followed by CTRL-O (turn printer on), but no other characters are allowed between the link and the end of a file. Links are saved on disk along with the text in a file.

To use the Autolink feature, press A from the system query status line to switch it on and off. Files may be linked in a forward, reverse, or circular fashion. Provisions for manual use of linked files are also included. Detailed explanations of all the Autolink features and how to use them are included in the program manual.

Videx™ 80-Column Board. Super-Text 40/80 includes the necessary routines to use the Videx board for full 80-column display. Using the 80-column board is simply a matter of loading the VIDEX file from the program disk into memory. The program must be rebooted to switch back to 40-column display mode. No changes in operating procedure need to be made when switching from the 40- to 80-column display mode. Control characters are displayed differently, as illustrated in the program manual.

Form Letter and Address Book Interface. Super-Text 40/80 is designed to work with both the Form Letter module and Muse's Address Book mailing list program. The three programs constitute a very capable personalized correspondence system. Offered as options, Form Letter sells for $100, and Address Book for $50.

HUMAN ENGINEERING

Logical, Easy to Use Commands. Although most commands are logical in their structure, Super-Text 40/80 requires some user familiarity to take advantage of all the features included. Careful reading of the manual and some experimentation will be a definite help in learning the control structure.

Verification of Potentially Dangerous Commands. With the exception of deleting a video page or the entire contents of memory, no verification is required before commands are executed.

Error Recovery and Emergency Procedures. The documentation devotes an entire chap-

ter to troubleshooting procedures. Some of the more common error recovery procedures are outlined in the particular chapter describing the mode from which they are commonly encountered. Error trapping in the program is quite effective and meaningful messages are displayed. In all instances, problems and procedures are clearly explained.

On-line Help. No tutorial or help files are included on the program disk. Several text files are included, however, to illustrate points discussed in the documentation.

DOCUMENTATION

User's Manual. I have seen documentation for four versions of Super-Text and can honestly say the Super-Text 40/80 manual (Fig. 6-28) is the best

Fig. 6-28. The Super-Text 40 /80 user's manual.

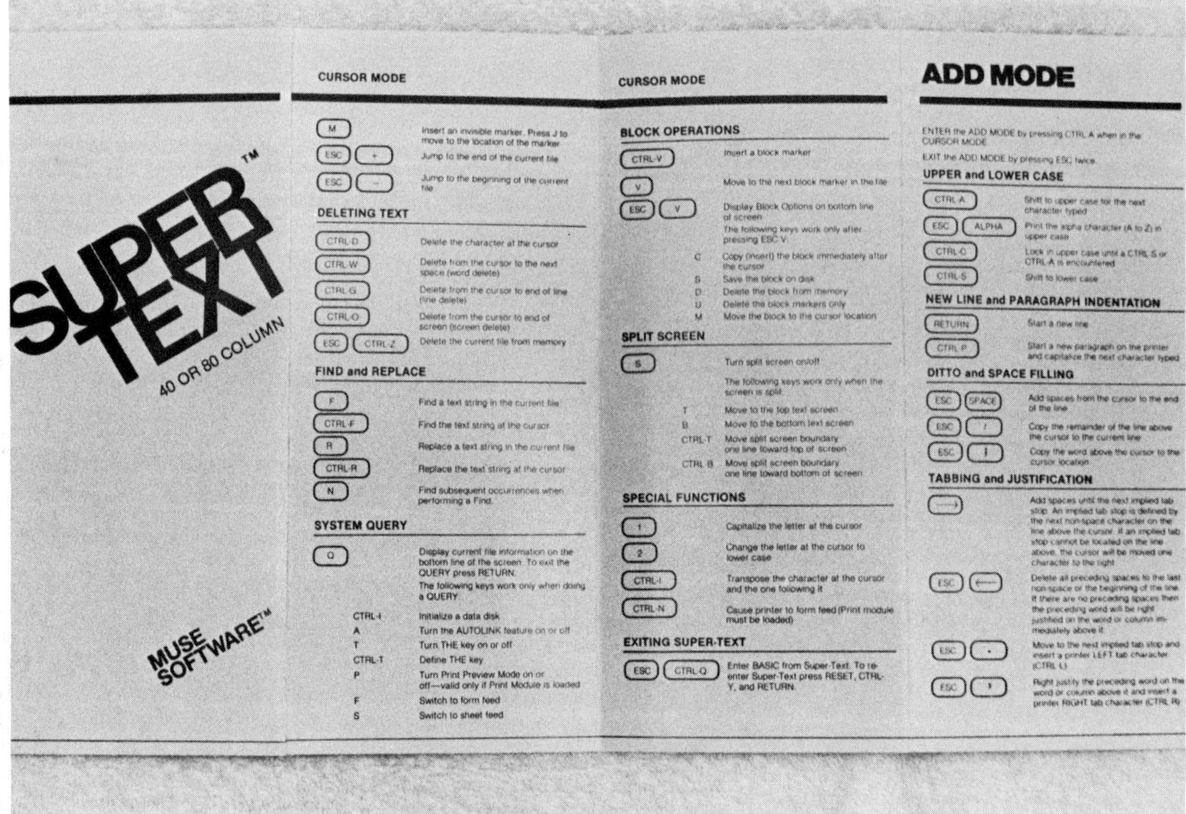

Fig. 6-29. A comprehensive reference card is included in the program package.

of the lot. Detailed explanations and use examples are included in the looseleaf binder. Chapters, identified by tab pages, discuss each of the modes of operation, special features, interfacing, and troubleshooting. A summary at the end of each chapter eliminates the need to dig through detailed explanations for answers to simple questions.

Reference Material. A comprehensive reference card is included with the program package. The card contains all the information necessary for day-to-day program operations (Fig. 6-29).

SUPPORT

Two copies of the program disk are included in the Super-Text 40/80 package. Muse will replace damaged or worn-out disks for $10 with no time limit.

I have had the opportunity on several occasions to talk with Muse regarding some minor problems with other programs and found them to be extremely helpful. If the answer to a question is not immediately available, every effort will be made to provide the information as soon as possible. There is certainly no reason to suspect that Super-Text 40/80 will be supported any less effectively.

IMPRESSIONS

Since I have used every version of Super-Text, my impression of Super-Text 40/80 may be somewhat different from those of someone using the system for the first time, but this is my favorite word-processing program for all-around use.

The documentation provides clear explanations of the procedures necessary to use the program effectively. The areas of printer interfacing, page numbering, and block operations are noticeably clearer than in previous versions. The actual processes for using these functions have also been improved considerably.

The feature I particularly like in Super-Text 40/80 are numerous. Convenient multiple disk access, logical commands, formatting capabilities from within text files, and user friendliness are some that immediately come to mind. Perhaps even more than any one feature is the "feel" of the program. Like an old shoe, I feel more comfortable using Super-Text 40/80 than I do with any other word-processing program in my library.

This is not a program for the occasional user. Both the program and documentation assume some word-processing sophistication. Infrequent users may find themselves spending an inordinate amount of time getting reacquainted with the program every time they want to use it.

The Executive Secretary

Publisher: Sof/Sys, Inc., 4306 Upton Avenue South, Minneapolis, MN 55410
Hardware Required: Apple II or Apple II Plus, 48K, Disk II, printer with interface card, lowercase adapter. Program supports several 80-column display boards: Hayes Micromodem, Thunderclock, and CCS clockcard.
Price: $250.00

The Executive Secretary (Fig. 7-1) is one of the most versatile word-processing programs available for the Apple II. In addition to the standard group of word-processing features. The Executive Secretary offers an unusually wide range of special features.

TEXT INPUT FEATURES

Upper and Lowercase Display. In the standard 40-column display mode, The Executive Secretary uses any of the add-on lowercase display devices to generate both upper-and lowercase letters on the screen. Shifting case is done with the shift keys, so your Apple must be modified to use this feature if it has not already been done. A "solderless" shift key connector and instructions for installation are included in the program package. CTRL-L is used as a shift lock/unlock command.

Video Display. Text displayed on the video screen includes both characters and commands typed there during the process of text input (embedded commands). During the process of text input, an inverse video line at the top of the screen reminds you of commands available. Directly below the command line, a scale identifies the possible print positions on the video screen (Fig. 7-2).

Word Formatting. A standard system of "word wrapping is used by the Executive Secretary, so that words too long to fit on one line are automatically shifted in their entirety to the next. No provisions are included for hyphenation or predefined paragraph indentation, although a tab may be set for the latter purpose.

Tabbing. Horizontal tabs are set using the tab set command > tb. In addition to the print position for each tab, L or R may be used to designate

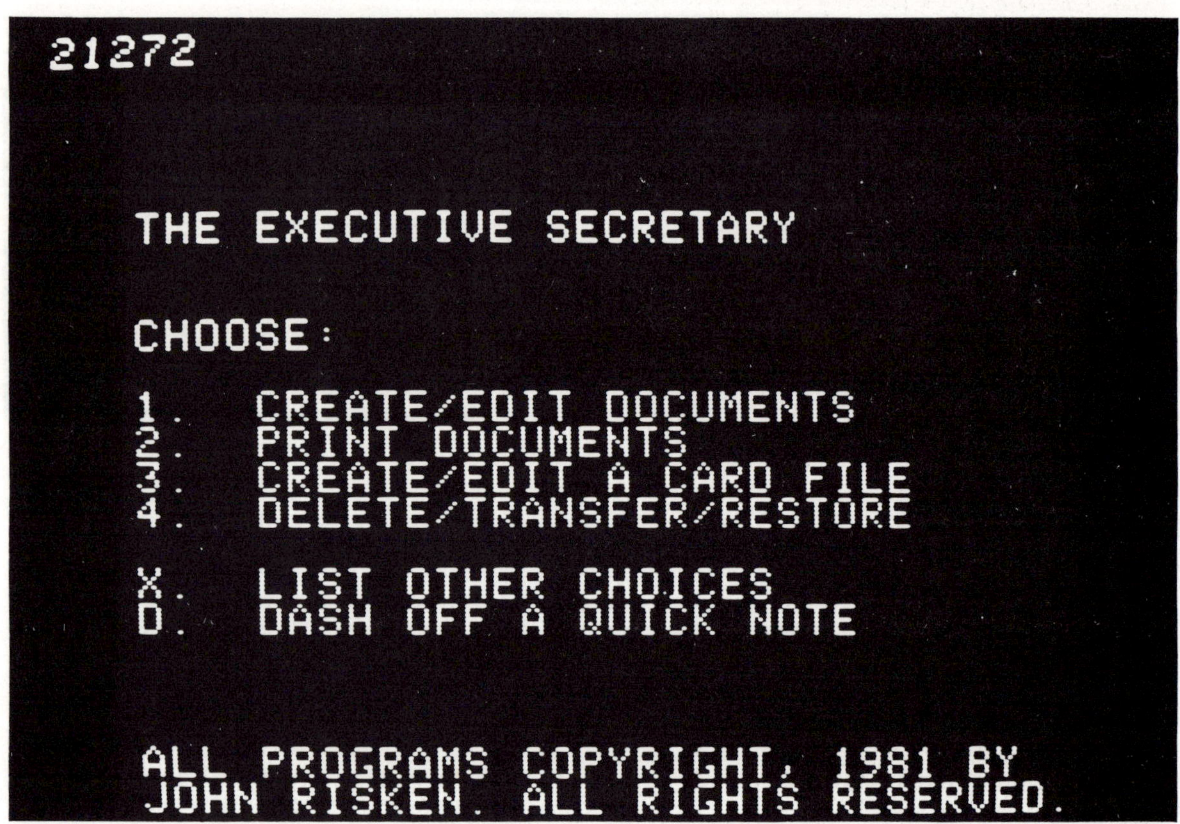

Fig. 7-1. The Executive Secretary title page menu.

whether text is to be left or right justified to the tab position (Fig. 7-3). Any number of tabs may be set (or reset) from within the text. Once tabs are set, pressing CTRL-T moves the print position to each tab stop. Trailing spaces at the end of a tab field and before the next CTRL-T symbol are ignored. When using the 40-column display, pressing CTRL-C allows you to continue lines of material to be tabbed.

Under normal circumstances, the spaces between tabbed fields are filled with blanks. The Executive Secretary allows you to specify another string of characters to be used instead of blanks. The fill-in command (> fi) is used for this purpose. For instance, to fill the spaces with periods, the command would be > fi ....

Also included is a system of commands used primarily to fill in forms. These allow you to specify both horizontal and vertical character moves. See the special features section for details.

Justification. Word-spacing justification to create flush left and right margins is selected with the > jn command and turned off by > jo. These commands may be inserted anywhere in the text. Lines to be centered on the printed page are preceded by >cn. After all the lines to be centered are typed, the centering off command (>co) is used to terminate centering operations.

Line Spacing. Although single or double spacing may be specified at the time of printing, a line spacing command may be embedded in the text for special purposes. The format of this command is >sp x, where x represents the number of lines to be left blank after each printed line.

Status Display during Text Input. There is a two-line display at the top of the video screen during text input operations. The first line appears in inverse video and displays the mode by the word TYPE, along with some commands available. The second line displays a scale for whichever display width you are using (40 or 80 column). Cursor position is indicated by a steady underline character. No further information is shown on the screen.

Page Specification Change. Virtually all of the normal page specifications can be readily adjusted during the process of text input through the use of embedded commands.

Text Files from Other Programs. The Executive Secretary will accept data from several other programs. See the special features section for more details.

Text from External Devices. Provisions are included for electronic mail exchange between two Apples equipped with the Hayes Micromodem and The Executive Secretary. See special features.

Formatting for Text Output. During text input operations, numerous commands may be embedded in the text. Each command is preceded by a wedge (>) followed by a two-letter command, a space, and the rest of the command. Each command must be located on a separate line. In addition to page-formatting specifications, embedded commands are used to set page breaks, headers, numbering, indentation, and so on.

Maximum Text Length per File. The user's manual for The Executive Secretary notes that the maximum length per file is about 3000 words. In keeping with the rest of the program's orientation, it further notes that an empty disk is capable of holding about 25,000 words.

Typing Speed. Occasionally the program will pause during the process of text input to do some housekeeping chores. During this period, text input is not accepted. The pauses are particularly noticeable when the amount of text contained is ap-

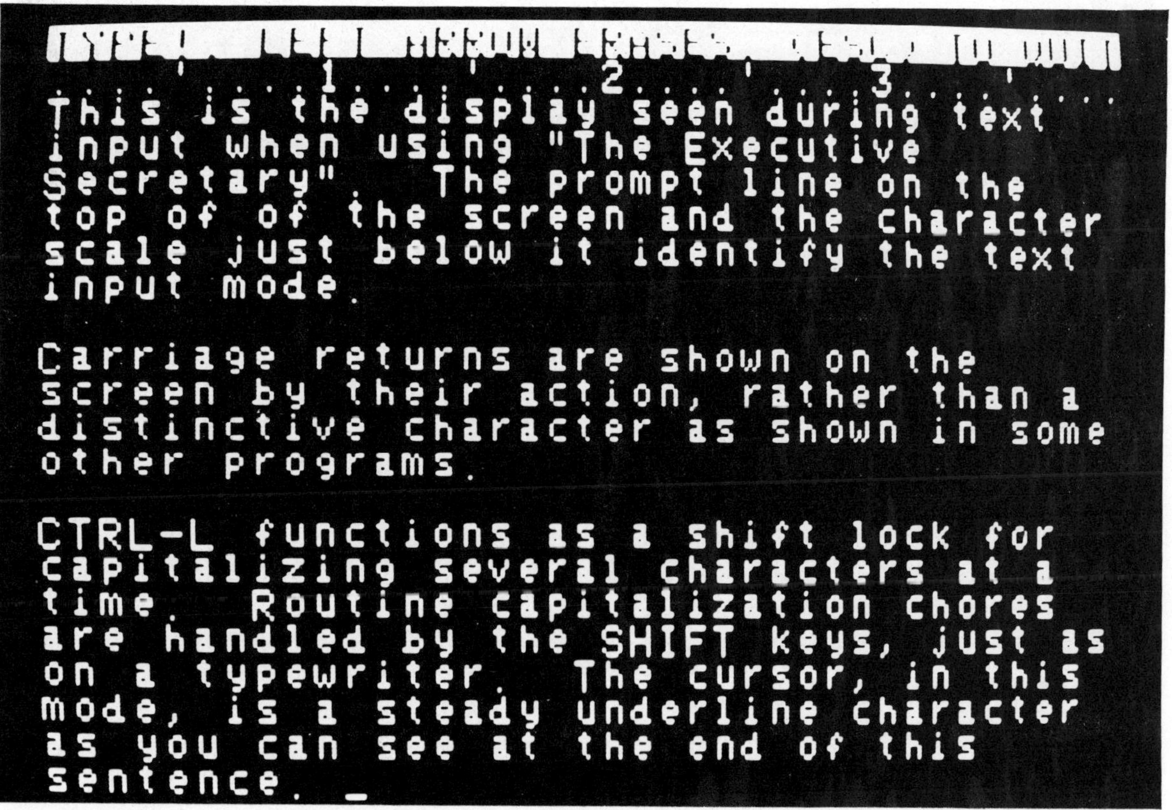

Fig. 7-2. The word "TYPE!" in the upper left corner of the display indicates that text input is in progress.

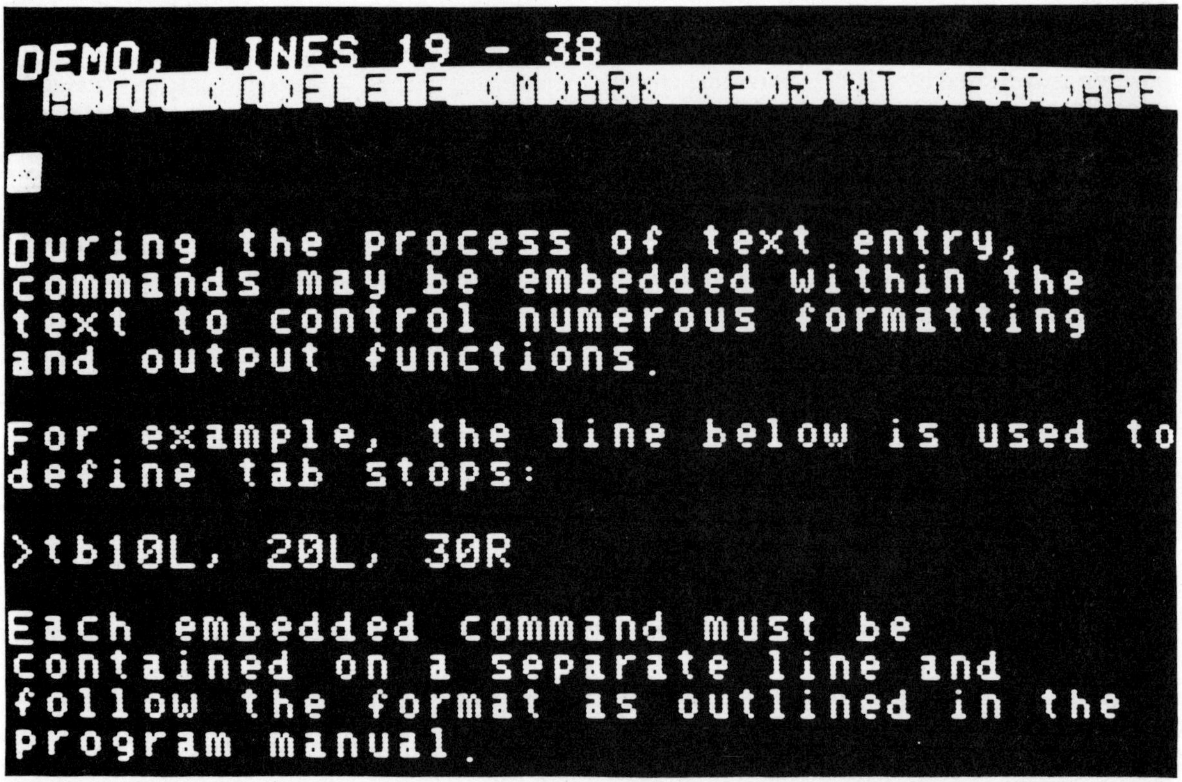

Fig. 7-3. Horizontal tabs are defined by character position in the printed line. Text may be either right or left justified to each tab stop.

proaching the limit that can be held in memory at one time.

EDITING FEATURES

Edit Marker Positioning. A distinctive cursor, called an edit marker in the manual, is used for editing operations. This marker is in the form of an inverse video up arrow ($\wedge$). In edit mode, this marker is moved by using the right and left arrow keys, RETURN, and the slash (/) key.

In operation, the RETURN key moves the edit marker up one line on the screen, and the slash key moves it down. Pressing the right arrow moves the marker one word to the right, and the left arrow moves it one character to the left. Holding the SHIFT key down and pressing the left arrow moves the marker back to the beginning of the line, pressing the right arrow moves the marker one space to the right, and RETURN and the slash move the marker up and down repeatedly.

Scrolling. The Executive Secretary has the capability of scroll through the text in either a forward or backward direction. Scrolling forward one screen page is done by pressing the semicolon (;); scrolling forward to the end of the document is done by pressing plus (+). To scroll backward one page, press minus (−), backward to the beginning of the text, press the equals sign (=).

Partial screen moves are provided by the B and F commands. Pressing b scrolls backward one line, B scrolls backward one-half a screen page. Similarly, f scrolls forward one line and F forward one-half a screen page.

Changing a Few Characters. The simplest way to change a few characters in the edit mode is to position the edit marker on the character following the last one to be changed and press A (for add). At this point, you may use the left arrow or shifted left arrow to delete the desired characters. Their positions may then be filled with the correct characters. Pressing ESC returns you to the edit mode.

Inserting Text. Adding text to an existing document is done by positioning the edit marker one character past the point where you wish to add the text. Pressing A (for add) will split the line at that point, with the text following the edit marker displayed at the bottom of the screen preceded by a slash (/). Any amount of new text may be added using the same commands described earlier in the text input section. Pressing ESC to return to the edit mode causes the text following the inserted material to be redisplayed in its proper position .

Deleting Text. There are several methods of deleting selected portions of text in a file. The method described earlier for changing a few characters will delete material if no new characters are typed. In edit mode, pressing d will delete the character following the marker and D will delete all characters up to and including the next space. CTRL-d will delete an entire line.

Block Operations. Blocks of text may be marked by positioning the edit marker one space to the left of the first character desired and pressing M. The process is repeated for the end of the block, except the marker is positioned one space to the right of the last character desired. Special block markers appear at the positions selected, and the first and last few characters are displayed at the top

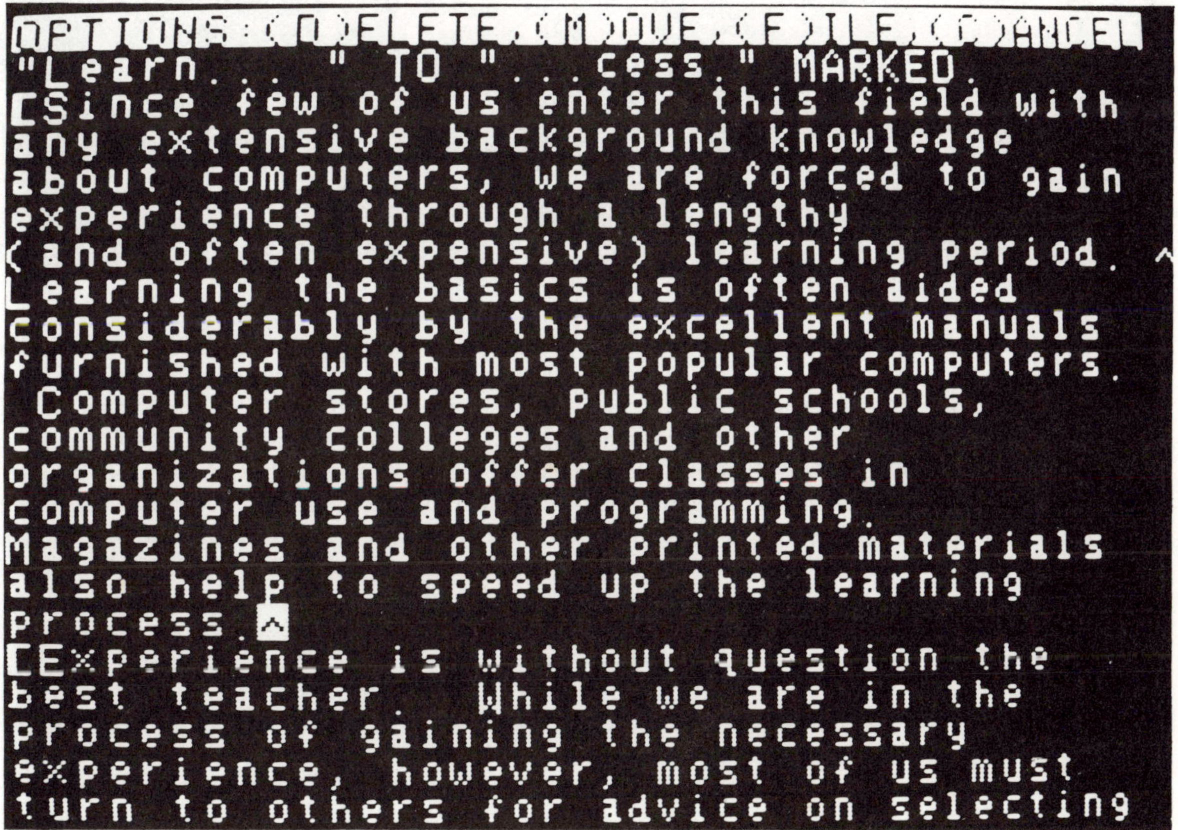

Fig. 7-4. Block operation commands are shown in inverse video at the top of the screen. The next line shows the range of characters marked as a block of text.

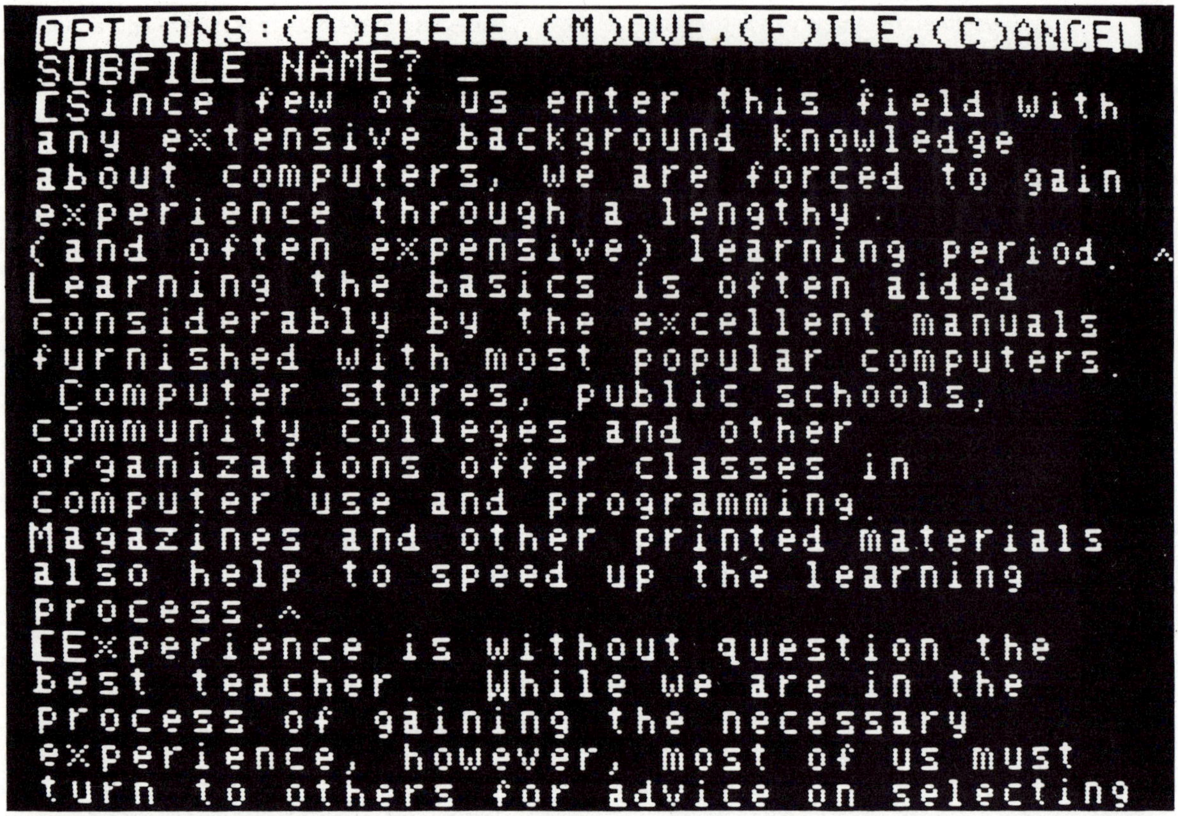

Fig. 7-5. Blocks of text may be saved in subfiles on a data disk.

of the screen. Blocks include the text between, but not including, the markers.

Once a block of text has been identified, it may be deleted, moved, or filed (Fig. 7-4). The deletion of a marked block is initiated by pressing D, after which the program asks if you want to delete the range you have marked. Answering Y deletes the block; any other response terminates the delete request.

Both move and copy provisions are included for text blocks. First, the edit marker is placed at the desired position in the text. Pressing M will move the block to the position selected, and you will be given the option of deleting the original marked range. Answering Y to the DELETE MARKED RANGE? prompt creates, in effect, a block move. An N response to the prompt merely copies the block at the edit marker and leaves the original marked block intact.

Blocks of text may be saved in subfiles on a data disk. If you press F, you will be asked for a subfile name (Fig. 7-5). Entering a name (in all capital letters), and pressing RETURN will save the subfile on your data disk and indicate its presence in the text (Fig. 7-6). Several methods are provided for retrieving the information contained in a subfile. See the text storage and retrieval section for more details.

Search and Replace. Initiating a search for a particular word in the text is quite simple (Fig. 7-7). Press S in the edit mode, and the program will respond with "SEARCH FOR WHAT?" Type in the desired word, and press RETURN. The line containing the word will be brought to the top of the page and the edit marker positioned to the right of the word (Fig. 7-8). Press S again to see the word being searched for or RETURN to locate other occurrences of the same word.

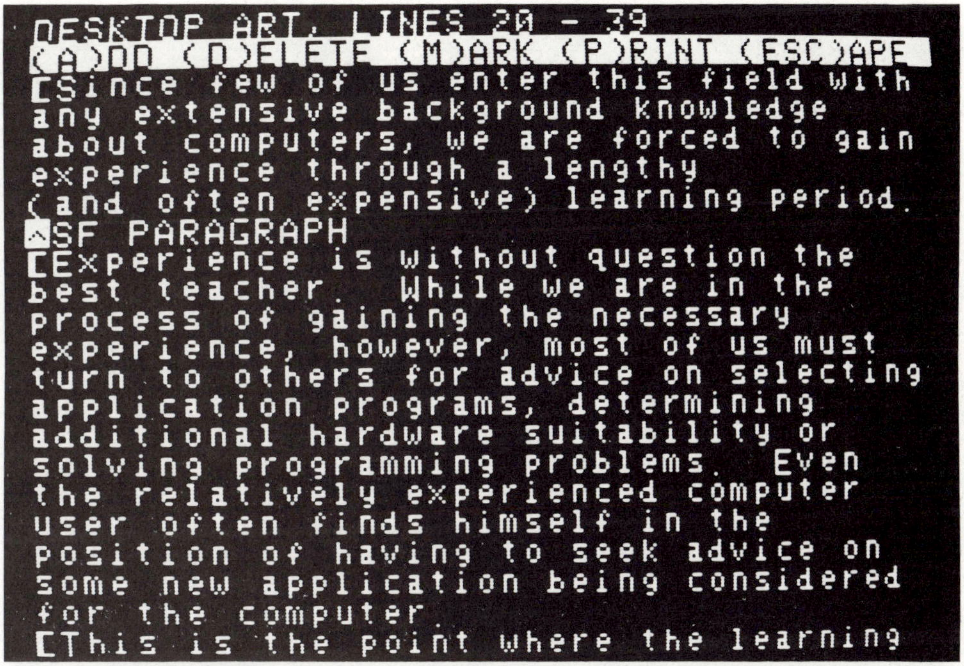

DESKTOP ART, LINES 20 - 39
(A)DD (D)ELETE (M)ARK (P)RINT (ESC)APE
[Since few of us enter this field with
any extensive background knowledge
about computers, we are forced to gain
experience through a lengthy
(and often expensive) learning period.
▲SF PARAGRAPH
[Experience is without question the
best teacher.   While we are in the
process of gaining the necessary
experience, however, most of us must
turn to others for advice on selecting
application programs, determining
additional hardware suitability or
solving programming problems.   Even
the relatively experienced computer
user often finds himself in the
position of having to seek advice on
some new application being considered
for the computer.
[This is the point where the learning

Fig. 7-6. The SF PARAGRAPH line indicates that a block of text from that location has been saved in a disk subfile named PARAGRAPH.

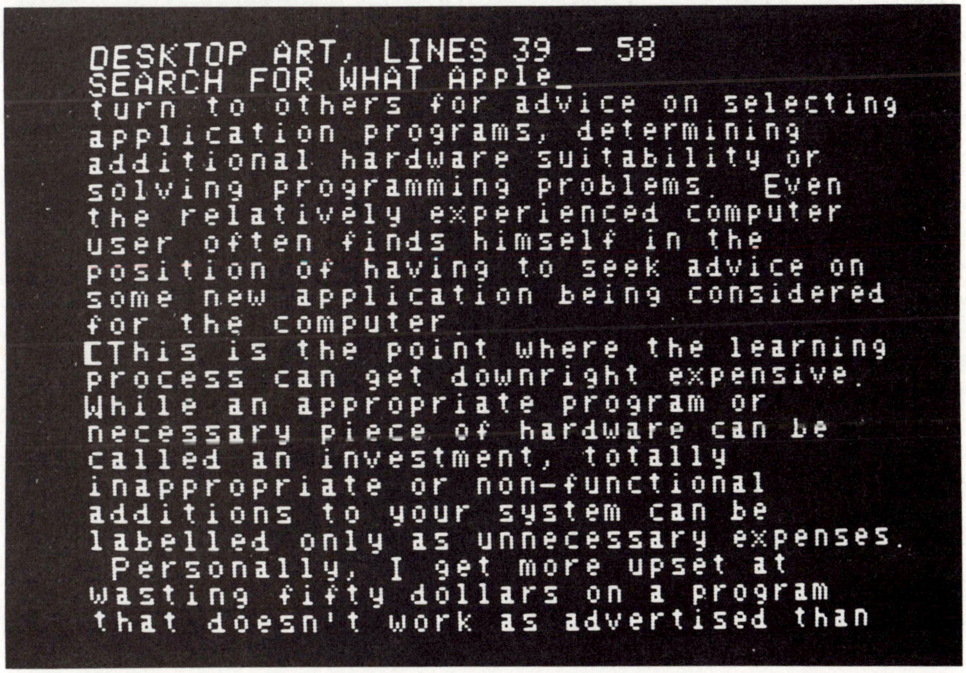

DESKTOP ART, LINES 39 - 58
SEARCH FOR WHAT Apple_
turn to others for advice on selecting
application programs, determining
additional hardware suitability or
solving programming problems.   Even
the relatively experienced computer
user often finds himself in the
position of having to seek advice on
some new application being considered
for the computer.
[This is the point where the learning
process can get downright expensive.
While an appropriate program or
necessary piece of hardware can be
called an investment, totally
inappropriate or non-functional
additions to your system can be
labelled only as unnecessary expenses.
   Personally, I get more upset at
wasting fifty dollars on a program
that doesn't work as advertised than

Fig. 7-7. Search operations are initiated by pressing S in the edit mode.

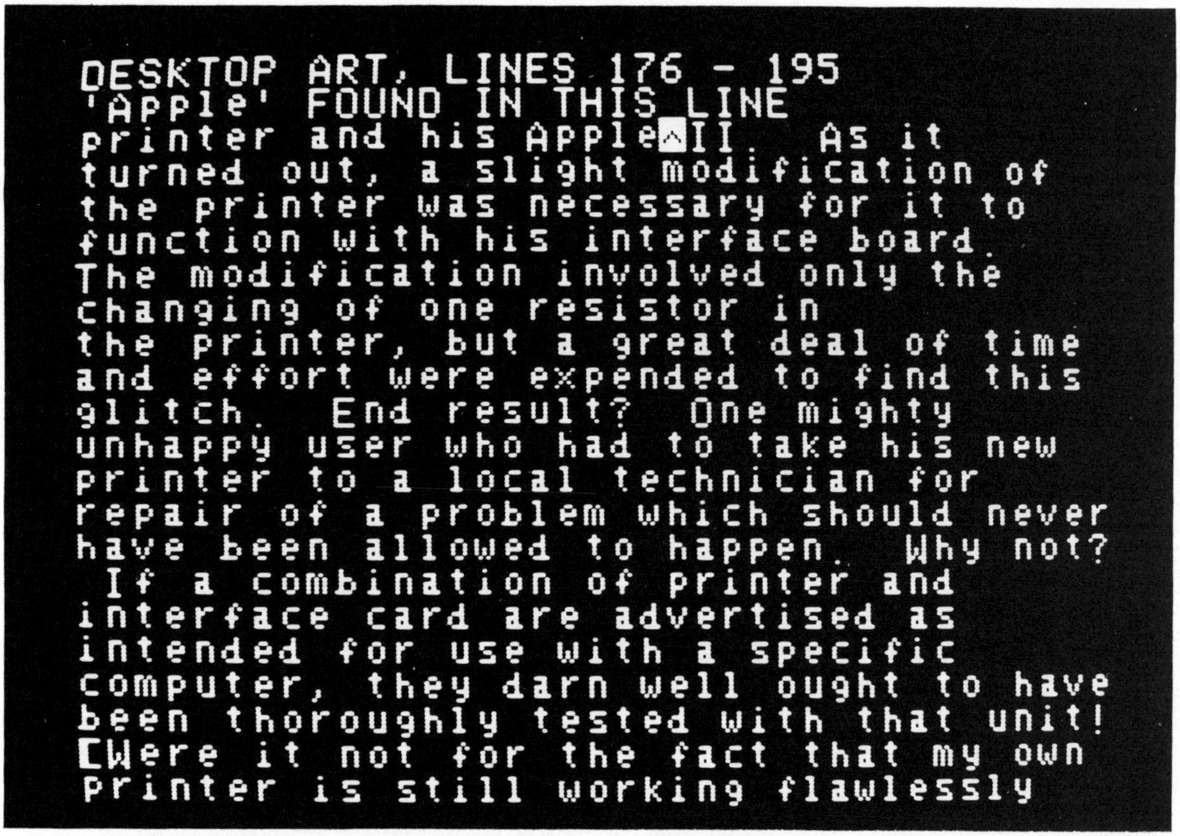

Fig. 7-8. The line containing the word or phrase that is being searched for is displayed at the top of the screen. The edit marker is automatically placed to the right of the word.

To make a single replacement, type r after search has located the word and placed it at the top of the screen. After r, type in the word to be substituted on the prompt line (Fig. 7-9). Multiple replacements are ordered by pressing R instead of r. When using the multiple replacement command, you will be asked to type R (replace the word), S (skip to the next occurrence), or Q (quit the search) at each occurrence of the specified word.

TEXT STORAGE AND RETRIEVAL

DOS Used. A nonstandard DOS, is used, preventing you from making back-up copies of the program disk or modifying the program. One copy of the disk is included with the program package, and the second is sent when the owner registration card is sent to Sof/Sys.

Data disks for use with The Executive Secretary must be initialized by the program, using option 5 from the menu shown in Fig. 7-10.

Text File Backup. Text file backup is carried out by selecting the transfer function from the file maintenance menu. Using this option, each file and its associated subfiles can be transferred to another data disk. Prompts are provided to guide you through the process. Essentially the same process is followed to rename and delete text files (Fig. 7-11).

Entire data disks may be copied using the COPY A program provided with your copy of Apple DOS.

Multiple Disk Drive Access. The initial configuration menu asks you to specify the number of disk drives you are using. This may be easily

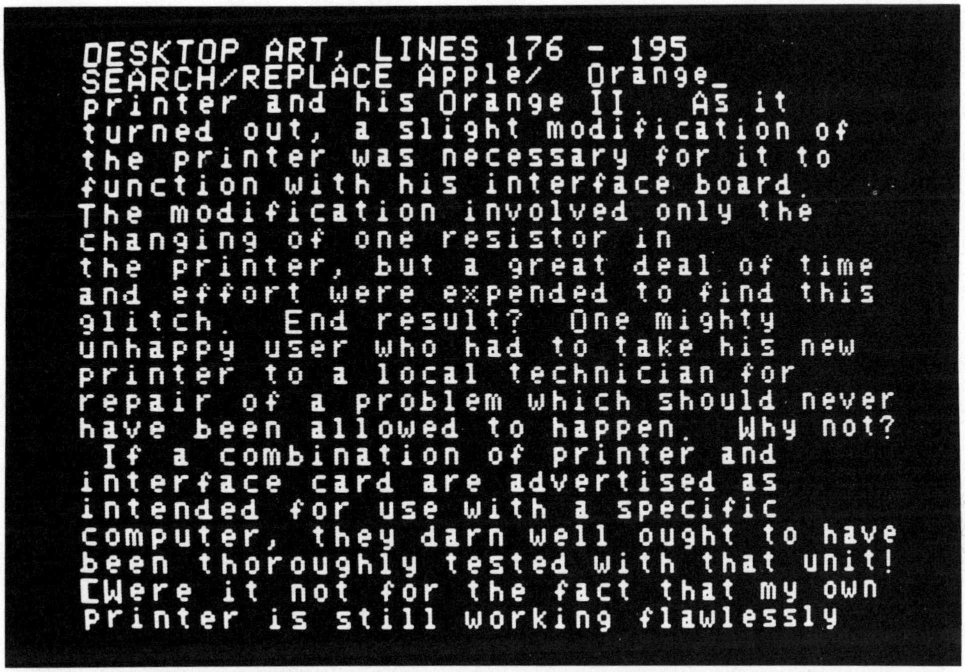

Fig. 7-9. Replace is specified after a specific word or phrase has been located by search.

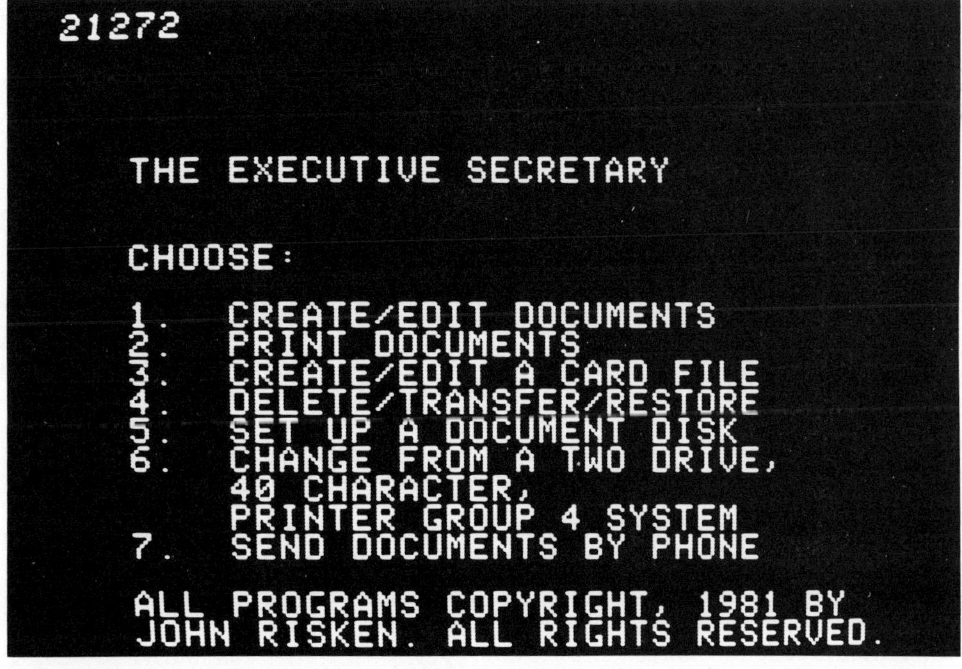

Fig. 7-10. The list other choices menu.

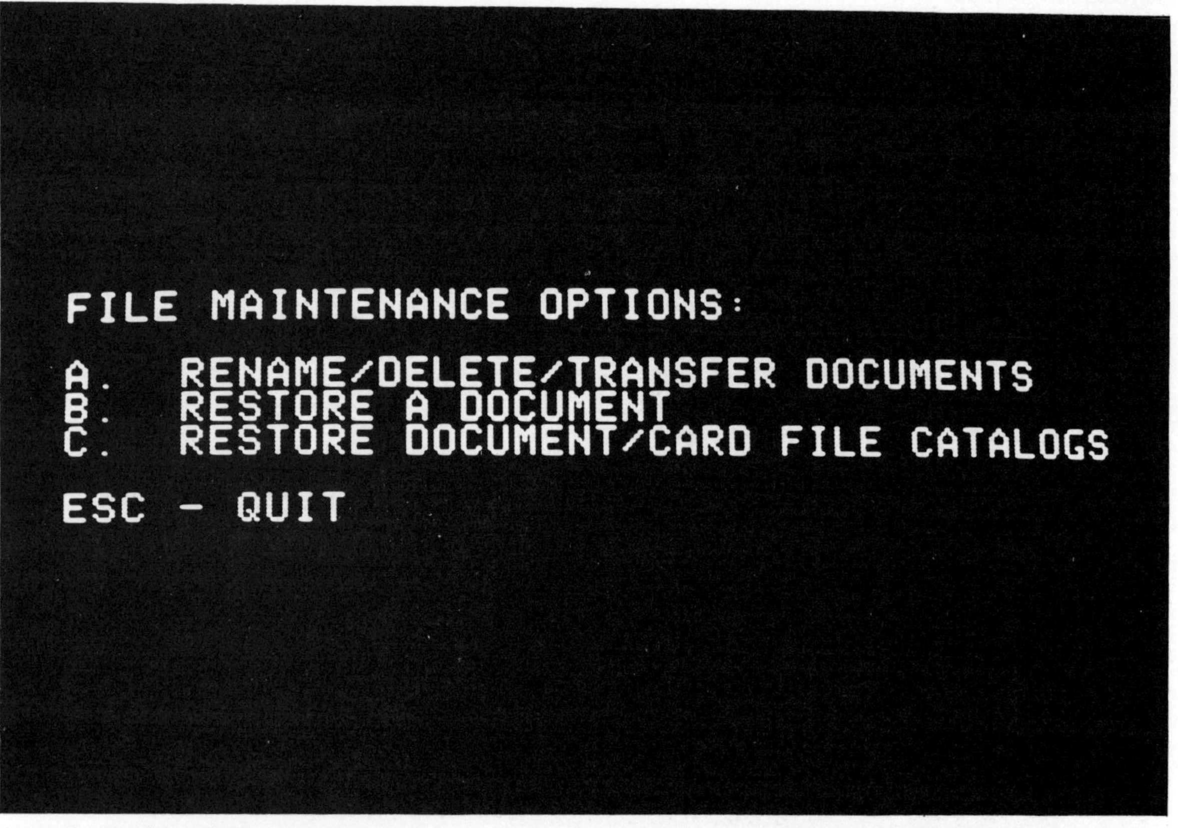

Fig. 7-11. The file maintenance options menu.

changed at any time. Except for transfer and a few other functions, the usual procedure is to leave the program disk in drive 1 and the data disk in drive 2.

Text File Creation and Documentation. Text may be stored on disks in either files or subfiles. For a more complete description of subfiles, see the block operations section under text input. Straight text file names are specified in response to the CREATE WHAT DOCUMENT: prompt following your selection from the add mode menu. Text file names must begin with a letter but may contain numbers or spaces. No length limitation is specified in the manual.

At the conclusion of text input operations, you are asked whether you want to save the file under the name specified, save it under another name, or not save it at all. If you choose either of the save options, the file will automatically be stored on your data disk (Fig. 7-12). If the CCS clock card or Thunderclock is installed in your system, documents will automatically be time stamped when they are saved. The size of each document is not indicated in the disk catalog, although the total amount of space remaining on the disk is (Fig. 7-13).

Files Compatible with Other Programs. The text files created by The Executive Secretary are, according to the manual, standard Apple text files. User-generated text files in the same format should be capable of being manipulated by The Executive Secretary, although I did not check this out myself. Several suggestions are offered in the manual for using files created by The Executive Secretary in your own programs. Provisions are included in the program for accepting and manipulating text files created by several other programs. For instance, Visicalc files may be printed by The Executive Secretary. See the special features section for further details.

124

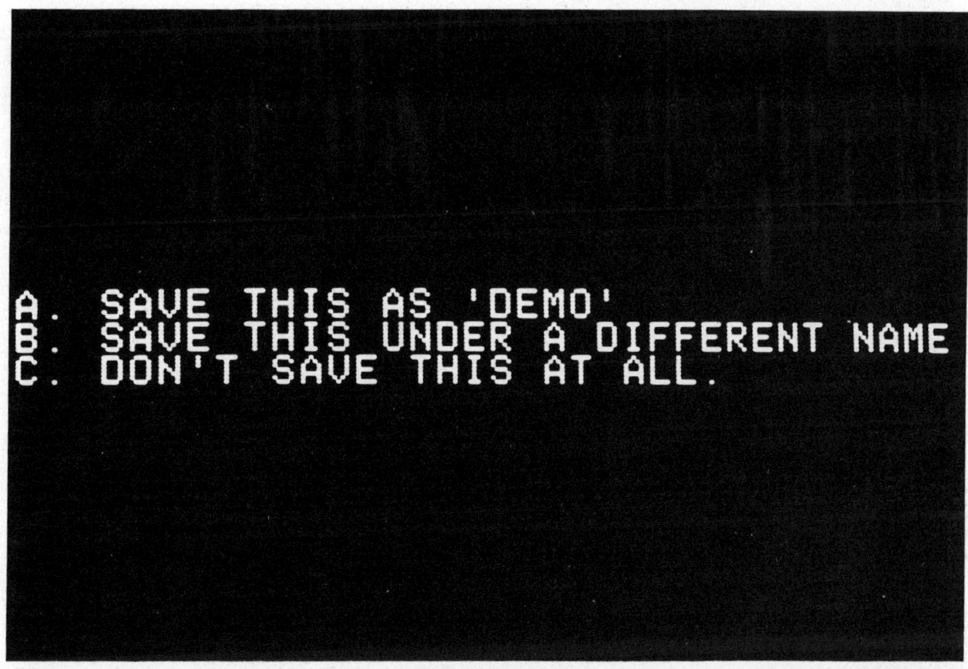

Fig. 7-12. Options presented when exiting text input operations.

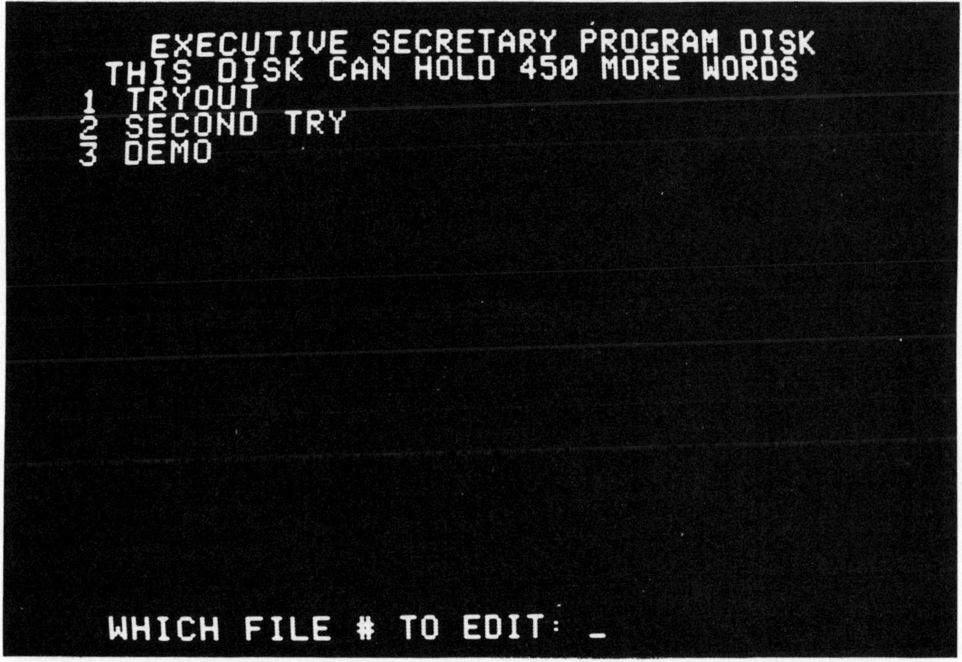

Fig. 7-13. The Executive Secretary data disk catalog indicates file name and number, along with the amount of unused space on the disk. Files for editing are selected by number.

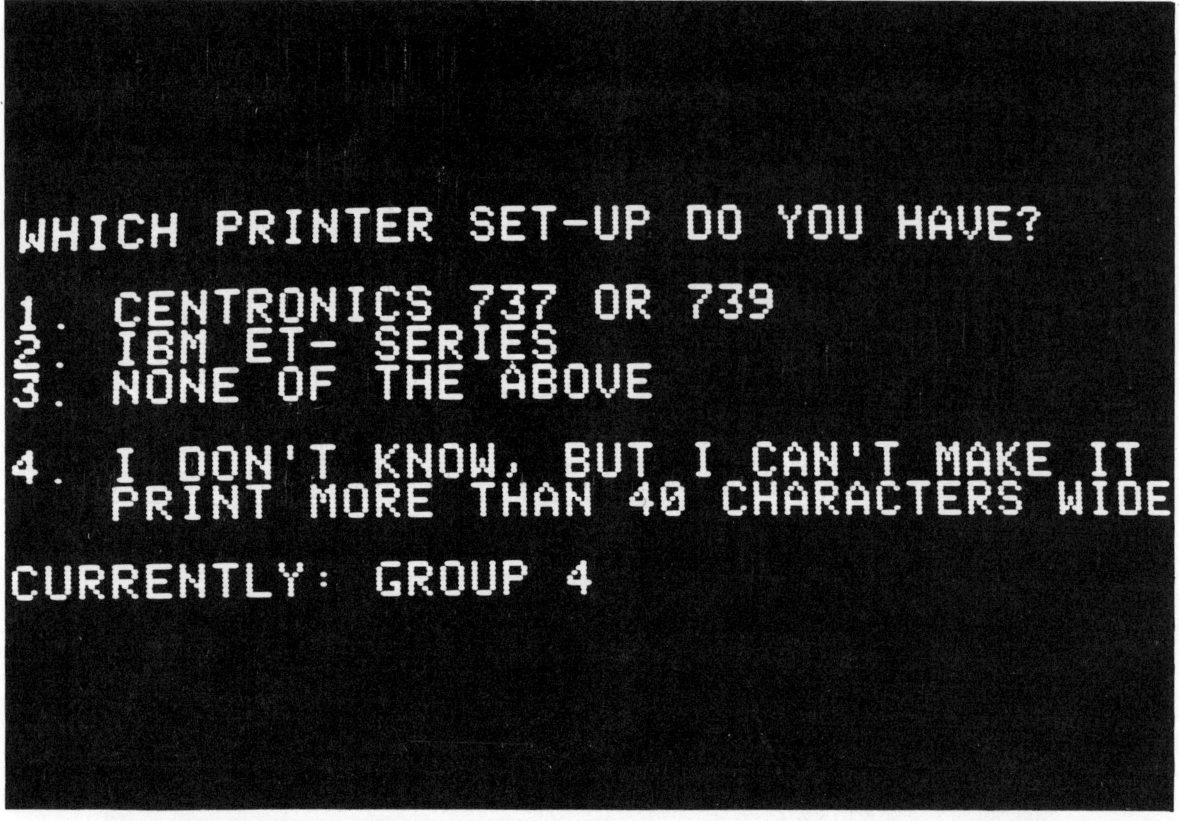

Fig. 7-14. Printer set-up may be reconfigured at any time using this menu.

OUTPUT

Printer Configuration. Selected in the initial set-up menu, printer options at first appear to be rather limited. The program asks which printer setup you have and proceeds to list a rather limited selection: Qume/Diablo without auto reverse, IBM-ET series, Centronics 737, other printers using the Apple card A2B0007 with P9 PROM, and all others. Simply select yours from this list. As noted in the manual, this program does work with a great variety of printers, most of which fall into the all others category. The configuration routine may be rerun at any time your system changes (Fig. 7-14).

Printer Control. I have used the program with two different printers, both hooked to my Apple parallel card, and no problems have been encountered. The program provides for the special features found on many printers (including my IDS 560). A somewhat unusual approach is taken to providing for special printer features, but it works very well. A system of abbreviations is provided to pass control codes from the text file to your printer.

The basic process involves spending some time with your printer manual (or dealer) investigating the control codes necessary to invoke your printer's features. For example, to select 16.8 CPI (small print for the bottom of a contract) on my 560 ASCII code 31 must be sent to the printer. You could use tc (for tiny characters) to designate this print size. The format for defining the abbreviation is >.tc #31. This abbreviation must be contained in any document before tiny characters are selected. Once the abbreviation is in place, typing .tc in the text will switch the print size to the small characters. Another abbreviation may be used to return to

126

normal characters. You may define any number of abbreviations to take advantage of all the features offered by your printer.

Although it sounds a little unwieldy, actually using this feature is rather simple if you set up a file of abbreviations used for your particular printer. This file can be merged with the one currently in memory whenever special features are called for.

Initiating Printing. Two modes of printing are available in The Executive Secretary, draft or document. Draft printing, selected by pressing P in the edit mode, will print a copy of your text from the edit marker. After pressing P, and RETURN to continue, you may select double spacing and line number printing. Pressing RETURN again will start printing the draft copy. Line numbers are provided for easy reference in later editing operations.

Document printing may be initiated by selecting option 1 (PRINT DOCUMENT) from the main menu (Fig. 7-15). After selecting the document desired from the disk catalog display, you may print to the screen or printer. Next the number of copies is requested. Finally, the print format is displayed for examination and possible alteration, prior to printing the document (Fig. 7-16). RETURN starts the actual printing process.

Justification. The Executive Secretary provides for justification of text using word spacing to achieve flush left and right margins. Proportional printing and infinite letter spacing are not supported.

Page Numbers and Headers. Page numbers can be printed in any position on any specified line of a page. The page numbering command is >pn x, y, where x is the line and y the character position on the line.

Headers may be set up to appear at the top of every page by using subfiles (see block operations).

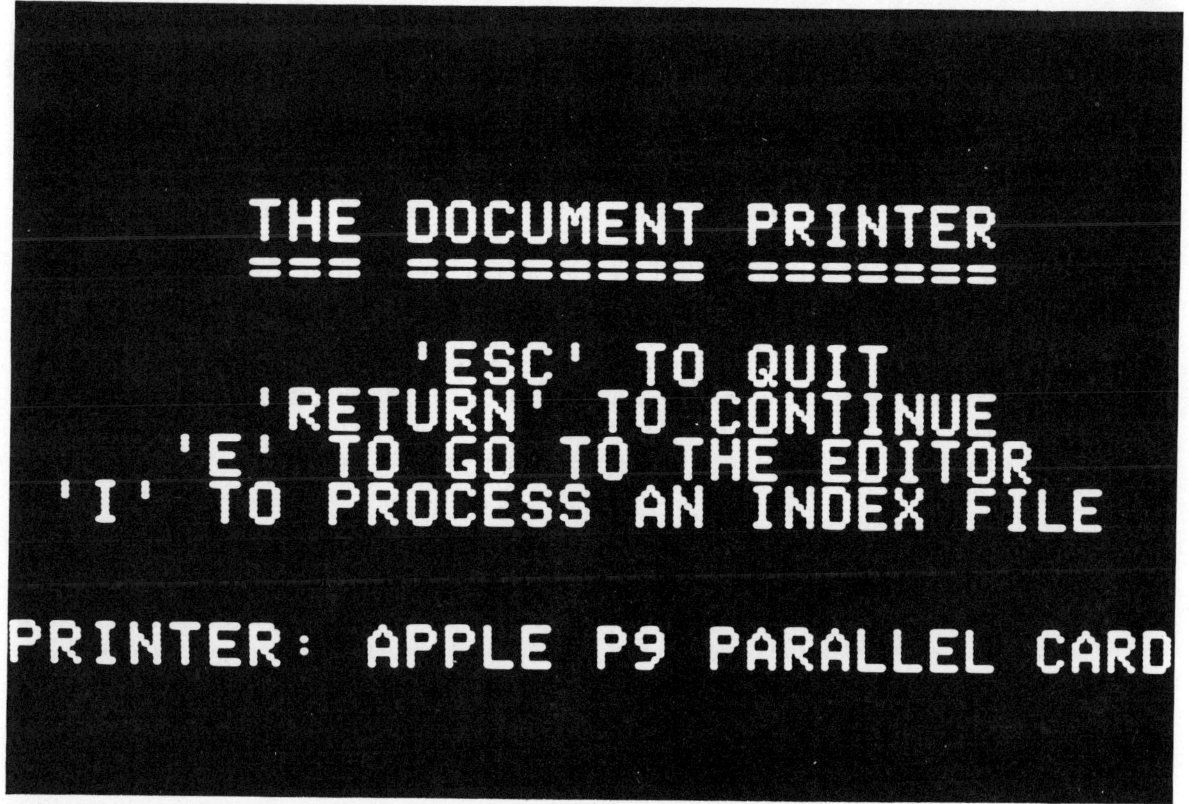

Fig. 7-15. Print mode options are clearly outlined in a series of brief menus.

```
CURRENT PRINTER SPECIFICATIONS. 'ESC'
LETS YOU CONTINUE. 'RETURN' MOVES YOU
DOWN THE PAGE. TO CHANGE AN ITEM, USE
LEFT ARROW TO ERASE, RETYPE, 'RETURN'.

SPACES IN LEFT MARGIN                      12-
# OF TYPED CHARACTERS PER LINE             66
# OF LINES ON SHEET OF PAPER               66
# OF LINES, TOP MARGIN                      6
# OF LINES, BOTTOM MARGIN                   6

STARTING PAGE #                             1
WHAT LINE TO PRINT PAGE # ON                0
# OF SPACES TO INDENT FOR PAGE #            0

SINGLE SHEETS (Y OR N)                      Y
LINES LOST AT TOP FOR PAPER BAIL            0

LINES TO SKIP BETWEEN LINES                 0

SKIP ACTUAL PRINTING UNTIL PAGE             1
```

Fig. 7-16. The print format is displayed and may be altered prior to printing a selected document or series of documents.

Any subfile can be printed as a page header as long as it is no longer than the entire page. In effect, the header file replaces the top margin specification in the format, so you must be careful to include blank lines where necessary to separate the header from the top of the sheet and text. Once a subfile has been created, it is specified as a page header by the command >ph FILE NAME. Page headers are changed in the text by simply specifying a different file name in a header command at the desired points.

Forms Control. Both continuous paper and single sheets are provided for by the program. You may specify the number of lines initially dropped by rolling the sheet up to the retainer bar in single sheet mode.

Printer Problems. No provisions are included for responding to error condition indications generated by many printers.

Text Insertion during Printing. A keyboard input command (> KD) provides the means to request input from the keyboard during printing operations. Up to 99 keyboard input commands may be used in the creation of a document. To use this capability, type each command on a separate line. For example:

>KD 1, FIRST AND LAST NAME
>KD 2, NUMBER AND STREET
>KD 2, CITY, STATE AND ZIP

In the text, input typed in response to these prompts is indicated by &01, &02, and &03. When the document is printed, the prompts will appear on the screen, and the text typed in will appear in the appropriate place in the text. If you are printing multiple copies of a document and wish to preserve the responses to one or more of the prompts for several documents, press SHIFT-RETURN instead of RETURN when you have finished typing the information.

Print Mode Display. When print mode is selected, you are first asked which document(s) from the disk catalog displayed are to be printed. Next, the (S)creen or (P)rinter prompt appears. Finally, the default print format for that file is shown, and you are asked to make any desired changes.

If you have selected (P)rinter, you are asked to press RETURN to begin printing. During printing, the PRESS ANY KEY TO INTERRUPT prompt is shown on an otherwise blank screen. When the document(s) have been printed, you may elect to print another copy, see the disk catalog, or return to the main menu (Fig. 7-17).

Screen Preview of Document. When initiating printing operations, you are given an opportunity to designate whether text will go to the (S)creen or the (P)rinter. If you are using the 80-column display mode, text can be printed to the screen in exactly the same fashion as it will appear on paper. For those without 80-column display capability, lines are broken on the screen to indicate their length in the printed document (Fig. 7-18).

Multiple Files or Copies. Printing documents consisting of material from multiple files is a relatively simple matter using The Executive Secretary. Text from subfiles or other text files may be set up to print in any desired sequence by using the >SF (file name) or >XT (file name) commands from within a document. If lengthy, complicated sequences of files are to be printed, a separate file can be set up just for the purpose of directing traffic.

Specifying multiple copies is even easier: Just type in the number of copies desired in response to the NUMBER OF COPIES prompt.

Other Print Commands. The Executive Secretary contains a large number of commands which may be used for special purposes during the

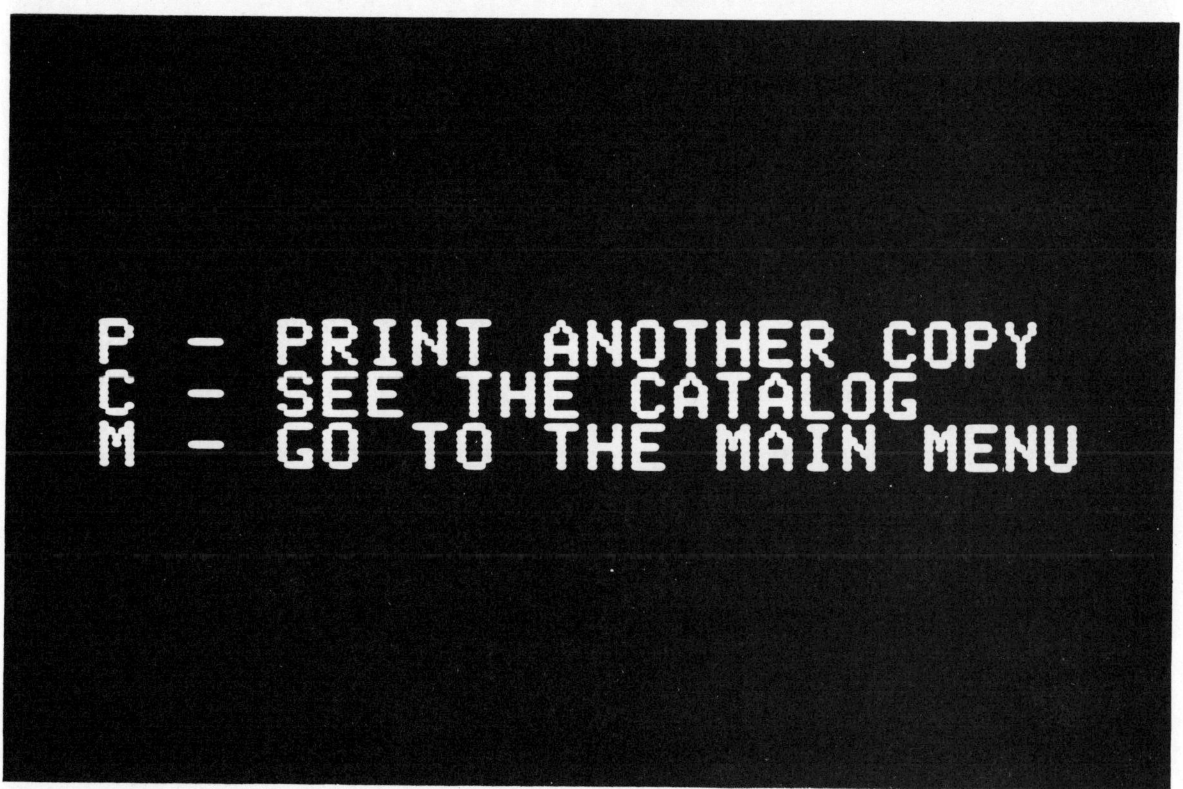

Fig. 7-17. Options presented at the conclusion of printing operations.

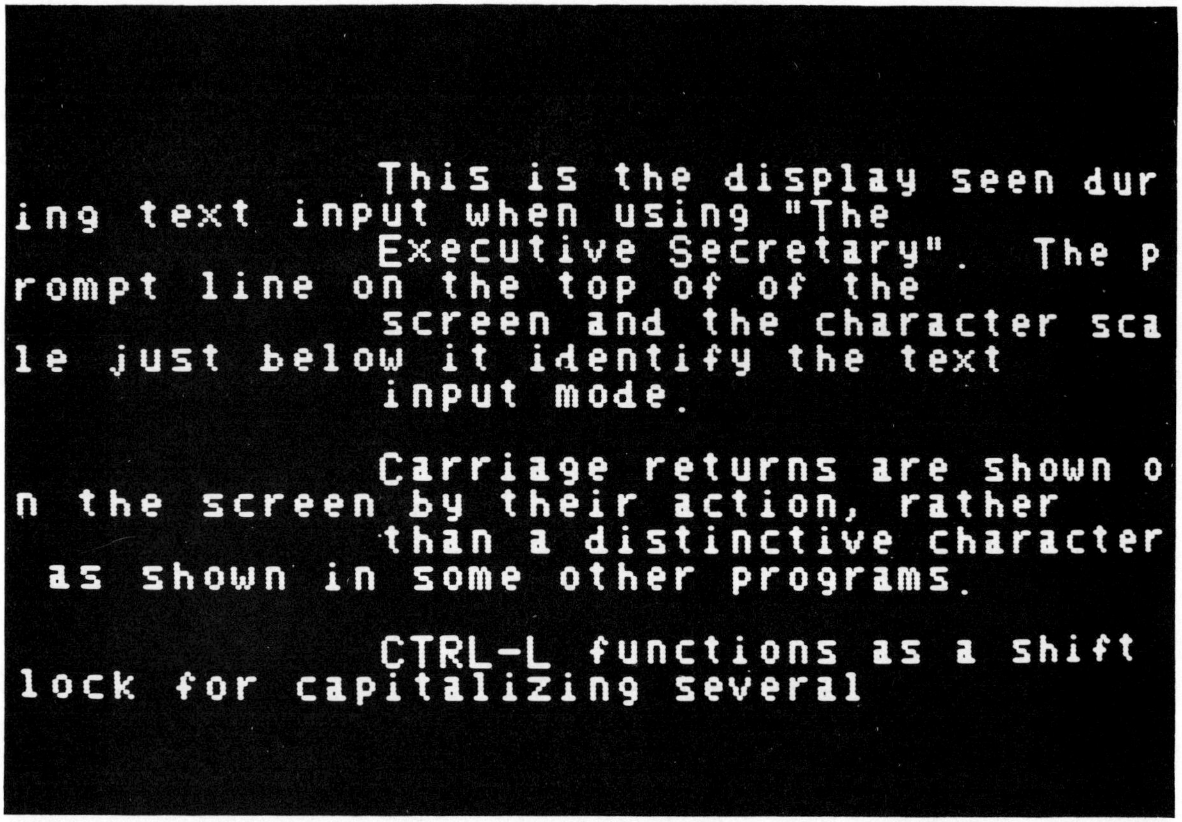

The following figure shows a screen display:

> This is the display seen dur
> ing text input when using "The
>   Executive Secretary". The p
> rompt line on the top of of the
>   screen and the character sca
> le just below it identify the text
>   input mode.
>
>   Carriage returns are shown o
> n the screen by their action, rather
>   than a distinctive character
> as shown in some other programs.
>
>   CTRL-L functions as a shift
> lock for capitalizing several

Fig. 7-18. Print preview as shown on the standard Apple 40-column screen.

printing process. The following are just a few of those available. Ordinary text inserted between a pair of address (>ad) commands will be used as typed in the text and stored for later printing on an envelope. Printing without reformatting (>nr) is used to print a copy of lines exactly as they were typed. For two-sided printing with bindings, the >bi command adds extra spaces to the left margin for odd-numbered pages and shifts the page number position. A "must have" (>MH) command allows you to specify the number of lines that must be available on the page before printing the text which follows, and >XT n (file name) specifies the number of lines that must be available before printing the file specified.

SPECIAL FEATURES

"Dash Off a Quick Note". This feature, selected from the main menu, allows you to short-out some of the normal input, editing, and printing procedures. As the name implies, this option is primarily used to type in a little bit of text and rapidly obtain printed copy for some specific purpose.

Outline Indentation. Although it may seem like a minor feature, the >oi commands, used for outlining with double levels of indentation, are quite unusual and very functional for those who use outlining often.

Printing Visicalc™ Files. Print files prepared by the popular Visicalc electronic spread sheet program may be incorporated into documents printed by The Executive Secretary. The procedure for doing this is clearly outlined in the manual.

Printing on Preprinted Forms. The Executive Secretary can handle preprinted forms using a combination of advance vertically (>av n), advance horizontally (>ah n), keyboard input (>KD), and text. Once these specifications have been set for a particular form, a file may be created to describe the layout.

Abbreviations. Most word-processing program users have developed some system of using abbreviations for frequently repeated portions of text within their documents. The Executive Secretary has provided special abbreviation commands which may be predefined and used at will throughout the text.

Counters. Nine counters, which can be used for any purpose, are available in The Executive Secretary. The counters are a1, a2, a3, etc. Counters may be used to keep track of specific sequential items in the text, recalling page numbers at a later time, or any other application required by the user.

Document Indexing. An alphabetical index of items contained in a block manuscript or lengthy document is one of the least favorite activities of any writer. The index cannot be completed until the material is printed in final form so page numbers are known. The Executive Secretary provides an automatic indexing system. To use this capability, an index file must be specified using the >SX (file name) command. During the process of text entry, items to be included in the index are marked with an >IX (item) command. Single entries or range of text may be identified.

Once the document has been printed, pressing I on the main print menu will allow you to access the index file. First, the file is sorted and merged. Then, you are asked to designate a column width and fill character for printing. Finally, an alphabetical index is printed.

Fig. 7-19. The Electronic Card File is a data base management system built into The Executive Secretary.

Fig. 7-20. When using The Electronic Card File, a file must be designated. In this case, NAMES is used for our demonstration file.

Electronic Card File. A data base management system, called the Electronic Card File, is included on The Executive Secretary disk (Fig. 7-19). This program may be used, among other possible applications, to store mailing list information for producing customized form letters.

Explicit instructions are included in the manual for setting up forms, adding information, sorting, searching, report formatting, etc. Rather than go into a lengthy explanation of the data base operations, I will use a series of figures to illustrate the process (Figs. 7-20, 7-21, 7-22, 7-23, 7-24, and 7-25). The Electronic Card File is a relatively simple, but effective, data base management system.

Provisions are included to use similar data from The Data Factory, CCA DMS, On-line Data Base, Information Master, and DB Master Utility Pack. Separate instructions are provided for using custom data bases for mail merging purposes.

Conditional Printing. The Executive Secretary is capable of printing customized form letters with information from one of the "card file" programs mentioned. The command IF is used to test the contents of various fields and print portions of text only if certain conditions are present. If the conditions specified are not met, all text is skipped until the next IF is encountered in the text. To further increase the flexibility of IF, several other commands may be used in conjunction with it: OR, AN, OR NOT, AN NOT, IF NOT. For numerical data, IF can test for less than, equal to, or greater than. Excellent examples of the various uses of conditional printing commands are included in the documentation.

Electronic Mail. If your computer is equipped with the Hayes Micromodem, you have

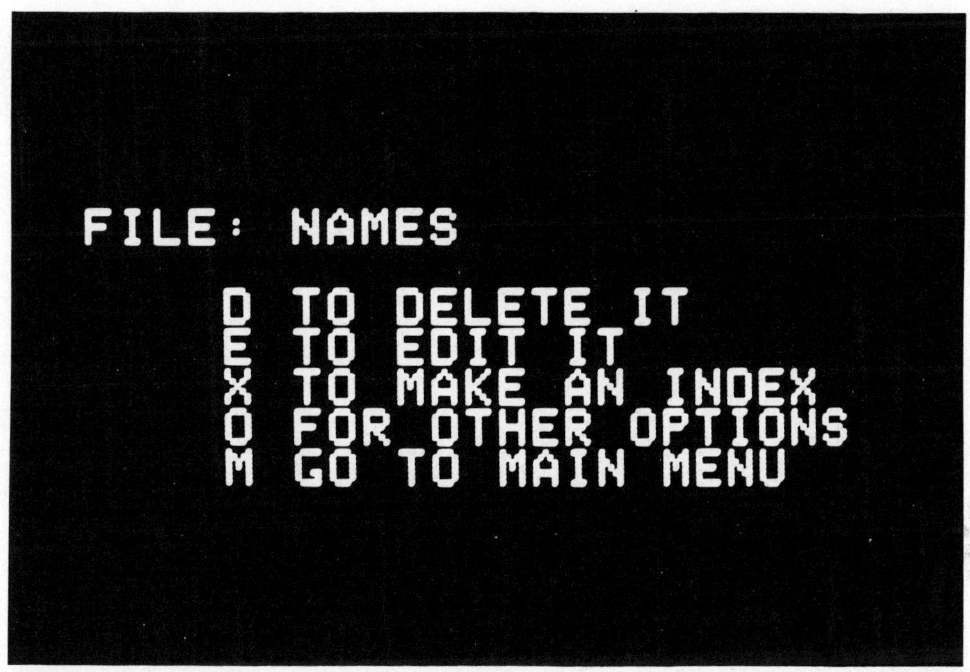

Fig. 7-21. Options for the use of the file are presented.

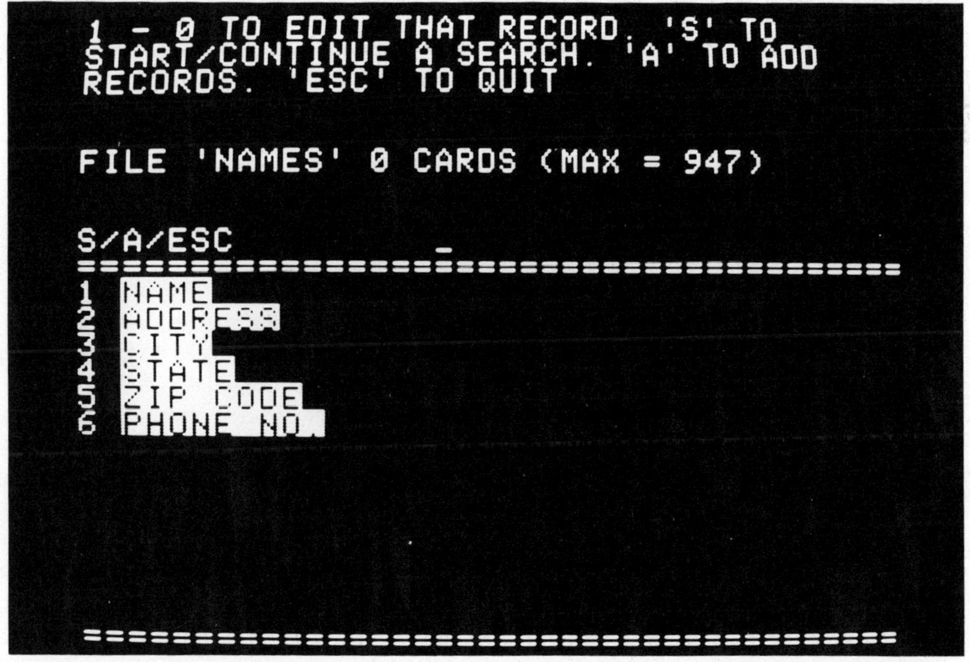

Fig. 7-22. The NAMES file will include records containing the six items of mailing list information.

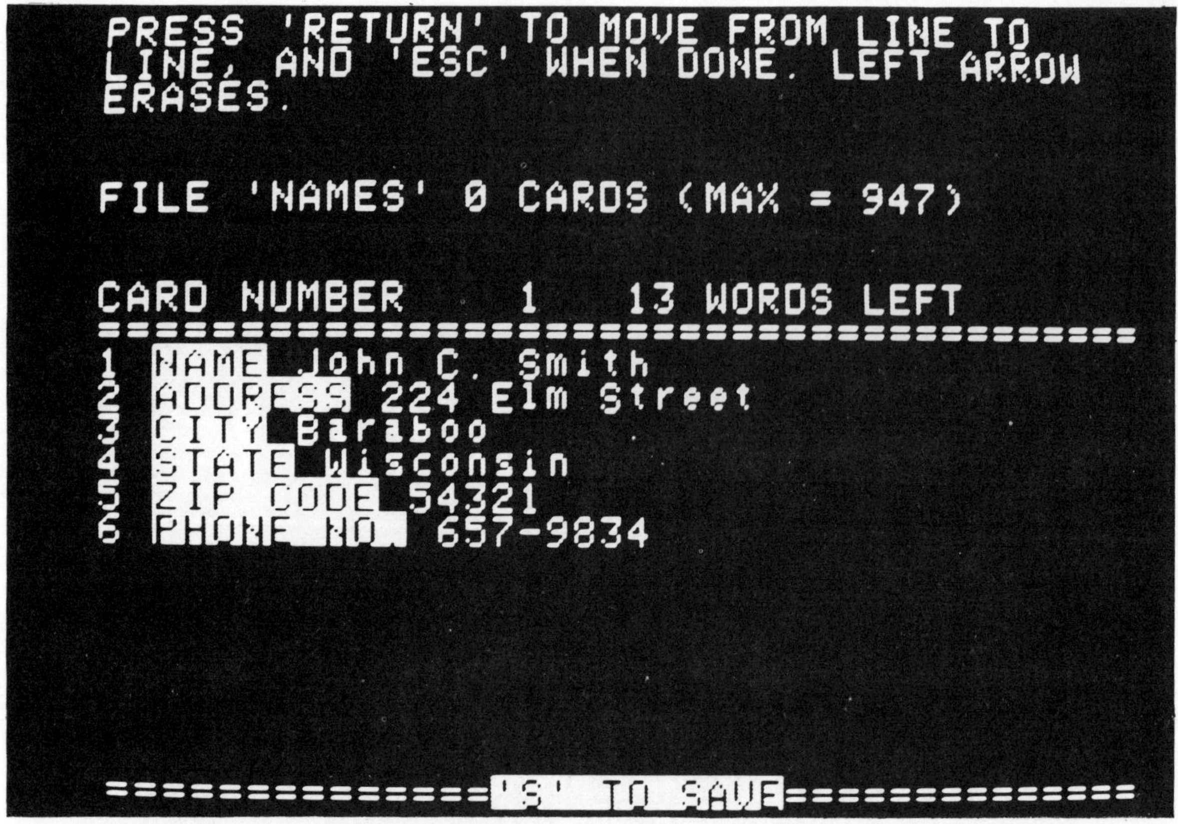

Fig. 7-23. Entering information into the mailing list file is simply a matter of following the on-screen prompts. When all the information has been entered, pressing S will save the record on disk.

electronic mail capabilities with The Executive Secretary, and you can transmit or receive documents from another computer similarly equipped. After selecting electronic mail from the main menu, you are given a choice of (S)ending or (R)eceiving documents.

For receiving, there is not much else to do. When the phone rings, your Apple will answer and accept documents. Each document is saved on disk under a unique name.

Sending documents is a little more complicated. You are first asked to enter a telephone number for the destination Apple. Next, you are asked to set a send-this-one marker for the appropriate files on the disk. If no clock card is contained in your machine, the system attempts immediate transmission. With a clock card, you are given a choice of sending the documents immediately or

waiting until a designated time. In either case, documents are transmitted in the same order in which they appear on the disk.

HUMAN ENGINEERING

Logical, Easy to Use Commands. For the most part, commands used by this program are quite logical, in that their names represent the words describing their action. In some instances, it is necessary to be familiar with the program to use special commands not routinely displayed in menus or prompts.

Verification of Potentially Dangerous Commands. Very few of the potentially dangerous delete commands require a second verification before executing. This may be due, in large part, to the system of life handling used by The Executive Secretary. Most of the time, changes are not permanent

134

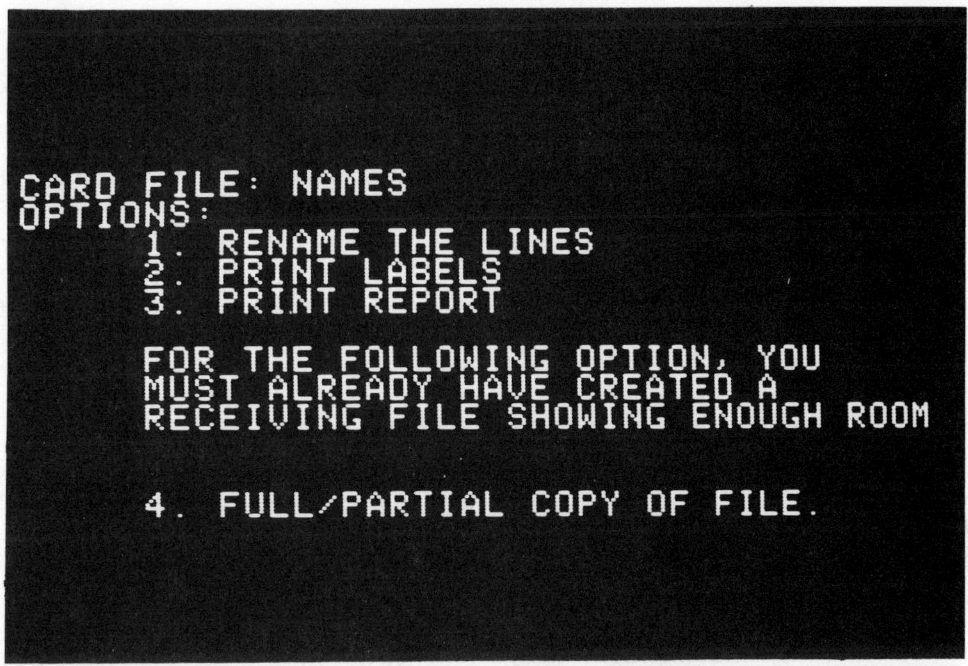

Fig. 7-24. Options available for the use of data contained in the card file.

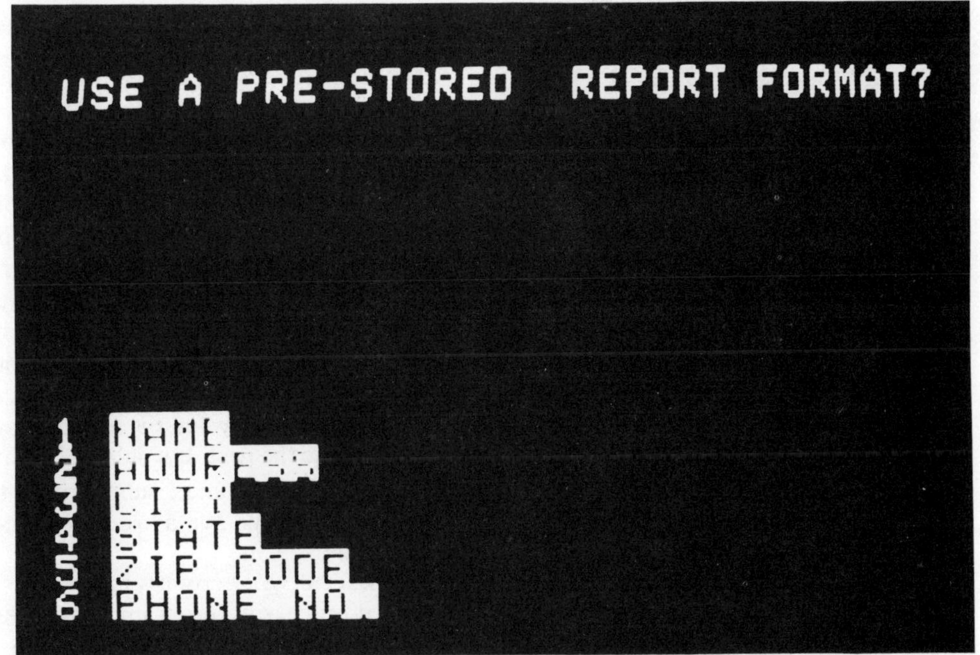

Fig. 7-25. The mailing list information can be printed using a prestored format, or a format can be designed for each specific application.

Fig. 7-26. The Executive Secretary user's manual.

until it comes time for actual disk operations. The original file is maintained on disk until specifically removed by the user.

Error Recovery and Emergency Procedures. Very little reference is made in the documentation to error recovery or emergency procedures.

On-Line Help. No tutorial or documentation files are included on the program disk.

DOCUMENTATION

User's Manual. Written in a tutorial fashion, the user's manual included with The Executive Secretary (Fig. 7-26) generally does an excellent job of explaining the features of the program to a word-processing beginner. An easel-type looseleaf book is used to cover the material and provide a convenient angle for reading while working at the keyboard. The material is divided into 25 lessons which get successively more complex as you progress through the manual.

Reference Material. A single copy of a rather extensive reference card is included with the program. Also to be found in the program package are the latest instruction update, instructions for installing the no-solder shift key adapter (included), and a plastic grid to aid in the layout of a printed sheet.

SUPPORT

The program package includes one copy of the program disk. When you have completed the registration form, a second copy will be sent directly from Sof/Sys. Damaged disks will be replaced for $7.50 upon their return. Registered owners can also receive an updated copy of the latest version of the program by returning their disk and sending $7.50. Telephone support is also offered for those needing a more immediate solution to a pressing problem.

IMPRESSIONS

The Executive Secretary is a program with a wide range of features. Sitting down with the documentation and learning them all could be a rather lengthy process, although this is certainly no reflection on the program itself. With flexibility and added features must come increased complexity.

Prompts and menus found in the program do a good job of guiding you through most of the processes involved in day-to-day use of the system.

Although the tutorial style of documentation is suitable for beginners in word processing, it tends to be somewhat wordy for those who have used other systems in the past. It would be helpful to see a short, concise reference summary of the program's commands and syntax requirements somewhere in the manual.

The Executive Secretary is a very sophisticated word-processing program for the Apple II. Many of the features it contains are quite rare in other programs available, particularly in a similar price range.

## Chapter 8

EasyWriter Professional System

Publisher: Information Unlimited Software, Inc., 281 Arlington Avenue, Berkeley, CA 94707
Hardware Required: Apple II or Apple II Plus, 48K, Disk II, 80-column display card (DoubleVision, Sup-R-Terminal, Smarterm, or Videx), video monitor, printer, and interface.
Additional Hardware Recommended: Cooling fan for Apple II, green phosphorous monitor, and letter-quality printer.
Price: $175.00

EasyWriter Professional System (Fig. 8-1) is one of the Apple II word-processing programs that requires a modest investment in additional hardware. Assuming that you already have an Apple system suitable for use with the other programs I have discussed, the 80-column display card is really the only required item. This no-nonsense program offers some very sophisticated capabilities and puts the 80-column display to very effective use.

TEXT INPUT FEATURES

Upper - and Lowercase Display. Upper- and lowercase letters are displayed on the video screen in the character set offered by the particular 80-column board you have installed. On an unmodified Apple II, ESC is used for shifting from lower- to uppercase and ESC-ESC as a shift lock. Instructions for modifying your Apple to use the shift keys are included in the program manual.

Video Display. 80 columns of text are displayed on the video screen. The exact format of that display depends primarily on which 80-column display card you are using (Fig. 8-2). Some cards offer a selection of character fonts. Unless your print lines routinely exceed 80 columns in width, entire lines are shown on the video screen as they will be printed.

Word Formatting. Within the margins specified, words too long to fit on one line are automatically shifted to the next. Spaces are used as the separators between words. No provisions for defining unbreakable spaces or hyphenation are included.

Indentation for the first line of a new paragraph and setting the left and right margins is specified by

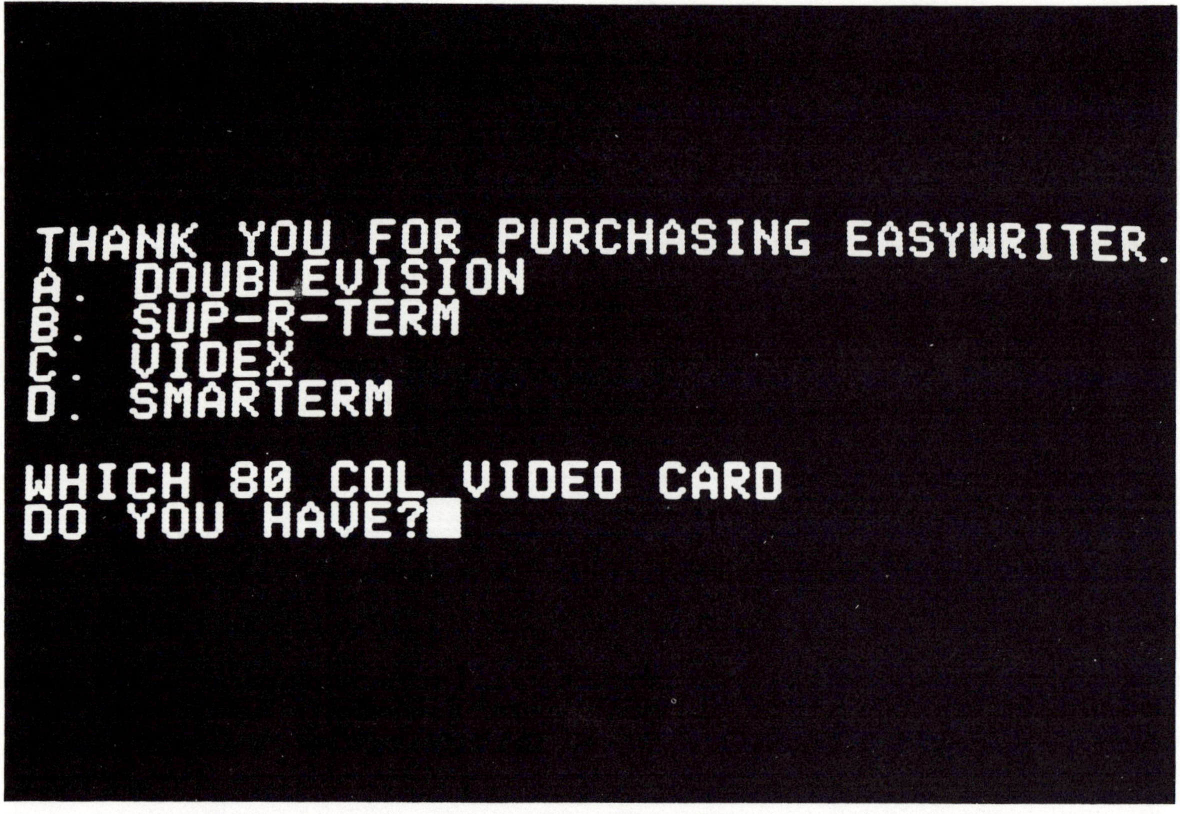

Fig. 8-1. The title page menu displayed by EasyWriter Professional System.

selecting M from the additional commands menu. The format for entering the desired value is left margin, right margin, indentation (Fig. 8-3). A letter I will be shown on the video display scale to indicate the position of paragraph indentation selected.

Tabbing. Horizontal tabs may be set using the additional commands menu (CTRL-N) from the editor. After typing T to designate tab set, you are asked to input the column numbers (separated by commas) for the desired tab stops. Press RETURN after entering the column numbers, and the tab stops are immediately indicated on the column scale shown on the screen.

CTRL-T is used to move from tab to tab when entering text. All the tab stops may be cleared by typing 0 instead of column numbers after selecting T.

Paragraph indentation may be predefined and is indicated by an I on the scale. The effects of tabbing and indentation are shown immediately during the process of text entry.

Justification. Word-spacing justification is switched on and off by pressing J from the additional commands menu (CTRL-N). The status of justification is indicated by JUST ON and JUST OFF messages on the screen, and the effects of justification are shown on the video display (Fig. 8-4).

EasyWriter Professional System is one of the few Apple II programs that supports incremental spacing and proportional spacing justification for those printers with the necessary features. See the output section for details.

Line Spacing. Single or multiple line spacing can be set during the process of text input using the embedded command (.SPACEn), where n is the number of spaces desired. Half-line feeds for printing either super- or subscripted text are available

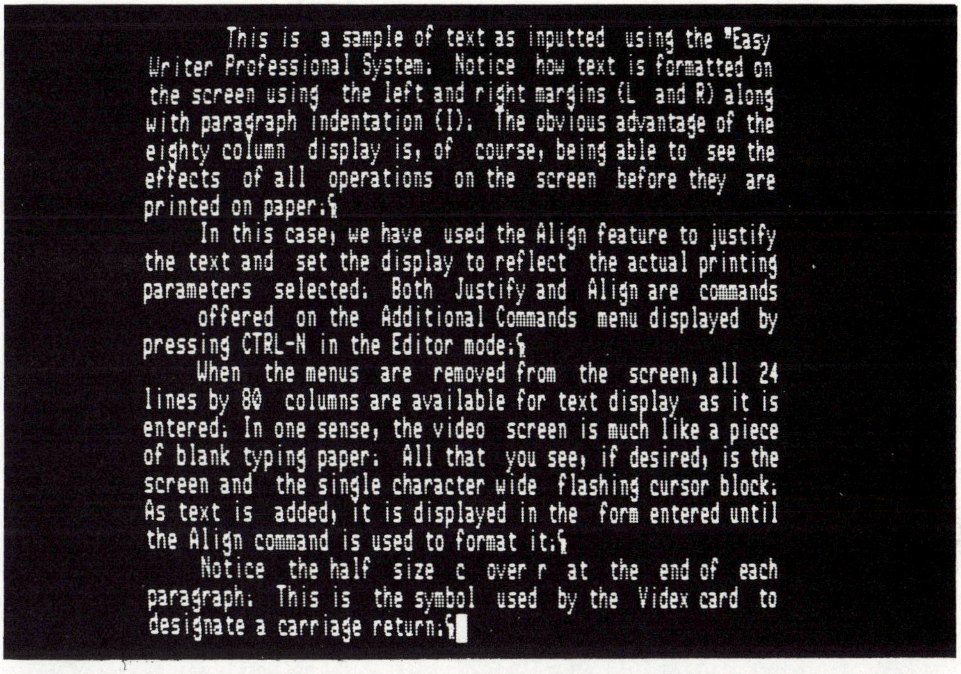

This is a sample of text as inputted using the "Easy
Writer Professional System. Notice how text is formatted on
the screen using the left and right margins (L and R) along
with paragraph indentation (I). The obvious advantage of the
eighty column display is, of course, being able to see the
effects of all operations on the screen before they are
printed on paper.
In this case, we have used the Align feature to justify
the text and set the display to reflect the actual printing
parameters selected. Both Justify and Align are commands
offered on the Additional Commands menu displayed by
pressing CTRL-N in the Editor mode.
When the menus are removed from the screen, all 24
lines by 80 columns are available for text display as it is
entered. In one sense, the video screen is much like a piece
of blank typing paper. All that you see, if desired, is the
screen and the single character wide flashing cursor block.
As text is added, it is displayed in the form entered until
the Align command is used to format it.
Notice the half size c over r at the end of each
paragraph. This is the symbol used by the Videx card to
designate a carriage return.

Fig. 8-2. This display of 80-column text lines was generated by the Videx board.

LEFT MARGIN= 0 RIGHT MARGIN= 65 INDENT= 0
ENTER:L,R,I
10,70,5
L
R

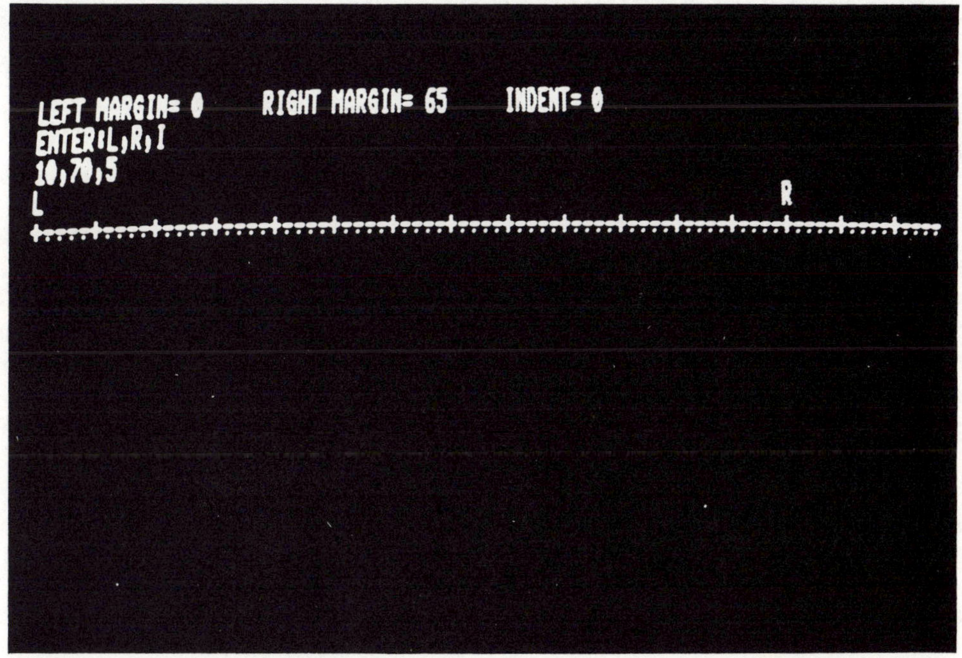

Fig. 8-3. Setting left margin, right margin, and paragraph indentation by specifying their positions relative to the left border of the paper.

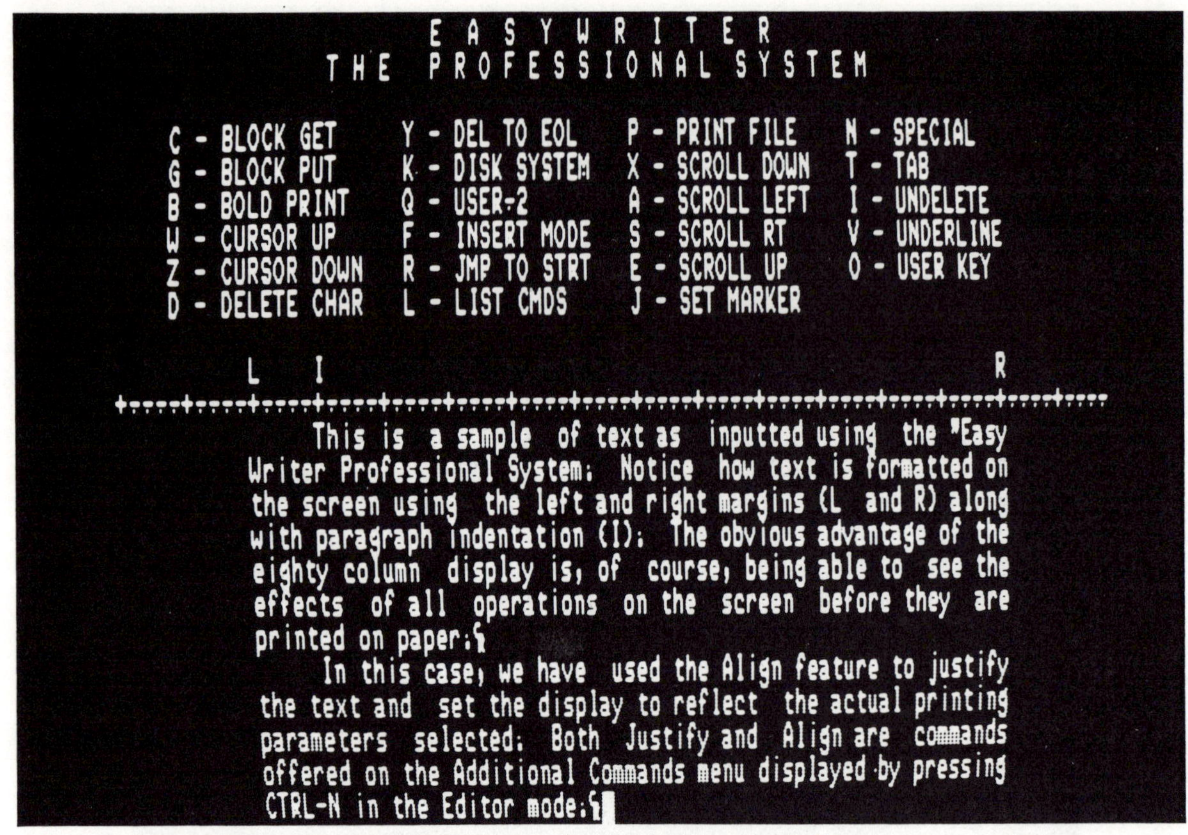

Fig. 8-4. The text shown below the line scale has been justified using word spacing.

for those with printers supporting this capability. A superscript is created by typing CTRL-Q U and the text to be superscripted. CTRL-Q D returns printing to the normal line. Subscripts are set by reversing the order of U and D in the CTRL-Q commands.

Status Display during Text Input. Operating mode, during normal input operations, is not displayed on the screen. Basically, what you see is what you enter. This is adequate if you are experienced with using EasyWriter Professional System. For those with less expertise, a help menu showing available commands and a character position scale which shows margins, indentation, and tab settings is displayed by pressing CTRL-L (Fig. 8-5). The additional commands menu may be selected by pressing CTRL-N (Fig. 8-6). Text input may continue while either menu is displayed.

Page Specification Change. During text input operations, the page specifications can be changed in either of two ways. Default characteristics for the entire document are accessed and changed through commands provided in the additional commands menu. Embedded commands can also be inserted in the text for page parameters which are to be altered at that point.

Text Files from Other Programs. A translate command is included to allow use of text files from earlier versions of EasyWriter Professional System, but no other program text files are provided for. Information Unlimited Software does offer The EasyMover which, among other functions, translates EasyWriter Professional System files into Apple DOS files and vice versa.

Text from External Devices. Although not provided directly in the program, EasyWriter Pro-

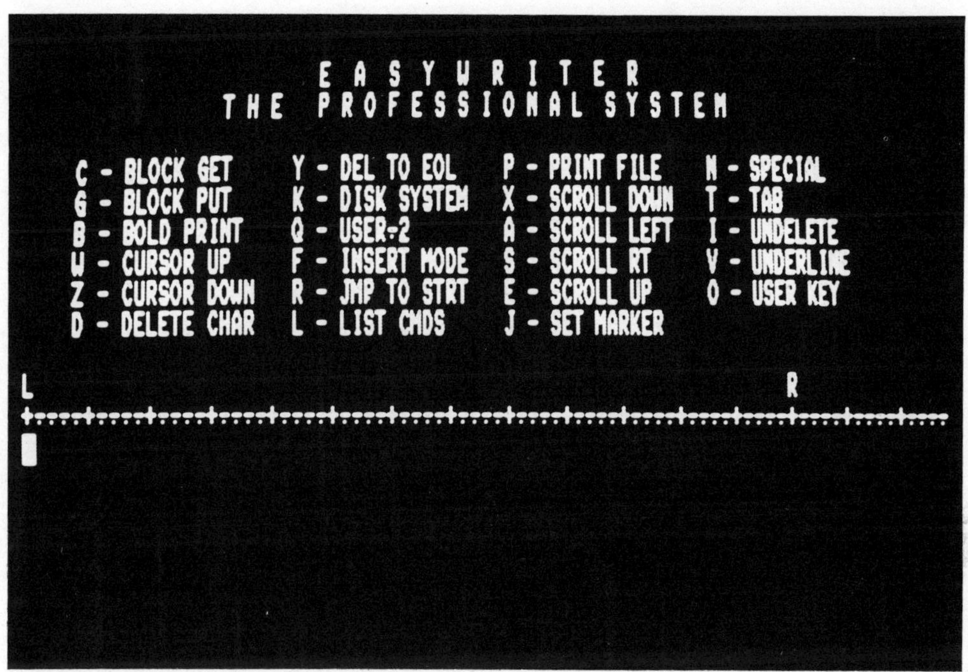

Fig. 8-5. The help menu, displayed by pressing CTRL-L, does not affect text currently being edited.

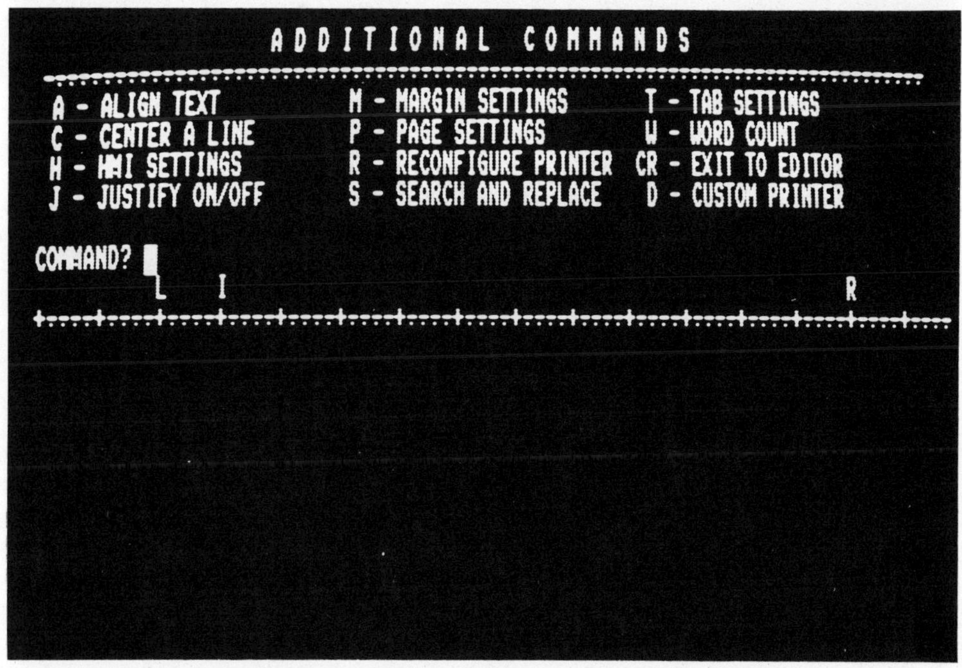

Fig. 8-6. The additional commands menu, displayed by pressing CTRL-N, lists other options available during editing operations.

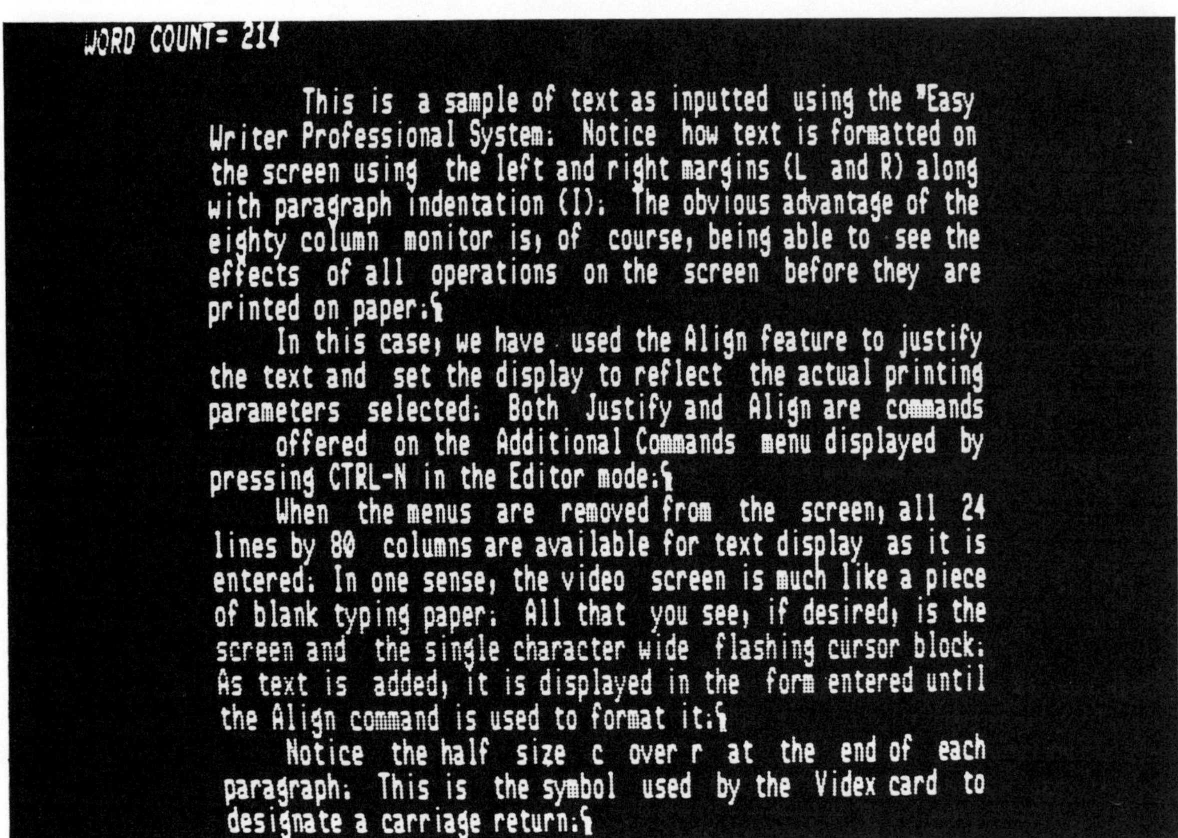

Fig. 8-7. A word count feature, shown in the upper left corner, is included for ease in estimating file length.

fessional System files can be transmitted and received using a modem and the EasyMover program.

Formatting for Text Output. Default formatting for text output is accessed and changed through the additional commands menu. Commands are included for using the special features of printers capable of underlining, boldface type, super- and subscripts, special character sets, and so on.

Maximum Text Length per File. Text files can contain a maximum of 10,000 keystrokes. A note in the program manual advises limiting files to about 5,000 keystrokes. During the process of text entry, the program signals the approach of maximum file length by producing a beep on every keystroke beginning at 256 keystrokes from the end of the file. For an indication of where you stand, a word count function is provided in the additional commands menu (Fig. 8-7).

EDITING FEATURES

Cursor Positioning. The Apple's left and right arrows are used to move the cursor in the appropriate direction. Additionally, CTRL-W moves the cursor up one line, and CTRL-Z moves it down. CTRL-T moves the cursor from tab stop to tab stop. The cursor commands can be used in conjunction with the REPEAT key for multiple moves.

Scrolling. Commands are provided for scrolling the text one screen page at a time. CTRL-X will advance one screen forward, CTRL-E moves one screen backward. Express moves are provided by CTRL-R (move to the beginning of the file) and CTRL-C (move to the end of the file). Horizontal scrolling, for text with lines wider than 80 characters, is provided by CTRL-A (move text to the left) and CTRL-S (scroll to the right).

142

Changing a Few Characters. For simple corrections or changes, move the cursor to the desired position, and type over the text to be changed.

Inserting Text. Text is inserted in front of the cursor, so it must be positioned to the character following the location where insertions are to begin. Once the cursor is properly located, pressing CTRL-F selects the insert mode (indicated by a solid, rather than flashing, cursor). After typing the characters to be inserted, RETURN is pressed to turn the insert mode off.

Deleting Text. Deleting a few characters is specified by pressing CTRL-D after positioning the cursor on the desired character. If the cursor has not been moved from the location of the final deletion, characters just deleted may be restored by pressing CTRL-I. Each successive press of CTRL-I will restore one additional character. CTRL-D will also delete a word if the cursor is placed on the space immediately preceding the word before CTRL-D is pressed.

Deleting all or part of a line is done with the CTRL-Y command. When CTRL-Y is pressed, all the characters from the current cursor position to the right margin of the line will be deleted. Larger sections of text may be deleted using the block operations discussed in the next section.

Block Operations. In order to use any of the block commands, a section of text must be marked using the following procedure. Position the cursor to the space in front of the first character to be included in the block, select insert mode (CTRL-F), and press CTRL-J to set a block marker. Now move the cursor to the space following the last character in the block, and again press CTRL-J.

Once a block has been marked in the above fashion, it can be moved to another location in the text. After moving the cursor back to the line preceding the block, press CTRL-SHIFT-P twice to clear the block buffer. Then press CTRL-C to move the text (maximum of 1024 characters) into a holding buffer in memory and delete it from its original location. Now, move the cursor to the location in the text where the block is to be inserted, and press CTRL-G. Finally, turn off the insert mode by pressing RETURN.

Saving a block of text in a separate disk file is somewhat more complicated. After marking the block as described above, CTRL-K is pressed to return to the disk system. Here, the text file in memory can be saved (without the block) or cleared from memory. If you want to save just the block, the latter course should be followed. Once the reset of the text file has been cleared, the block is retrieved from the buffer (CTRL-G) and may be saved in a disk file under a different name.

Text is deleted in blocks by marking the desired material, then saving the file in memory without it. Blocks can be inserted into other documents, using the procedures outlined in the manual. The process seems excessively complicated at first but can soon be learned well enough to accomplish the desired block operations.

Search and Replace. Typing S from the additional commands menu initiates both search and replace operations. After typing S, you are asked for the search word. Spaces should be entered preceding and following the characters typed to identify them as a complete word; otherwise, the program will locate the string no matter where it occurs. When you have specified the search word, you are asked to supply a replacement. Pressing RETURN instead of entering a word will designate a simple search operation. As each occurrence of the word is located, you are asked to press C, B, or X to continue, move backwards, or exit the search.

As you would expect, entering a word or phrase in response to the REPLACE WITH prompt adds replace to the search function (Fig. 8-8). You are asked if all or some of the search words should be replaced. If you indicate all, each occurrence of the word is automatically replaced in the file. Electing to replace only some of the occurrences will cause the program to pause at each and ask if you would like to K (keep), D (delete), or R (replace, the word in question or X-(exit), the replacement mode (Fig. 8-9). Search and replace can be used with linked files for multiple file operations.

TEXT STORAGE AND RETRIEVAL

DOS Used. A nonstandard DOS is used on the program disks, which must be used to initialize data

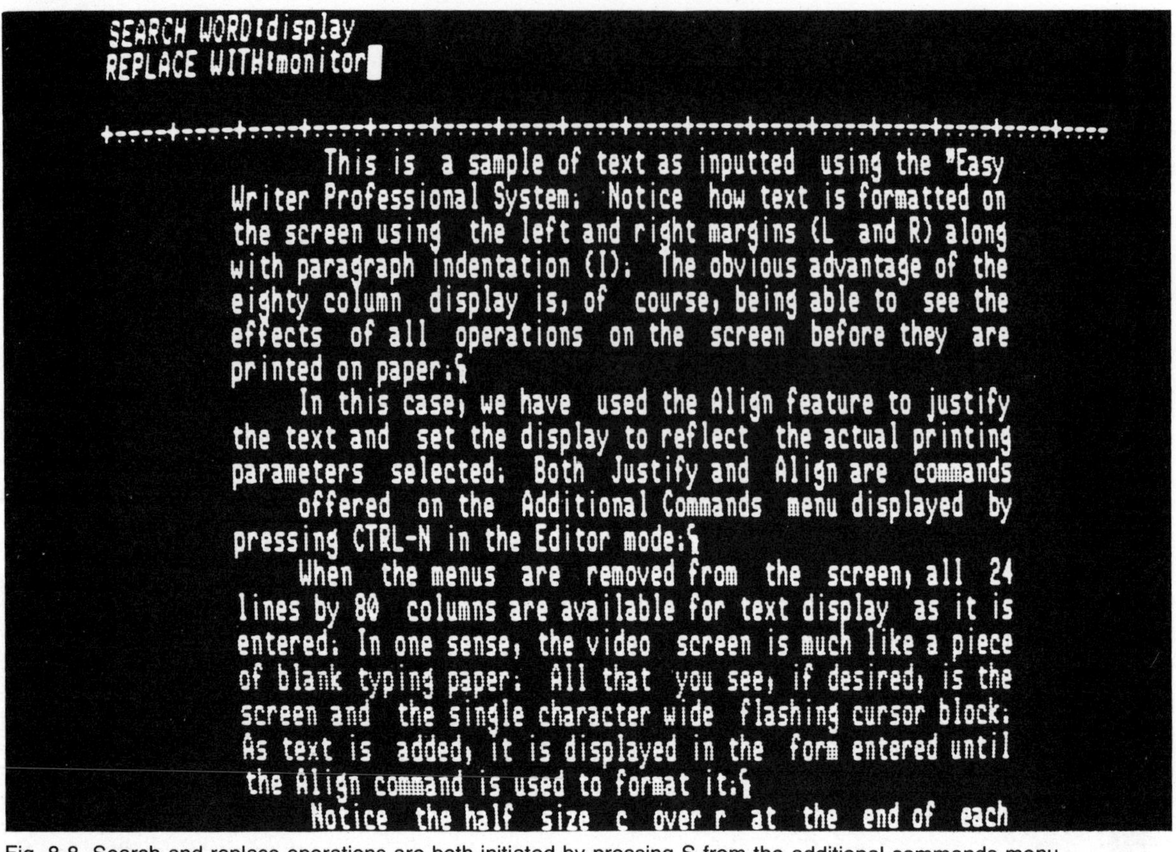

Fig. 8-8. Search and replace operations are both initiated by pressing S from the additional commands menu.

disks. Two copies of the program disk are included in the program package.

Text File Backup. Back-up copies of text files may be made in either of two ways. When saving a file on a data disk, save it on a back-up disk at the same time. This is done by using the file save command once for each disk. The newest revision of EasyWriter Professional System includes a dual-disk copy program so you can automatically make back-up copies of your data disks.

Multiple Drive Access. The latest revision of EasyWriter Professional System includes provisions for multiple drive access. All previous versions have operated with only a single drive. After the program has been booted, data disks can be inserted in both drives. From that point, you can switch back and forth by specifying 1 or 2 from the disk system. Data may be retrieved and saved from either disk. A copy program is included for data files (Fig. 8-10).

Text File Creation and Documentation. Text files are limited to the size of memory available with the program booted, approximately 10,000 characters. File names are limited to a total of 9 characters and spaces. No more than 31 text files, regardless of their length, can be saved on any data disk. All disk operations are done in the disk system. Entering the disk system is done be pressing RETURN after booting the program or pressing CTRL-K from the editor mode.

Once you have entered the disk system, a help menu listing all of the available commands is displayed. The disk system also displays a status line showing the name and size of the file currently being worked on, percentage of the disk presently being used to store files, and a catalog of the other files on the disk (Fig. 8-11).

To create a disk file or save a current file under a different name, press S (save), and the program will ask for a file name. After the name is entered, the file will be saved on the data disk currently in the drive. You may also create a back-up copy of the file by repeating the S (save) process on another data disk.

If you have completed revisions on a file currently on the disk, the updated version may be substituted for the current file by pressing R (revise). After you press R, the program will ask for verification and then save the updated file on disk. Deleting a file from the disk is accomplished by pressing D (delete), supplying the file number when prompted, and responding Y to the ARE YOU SURE? prompt.

Disk files may be protected from revisions or deletions by typing P (protect) and the file number when prompted. Protected files may be examined or appended but are protected from change or deletion. The protective lock on a file may be removed by pressing U (unprotect) and supplying the file number when asked.

Loading a file for work with the editor mode is selected by pressing G (get) and the file number. Actually entering the editor from the disk system is done by pressing E.

Several other commands are available in the disk system. A (append) will attach a file from the disk to the one currently in memory (as long as their combined length does not exceed 10,000 characters). C (clear text) erases text currently in memory and requires verification before proceeding. T

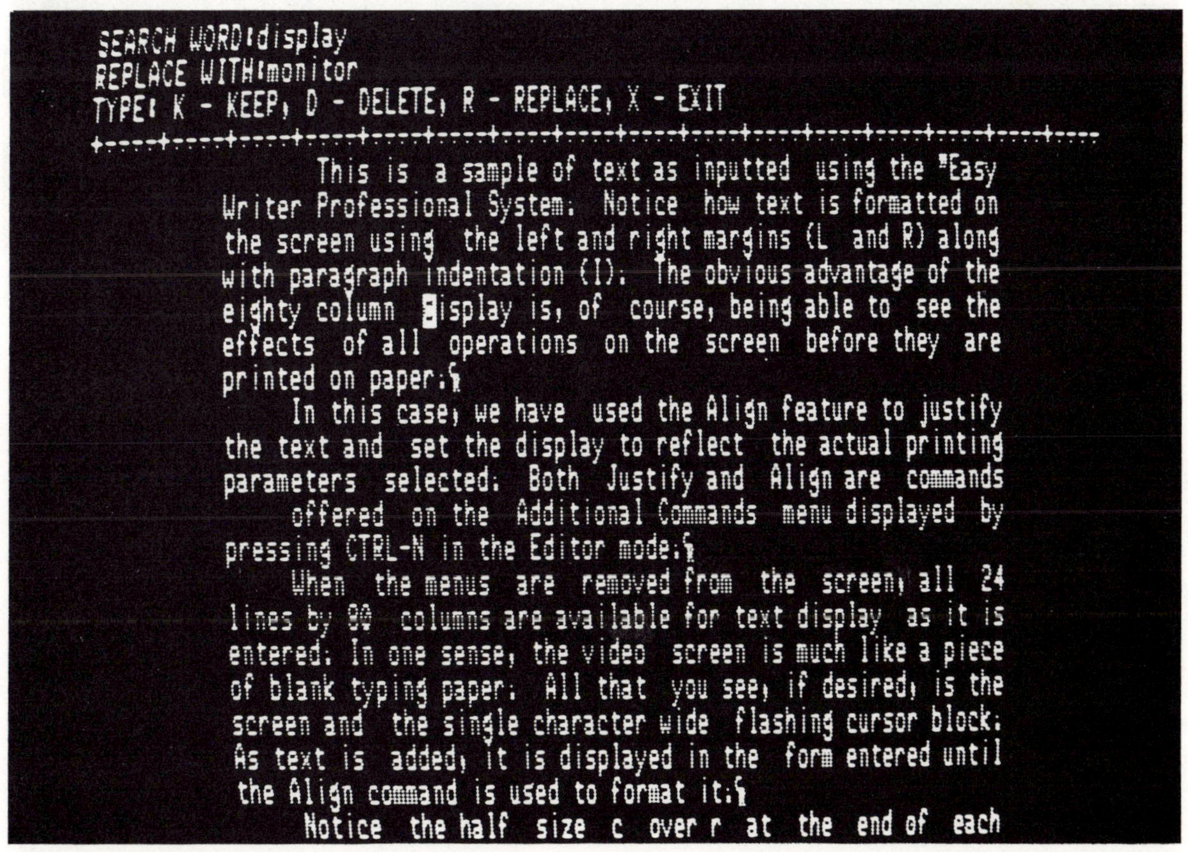

Fig. 8-9. Replacing only some occurrences of the search word or phrase is controlled by the commands shown above the scale line.

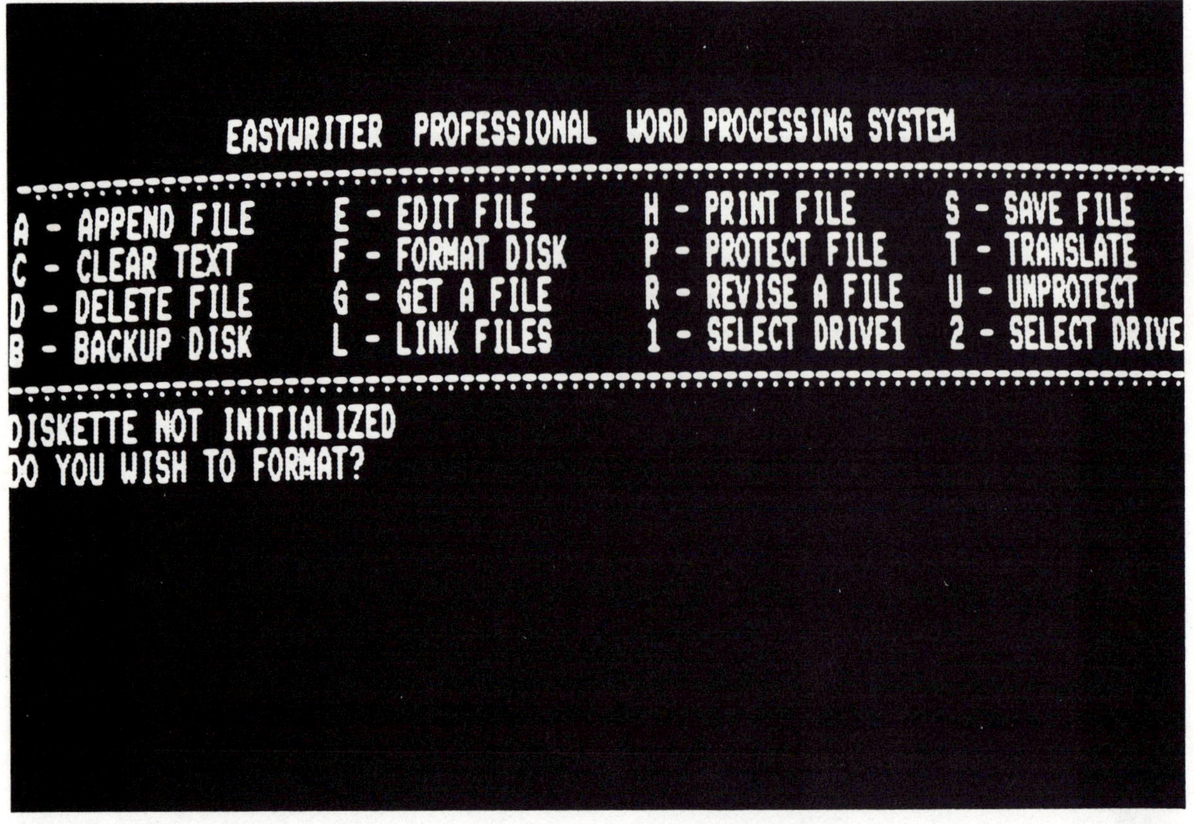

Fig. 8-10. The disk system help menu lists commands available for disk operations.

(translate) allows you to update text files from earlier EasyWriter versions to the current format. H (print) and L (link) will be discussed in the output section.

If you are using multiple data disks to locate or save a file, each disk may be catalogued by pressing the space bar after it is inserted into whichever drive is currently in use.

OUTPUT

Printer Configuration. On first use of the program or by pressing C after subsequent boots, printer configuration and other program parameters can be defined. After asking which 80-column display you are using, the program requests specific information regarding your printer. First, you must identify the slot in which the printer interface card is located. Next, you are asked to select your printer from the following list:

1. Diablo/Qume
2. Spinwriter
3. Proportional
4. Other
5. Spinwriter (5530)

After designating your printer type (using the guidelines in the program manual), you are asked to answer a series of questions regarding your printer's capabilities. Auto line feed, form feed, bidirectional printing, shift key modifications, and parity status are requested (Fig. 8-12). Finally, you are directed to identify the type of printer interface card you are using. If a custom machine-language printer interface program is required to operate your printer, it can be loaded to the EasyWriter disk using a routine provided in the configuration (Fig. 8-13). Once this process has been completed, it needs to be redone only if changes are made in your system.

Printer Control. EasyWriter Professional System provides for control of special printer features in two ways. Special nonprinting control characters are entered directly in the body of the text by preceding them with a CTRL-O. Commands requiring a number of characters may be used, although each nonprint character must be preceded by CTRL-O.

A user-definable (.USER) command may be used to print special characters not normally available from the Apple keyboard or to send control character sequences to the printer. The program manual does an excellent job of explaining and illustrating the use of both types of .USER commands. New in the latest revision of EasyWriter is a programmable end of line character, required to oper-

ate special printer features. Samples of commands for the Centronics 737, Sanders Media 12/7, and Epson MX-80 and MX-100 are provided in the manual.

Initiating Printing. Printing is requested from either the disk system (by pressing H) or the editor (by pressing CTRL-P). Since printing starts immediately after receiving the command, be sure your printer is turned on and the paper is aligned before selecting the print mode.

Justification. When you have specified justification in the text, the standard word-spacing justification is used. This program will support the use of printer capable of justifying proportionally spaced characters through its own software. In this case, control codes must be sent to the printer for setting margins, line length, character font, and so on. To use this capability, you select the propor-

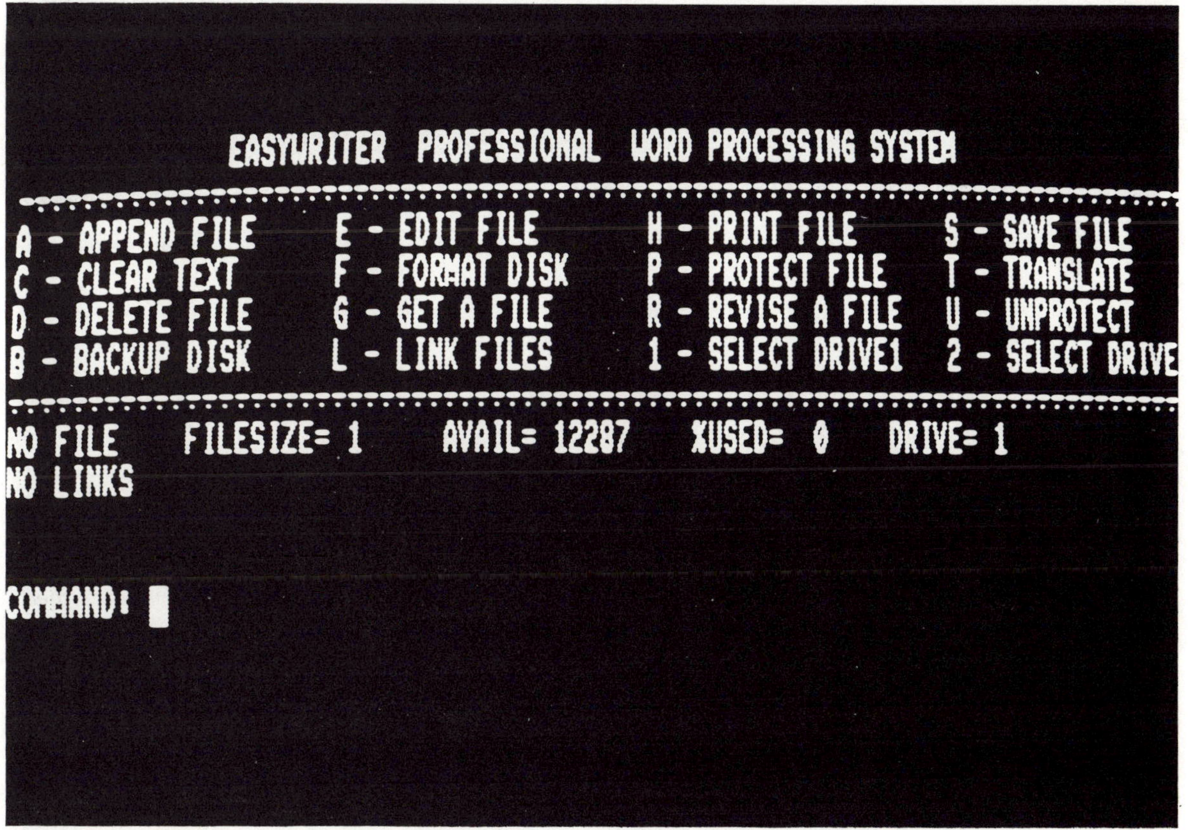

Fig. 8-11. File status is displayed along with commands in the help menu when cataloging a disk.

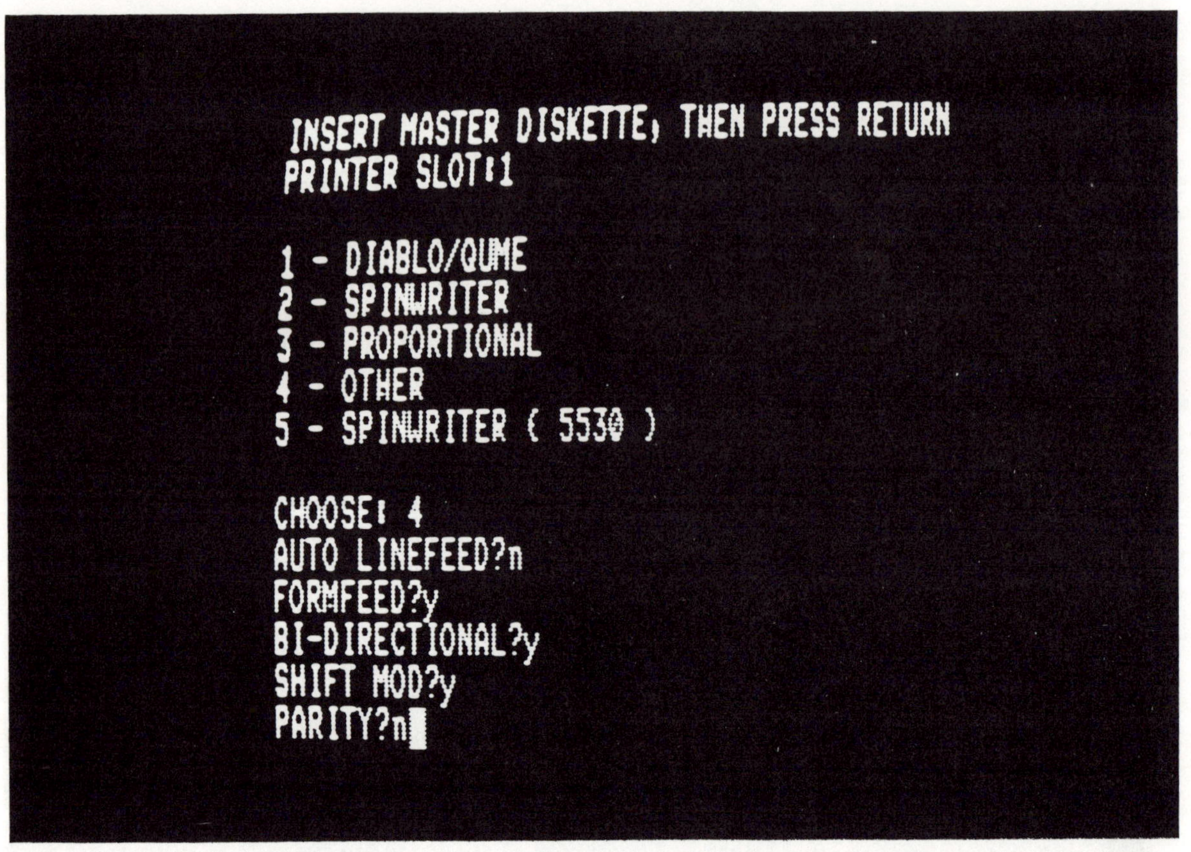

Fig. 8-12. The first printer configuration menu asks for specific information about the type of printer you will be using.

tional option in the configuration routine. Easy Writer Professional System correctly does not transmit carriage returns and line feeds when operating in the proportional mode.

Headers, Footers, and Page Numbers. Up to three headers or footers may be included on each page. Embedded commands of the form .TITLEA,row,text are used to specify both the location and text for each of the desired titles. Spacing from the left margin is determined by the number of spaces entered following the row comma and preceding the actual text. If no spaces are included, headers or footers will begin printing at the left margin. Titles can be changed in the text at will or deleted by retyping the title command with no text following the row number.

Page numbering is selected from the additional commands menu by typing the letter P. The pro-gram will ask for the beginning page number and start numbering the text. The embedded .PAGE, row,column command will determine the location on the printed page where the number will appear. Adding a second column number to the page command allows for different numbering locations on alternate pages. Numbering is suppressed by the command .PAGE 0,0.

Forms Control. The length and width of forms are specified in the default format file and are modified by properly embedded commands. By default, EasyWriter Professional System assumes that you will be printing on continuous paper and will not need a pause between sheets. To force a pause for single sheets, the command .FORMSTOP should be embedded in the beginning of the document. With .FORMSTOP in effect, pressing the space bar will resume the printing operation after a new sheet of paper is inserted. To return to printing on continuous forms, type .FORMSTOPOFF.

Printer Problems. No provisions are included in the program for response to error indications generated by the printer.

Print Mode Display. Text is readied for the printing process by using embedded or default values for margins, indentation, page length, tabs, and so on. HMI (horizontal motion index) character spacing is also adjustable from within the program.

Once you have completed work on your text file, alignment is done to visualize the final printed appearance by selecting A (align) from the additional commands menu. If there are some areas of the text that you do not want realigned, they must be protected from this command by using special markers that are available.

During the printing process, a temporary pause results from pressing X. Printing operations halt until the space bar is pressed. Two presses of X will stop the printing operation in progress. Pressing the left arrow twice will slow down the printing process, and the right arrow returns it to normal output speed. Internal pauses may be programmed into a file using a CTRL-Q,CTRL-S embedded commands. In this case, printing will pause until another key is pressed.

Multiple Files of Copies. There are no provisions for printing multiple copies of a file. Several files may be linked together (using the link capability of the disk system) for the purpose of printing a document longer than that permitted by one file on the disk.

HUMAN ENGINEERING

Logical, Easy to Use Commands. Easy-Writer Professional System is one of the few word-processing programs I have seen that func-

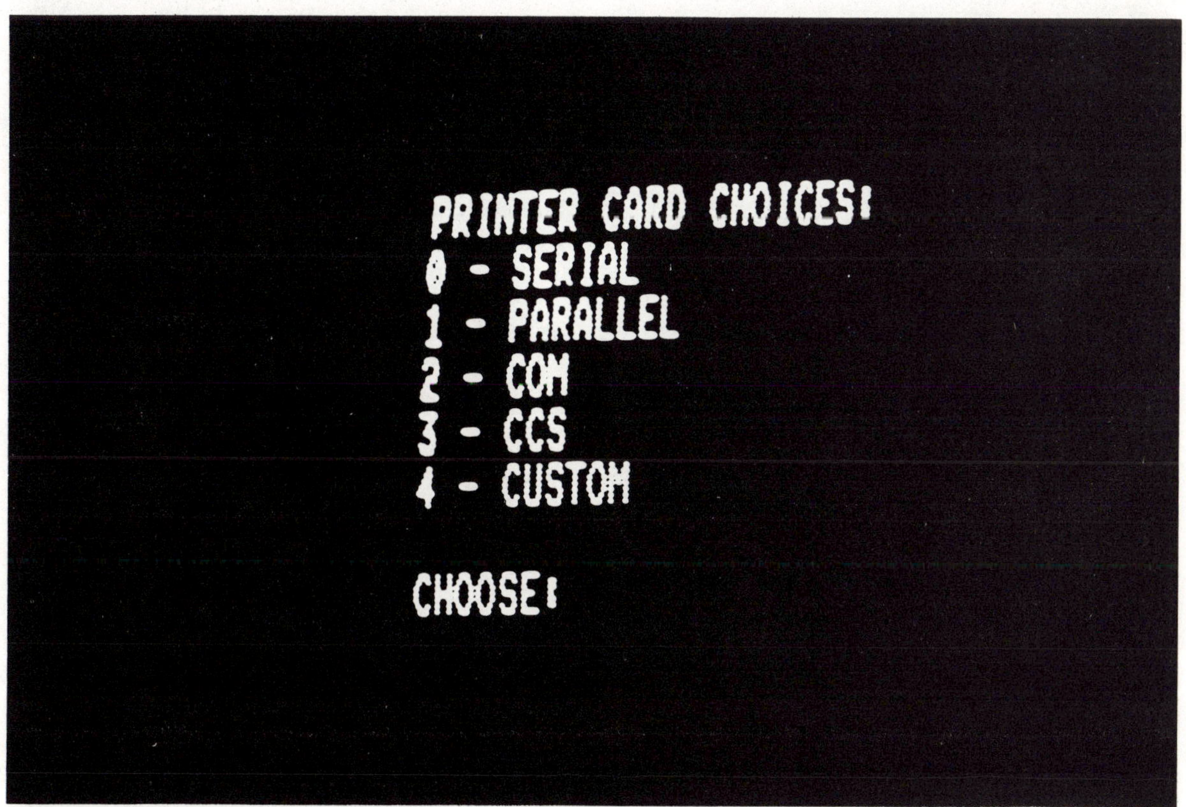

Fig. 8-13. Printer interface information is entered by making a choice from this menu.

tions effectively on two levels. If you are a more sophisticated user you can pretty much go your own way without a lot of interference from excessively wordy menus and unnecessary frills. Beginners will appreciate the provisions for having all commands displayed and accessible at all times.

Most of the commands are logical and easy to use. The only area of possible exception is that of block operations. Confusing commands and a large number of steps to accomplish relatively simple operations are not in keeping with the quality of the rest of the program.

Verification of Potentially Dangerous Commands. Beginners should have few qualms about using this program, from a standpoint of potential data loss. Effective verification requests are made at virtually every step where data could be inadvertently deleted or changed. Even those of us with a little more experience have often breathed a huge sigh of relief when given a chance to back away from an operation we really hadn't intended to initiate.

Error Recovery and Emergency Procedures. A section of the manual is devoted to error recovery and emergency recovery procedures. Three areas are covered: accidental reset, power failure, and damaged disks. While that may cover 95% of the potential problem areas, there are other possible problems that are not mentioned. The most important concept presented in the section is: Back up data disks frequently.

DOCUMENTATION

User's Manual. The manual included with EasyWriter Professional System is, in many ways, a welcome relief from the tedious tutorials furnished with almost every other program these days. Tutorials are great for beginners, but after an initial trip through all the lessons, reviewing the particulars of just a command or two can be confusing if the tutorial is not properly constructed. The Easy Writer Professional System manual presents commands in a logical sequence and defines each command well enough so you know how to use it. The index and table of contents help to quickly locate a specific command for review. Lest you think beginners have been neglected, a short tutorial introducing word processing to beginners is included in this manual.

Reference Material. An information card, listing all the commands and some syntax requirements, is included. The effective use of on-screen menus all but eliminates the need for this reference card once the program has been used a few times. Labels for data disks are also included (a nice touch).

SUPPORT

An extra copy of the program disk is included in the program package, along with order forms for a replacement or back-up disk. Owners can purchase revisions or updates to the system at a nominal cost.

Warranty coverage for the program disk is provided for 90 days, during which time replacements may be obtained for defective disks at no cost. After 90 days, defective disks are replaced for $20.00. Enhancements and upgrades are furnished at a discount as they become available.

On the occasions I have had to contact Information Unlimited Software by telephone for answers to questions or problems, I have found them extremely helpful. There is certainly no reason to think your experience should be any different.

IMPRESSIONS

EasyWriter Professional System is a no-nonsense word-processing system designed, as the name implies, for the professional user. Although beginners can learn to use it, most of the features included are oriented to the professional writer who demands an essentially utilitarian approach to word processing.

Personally, I like the way the program and documentation are set up. A lot of the marginally useful features found in other systems are noticeably lacking, but what remains is a real workhorse that will do what you want it to with a minimum of fuss.

## Chapter 9

Printers, Hardware, and Supplies

For successful word-processing operations you will need some hardware and supplies, particularly a printer. The capabilities and features offered by your printer will often determine the total success of an entire system. The end product is produced by the printer. No matter how sophisticated the rest of your system is, it is the finished appearance of the impressions on paper produced by the printer that determines how the recipient will judge both you and your operation.

COMPUTERS

Microcomputers, so far, have been treated in a rather generic sense. A microcomputer uses a processing chip designed for 8- or, more recently, 16-byte words. Memory has traditionally been limited to 48K or 64K, although ingenious methods of getting around that limitation (such as software selected "banks" of memory and frequently used program routines in ROM) are routinely being used today.

Most computers suitable for word processing have a keyboard capable of producing all the standard characters and a video interface, or display, capable of showing them. Some method of attaching a printer must be provided. This leaves the field pretty wide open, doesn't it? There are word-processing programs available for virtually every computer on the market.

In addition to the Apple II, some of the more popular computers for word-processing applications include the TRS-80 Models II and III from Radio Shack. The TRS-80 Model III (Fig. 9-1) is a relatively low cost, expandable computer that has proven to be a very popular choice for word-processing applications. The Model III will hold up to 48K memory, an RS-232 interface, and two disk drives in its integral keyboard and video display cabinet. The TRS-80 Model II (Fig. 9-2) is a very capable business machine. Capable of handling 64K memory and multiple 8-inch disk drives, this unit features a professional video display and keyboard.

I will not attempt to offer guidelines for computer selection here, except for those features that pertain directly to word processing. There are many excellent books and periodicals that can help

Fig. 9-1. The TRS-80 Model III. (Courtesy of Radio Shack, a division of Tandy Corp.)

you make an intelligent selection from the ever-increasing number of excellent small computers on the market. From a word-processing viewpoint, the following features are necessary in a computer:

1. Keyboard with all standard characters accessible, preferably including functional shift keys for upper- and lowercase selection.

2. Some method of video display that allows you to see on-screen what is happening in the computer's memory. Most microcomputers include this capability, although not many approach the standard 24-line by 80-character display.

3. Enough memory capacity to allow use of a word-processing program and reasonably long text files.

4. Some form of external storage system for program and text files. Most often, this takes the form of a 5-and-1/4-inch "mini-floppy" disks.

5. The ability to output text to a printer for finalization of the word-processing operations.

ADD-ONS

If your computer can meet most of the word-processing criteria, add-on peripherals can help it to meet the rest. For example, the unmodified Apple II is capable of dealing only with uppercase letters. Many inexpensive lowercase adapters allow both upper- and lowercase characters to be displayed. With the Apple, the screen is capable of displaying 24 lines of 40 characters in width. Wider line displays, up to 80 characters, may be obtained through the use of plug-in adapters (Figs. 9-3 and 9-4) or generated (in some cases) by the word-processing program itself.

Similar add-ons are available for most of the popular microcomputers presently on the market. If your computer is capable of handling most of your business or personal applications, chances are that you can successfully use it for word-processing programs.

PRINTERS

The ultimate producer of word-processing operations is the printer. No matter how sophisticated the program or efficient its operations, the appearance of printed output is often the sole criteria of quality applied by the recipient. It's kind of like the scorecard used in a golf game; there are spaces provided only for the scores, not detailed explanations of how they were obtained. This is as it should be. The final product of any word-processing operation should look like it was flawlessly produced, regardless of the method employed to do so.

Computer printers are described in categories denoting the number of characters printed at a time and the method of transferring those characters to paper. Line printers have several print actuators, usually one for each print column, fired concurrently. Full lines are printed once they are received in the printer line buffer from the data source. Serial

Fig. 9-2. The TRS-80 Model II microcomputer. (Courtesy of Radio Shack, a division of Tandy Corp.)

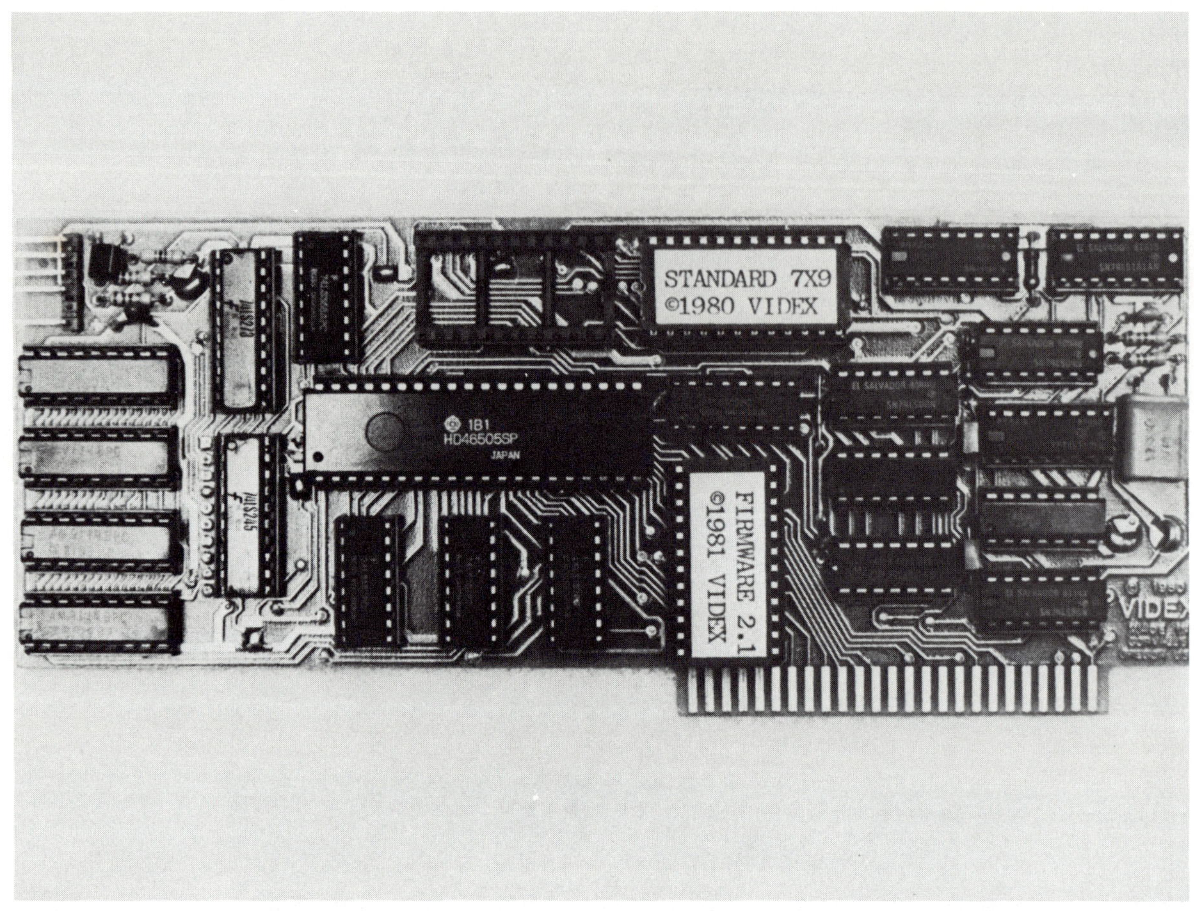

Fig. 9-3. An 80-column display can be obtained on the Apple II by using a plug-in card such as the one manufactured by Videx.

printers, on the other hand, have one print head moving to print a character in each column. Depending on the speed of the printer, characters may be printed as received or stored in a data buffer for printing on a delayed basis.

Both line and serial printers can be divided into categories depending on their method of transferring an image to paper. Impact printers, probably the most common example of which is the typewriter, operate by having the character strike an inked ribbon, which in turn makes an impact on the paper and leaves an impression. Nonimpact units do not actually strike the paper but use other methods of leaving an image. Further subdivision is possible by describing the method of character production. Impact line printers may use embossed drums, print wheels, moving chains, trains, belts, or bands. Nonimpact line printers may use electrostatic heads, ink jets, or laser beams.

Serial printers may also be divided into impact and nonimpact groups, with methods of character production differing somewhat from those of the line printers. Impact character production in serial units is most commonly accomplished by formed character print elements (daisy wheels, "golf balls," or thimbles) or dot-matrix heads. Nonimpact printers are most often thermal, electrostatic, or ink jet based.

Speed ratings, stated in LPM (lines per minute) for line printers and CPS (characters per second) for serial units, are commonly used as yardsticks for measuring the suitability of a printer for a particular application. Line printer speeds range from 300 to over 20,000 LPM, while serial printers commonly operate in the range of 15 to 900 CPS.

The line printer is best suited for applications involving large quantities of printing at premium speeds. Prices for this type of printer start in the vicinity of $5000 and can run well over $200,000. Few small businesses and even fewer computer hobbyists have either the applications or the financial resources necessary to justify the purchase of a line printer.

Serial printers are available in many configurations that are suited to the lower printing volume applications typical of most (if not all) micro-computer-based word-processing system users. Prices start at well under $1000 and are decreasing because of increased competition. All but the most deluxe serial units cost less than the lowest priced line printers.

Printer Interfacing. In order to use a printer with your computer, some method of interfacing must be employed. Printers are designed to receive data from your computer either through a serial (one bit at a time) or parallel (eight bits at a time) interface, although an increasing number of printers are available with either configuration (or both) as options. Most small computers are capable of supporting either serial or parallel interface devices when equipped with the proper hardware. The Apple, for instance, offers both serial and parallel interface cards as plug-in accessories. Some computers are supplied with one or the other type of printer interface built in.

It is incumbent on you and your computer supplier to be sure that your word-processing pro-

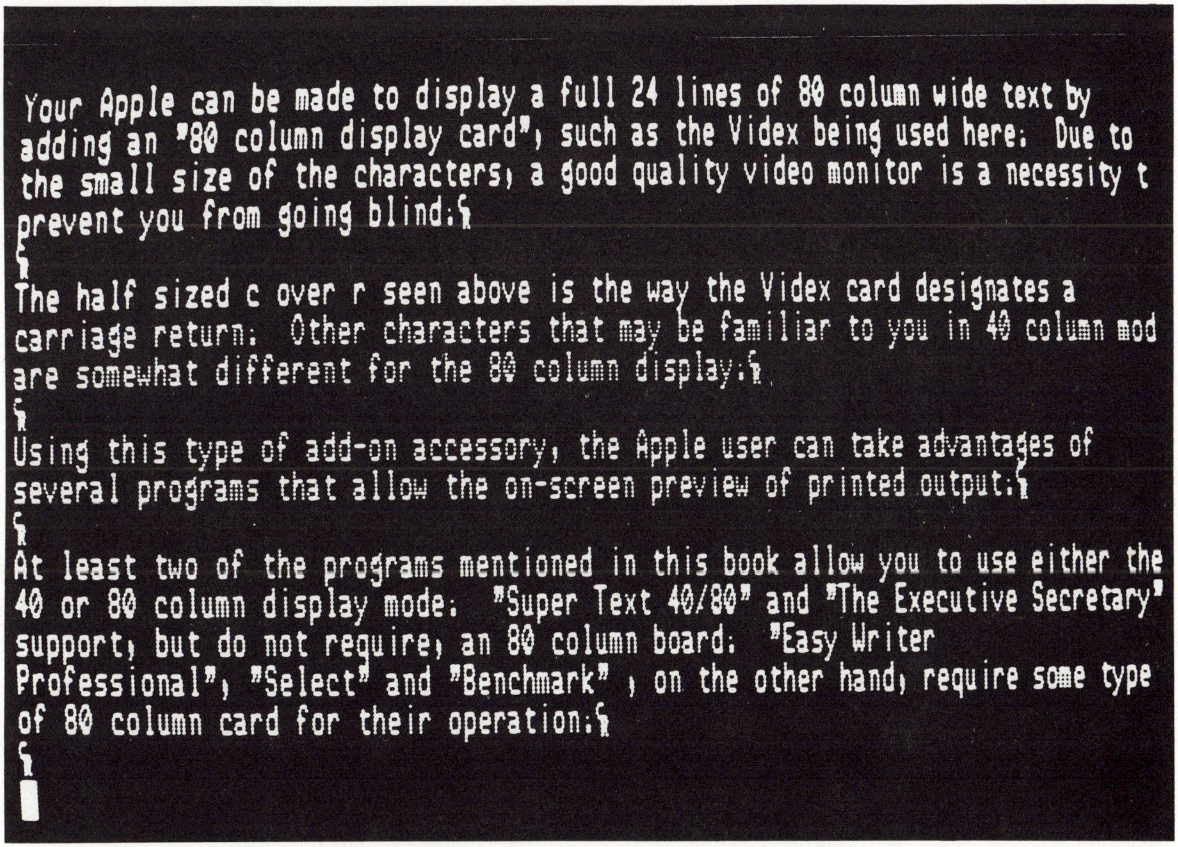

Fig. 9-4. The standard 24-by-80 video display as generated by the Videx plug-in card.

gram, compute, and printer are all compatible in terms of the type of printer interface they will support. Choose carefully and you should experience no compatibility problems.

PRINTER CHARACTERISTICS

There are some general characteristics of printers that you will want to consider before looking at the information on specific units.

Print Quality. This is one of the most important characteristics for most word-processing applications. Highest quality print is obtained through the use of formed character elements such as type balls, daisy wheels, or thimbles. Dot-matrix printers are a close second in this area, and the gap is narrowing. Promising new developments, such as low-priced ink jets, voice coil-controlled stylus, and laser xerography, will undoubtedly enhance the print quality of dot-matrix units in the future.

Speed. Speed and print quality are inversely proportional. Those printers producing the highest quality output are significantly slower than those designed for less precise character production. Speed ratings must be read carefully, however, since both CPS and LPM figures can vary considerably with character density, line length, and duty cycle. Bidirectional printing capability significantly increases the throughput LPM, since no time is lost while the print head returns to the first print column after each line. Logic-seeking printing capability further increases throughput, since no time is wasted on blank lines or spaces.

Paper Handling. Pressure feed systems handle either single sheets or rolls of paper. Pin or tractor feed systems require perforated paper stock to operate properly. Several units now on the market offer both feed methods, while others can be equipped for the method of your choice. Nonimpact printers usually require specially treated, paper, while most impact units use plain paper. Vertical formatting, either by switch selection or under software control, is a commonly offered feature.

Character Format. Variable-size character fonts are offered in the majority of printers presently on the market, however, different methods are used to accomplish the size change. Inter-changeable print elements are used in the formed character units, while dot-matrix print sizes are varied by a switch or software selection. Graphics capability enables you to select from an almost infinite variety of fonts, since the printer is able to reproduce almost anything generated on your video display. At the very least, your printer must offer the full 96 ASCII characters to be useful for word-processing applications.

Other printer features to watch for include built-in self-test, memory buffer size and expand-ability, available options, service policies, warranty, and reliability data.

PRINTER SPECIFICS

Printers can be divided into two broad categories according to their method of producing characters. Within the formed character and dot-matrix groups, I will describe and illustrate several of the more popular units on the market today. Printer technology is changing rapidly, and newer and better versions of many of these printers will probably be available by the time you read this. The illustrations will serve to show the range and extent of features available for word-processing printers.

Formed Character Printers

This group includes all the printers that use a character element to produce letters. The most popular types of print elements are daisy wheels, type balls, or thimbles. The print, or daisy wheel is the closest to being an industry standard and is used in more formed character printers than any other type of element.

Numerous character fonts are available for printers of this type and may readily be interchanged in most printers. Ribbons are usually contained in some type of cartridge carrier that is easily replaced.

Starwriter/Starwriter II. These two printer models (Fig. 9-5) look identical and, in many ways, perform in the same fashion. Using standard daisy wheel, the Starwriter prints at 25 CPS, while the Starwriter II speeds along at 45. Both printers handle paper up to 15 inches wide and print up to 136 columns per sheet. Either serial or parallel interfacing is available.

Manufacturer: C. Itoh Electronics, Inc., P.O. Box 66903, Los Angeles, CA 90066.

Diablo Model 620. The new, third generation Model 620 printer (Fig. 9-6) from Diablo offers up to 25 CPS bidirectional printing using "drop-in" printwheels with automatic "self-homing" positioners. Bidirectional paper and carriage movement permits plotting and graphic output from programs with these capabilities. Serial interfacing is required, with data transmission speeds switch selected at either 110 or 300 baud.

Manufacturer: Diablo Systems, Incorporated, 24500 Industrial Boulevard, P.O. Box 5003, Hayward, CA 94545.

3500 Spinwriter™ Printer. The new 3500 series of formed character printers (Fig. 9-7) uses the popular NEC print thimbles. These thimbles resemble a daisy wheel except the petals are not folded completely back. Numerous character fonts are offered in the thimble configuration. The 3500 series of printers will print at speeds of up to 33 characters per second on paper that is a maximum of 16 inches wide. Several forms handling and ribbon cartridge options are offered. Most of the popular enhancement features (bold printing, underlining, offset printing, super- and subscripts) are supported by the printer. Either parallel or serial interfacing may be specified by ordering the appropriate model from the 3500 series.

Manufacturer: NEC Information Systems, Inc., 5 Militia Drive, Lexington, MA 02173.

F-10 Printmaster. The Printmaster (Fig. 9-8) is one of the newest daisy wheel printers on the market. Compact size, low noise operation, and

Fig. 9-5. The Starwriter /Starwriter II daisy wheel printer. (Courtesy of C. Itoh Electronics.)

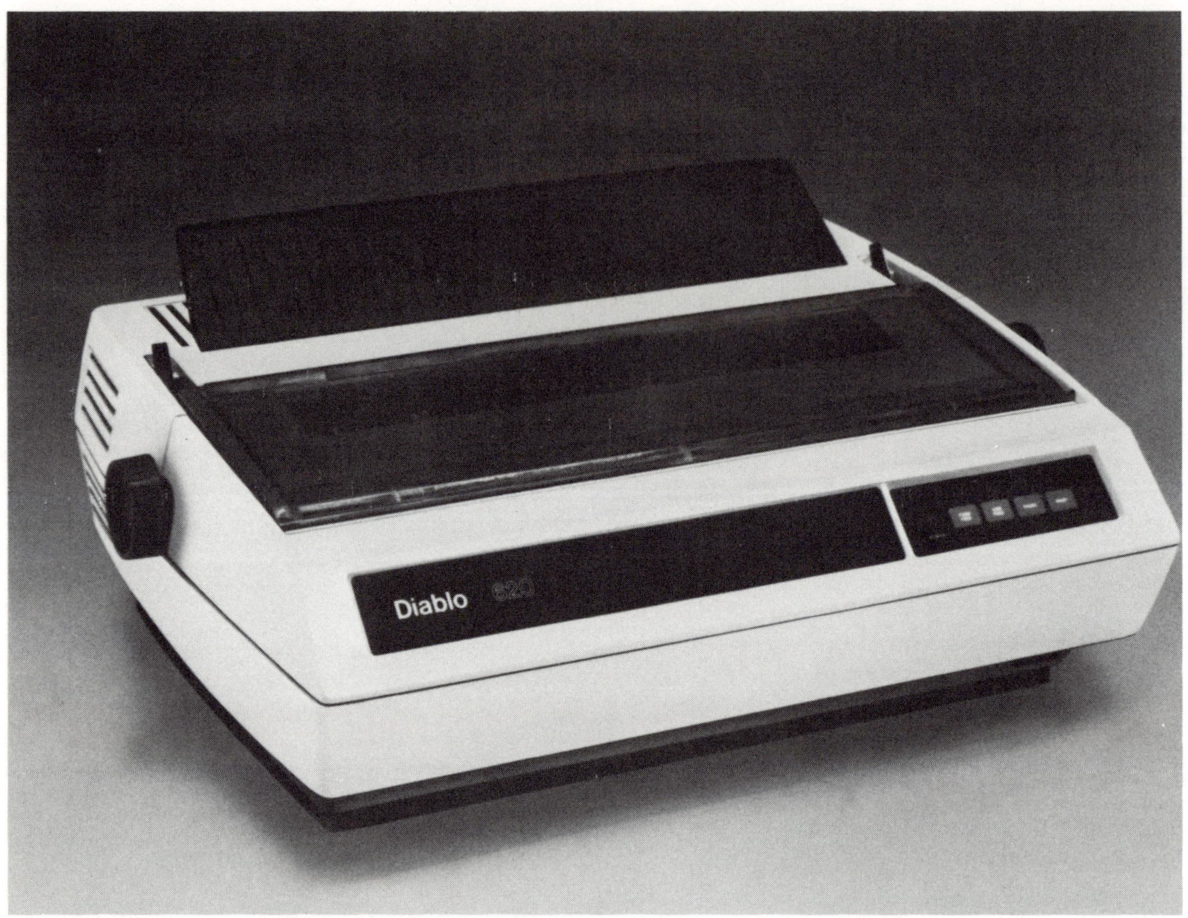

Fig. 9-6. The Diablo Model 620 formed character printer. (Courtesy of Diablo Systems, Inc.)

built-in special features make this one of the most interesting new units available. Many word-processing functions, such as special characters and proportional spacing, are built into the printer's electronics. The ability to use standard print wheels and ribbon cartridges insures a steady supply of competitively priced materials. Serial or parallel interfacing is offered. The F-10 Printmaster is offered in two text speed versions, 40 CPS and 55 CPS.

Manufacturer: C. Itoh Electronics, 5301 Beethoven Street, Los Angeles, CA 90066.

Diablo Model 630 KSR (Fig. 9-9). The 630 KSR is one of the newest members of Diablo's expanding 630 family of 32- to 40-CPS formed character printers. The 630 KSR offers a comprehensive set of terminal communications capabilities which include a 16-byte input buffer, expanded 2,688-byte print buffer, word-processing firmware features, extensive diagnostics for host control, and serial transmission rates ranging from 110 to 9600 baud.

Manufacturer: Diablo Systems, Incorporated, 24500 Industrial Boulevard, P.O. Box 5003, Hayward, CA 94545.

Dot-Matrix Printers

Printers which fall into the dot-matrix method of generating characters show a very wide range of capabilities. Print qualities run from excellent to

158

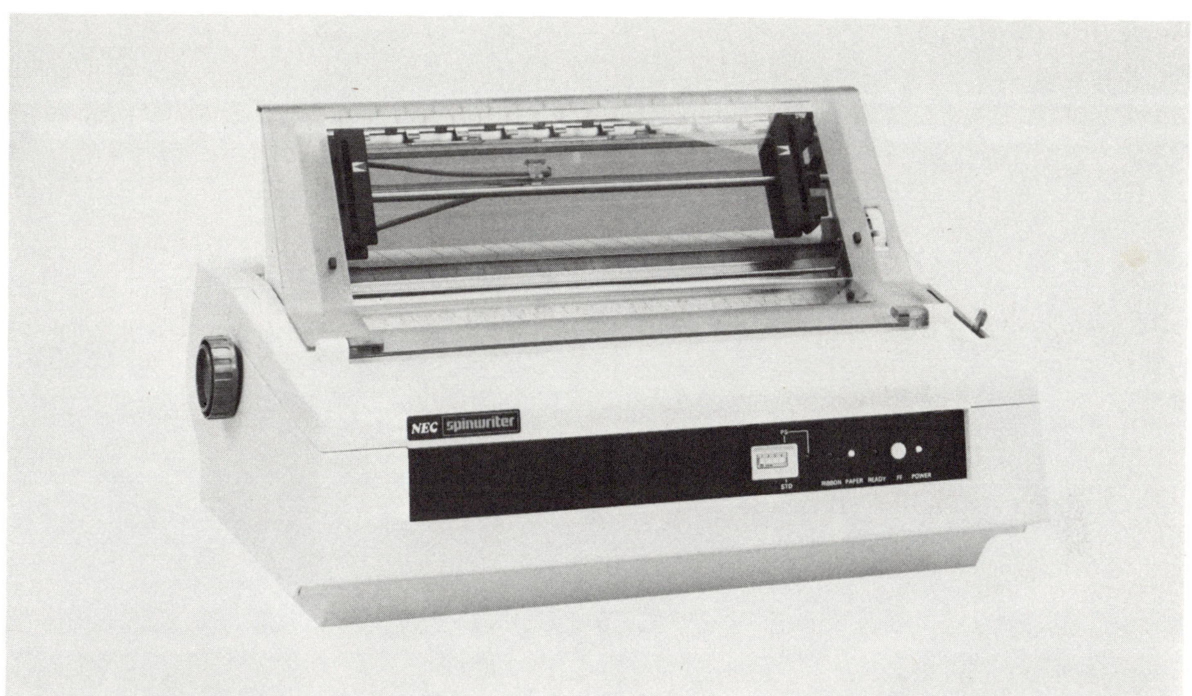

Fig. 9-7. The NEC 3500 Spinwriter uses a formed character thimble to produce letter-quality output. (Courtesy of NEC Information Systems and Hutchins Photography, Inc.)

Fig. 9-8. C. Itoh's F-10 Printmaster daisy wheel printer. (Courtesy of C. Itoh Electronics.)

Fig. 9-9. The Diablo Model 630 KSR formed character printer /terminal. (Courtesy of Diablo Systems, Inc.)

barely legible, speed from very fast to moderately slow, and special features from multitudinous to nonexistent. This segment of the printer market is growing by leaps and bounds. Tomorrow's printers will be more capable and cheaper than those available today, and today's printers are light years ahead of those available five years ago. Competition for consumer dollars is particularly acute in this segment of the printer market, so be alert for new and improved versions.

DIP-95. The DIP-95 (Fig. 9-10) is the top-of-the-line unit in a series that includes several other models. This printer incorporates a 9-by-9 and 11-by-9 dot-matrix configuration to produce lowercase descenders and letter-quality printing, in addition to being able to reproduce graphics. Several charac-

ter sets are offered in software. Bidirectional printing, several paper handling options, and good life expectancy make the DIP line of printers quite interesting.

Manufacturer: DIP, Inc., 745 Atlantic Avenue, Boston, MA 02111.

MPI Model 150G. The MPI printers (Fig. 9-11) offer an interesting switching capability now becoming more common in dot-matrix printers. For data printing, a 7-by-9 matrix is used, and an 11-by-9 matrix is used for correspondence-quality printing. Of course, the data-printing mode is faster than the correspondence-quality mode. Both modes utilize the logic-seeking, bidirectional printing capabilities of the 150G. Special character fonts may be loaded into the printer and selected by a

160

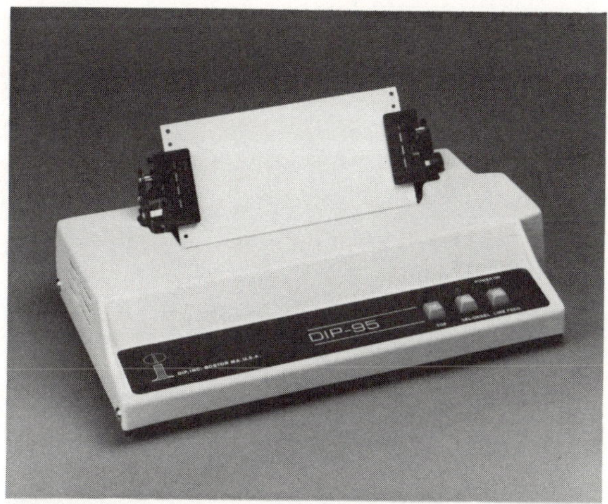

Fig. 9-10. The DIP-95 dot-matrix printer. (Courtesy of DIP, Inc.)

series of switches on the front of the unit. Either parallel or serial interfacing is offered. The 150G represents one of the newest printers on the market and, as such, offers an impressive array of features for a reasonable price.

Manufacturer: Micro Peripherals, Inc., 4426 South Century Drive, Salt Lake City, UT 84107.

Printronix MVP. The MVP is a selectable mode printer that features several important advancements in matrix line printer technology (Fig. 9-12). The MVP is a line printer, because it uses a "hammerbank" rather than a moving print head to produce characters. Three operator or software selectable print modes are offered:

1. Correspondence quality offers a maximum dot density of 100-by-100 per inch and prints at a speed of 80 lines per minute (LPM).

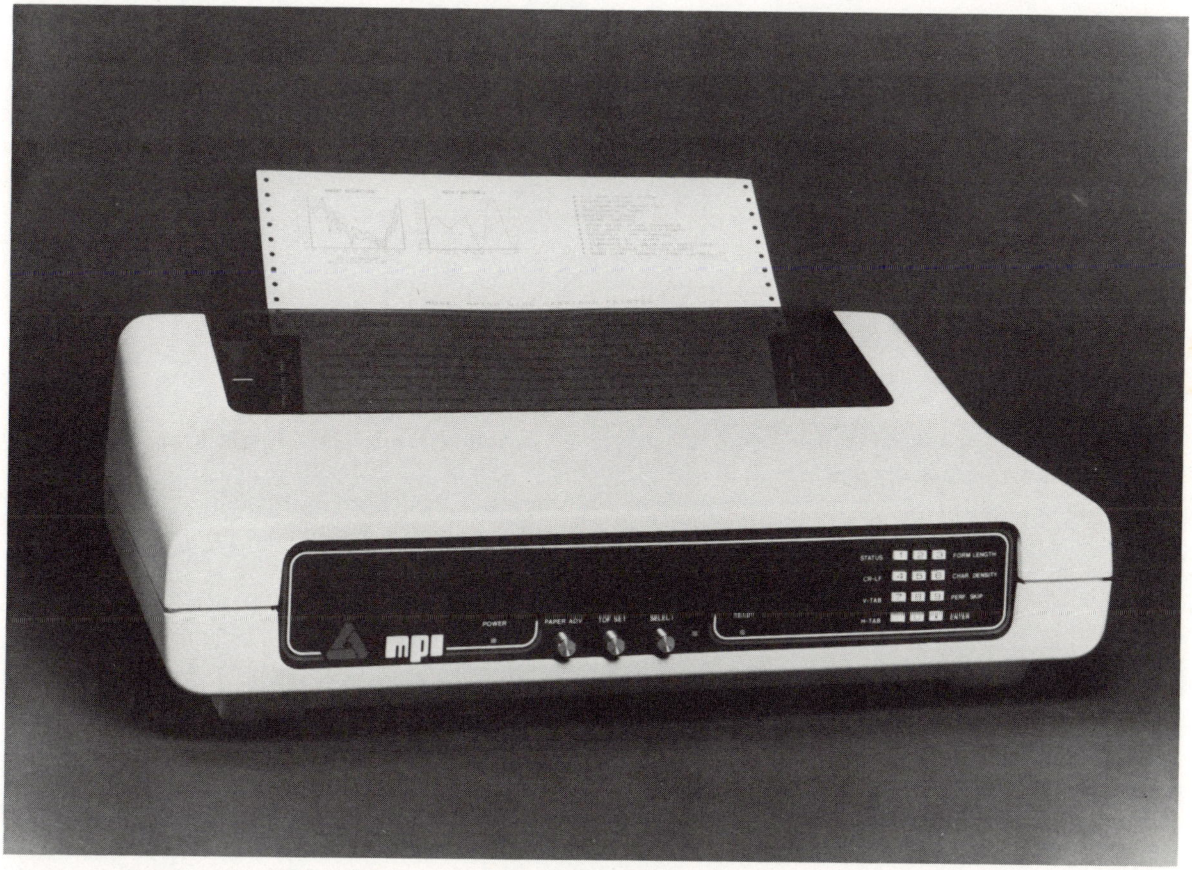

Fig. 9-11. The MPI 150G dot-matrix printer. (Courtesy of Micro Peripherals, Inc.)

Fig. 9-12. The Printronix MVP dot-matrix printer (Courtesy of Printronix, Inc.)

2. Data-processing quality offers a dot density of 60-by-72 dots per inch and prints at 150 LPM.

3. Compressed character printing on reduced format, 66.7-by-66.7 dots per inch, prints at 200 LPM.

Double height printing, character printing, underlining, and vertical formatting are included. A complete repertoire of printing capabilities, including 6-part forms, business graphics, plotting, forms generation, labeling, OCR, and bar codes are offered. Options include special and expanded character sets, multilanguage output, manual forms length selector, and RS-232 interface.

Manufacturer: Printronix, Inc., P.O. Box 19559, Irvine, CA 92713.

Anadex Model DP-9001. From the grafix-PLUS series, the DP-9001 (Fig. 9-13) from Anadex combines high density graphics with correspondence-quality dot-matrix printed characters. Lowercase letters include descenders, and provisions for underlining are included. Print is bidirectional. Four character densities are available: 10 characters per inch (11-by-9 matrix, 120 CPS print speed), 12.5 characters per inch (7-by-9 matrix, 150 CPS), 15 characters per inch (7-by-9 matrix, 180 CPS), and 16.7 characters per inch (7-by-9 matrix, 200 CPS). All four character sets may be printed double width.

A universal interface is built in, as are vertical formatting commands, a 700-character buffer, and self-test mode. Ribbon cartridges have a life expectancy of over 6 million characters. Fanfold paper, fed by form tractors, may range from 1.75 to 9.5 inches wide.

A new and improved version of the DP-9001, the DP-9001A, is now in production. The new model features a redesigned case, quiet operation (54 dB or less), expanded buffer, and a second, high resolution graphics mode featuring up to 150-by-72 dots per inch. Figure 9-14 shows the attractive new case used for the Anadex printer line.

Manufacturer: Anadex, Inc., 9825 DeSoto Avenue, Chatsworth, CA 91311.

Malibu Dual-Mode 200. The 200 is a printer designed for both data- and word-processing applications (Fig. 9-15). For data-processing printing requirements, the Malibu will print all 96 ASCII characters in a standard 9-by-9 font at 165 to 250 CPS. Descenders and underlining are included.

For word-processing use, the letter mode uses a dual-pass technique to produce characters which rival those from formed character printers at speeds of 42 to 70 CPS. A total of six different character fonts can be stored in the computer's ROM, each usable in either the high speed data-processing mode or slower letter-quality mode. In addition, graphics with resolution of 120-by-144 dots per inch can be printed.

Either single sheet or continuous fanfold paper is accepted. Both serial and parallel interfacing are

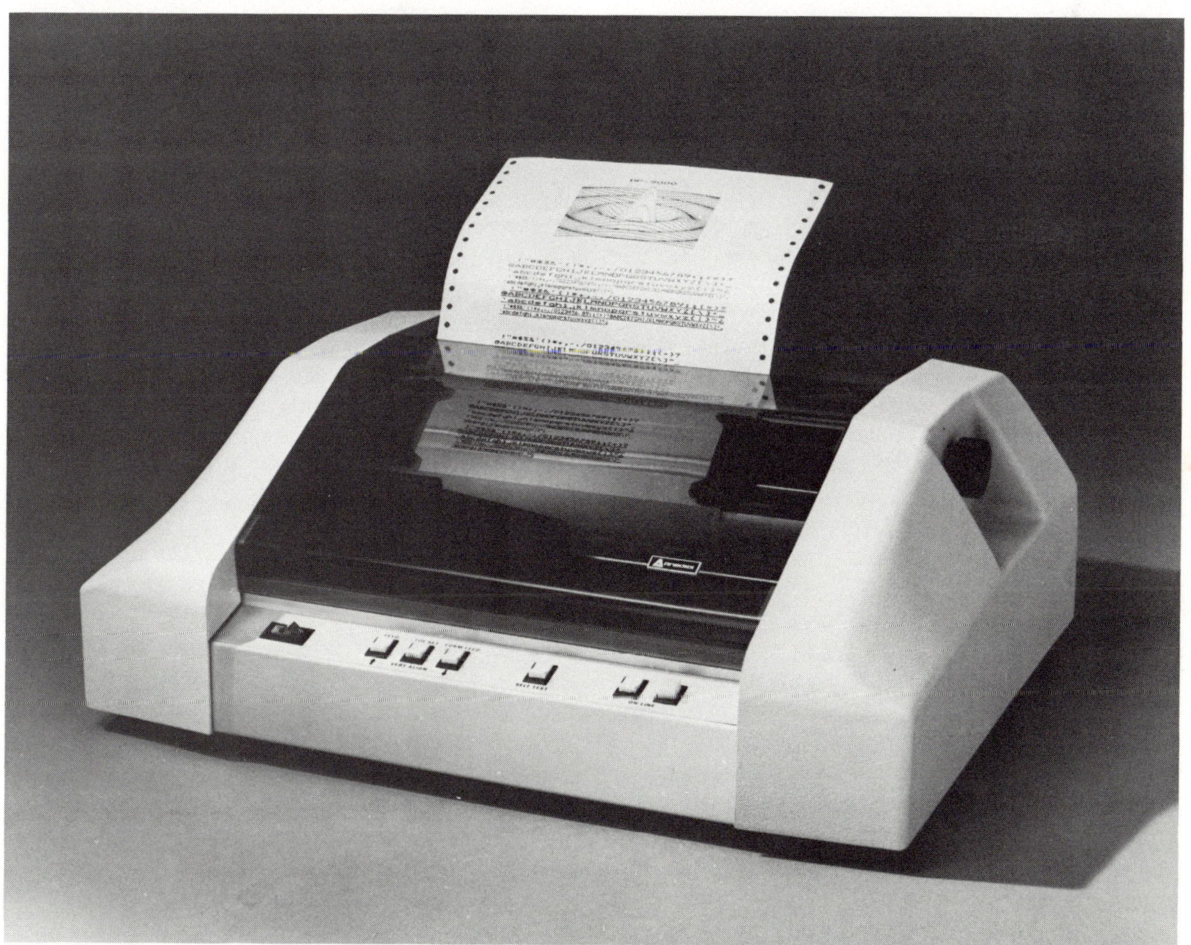

Fig. 9-13. The Anadex DP-9001 dot-matrix printer. (Courtesy of Anadex, Inc.)

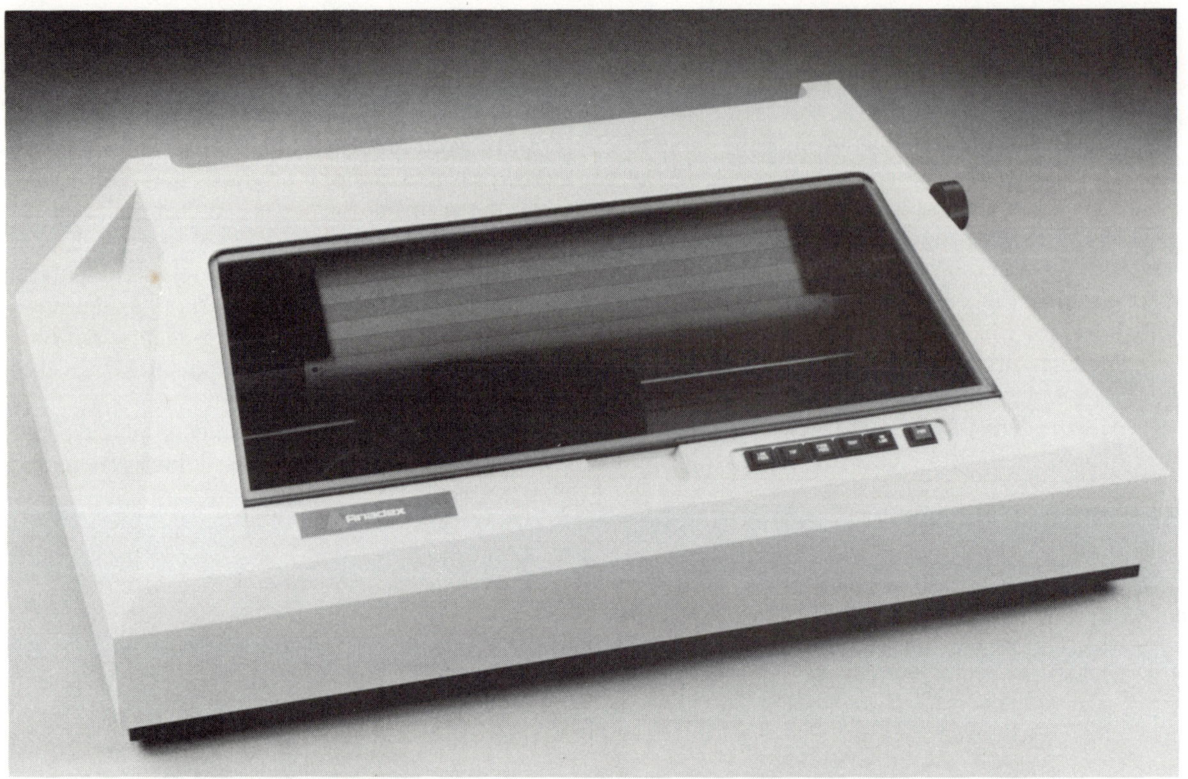

Fig. 9-14. The Anadex A line of printers features a case designed for quiet operation. (Courtesy of Anadex, Inc.)

provided. The ribbon cartridge features a life expectancy of 15 million characters. Full front panel controls are included, although most of the printer's functions can also be software selected.

This printer offers a host of features for the serious word-processing user. You may want to check on current availability if the Malibu appears to meet your needs.

Manufacturer: Malibu Electronics Corporation, 2301 Townsgate Road, Westlake Village, CA 91361.

Florida Data OSP 120 and OSP 130. These printers feature high speed printhead technology, triple paper path, and sophisticated electronics (Fig. 9-16). Print speeds range from 600 CPS in draft mode, 150 CPS in two-pass correspondence, and 100 CPS in three-pass letter-quality mode. Automatic or manual cut sheet or tractor feed modes for sheets up to 15 inches wide are standard. Numerous interface, character fonts, graphics, and accessory options are available.

Manufacturer: Florida Data Corporation, 600 D John Rhodes Blvd., Melbourne, FL 32935.

TRS-80 Printers. Several printers are offered by Radio Shack for the popular TRS-80 series of computers:

1. Line Printer VII (Fig. 9-17) is a low cost unit that features two character fonts (5 or 10 characters per inch, 5-by-7 matrix), and high density graphics printing. Print speed is 30 CPS. Forms tractors are adjustable to accommodate fanfold paper from 4.5 to 9.5 inches wide. Both parallel and serial interfacing schemes are provided.

2. Line Printer VIII (Fig. 9-18) offers many features of interest to word-processing users. Letter-quality monospaced or proportionally spaced characters can be printed in densities ranging from 4.35 to 22.2 characters per inch. The dot-matrix configuration used is 9-by-8. Underlining,

Fig. 9-15. The Malibu Dual-Mode 200 printer. (Courtesy of Malibu Electronics Corporation.)

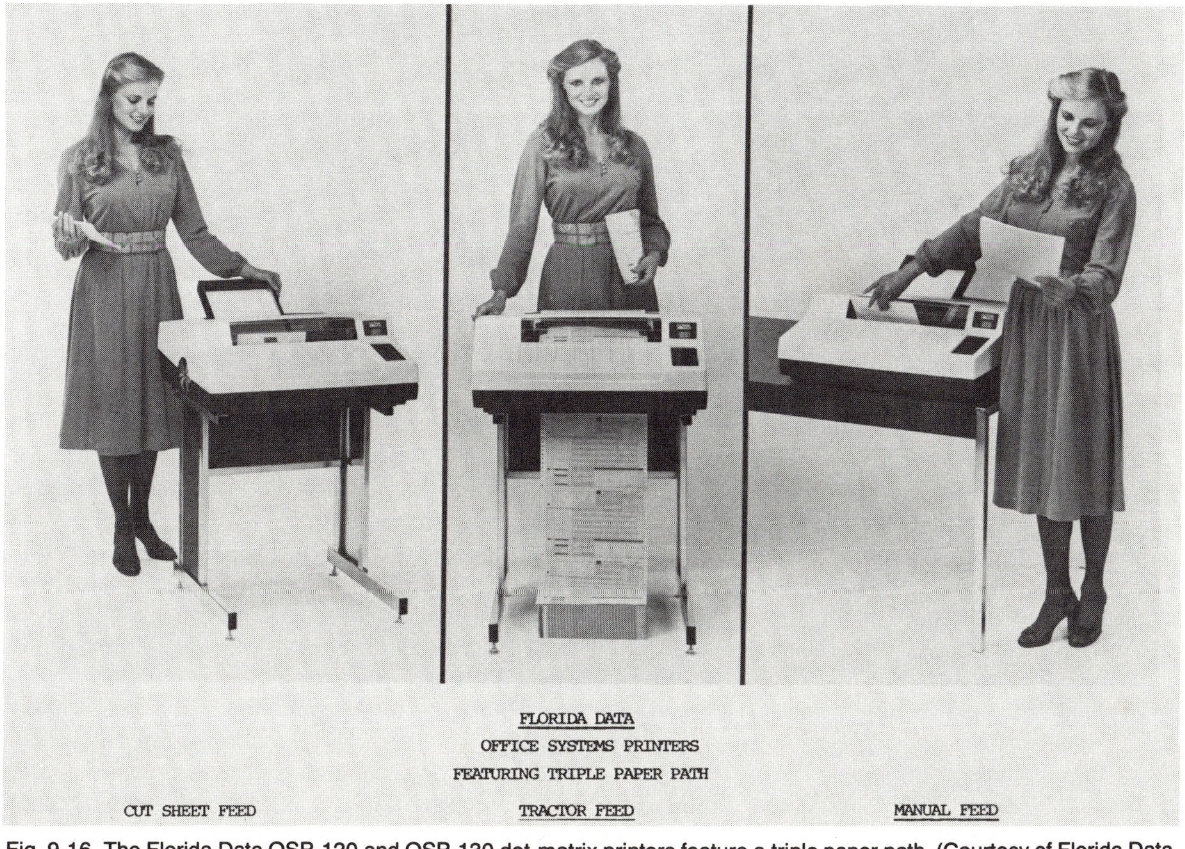

Fig. 9-16. The Florida Data OSP-120 and OSP-130 dot-matrix printers feature a triple paper path. (Courtesy of Florida Data Corporation.)

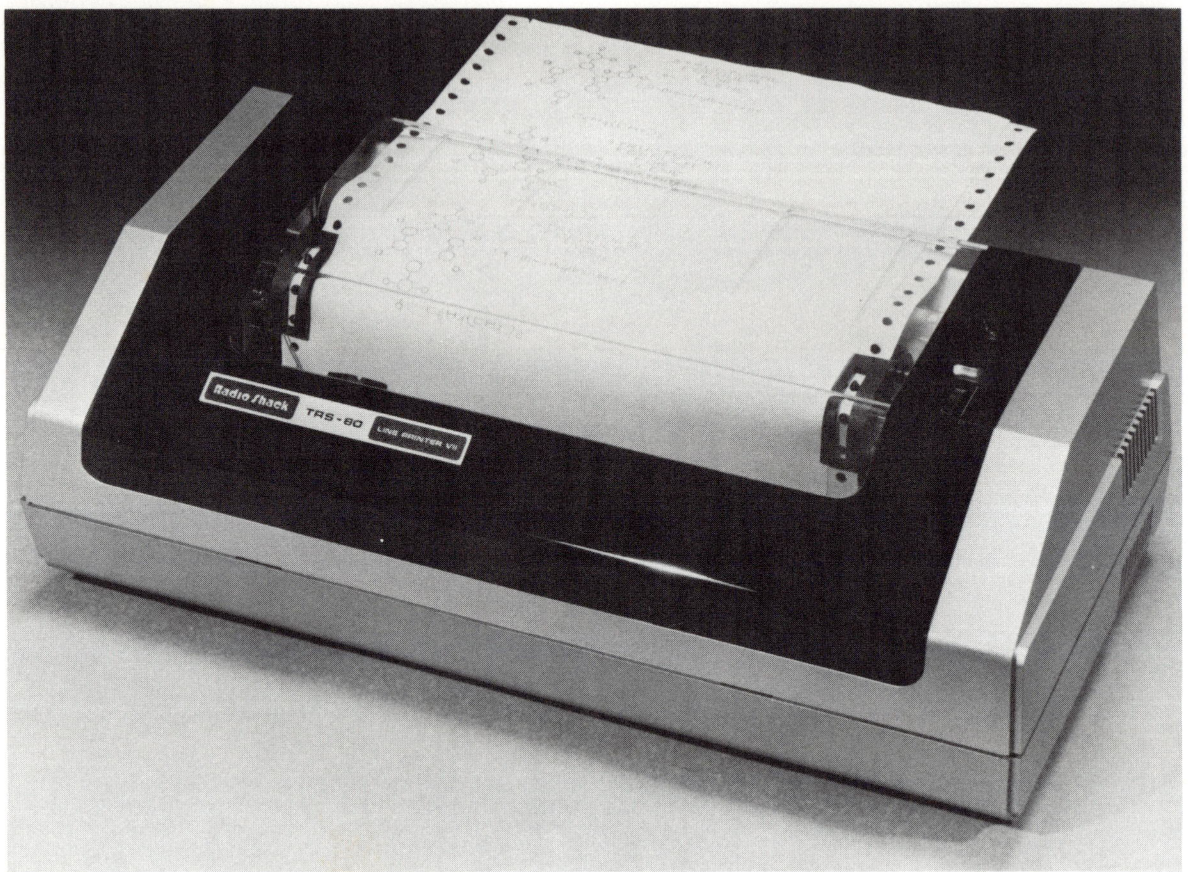

Fig. 9-17. The TRS-80 Line Printer VII. (Courtesy of Radio Shack, a division of Tandy Corp.)

superscripts, subscripts, upper- and lowercase English letters, European symbols, block graphic characters, and selectable parallel or serial interface are included. Fanfold, roll, or single sheet paper of up to 9.5 inches may be used.

3. Line Printer V (Fig. 9-19) is a high speed, bidirectional, logic-seeking printer. Upper- and lowercase characters with descenders can be printed in densities of 5, 7.5, 10, and 15 characters per inch at 160 CPS. A 10-character per inch bold print mode is also included. Underlining, 26 European characters, and 30 graphic patterns are standard. Fanfold paper up to 15 inches wide may be used. Parallel interfacing is used.

Manufacturer: Radio Shack, Inc., 1300 One Tandy Center, Fort Worth, TX 76102.

Prism 80 and Prism 132. The Prism series (Fig. 9-20) from Integral Data Systems represents a unique modular approach to obtaining the printer features you need. The basic Prism, either the 80 (for paper up to 9.5 inches wide) or the 132 (for sheets up to 15 inches wide), offers an impressive array of features.

Standard print densities of 10, 12, and 16.7 characters per inch can be printed in single or double width, mono or proportional spacing. Up to four 96-character sets may reside in the printer at one time. Automatic justification, horizontal and vertical tabbing, reverse paper feed, and inifinite adjustment of character positioning are included. Bidirectional printing at speeds of up to 150 CPS with logic-seeking capability is standard. Fanfold and cut sheet paper-feeding systems are built in. Both serial and parallel interface circuitry is in-

166

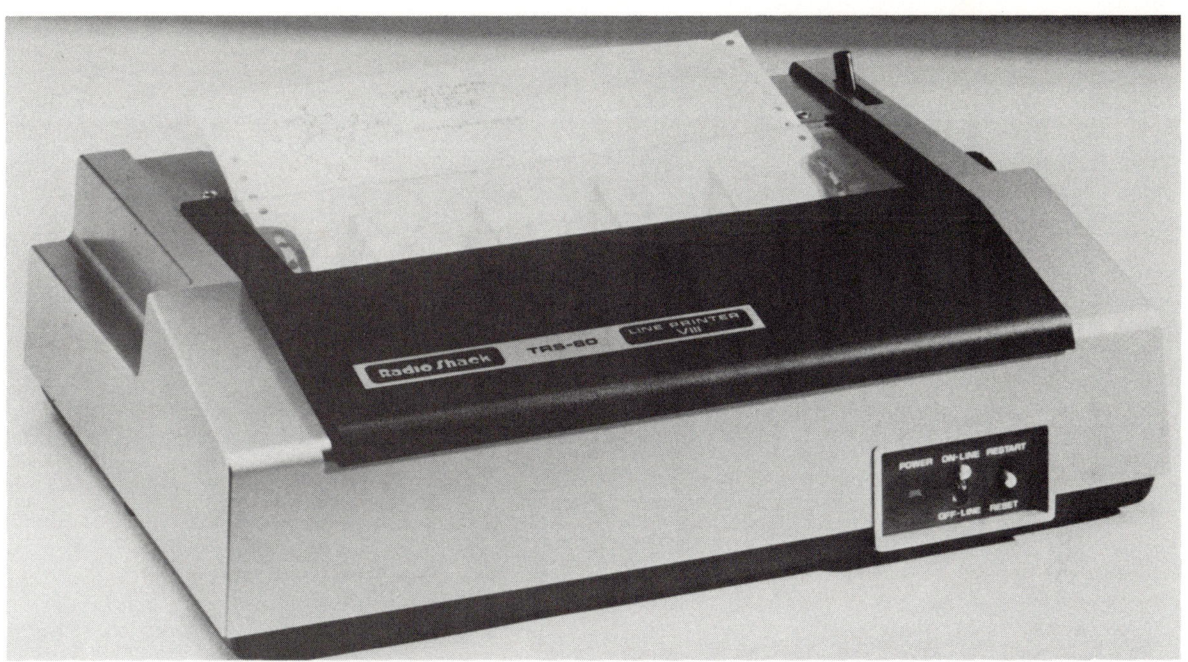

Fig. 9-18. The TRS-80 Line Printer VIII. (Courtesy of Radio Shack, a division of Tandy Corp.)

Fig. 9-19. The TRS-80 Line Printer V. (Courtesy of Radio Shack, a division of Tandy Corp.)

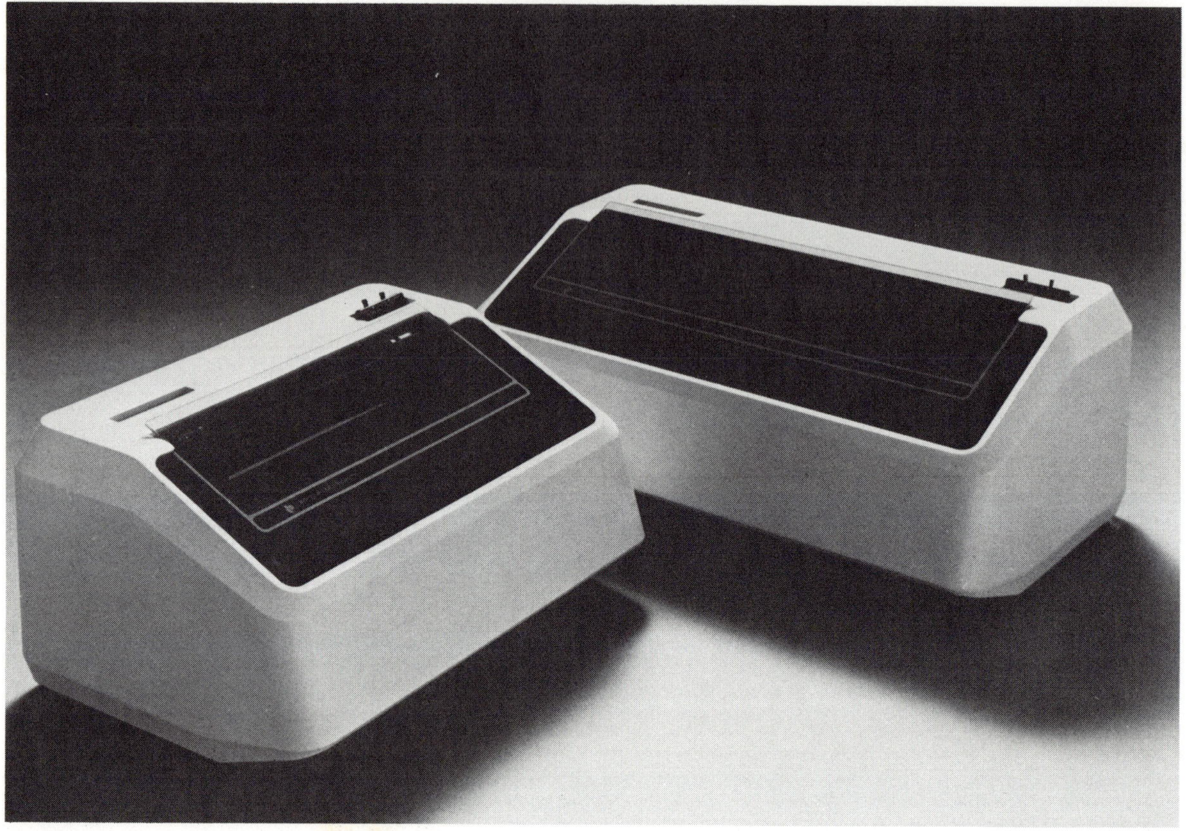

Fig. 9-20. The Prism 80 and Prism 132 dot-matrix printers. (Courtesy of Integral Data Systems, Inc.)

cluded. A ribbon cartridge is used to provide exceptionally long useful life. Features that may be added for an additional cost include:

1. Sprint Mode. This allows you to select a standard density print matrix rather than the normal high (24-by-9) density matrix used. Print speed in this mode, used primarily for draft- and data-processing applications, exceeds 200 CPS.

2. Auto Cut Sheet Feed. This is a mechanism which positions each sheet to a preprogrammed starting line, with subsequent positioning software selectable.

3. Dot Plot™ Graphics. This option provides raster graphics at a density of 84-by-84 dots per inch.

4. Prism Color. This module allows the use of any three four-zone ribbons for producing copy in up to eight colors. The ribbon options include black with three process colors (cyan, magenta, and yellow) for color mixing, black with three primary colors (red, blue, and green), and black only. Although the primary use for color capability is graphics, word-processing applications are sure to follow in the very near future.

Manufacturer: Integral Data Systems, Inc., Milford, NH 03055.

Comprint 912. The 912 series of printers from Comprint (Fig. 9-21) uses an electroresistive print head and specially treated (electrosensitive) paper, rather than the usual impact head and ribbon arrangement found in other printers in this section. Paper is supplied in the form of a 300-foot roll, which is stored inside the printer. Excellent photocopies can be made from the output. Printing speed is 225 CPS (unidirectional) using a 9-by-12 dot matrix. Lowercase descenders are included. The 912-GO offers graphics capability with resolution of 100 dots per inch. Either parallel or serial interface units may be specified. These printers are surprisingly inexpensive and could be used in word-processing applications if desired.

Manufacturer: Computer Printers International, Inc., 340 E. Middlefield Road, Mountain View, CA 94043.

Epson MX-80 F/T. The MX-80 F/T is one of the popular MX series of printers offered by Epson (Fig. 9-22). Featuring bidirectional logic-seeking printing at 80 CPS, the MX-80 F/T will print 5, 8.25, 10, and 16.5 characters per inch. A full ASCII 96-character set with lowercase descenders and 9-by-9 dot matrix is standard. Emphasized, double, and double emphasized printing modes may be selected.

Friction fed single sheets or rolls or fanfold pin fed paper up to 9.5 inches in width may be used. A Centronics-style parallel interface is standard, although serial may be ordered. An inexpensive print head, which is discarded and easily replaced when it has reached the end of its useful life, is unique. A ribbon cartridge is rated at a life expectancy of 3 million characters. Vertical and horizontal tabs can be set and both line and form feed commands may be user programmed.

Other printers in the Epson line share most of the MX-80 F/T's features, while adding some of their own. The MX-100 (Fig. 9-23) for instance, includes GRAF-TRAX and accepts paper up to 15.5 inches wide. Prices are quite inexpensive for the range of features offered.

Manufacturer: Epson America, Inc., 3415 Kashiwa Street, Torrance, CA 90505.

New Trends in Printers

Printer technology has advanced dramatically in the last five years and shows every promise of continuing to do so. A glimpse into the future is offered by some of the units just described. Features such as multicolor printing, graphics en-hancements, selectable draft- or letter-quality print mode, faster printing speed, and diverse paper-handling capabilities will certainly become more widely available.

Alternative methods of producing characters will be introduced as time goes on. Manufacturers are talking about using a high speed stylus, laser beams, xerography, and numerous other alternatives to the formed character and dot-matrix methods commonly employed today. Print heads are destined to become disposable and much less expensive than they are presently.

Noise reduction and mechanical simplicity are receiving a great deal of attention. These efforts will be reflected in printers on the market in a few years. Price has shown a great deal of competitive pressure. The features available today for under $1000 would have cost (if they had been available) more than double that just a few years ago.

Wherever the future of printer technology leads, users of word-processing systems are certain beneficiaries. A lot of time and effort is expended by printer manufacturers to offer the best product for the smallest amount of money. If the price/feature relationship continues as it has in the past, all of today's printers will be outmoded in a few years.

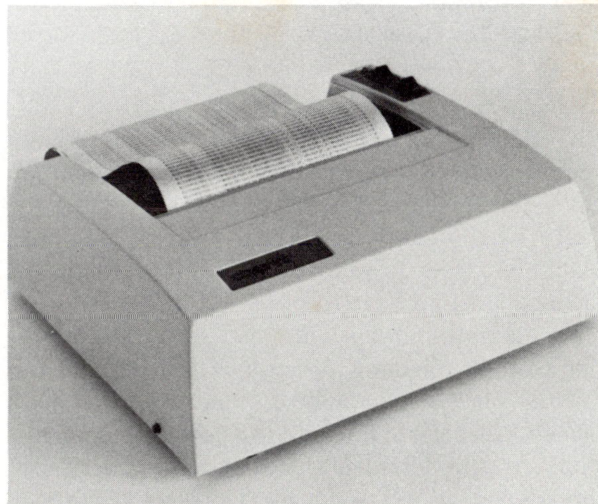

Fig. 9-21. The Comprint 912 series of electrostatic printers. (Courtesy of Computer Printers International, Inc.)

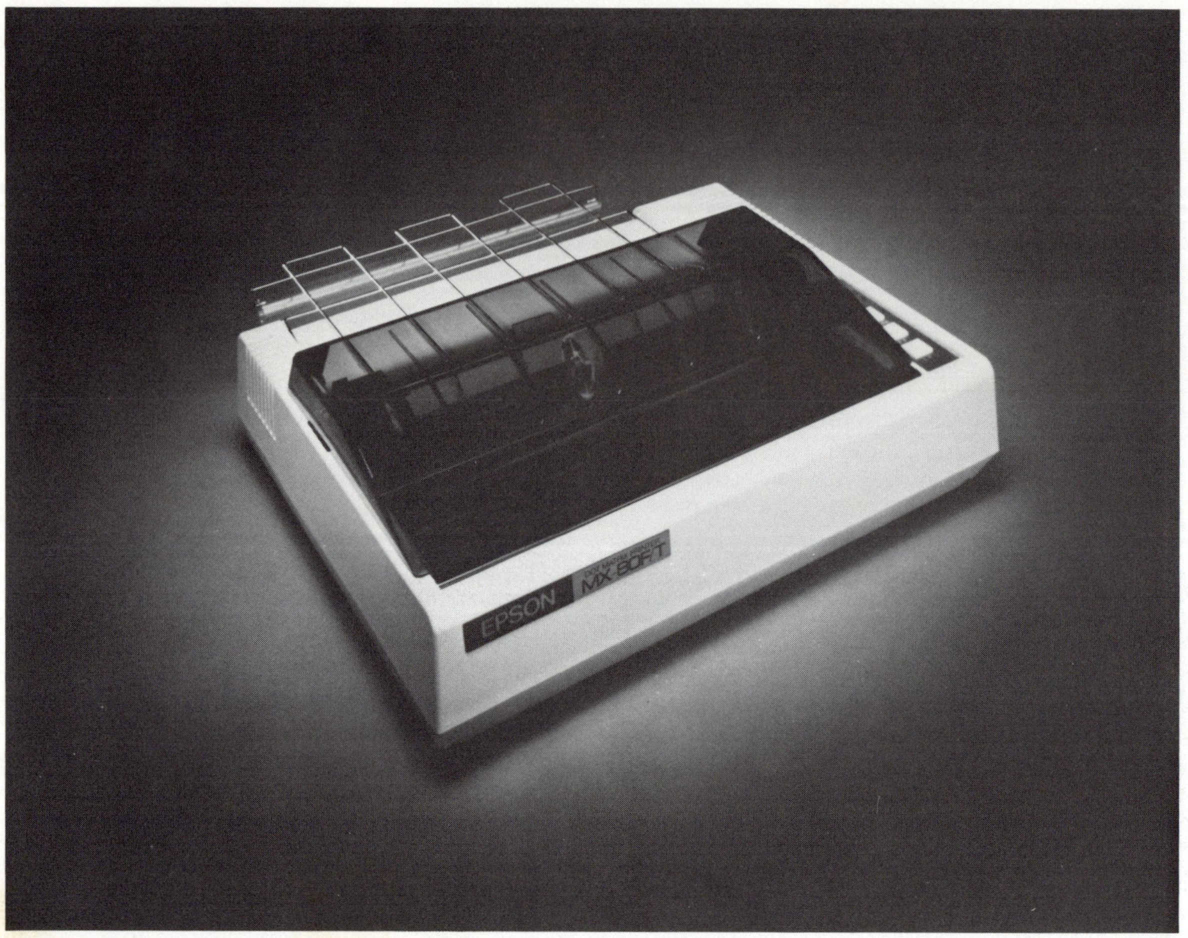

Fig. 9-22. The Epson MX-80 F/T dot-matrix printer. (Courtesy of Epson America, Inc.)

SELECTING A PRINTER

Before considering the relative merits of individual printer models, you will need to construct some general selection criteria. These preliminary criteria should be based on your system capabilities, your own abilities, and your intended applications.

Your system capabilities are an obvious starting point in selecting a printer. Things to look for include input/output configuration and availability, speed, character set output, and potential modifications. You may discover that your computer is capable of handling only serial interfacing for printers; if such is the case, one of your selection criteria has already been decided.

Peripherals, software, or modifications neces-

sary for your printing applications may not be available from the manufacturer of your computer. For each of the more popular microcomputers, a group of "second source" suppliers has emerged. One of these sources may have just what you need. Check with your local dealer, or read the ads in computing magazines for information on the latest offerings.

Your own abilities and interests should be strongly considered in setting selection criteria. If you are the original hardware klutz, simple hookup and operation may be one of your primary printer selection criteria. Those blessed with greater mechanical and programming ability can consider complicated printing units that are difficult to interface.

Intended applications will determine the next

of your selection criteria. This may sound obvious, but it still remains the single most important consideration you will make in selecting a printer. Be realistic in assessing your potential applications, but leave some flexibility for the additional applications that will crop up as more sophisticated software and hardware become available.

Your printer may not have to be a letter-quality unit, if this application is one you will use only occasionally. On the other hand, if you plan to do a great deal of correspondence where quality is a deciding factor, go for the best printer you can find, regardless of the cost.

Once you have developed preliminary selection criteria, the rest will fill in as a result of consid-

erations unique to your situation. Such things as budget and space limitations, ease in obtaining paper and ribbon supplies, brands carried (and recommended) by your local dealer, delivery delay, and manufacturer's reputation will influence your decision.

To illustrate the interaction of these factors in a practical situation, let me share with you the criteria I recently used in selecting a new printer for my system. My Apple II computer has either serial or parallel output cards available. Since I already owned a parallel card, I wanted the printer to be able to work with it. Line length output is adjustable in software, and graphics are included. Although input and output are uppercase only on the unmod-

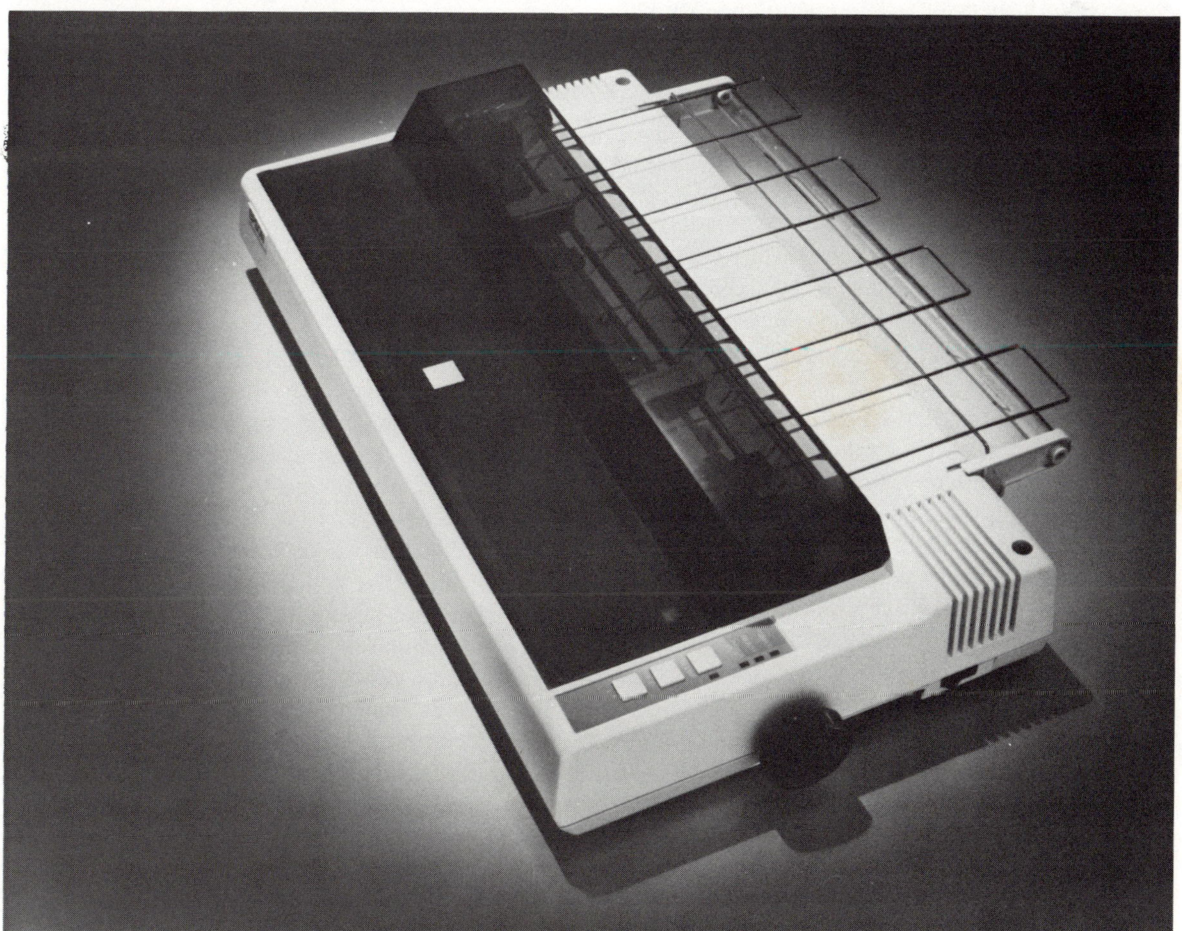

Fig. 9-23. The Epson MX-100 printer. (Courtesy of Epson America, Inc.)

ified Apple, my unit has a hardware modification to output either. My hardware abilities are quite limited, so I wanted a printer that was simple to interface and operate.

My intended applications revolved primarily around word processing, although I also use the computer for program listing and development, business form printing, and numerous other chores. Graphics capability, not present in my last printer, was desirable but not a real priority consideration.

Based on the preceding factors and several other considerations, I went shopping for a new printer armed with the following criteria:

1. Full 96-character ASCII capability, selectable character fonts, and built-in graphics.

2. Good print quality. This goes almost without saying, but I was specifically looking for lowercase letters with descenders. My last printer did not have descenders, although the print quality was good.

3. Tractor or pin feed. Since I do quite a volume of printing, the convenience of not having to tend to paper feeding is important.

4. Reasonably fast printing. My old printer was capable of printing 125 characters per second, so I was interested in at least that much speed capability. Bidirectional logic-seeking features were also highly desirable.

5. Easily interfaced to the Apple II. Since I already owned the parallel interface card, this was a primary consideration.

6. Relatively quiet operation. Since most of my work is done late at night, this is a most important factor. My old printer used a solenoid to advance the paper and was relatively noisy. I wanted the new printer to use stepper motors and be as quiet as possible.

7. Other features on my list included fairly compact size, capability to use plain paper wider than 9.5 inches, and relatively low cost.

As you may have guessed, there were many printers available that met or exceeded all of my criteria. I found it extremely helpful to list my criteria in order of priority.

Once you have developed your criteria in order of priority, collect information on all the printers that could be potential purchase candidates. Information can be gathered from a variety of sources. Your local computer store will have literature on the brands they carry. Advertisements in magazines provide a way of contacting manufacturers or distributors of other units. Other computer owners are often happy to demonstrate, or at least tell you about, their printers. Applying your selection criteria to information gathered should help narrow the selection to a few units from among the multitude on the market. A "hands-on" demonstration, if possible, of each purchase candidate will aid immeasurably in your final selection.

Printer technology is advancing rapidly. Units with infinitely more capacity and smaller price tags are on the horizon, although this won't help you if you need a printer now. While purchasing a printer wih ample capacity is certainly a good idea, over-buying today's technology may leave you with outmoded potential in a few years. The logical approach to printer selection is to purchase as much capacity as you need for the immediate future, with the intention of trading up as new developments appeal to you and are supported by the programs you most frequently use.

MISCELLANEOUS WORD-PROCESSING NEEDS

Word-processing activities require much more than just a computer and printer for day-to-day operations. These needs can be divided into two general categories: hardware and supplies.

Hardware. The term hardware has been used to mean computer equipment. Here, it includes furniture and other nonexpendable items typically needed for word-processing operations. Most furniture needs can be thought of simply as providing a place to put everything, including yourself. Your work area may include a desk specially designed to hold a computer and necessary peripherals, a printer stand complete with paper holder and catcher, and files for holding both printouts and data disks. Even a simple item such as a chair becomes a major comfort consideration when you spend a great deal of time in it. You need not refurnish your office or work area for word processing, however, you should provide furniture adequate for the intended purpose.

Other popular hardware items include copy holders to hold papers in the correct position for keyboard operations, glare shields for elimination of video display reflections, and disk holders. If your word-processing activities involve dictation, transcribing equipment must also be furnished.

Supplies. The appetite of most word-processing systems for expendable supplies is insatiable. Paper, envelopes, ribbons, and disks are used at an astounding rate. Depending on the capability of your system, special items may be needed for daily operations. Paper, for example, comes in many forms and shapes. Letterhead can be supplied in individual sheets, printed on fanfold paper, or glued to a fanfold carrier sheet. You will need an adequate supply of each variety normally used, if you want to keep operations moving smoothly. If your printer requires fanfold sheets, special ordering may be required. Anticipating these needs will insure an uninterrupted flow of production from your word-processing system.

Printer ribbons seem always to go at the wrong time, so you should always have extras on hand. Similarly, you should have plenty of extra disks, tapes, labels, and any other items required.

Purchasing Needed Items. Some of the items needed for word-processing applications can be obtained from your computer dealer or local business supply store. If you have difficulty in locating a specific item or do not have a local source for your needs, there are numerous firms that specialize in supplying word-processing hardware and supplies by mail. Names and addresses of these firms can be obtained through their ads in magazines, telephone directories, or newspapers.

The following offer word-processing supplies by mail. It is not a complete list, but provides you with some places to contact.

ABM Products
8868 Clairemont Mesa Boulevard
San Diego, CA 92123
(800) 854-1555
General word-processing supplies

Alpha Computing Supply, Inc.
9625 Mason Avenue
Chatsworth, CA 91311
General word-processing supplies

American Word Processing Company
18730 Oxnard Street
Tarzana, CA 91356
General word-processing supplies, furniture, and books

Atlantic Cabinet Corporation
P. O. Box 100, Interstate Park
Williamsport, MD 21795
Computer system work stations

Fidelity Products Co.
5601 International Parkway
P. O. Box 155
Minneapolis, MN 55440
(800) 328-3034
General word-processing supplies

Image Materials Corporation
185 North Wacker Drive
Chicago, IL 60606
(800) 621-2266
General word-processing supplies

Inmac
2465 Augustine Drive
Santa Clara, CA 95051
Inmac has several sales and distribution centers.
General word-processing supplies

Jade Computer Products
4901 West Rosecrans Avenue
Hawthorne, CA 90250
(800) 421-5500
Primarily hardware

Moore Computer Supplies Catalog
P. O. Box 20
Wheeling, IL 60090
(800) 323-6230
General word-processing supplies

Nebs Computer Forms
78 Hollis Street
Groton, MA 01471
(800) 225-9550
Custom forms and paper supplies

Uarco Incorporated
121 North Ninth Street
DeKalb, IL 60115
(800) 435-0713
General word-processing supplies and furniture

Visible Computer Supply Corp.
3626 Stern Drive
St. Charles. IL 60174
(800) 323-0628
General word-processing supplies

Vista Information Products
1534 East Edinger, Suite 8
Santa Ana, CA 92705
(800) 854-7135
Primarily disks, ribbons, printwheels, etc.

Xerox Corporation
Route 303 and Bradley Road
Blauvelt, NY 10913
(800) 431-1666
General word-processing supplies

WHY YOU NEED A GOOD PRINTER

There is a lot more to word processing than just buying a computer and a program. In a very real sense, the computer and program are not nearly as important as the printer and paper. Even the most perfectly typed document suffers immensely if the printing and paper are of substandard quality. Nothing cries COMPUTER more quickly than draft-quality printing on an important letter. The very best word-processing systems are those that remain invisible to the intended recipient of the end product.

We've all seen the computer generated letters, "personalized" by crudely inserting your name (usually misspelled) a few times in the text. Word-processing users are seldom allowed the luxury of being that obvious. Correspondence, contracts, and documents must be error free and letter perfect if they are to make the desired impression. Careful attention to the details of print quality, paper grade, and other subtle factors will insure that you create a positive impression with your word-processing operations.

## Chapter 10

Tab stops may be set and used in several ways. The Word Handler
displays the tab stops on the bottom of the screen and the effects
of tabbing directly in the text:

Name	Phone	Computer	Disks?
Adams, P	555-1416	Apple II	Yes
Jones, J	324-5672	TRS-80	No
King, A.	677-9024	Zenith	Yes
Smith, R.	555-3831	Apple III	Yes
Wilson, T	555-4871	Atari	No
Young, L.	978-3421	IBM	Yes

Small Business and Home Applications

One vital question remains unanswered: Once you have word processing, what do you do with it? The advertisements and demonstrations tell you about the slick features of each program. What they fail to explain, however, is how these features relate to the practical applications you have in mind. More importantly, very little attention is paid to helping you come up with some applications that may never have occurred to you.

The time to think carefully about the sum total of your own possible applications is before a major investment in computer equipment and programs has been made. These considerations will have a direct bearing on the capabilities you need in your own system, and whether or not you really need a word-processing system at all. The next chapter will discuss the "whether or not" question more fully. This chapter offers a few suggestions regarding possible word-processing applications in typical small business and home situations.

Actually, differentiating between the two situations may be a little artificial. Often a microcomputer serves in more than one capacity and environment. The same computer that keeps the books for a small business may be used for word processing, entertaining your kids, tracking stocks, and a host of other home applications.

No doubt you will be able to think of many more potential applications for a microcomputer-based word-processing system than will be discussed here. Why potential? Ideally, you have looked over the information presented so far and have a pretty fair idea of what word processing involves. Perhaps by now you have developed an interest and have some applications in mind. More likely, however, you have an application or two in mind but would like a few more ways to justify the cost of a system. Possibly, you would like to know a little more about the kinds of chores you can do with a word-processing system.

Whatever your motivation, it is time to take a few pages and look at some practical applications for word-processing systems. Wherever special features are needed for specific applications, they are noted. For the most part, the applications outlined in this chapter should be within the capability of any word-processing program and small computer.

BUSINESS LETTERS

Simple business letters can be produced rapidly using a word-processing system. The primary advantage of a word-processing system, in this situation, is the ability to edit and format the letter on screen prior to printing. If your word-processing system is equal to the task, the recipient of your letter should have no inkling as to the method of production. Copies may be printed, if necessary, and the letter saved on a disk for future reference.

If your business correspondence seems to use a lot of repetitive material, small disk files can be set up to handle standardized portions. You may decide to set up a few standard paragraphs which can be inserted into letters as required.

As an example, let's assume you are the owner of a small computer software company. Since you can't yet afford a secretary, you are charged with answering inquiries from both retailers and potential customers regarding your program line. Using word processing, the following paragraphs could be set up as separate disk files:

Paragraph 1

Thank you for your recent inquiry regarding our new line of microcomputer programs. As you will see from the literature enclosed, we have introduced some exciting new products.

Paragraph 2

Computer retailers, like yourself, will appreciate the special sample package described on page 7. This provides an opportunity to examine each of the new products on your own computer.

Paragraph 3

Our products are sold only through established retail outlets. Please consult the Authorized Dealer List enclosed to find the retailer in your area.

Paragraph 4

Special discounts for quantity purchases are noted on the dealer price list enclosed. We hope you will decide to feature our complete line in your store and look forward to receiving your order. Rest assured it will receive our usual prompt attention.

Paragraph 5

Reviewers and computer users have been unanimous in their praise for our new programs. Please visit your local dealer and let him show you the sophisticated features included in our products.

Paragraph 6

Sincerely,

John J. Smith

This is an example of a two-tier correspondence system that can save you a great deal of time and effort. Answering an inquiry from a dealer consists of typing in the name and address, telling your word-processing system to insert paragraphs 1, 2, 4, and 6, and printing the letter (Fig. 10-1). Similarly, a customer inquiry follows the same procedure with paragraphs 1, 3, 5, and 6 (Fig. 10-2).

Although the majority of your letters may not be that simple, the concept of constructing a group of "canned paragraphs" is. If your word-processing program is capable of merging text from disk files into a document (most are), this type of system is well within your reach.

Further sophistication for the simple business letter is provided using a series of preconstructed letters into which you insert specific information. Some programs provide an automatic system of prompting input from the keyboard, although you can do the same thing manually using the insert or change commands found in all systems. Another method of inserting specific information is with the replace command contained in most word-processing programs. To use this approach, type (NAME) as the search string and specify the desired replacement. Do the same with all the other variables you have inserted into the text of each letter.

Continuing our previous example, let's set up a slightly different customer response letter using capital letters enclosed by parentheses to indicate the points where specific information is to be typed (Fig. 10-3). Save the letter in a file on your data disk. Each time this letter is to be used, retrieve it from the disk, and insert the proper information using one of the commands discussed above.

Either of these approaches is suitable for a small volume of correspondence and will provide a savings of time and effort. Larger numbers of letters, personalized or not, require a slightly different approach (see the mailing list merging section).

BUSINESS FORMS

Any business, larger or small, must deal with a certain number of forms. Purchasing, invoicing, estimates, accounts receivable statements, inventory, and numerous other business activities have their own distinctive forms.

You can buy forms for these purposes, of course. In that case, your word-processing system can be taught to fill in the appropriate blanks through the use of a print format routine. Often this is a tedious process unless the forms have been designed for computer use.

Alternately, your word-processing system can print all, or any portion of, the form headings and

```
May 25, 1982

Mr. Frank C. Hollis
Frank's Computer Center
P.O. Box 111
Muscatine, IA 52761

Dear Mr. Hollis,

Thank you for your recent inquiry regarding
our new line of microcomputer programs.  As
you will see from the literature enclosed, we
have introduced some exciting new products.

Computer retailers, like yourself, will
appreciate the special sample package
described on page 7.  This provides an
opportunity to examine each of the programs on
your own computer.

Special discounts for quantity purchases are
noted on the dealer price list enclosed.  We
hope you will decide to feature our complete
line in your store and look forward to
receiving your order.  Rest assured it will
receive our usual prompt attention.

Sincerely,



John J. Smith
```

Fig. 10-1. The response to a retailer inquiry is assembled from the paragraph files shown in the text.

May 25, 1982

Mr. William C. Marshall
3619 Fairmeadow Lane
Granite City, PA 23456

Dear Mr. Marshall,

Thank you for your recent inquiry regarding
our new line of microcomputer programs. As
you will see from the literature enclosed, we
have introduced some exciting new products.

Our products are sold only through established
retail outlets. Please consult the Authorized
Dealer List enclosed to find the retailer in
your area.

Reviewers and computer users have been
unanimous in their praise for our new
programs. Please visit your local dealer and
let him show you the sophisticated features
included in our products.

Sincerely,

John J. Smith

Fig. 10-2. A few different "canned paragraphs" generate this respone to an inquiry from a potential retail customer.

format. A little time spent designing an output format may mean you don't have to purchase special forms for some operations. Figure 10-4, for example, shows a simple purchase order form that was designed using a word-processing program. Once a form has been designed, it can be saved in a disk file for later use. Distinctively marking the points for input from the keyboard will save confusion when the format is used repeatedly. This type of application is particularly well suited to word-processing programs that have effective horizontal tabbing capabilities. Setting the tabs in the format of the form will save spending a lot of time getting information in the proper location on the face of the form. A completed purchase order using the format designed earlier is shown in Fig. 10-5.

A SIMPLE MAILING LIST

Perhaps you occasionally need mailing list information but don't have a specialized program for that purpose. Almost every word-processing system can be used to construct such a file. Text files are not particularly selective about the type of information they contain. There is no reason you can't construct a file containing name and address information and manage it effectively without spending the money for a separate mailing list management system.

Here's the secret: Set up a format that will be of use to you in the future. Your simple mailing list could contain lines for name, company, address, city, state, and zip code. Let's say, for example, that you plan to print this information on mailing labels that are one inch high and three inches wide. Translating that to word-processing terms, each label will hold six lines containing a maximum of 30 characters each. Create a file with those output specifications, and you're in business. As you type each entry, be sure to include the proper number of blank lines, and your labels will print beautifully. To avoid confusion, you may want to add some insignificant character in the first or last line of each record to designate where spaces should occur. The sample mailing list shown in Fig. 10-6 was typed in

```
(DATE)

(NAME)
(ADDRESS)
(CITY,STATE,ZIP)

Dear (NAME),

Thank you for your recent inquiry regarding
our new (PROGRAM) program for the Apple II
personal computer.  I have enclosed a brochure
which describes the program's unique features.

Reviewers and computer users have been
unanimous in their praise for the exciting
capabilities included in (PROGRAM).  Extensive
documentation and reference material are an
integral part of the program package.

Please note that our products are sold only
through established Apple dealers.  Your local
dealer, (DEALER NAME), would be happy to
demonstrate this program for you and answer
any questions you may have.

Sincerely,



John J. Smith
```

Fig. 10-3. Entire letters may be saved in disk files and personalized for the intended recipient by inserting the proper information in place of the titles enclosed in parentheses.

```
                    PURCHASE ORDER

                       LeSoftware
                    3224 Magnolia Ct.
                  Bettendorf, IA 52722

         Date:                    Order No.:

         To:




         Please ship the following items:

         Quan.      Description       Each  Total
         -----    ------------------  ------ ------








         Ship Via:

         Bill To Account Number:


         Thank you for your prompt attention to
         this request.  Please advise if any of
         the above items are out of stock or
         backordered.
```

Fig. 10-4. Simple business forms, such as the purchase order shown here are designed and saved as disk text files.

exactly that manner, using an asterisk as the record separator.

How do you manage your mailing list? First I will define what is meant by management. The primary management needs for mailing data of this sort are some method of adding, deleting, or revising records. Your word-processing program is entirely capable of handling all three functions. Using the add, delete, and change functions of my program, the mailing list data was revised as shown in Fig. 10-7.

You can take advantage of special features offered in any specific word-processing program to aid in the management of your data. Linked files, for instance, may be constructed to handle lists too long to be fully contained in one file. Search can be used to locate a record or emulate a rough sort function by multiple occurrence searching. To "sort" your list by zip code, specify the desired zip as the string and do a multiple search. Marking each record as a block of text and adding it to a separate disk file will allow you to construct a sorted list.

A DATA BASE

You are not limited to mailing list information for the type of file discussed in the last section. Any data which lends itself to storage in a predefined format can be used. Groups of records organized in this fashion make up a data base. Crude, perhaps, but a data base none the less. Elaborate programs are available for the management of information contained in a data base (called, logically, data base management systems). If your data and management needs are limited to relatively simple information like the mailing list discussed earlier, use your word-processing system. I have used this approach for storage of names of programs contained on the disk in my library, sources of information for articles, location of specific items in an inventory, Christmas card lists, monthly scheduling reminders, and a host of other chores.

If it seems like a lot of trouble to construct and use data files in this format, consider the convenience of being able to print hard copies of your data using the versatility of your word-processing program. I have used programs designed specifically for mailing list management that will print information only in uppercase and in a rigidly defined format. My word-processing mailing list files can be

```
                     PURCHASE ORDER

                      LeSoftware
                   3224 Magnolia Ct.
                 Bettendorf, IA 52722

   Date: May 25, 1982      Order No.: 11721

   To: Barton Computer Products
       316 West 25th Avenue
       Waterloo, IA 52304


   Please ship the following items:

   Quan.       Description        Each   Total
   -----       -----------        ----   -----
     5     Floppy disk mailers     .95    4.75
    10     Literature holders    15.50  155.00
     1     Magnetic sign holder  9.80    9.80
   100     #7 Mailing labels       .05    5.00
    50     Bulk Rate labels        .10    5.00




                              Total  179.55

   Ship Via: United Parcel Service

   Bill To Account Number: LS00-0002


   Thank you for your prompt attention to
   this request.  Please advise if any of
   the above items are out of stock or
   backordered.
```

Fig. 10-5. Using a predesigned form is simply a matter of retrieving the file from disk and inserting the required information with each use.

*

John C. Adams
114 Friendly Lane
Watertown, VT 13452

*

William R. Baker
Heavy Industries, Inc.
40 Industrial Park
Milwaukee, WI 54343

*

Mabel J. Connors
R.R. #1 Box 270
Podunk Junction, MI 49767

*

Charles B. Duncan
Sunnyvale Nursing Home
321 W. Pleasant Street
Anytown, AZ 87698

*

Ezra K. Franklin
P.O. Box 249
Centerville, KY 44521

*

Paul C. Granlund
Executive Director
Community Health Center
7428 North Plaza Blvd.
Bigtown, NV 99835

Fig. 10-6. A simple mailing list as implemented with a word-processing system.

printed on labels, full pages, or in groups of any specified size. Data can be added, deleted, changed, and manipulated almost as easily with the word-processing program approach as with the specialized program.

MAILING LIST MERGING

If you maintain a mailing list for any purpose, setting up a personalized correspondence system is relatively easy. Most word-processing programs include either built-in or optional add-on provisions for merging text with mailing list information. Several programs already have a built-in specialized mailing list management system.

The simplest use of this type of capability is adding name and address information to the heading of a preconstructed letter or document. Since each letter is individually printed, the typical "form letter look" is eliminated. With some imagination and a capable program, you can construct letters and documents that contain personalizing information in several locations. Most programs that offer mailing list merging capabilities include provisions for printing any data contained in the mailing list files anywhere in the text of a document.

Conditional Printing

Going one step beyond simple mailing list merging involves printing different passages of text at several locations, depending on some specified condition being met or not met in the mailing list data. This capability is called conditional printing and is available in many sophisticated word-processing programs.

Some programs offer conditional printing through the use of IF-THEN statements in the text. To use this feature, you can specify conditions (IF) and what will happen if they are met (THEN). For instance, IF CITY=CHICAGO THEN print something like, "The last time I visited Chicago was during the famous blizzard of 1981." Multiple IF-THEN statements may be used. We could add IF CITY=LOS ANGELES THEN print, "I hope the sun is still shining in my favorite city." As your letters are printed, each recipient in Chicago will get the blizzard message, those in Los Angeles will enjoy the sun, and letters to any other city will not have either message.

Although the actual syntax of the logic commands may vary, conditional printing involves some variation of the IF-THEN capability. I have seen some programs that add AND, OR, NOR, NOT, and several other commands to the basic IF-THEN.

CONTRACTS AND LEGAL DOCUMENTS

Word processing has proven a valuable aid to those who must frequently deal with contracts and legal documents. The primary advantage offered here is the capability to construct predefined clauses that can be assembled in any desired order. Each clause is typically saved in a separate disk file for easy access. This same approach can be used by many professionals to assemble diagnostic summaries, progress reports, service descriptions, etc.

A secondary benefit is the ability to proofread, edit, and revise the document prior to final printing. Since most legal documents must be error free, printing an acceptable copy after making a few changes on the screen is a lot easier than retyping an entire document by hand.

OTHER APPLICATIONS

Many businesses offer special items or bargains which change at fairly regular intervals. Word processing is a natural for this type of application. If a restaurant changes the special with the day of the week, seven disk files will handle the job of printing new lists daily. Each Friday's specials could be printed for clipping to a menu as shown in Fig. 10-8. The number required may be smaller or larger, depending on the frequency of change. Many restaurants could benefit from keeping their entire menu in a disk file so minor changes could be made without having to redo the whole thing. If your business uses price lists in any form, committing them to word-processing disk files allows for selective revision and reprinting.

Writers

Writers write, right? Of course, what writers write depends largely on their particular areas of interest and expertise. The traditional picture of a writer sitting at an old typewriter surrounded by huge stacks of crumbled, discarded sheets of paper has gone the way of the horse and buggy. Today's

```
*

    John  C.  Anderson
    114  Friendly  Lane
    Watertown,  VT  13452

*

    Henry  C.  Banks
    Heavy  Industries,  Inc.
    40  Industrial  Park
    Milwaukee,  WI  54343

*

    Charles  B.  Duncan
    Sunnyvale  Nursing  Home
    321  W.  Pleasant  Street
    Anytown,  AZ  87698

*


    Phillip  C.  Dykstra
    1417  Grand  Avenue
    Middletown,  ND  35751

*


    Ezra  K.  Franklin
    P.O.  Box  249
    Centerville,  KY  44521

*

    Paul  C.  Granlund
    Executive  Director
    Community  Health  Center
    7428  North  Plaza  Blvd.
    Bigtown,  NV   99835
```

Fig. 10-7. Managing a word-processing-based mailing list is simply a matter of using the editing commands available. In this example, several items have been changed from the first list.

```
                    FRIDAY SPECIALS

                 YOUR CHOICE......$3.95


        Baked Chicken.

            One-half chicken served with our famous
            coleslaw, baked potato, green beans and
            honey glazed rolls.   Includes beverage.



        Broiled Whitefish.

            Our most popular dish!  Includes green
            salad, baked potato, spring peas and
            honey glazed rolls.   Served with hot
            butter and tartar sauce.


        Spaghetti And Meatballs.

            For hearty appetites, this Italian
            specialty is just what the doctor
            ordered.  Pasta smothered in our secret
            sauce and topped with seasoned
            meatballs.  Served with tossed green
            salad and warm garlic toast.


        Top off your meal with a piece of our homebaked
        pie.  Today's selection includes:  Apple, Cherry,
        Coconut Cream and Pecan.
```

Fig. 10-8. This list of daily special menu items is easily printed in any quantity from the word-processing program on which it is stored.

writer is more likely to be found staring intently at a video display and typing characters noiselessly onto the screen.

As a writer, I have found word processing to be an indispensible tool. Consider the process of writing a book such as this. When entering text, I define words or phrases likely to be used repeatedly. Each of these phrases is typed as an abbreviation. For instance, I used WP to represent "word processing." Once text entry is completed, the search and replace function of my program substitutes word processing for WP. Obviously, a great deal of time is saved when numerous abbreviations can be used in typing a lengthy manuscript.

Being able to back up and type over each error character saves a great deal of time, and you don't have to concern yourself with line length and pres-

sing RETURN more than infrequently, because these functions are handled automatically by any word-processing program. Editing the text is a relatively simple process. Words are added, deleted, moved, and shuffled to achieve a satisfactory arrangement. If a page or paragraph is out of place, block operations rectify the problem.

Each chapter can be contained on a data disk on which files have been automatically linked together for printing. Before actually printing each file, you can preview it on the video screen to spot any obvious formatting errors. You can produce a double-spaced copy for the publisher, and by changing a couple of line commands in the first file on each disk, print a second copy (single spaced and numbered differently) for your own files.

Writers of technical material can appreciate

having comprehensive mathematical functions in their word-processing programs. The ability to do calculations within the text saves an additional separate set of operations before sitting down to compose and type material. Subscripting and superscripting capabilities are certainly helpful in many technical writing applications.

The day is not far off when writers will submit disks of material rather than hard copy to publishers. Editing will be done right on the disks and typesetting finished without ever printing a page of hard copy. There are already several publications doing exactly what I have just described. The practice will certainly become more widespread in the future, as will using a modem to transmit text from one microcomputer to another.

Specialized Writing

Within the broad category of writers, there are many types of specific writing applications that place different demands on a word-processing system. Technical writers can use mathematical capabilities, superscripts and subscripts. How about printing a graph or schematic drawing in the text of a document? There are some word-processing systems capable of doing just that.

Playwrights and screenwriters need, among other things, extensive temporary margins to handle the various requirements of stage directions and dialog. Write-On! has these capabilities built in, and most programs will allow definition of temporary margins and indentations that will suit these demands quite adequately. Any changes needed in the script can be made on the screen and a revised copy printed without having to retype all the material that is unaltered.

Personal correspondence and writing applications can be handled by word-processing systems. If you are a prolific letter writer, you will probably find yourself writing essentially the same things to several different people. How about setting up some standard paragraphs and inserting them into your letters as needed? Got a few recipes you're very proud of? Set them up in a disk file, and print a copy or two when you get a request. Not only will the recipe look more professional, but you will be sure the proportions are printed clearly enough so you won't be blamed when the cake falls. Many of the ideas mentioned earlier are appropriate for personal use. A data base may be constructed for shopping lists, household inventory, or telephone lists, just to mention a few.

Church and Social Club Secretaries

The church secretary or social club newsletter editor must often type material that is not only repetitive but difficult to format for final printed appearance. Have you ever looked at a typical church bulletin? You know, the folded 8½-by-11 sheet that has at least three surfaces for typed material (assuming the front cover is preprinted). Can you imagine the hours it takes to layout and type that material?

There is a better way. Let's take the church bulletin as an example. Most church services follow a fairly standardized format, with only a few items changing from week to week. You can set up a word-processing file to handle the majority of the work. If your church has several different types of services, set up a file for each. After selecting the proper file, type in the current date, hymn numbers, and whatever other changes need to be made (Fig. 10-9). Since the format is already defined, the job has been cut to a few minutes rather than hours.

Some churches and social organizations publish a periodic newsletter. If your organization is like ours, material for the newsletter does not come in all at once. With a word-processing system, you can type it in final form as you receive it instead of waiting until the last minute to do everything.

If you have to produce a newsletter, set up a standardized format for the printed output. Using this format, set up one disk file for each month of the year. As material is received, place it into the disk file for the appropriate month. Special events, particularly, are often set up far enough in advance that you may want to include information regarding them in several issues. There is no need to type the information more than once, since it can be set up as a block and added to several files at once. Monthly reminders can be handled in the same fashion. If you're also responsible for mailing, you might con-

```
             COMMUNITY BIBLE CHURCH

                     (DATE)


        Worship begins with silent prayer.
        Prelude
        Order of Confession              Page 56
        Entrance Hymn                    No.###
        Greeting                         Page 57
        Prayer of the Day                Insert
        The First Lesson                 Insert
        Psalmody                         Insert
        The Second Lesson                Insert
        Verse                            Page 62
        Gospel                           Insert
        Pulpit Hymn                      No.###
        Sermon (TITLE)
        Nicene Creed                     Page 63
        The Prayers                      Insert
        Anthem (NAME)
        Offering
        Offertory                        Page 66
        The Lord's Prayer                Page 76
        Closing Hymn                     No.###
        Benediction                      Page 76
        Threefold Amen and Silent Prayer
                    * * * * * * * * * *
```

Fig. 10-9. Formats for setting up bulletins and newsletters such as the one shown, can be created for each different service used throughout the year.

sider the simple mailing list described earlier if your word-processing system does not include other mailing capabilities.

Students Large and Small

Although it might be a bit difficult to justify purchasing a system for your first grader, children can be taught to handle word-processing programs with ease. The home or school is an ideal place for a student to learn that a computer is capable of doing more than just playing games.

As students progress from early elementary to the middle and high school years, the amount of writing they are expected to do increases dramatically. Somewhere along the line, they discover that neatly typed papers make a better impression than pencil smudged, dog-eared looseleaf sheets. Your children can start off with a simple word-processing program as soon as they show an interest. The value of word processing to college students should be quite apparent. Well-prepared papers are expected in most courses. In the next few years, a personal computer with word-processing ability may become as much a part of college life as the typewriter is today.

MAKING A LIST OF YOUR NEEDS

Virtually every computer owner I have met who has word-processing capability has outlined at least several unique applications. The pharmacist who prints prescription labels and instructions, the dress shop owner who sends personal letters to every newly engaged couple in the area, the mortician who sends reams of letters (many of them signed "Eventually Yours"), the housewife who prepares resumes in her spare time, part-time writers, and radio amateurs who prepare QSL cards have all offered suggestions. The range and diversity of word-processing uses are far beyond the wildest imagination of all but the most dedicated computer advocates. Take a little time to think about your own situation. List a few of your primary potential applications and then try to determine how many additional things word processing could do for you.

## Chapter 11

Is Word Processing for You?

In order to help you make this important decision, this chapter discusses the pros and cons of microcomputer-based word processing. The material is divided into two sections: one for those who don't already own a computer, and the second for those who do.

SELECTING A COMPUTER FOR WORD PROCESSING

If you are contemplating the purchase of both a computer system and a word-processing program, you are at financial disadvantage compared to those who already own the necessary hardware. In practical terms, the cost of even the most elaborate word-processing program is small compared to the cost of a total system. If the prospect of spending $3000 to $5000 for a computer and the necessary peripherals to handle word processing does not appeal to you, perhaps you are not yet ready to purchase an entire word-processing system. If you're willing to spend the money required, read on.

There are many good references available on choosing and buying a computer system, which you should consult. Some characteristics of computers that make them especially well suited for word processing can be easily identified. Some of the readily available accessories are also of definite value for word-processing applications.

The Computer Itself. Most microcomputers are not purchased exclusively for word-processing applications. With the great diversity of application programs available, many computers are purchased to do a multitude of chores. While any number of computers may be suitable for most of your applications, some foresight in the initial selection will greatly increase the utility of your computer for word-processing applications. In addition to other considerations you will be making, think about some of the factors discussed in the next few pages before making your final selection.

Memory Size. Handling text files of any significant size requires a lot of memory, particularly when the "overhead" required by the program is added in. Most microcomputers are capable of managing at least 48K of random-access memory (RAM), either internally or on plug-in cards. Standard units seldom include that much. Since memory is a relatively inexpensive addition, be sure you select a unit with a full complement. When purchased with a computer, additional memory is usually installed and tested by the dealer prior to delivery of the computer.

Another consideration when determining the amount of usable memory in a computer is the ROM Read-Only Memory) included. Many computers include ROM-based operating systems, languages, disk operating systems, and utility routines. Others offer these functions in ROM as options, which I would recommend you seriously consider purchasing. Generally, the more functions provided in ROM, the better. Not having to use the Random Access Memory for computer overhead operations frees it up for program and file use.

The Keyboard. Whether you are selecting a computer with a built-in keyboard or a terminal for one without, the layout and feel of the keyboard plays an important role in how successful your word-processing efforts will be. Every keyboard bears a strong resemblance to every other one. A few of the keys, particularly function keys, may vary in their location. Keyheads may be round, square, or any other shape that permits fingers to reach them easily. The arrangement of letters and numbers follows the widely accepted QWERTY standard in most cases.

The primary difference between keyboards is a subjective quality called "feel." Feel can be thought of as a combination of all the physical factors that make a keyboard comfortable for you to use. The angle at which the keys are placed, the indentation on their faces (if any), and the spacing between them play a part in determining how a keyboard feels in use. I have used a great many keyboards and developed some very definite likes and dislikes. Rating keyboards, I would have to place my old portable typewriter at the bottom of the list and the silky smooth keyboard used on the Hewlett-Packard display terminals at the top. My Apple II keyboard, although adequate in most respects, lacks the smooth feel of the Hewlett-Packard units rated tops on my list. The standard office typewriter keyboard with indented keytops and some degree of tactile feedback will provide at least

adequate operating comfort for most word-processing operations.

The best way for you to judge the keyboard on a computer or terminal is to use it. Don't just plunk at a few keys when the salesperson isn't looking. Sit down, and do some serious typing on it. Look for speed, accuracy, key pressure required, tactile feedback, and smoothness, and form your own opinion. Try several different keyboards, and the sense of feel will come through loud and clear. Remember, if you are going to be doing serious word processing, the keyboard will be the most heavily used part of your computer. Choose it wisely!

Video Display. The video display is also important in word processing. Some video monitors are built in and others must be added on. You will spend many hours staring at the video screen, so spend a few minutes choosing the best one for you. In judging a video display, look at clarity, contrast, stability, size, and human engineering. Clarity becomes more important as the density of characters displayed increases. If you plan to display 32- or 40-character lines, a television set and RF modulator may be entirely adequate. A video monitor is usually required for any denser display.

Contrast between displayed characters and the background is a little deceiving at first glimpse. In the store, nice white characters against a dark black background look very nice. Spend a few hours staring at them, and you may change your mind. Too much contrast is just as bad as too little. Look for a wide range of adjustment to suit your own taste.

Stability is one of the few absolutes when you are judging a video display. If the characters jump up and down or sideways, the video display will not be suitable for word processing. Any amount of time spent working with a display that's doing the jig will give you an economy sized headache.

Size of the actual display tube, assuming the entire surface of it is usable, is also a bit deceiving. You might think bigger is better, and this is usually the case. Too large a display can impair readability, and similarly you would have a tough time reading off a three-inch screen for any length of time. The easiest way to judge screen size is to set up the system as you plan to use it and see if the size suits you.

Human-engineering factors, such as angle of the screen, provisions for glare reduction, shape of the characters, and adjustments provided, are also important. Spend enough time with the various display options to insure that your needs have been adequately met.

I have used several video display units. My first was a small, black and white portable television set with an RF modulator. This proved adequate for most of my word-processing applications, and I used it for quite some time. When the black and white died, I went to a 15-inch Sony color television with the same modulator. Again, this was adequate as long as I kept the screen at least two and a half to three feet away from the keyboard, since the characters appeared to be quite a bit larger than I was accustomed to seeing them. Recently, I treated myself to a video monitor with a green phosphorous screen. The monitor, at least for word-processing purposes, is head and shoulders above the other two display units I used. The Sony still sits next to the computer but gets very little use when the word-processing programs are being used.

Mass Storage Systems. Tape cassette and/or floppy disk storage systems are available for every microcomputer on the market. Although tape has some distinct advantages, most word-processing programs are oriented to the use of floppy disks. Some computers offer a selection of either 5- and-¼-inch (mini-floppy) or 8-inch floppy disk systems. Either size may be used for the application discussed in this book, although some of your other programs may mandate the use of one or the other. One drive is a practical minimum; two are necessary for all but the most rudimentary file-handling applications. If the computer you are considering is capable of managing more than one drive, purchasing two is strongly advised for serious word-processing applications.

Hard disk storage systems are becoming increasingly popular and are supported by many of the programs presently available. Vastly increased storage capacity and fast file-handling operations are the primary advantages to hard disks. These advantages must be carefully weighed against the cost difference, which is considerable. I suspect the cost of hard disk storage systems will be reduced significantly in the near future, which will decrease the cost differential.

Standard cassette tape storage for day-to-day word-processing operations is almost impossible. The amount of handling necessary for simple file manipulation is prohibitive. There are some cassette, and "string" tape systems that are more suitable. The major advantage of any tape-handling system over disk-based storage is cost. Your computer shopping budget will dictate which type of storage system you can purchase. If cost is a limiting factor, and some alternative forms of tape-handling systems are offered for your computer, perhaps they will prove a viable alternative to floppy disks.

Other storage systems are being introduced, such as the RAM-based "disk emulator," which uses a large amount of random access memory (periodically refreshed and protected from power failure by a battery) as a mass storage medium. Provisions to make periodic back-up copies of the contents of this type of storage on standard media are usually provided. Combination units featuring hard and floppy disks are also available.

Whatever method of mass storage you select, be sure it has enough capacity and versatility to be effectively used for word-processing purposes. Look over the program description chapters and some of the listings in the Appendix to see which mass storage systems are supported for the particular computer you are considering.

Interface Potential. Most popular computers allow the use of either parallel or serial interface configurations for peripheral devices. Chapter 9 discussed the importance of printer interfacing. If you are considering a specific type of printer, be sure the computer you are considering can handle the job.

Operating Convenience. Some computers are simple to operate, some are not quite so simple, and a few are downright complicated. Operational simplicity and convenience are important if you are less interested in the hardware than the job it is suppose to be doing. Initial start-up and in-use features should be evaluated. How many steps are required to load a program? What about management of peripherals such as disk drives and printers? What is the potential for errors in operating procedures, and what provisions for recovery from errors are included? Look carefully at the manuals, and ask questions during demonstration sessions to determine whether the operating convenience of a specific computer is within your acceptable range.

Identifying Your Requirements. When you are selecting a computer for more than one application, some compromises are necessary. You need to balance the requirements of your potential applications against the practical limitations of hardware availability and your budget. Look carefully at your list of applications, and determine which is most important. Rate the rest in order of importance, and look for the features best suited to those applications at the top of your list.

If you intend to spend 90% of your time with financial accounting and plan to use word processing for an occasional letter, don't give word-processing requirements a second thought. The writer who plans to use word processing 90% of the time and may try a few additional applications will certainly not give the financial-accounting capabilities a second thought. If you fall somewhere between these two extremes, compromise where necessary to buy the best unit for your own purposes.

Most computers can be used for numerous purposes and adapted for many others by using add-on hardware. The computer you purchase depends on what you feel is adequate for your applications. Shop around, look carefully, study the literature, and try before you buy. A computer system is a major purchase (at least in my financial circles), and you should base your decision on carefully considered factors.

WORD PROCESSING FOR YOUR COMPUTER

If you presently own a microcomputer or have decided to purchase one for word-processing purposes, the major portion of your purchase has been made. Now you must select the best program for your applications. The cost of word-processing programs for microcomputers is modest in comparison to your hardware expenditures. As new programs are introduced, you can update software many times before having to significantly change the computer equipment.

In order to select a specific program, you will spend time looking at the lists I asked you to compile in previous chapters. By the time you complete this examination, selecting a program from what is available will be a relatively simple process.

Your Potential Applications. Divide your list of potential applications into four groups: definite and immediate, possible and immediate, definite in the future, and possible in the future. Your definite and immediate list should include those needs that prompted you to consider word processing in the first place. Possible and immediate applications are those that sound practical, but which may not have occurred to you before you began to consider word processing. My own lists for these two categories would look something like this:

Definite and immediate

1. Short articles (5-10 pages)
2. Lengthy manuscripts (200-300 pages)
3. Business and personal correspondence
4. Management of small data bases for location of articles, program library, telephone numbers, etc.

Possible and immediate

1. Mailing list management and printing of personalized form letters
2. Printing labels or small clip-on sheets of special values for my wife's cosmetics sales activities
3. Constructing predefined formats for professional reports, business forms, and newsletters

With a little thought and imagination, your list of immediate applications can reflect the situations in which you could utilize a system today. If you already own a word-processing program and are thinking of updating it, following the same process will help you to select one adequate for your needs.

The second group of potential applications, those for the future, can reflect uses that you would like to implement once your skills are equal to the task. Just buying a word-processing program and learning the basics of its use will allow you to handle your immediate applications. Some of the special capabilities found in many programs will let you "grow into" a few of your future applications. Again, taking my own situation as an example, the following future applications lists could be constructed:

Definite in the future

1. Exchange of text files via a modem, such as electronic mail through a time-sharing computer service

2. Submission of article and manuscript files on floppy disks instead of printed pages

3. Editing and formatting listings of other programs in my library and under development

Possible in the future

1. Inclusion of graphic information in printed document files

2. Interchanging data with other programs for purposes of printing business reports, customer data, etc.

3. Adding, spelling, checking, and grammatic evaluation of text files intended for construction of articles and manuscripts

Although these sample lists are rather short, there is no reason that yours would have to be. Target your applications carefully, and place them in priority order. Revise and rework your lists until you feel comfortable with them. You will find them immensely helpful in deciding which, if any, program is best suited to your needs. By leaving some room for future expansion, the same lists will come in handy if you update a program.

Look again at the lists you just compiled. If you didn't come up with several definite applications for word processing, you may decide not to consider purchasing a program at this time. Let's say, for instance, that your primary potential application involves the occasional production of short business letters. Do you need the hassle and expense of word processing for something that any typewriter could handle adequately? Do you feel that the expense of a program (and computer system, if you don't already own one) could make you more productive? Are you willing to take the time and effort required to learn to use a program? Take a few minutes to sit back and reflect on these questions.

Your Features Shopping Lists. Go back to the two shopping lists you made while looking through the program features sections. Look again at those features you considered important and those you didn't. Are those features relevant to your potential applications? Rank the features in priority order. As an example, I could construct the following lists for my own word-processing applications:

Important Features

1. Upper- and lowercase input and direct display on the video screen

2. Convenient formatting, tabbing, and indentation capabilities with results shown directly on the screen

3. Provisions for lengthy text files and convenient access to them. Linking capabilities for printing multiple files at once

4. Dynamic editing features with heavy emphasis on ease of use

5. Block operations that allow dynamic management of sections of text, provisions for temporary storage, and appending blocks to existing text files

6. Control functions for special features included in my printer, such as character font selection, vertical formatting, and proportional spacing

7. Search and replace operations oriented to full words and phrases. Prompted replacement, used regularly to fill in abbreviations, is particularly important. Multiple search and replacement is desirable

8. On-screen preview of printed documents, including page numbering and breaks

9. Provisions for printing headers and footers, especially those which include some provision for page numbering in the header text

1. Built-in mailing list management system or form letter capability, since I already have separate programs for those purposes

2. Provisions for automatic telephone dialing or modem management

3. Extensive user prompting or tutorials, since I have used word processing for some time

4. Extensive mathematic functions

5. Provisions for security from undesired access to program text files

6. Use of foreign language or decorative print fonts.

Although I have included just a few of the many features from my lists, I think you get the idea. Look carefully at your own lists. If you didn't compile them earlier, it might be helpful to do so at this time.

MATCHING HARDWARE AND FEATURES

You have listed a group of features that you want for your word-processing system. Now it's time to look carefully at your computer and peripherals to see if they are equal to the demands. If not, you may have to trim some of the features from your list or look for some method of circumventing the limitation (using an add-on peripheral, for instance). Specifying 80-character lines when your computer will handle only 40, multiple disk access for systems that will handle only one disk, and extensive character font selection for printers that have only a few fonts available are some of the most common areas of conflict.

A few of your requirements may be met by the specific program itself, so don't be discouraged if all your requirements can't be met by your hardware. The Apple can display only 40-character lines without the addition of a relatively expensive hardware adapter. A few word-processing programs get around this limitation by generating character sets in software that display 60 to 80 character lines.

This process can also go in the opposite direction, and you may have more hardware capacity than most programs can handle. If you have five disk drives, and your requirements specify only two, perhaps your requirements should include some method of utilizing the other three drives. Owning a printer capable of printing in several colors is great, but programs to use that capability are rare. Set your requirements to get the most effective use of all the hardware you have.

Shopping for a Program. It is time to narrow the field of word-processing programs to a couple that look promising for your applications. The process may be something of an anticlimax, since you have spent a lot of time laying the groundwork. You already have a good idea of what you want the program to do and how it will go about doing its job.

From the list presented in the Appendix and whatever other information you can gather, eliminate those programs that obviously do not meet your requirements. Those that look like good possibilities should be investigated further, either at your local store or by requesting more specific information from the program supplier. If possible, narrow your group down to no more than two or three programs.

Once you have decided to look carefully at just a few programs, ask your dealer to let you try them in the store, if possible or try to arrange a money-back trial period at home. Sit down at a computer with each program and try a few of your definite and immediate applications. Type a letter or two, copy some text from an article you are working on, fill in a few forms, and do whatever else strikes your fancy. If a salesperson is available to help you, so much the better. Do not rely on a demonstration to answer your questions. Try it yourself.

During this process you will realize that each program has its own "personality" and "feel." Much like the keyboard feel discussed earlier, programs tend to combine their features in such a way as to make you comfortable or uncomfortable with the way they operate. Even programs with virtually identical capabilities have a different operating feel. If all other things seem equal, buy the one that feels most comfortable for you to use.

Appendix

Word-Processing Programs

This section lists word-processing programs and two spelling check programs offered for microcomputers. This list of programs will give you an idea of what is available for specific computers and provide buying information for programs with special features. With a little persistence, you can probably locate several more programs for your computer system.

This information has been gathered from manufacturers' data sheets, advertisements, program manuals, and product announcements. Although every effort has been made to insure accuracy, this listing may inadvertently contain some outdated or inaccurate information. You are advised to seek further information from your dealer or the program supplier before making any decisions regarding the suitability of program for your own use.

The listing format includes the following: program name, publisher's name and address, computer system requirements, description, my impressions (if applicable), price, and add-on or compatible programs offered. In the description section, I avoided repetitive lists of features found in almost every word-processing program and concentrated on special features and unique capabilities.

WORD-PROCESSING PROGRAMS

Applewriter™

Publisher: Apple Computer Corp., 10260 Bandley Drive, Cupertino, CA 95014.

Computer system requirements: Apple II or II Plus, 48K, Disk II (DOS 3.3), printer, and interface card.

Description: AppleWriter is a surprisingly capable menu-driven word-processing program. All the standard word-processing functions, with the exception of tabbing, are present. All text is displayed in uppercase letters on the screen, with capital letters identified by inverse video. A tutorial is included on the program disk.

Comments: AppleWriter is one of the most popular word-processing programs available for the Apple II. In spite of its uppercase and tabbing limitations, many Apple owners have found that it handles their word-processing applications very capably.

Price: Suggested retail price is $75.00.

The Benchmark Word Processor™

Publisher: Metasoft Corporation, 711 East Cottonwood Lane, Suite E, Casa Grande, AZ 85222.

Computer system requirements: Apple II CP/M, Northstar DOS, Northstar CP/M, Northstar Advantage, 8-inch single density CP/M, Zenith, Vector, Superbrain, Sharp, Xerox 820, or NEC PC-8000.

Description: Operational features include help panels, error messages that are easy to understand, default parameters defined for frequently occurring events, dynamic text formatting, automatic pagination, and a short training time for new operators.

Disk operation features provide for 30-character document titles, automatic recording of data and time of document creation or revision, preservation of both operator's and author's initials, automatic revision level tracking, and document and disk space size display.

Document-handling functions include single or double disk copying of disk files, deletion of multiple documents in a single operation, discretionary deletion of original document on revision, document append, and multiple printout queued files.

Format control includes settings for both horizontal and vertical pitch, word wrap "hot zone," first and last print line, and page format storage on disk. Horizontal tabs may be normal, indented, decimal aligned, flush right, centered, dot led, or underscored.

Proportional spacing and other special printer features are supported. Interactive printing permits the program to function as a typewriter for short letters. Versatile header and footer commands are included.

A maximum of 52 different phrases, of up to 2000 characters each, can be defined and used directly from the keyboard. Any format or format combination may be defined as a phrase.

Comments: I have examined the documentation for the Benchmark and found it to be most comprehensive and helpful. The command structure provided is awesome in its capabilities. Heavy emphasis has been placed on creating a program that features ease of operation coupled with efficient performance in an office environment. The documentation does a good job of instructing the inexperienced user in program operations and capabilities.

Price: Suggested retail price is $499.95.

Add-on or compatible programs: The Benchmark Mail List has been designed to work either as a stand-alone program or with the word-processing program. Many capabilities are built into both programs for efficient management of mailing list data. Price: $250.00.

EasyWriter Professional System™

For publisher and detailed examination data, see Chapter 8.

Price: Suggested retail price is $175.00.

Add-on or compatible programs: EasyMailer Professional System is a continuous letter-writing program designed for use with EasyWriter. Price: $175.00. EasyMover is an electronic Mail system that transmits EasyWriter files from one Apple to another via phone lines and translates EasyWriter files from and to Apple DOS. Price: $99.95.

EasyWriter II™

Publisher: Information Unlimited Software, Inc., 281 Arlington Avenue, Berkeley, CA 94707.

Computer system requirements: IBM Personal Computer.

Description: EasyWriter II is a version of EasyWriter Professional System developed for the IBM Personal Computer. You may find the information in Chapter 8 helpful, at least for background purposes. The IBM version combines the menu-driven approach seen in EasyWriter Professional System with the function keys found on the IBM. Some of the new features added include automatic pagination while typing, decimal tabbing, simplified headers and footers, built-in help function, and print spooling.

Comments: As you probably noted in Chapter 8, EasyWriter Professional System is an excellent word-processing program. EasyWriter II offers some additional sophistication that takes advantage of the features of the IBM Personal Computer.

Editrix 1.0™

Publisher: Data Transforms, 616 Washington Street, Denver, CO 80203.

Computer system requirements: Apple II, 48K, Applesoft in ROM, Disk II (DOS 3.3), Graphtrix 1.3 (companion program from Data Transforms), parallel interface card, and one of several popular printers with graphics capabilities.

Description: Editrix is a screen-oriented word processor for the Apple II that offers a full range of the features one would expect. In addition to the standard features, this program allows graphics displays to be printed directly into your document.

Comments: Editrix is one of the few word-processing programs that takes advantage of the Apple's graphics capabilities.

Price: Suggested retail price is $75.00. Also requires Graphtrix, retail price $65.00.

Add-on or compatible programs: Graphtrix is required for use of Editrix. It also allows insertion of graphics into text produced by the Applewriter word-processing system.

Electric Pencil™

Publisher: IJG Computer Services, 1260 West Foothill Boulevard, Upland, CA 91786.

Computer system requirements: TRS-80 Models I, II, and III. CP/M systems with memory mapped video.

Description: Electric Pencil is one of the classics in microcomputer word-processing programs and offers an extensive list of standard features. The latest version features more extensive debugging, help menus, and revised documentation. The package runs on a variety of TRS-80 systems, is compatible with all lowercase modifications, and uses standard TRS-80 mnemonics for file commands.

Price: Suggested retail price is $85.95.

The Executive Secretary™

For comprehensive information and detailed examination of The Executive Secretary, see Chapter 7.

The Final Word™

Publisher: Mark of the Unicorn, P.O. Box 423, Arlington, MA 02174.

Computer system requirements: Requires 56K CP/M system and video terminal with cursor-positioning sequences. Standard versions are available in 8-inch format for TRS-80 Model II, Vector Graphics, and Altos. Compatible versions are offered for the HP-125, Xerox 820, Cromeco, Micropolis, Ohio Scientific, and Dynabyte system. 5-and-¼-inch disk versions for the Heath/Zenith Z-89, Northstar, Apple, Superbrain, And IBM Personal Computer are also available.

Description: The Final Word features automatic generation of table of contents, indexing, footnoting and chapter/section numbering, enhanced command sets, multiple buffers and windows, deletion recovery, true proportional spacing, and simultaneous printing while editing.

Price: Suggested retail price is $300.00.

Letter Master™

Distributor: Monument Computer Service, Village Data Center, P.O. Box 603, Joshua Tree, CA 92252.

Computer system requirements: Apple II or Apple II Plus, Disk II.

Description: Menu-selected operating modes allow the entry, storage, recall, editing, and draft and final printing of reports and letters. In addition to a standard range of word-processing features, the program includes automatic pagination, copy designation, user-programmable line spacing, and justified and unjustified text on the same page. Mailing list and form letter writing elements are included in the program.

Price: Suggested retail price is $139.95.

Letter Perfect™

Publisher: LJK Enterprises, P.O. Box 10827, St. Louis, MO 63129.

Computer system required: Apple II or Apple II Plus, Disk II, 80-column display or lowercase adapter. Also available for the Atari 400 or 800.

Description: Features fast machine-language operation, screen preview of printed text, supports printers with proportional or incremental spacing, ability to transmit control codes from within the body of the programs, and other normal word-processing operations.

Price: Suggested retail price is $149.95.

Add-on or compatible programs: Data Perfect, by

LJK, provides the capability to perform data base merging operations.

LetteRite™

Distributor: Monument Computer Service, Village Data Center, P.O. Box 603, Joshua Tree, CA 92252.

Computer system requirements: Apple II or Apple II Plus, Disk II.

Description: This system allows for the entry, editing, printing, and disk storage of letters or small reports. Instructions for operation are on the screen, and menus are presented as needed. Entry of both upper- and lowercase letters is permitted. The program may be used with either one or two disk drives.

Price: Suggested retail price is $69.95.

Magic Wand™

Publisher: Peachtree Software Incorporated, 3 Corporate Square/Suite 700, Atlanta, GA 30329.

Computer system requirements: Apple II CP/M, Northstar CP/M, Superbrain, Micropolis, or 8-inch standard CP/M.

Description: Magic Wand includes all the standard word-processing commands, plus provisions for underscoring, boldface printing, subscripts and superscripts, variable pitch control, incremental spacing, and print spooling. In addition, variables may be defined, conditional printing statements structured, and numerous other commands used as the operator becomes more proficient with the system.

Comments: Magic Wand is one of the classics in the word-processing program market and offers a most impressive array of features to the user.

Add-on or compatible programs: Magic Spell is used for locating spelling mistakes and typing errors in Magic Wand files. Magic Messenger provides electronic mail capabilities. Magic Address adds mailing list management capabilities.

Magic Window™

Publisher: ARTSCI, Inc., 10432 Burbank Boulevard, North Hollywood, CA 91601.

Computer system requirements: Apple II or Apple II Plus, 32K (48K recommended), Disk II, printer, and interface card. Also directly supported are lower-case adapters and the Apple Language System.

Description: Magic Window is a very capable and popular word-processing program for the Apple II. A unique method of text display is featured. During text entry, the cursor remains fixed in the center of the screen, and text passes by. The effect is similar to that seen when typing on a standard typewriter. A window of 40 characters, 20 on either side of the cursor, displays the area of text around the cursor (but not the whole line).

This program is screen oriented. Most formatting commands show the effect, as opposed to the command itself, on the video display. The editing mode commands are structured in such a way as to give the effect of a whole keyboard full of predefined function keys.

Comments: Magic Window offers an interesting alternative to the usual method of screen display of text. Most users I have talked with are very pleased with this feature and overall operation of this program.

Add-on or compatible programs: Magic Words provides the ability to locate and correct mistakes in spelling. Over 14,000 words are included in the dictionary, which may be expanded by the user. Magic Mailer allows the insertion of names, addresses, or other related data from a mailing list to individualize documents.

Price: Suggested retail price is $99.95.

Maxi Pros™

Publisher: Aardvark Technical Services, 2352 South Commerce, Walled Lake, MI 48088.

Computer system requirements: Ohio Scientific or TRS-80 Color Computer.

Description: Maxi Pros is a word-processing system featuring all the standard commands and capabilities. A learning aid is provided to teach all the basic commands through the use of examples. Text may be stored or recalled from disk, edited, and formatted for printing. The program is written in BASIC and may be modified by the user.

Price: Suggested retail price is $39.95.

Memorite III™

Publisher: Vector Graphic, 500 North Ventu Park Road, Thousand Oaks, CA 91320.

Computer system requirements: Vector Graphic

computers, 56K, one or more disks, CP/M.

Description: Provides all the standard word-processing features and several specialized functions. List management capabilities, including sorting, are standard. Information from the lists can be merged with standard or custom letters or printed on labels. The program can substitute phrases for predefined abbreviations and supports electronic mail.

An interesting feature: the instruction manual is included in the software package so any topic, the table of contents or the entire manual can be printed on demand.

Price: From $450.00.

Mince™

Publisher: Mark of the Unicorn, P.O. Box 423, Arlington, MA 02174.

Computer system requirements: 56K CP/M system, video terminal which has cursor-positioning character sequences. Disks normally supplied in 8-inch single density. Contact publisher for information on additional systems supported.

Description: Mince is an interactive text-editing program that offers automatic virtual memory, multiple file display, recovery of deleted information, "try out" capability to see what the effect of a command will be before finalizing it, tabbing by increments, and a host of other sophisticated features. Two introductory lesson sets are included: one for the nontechnical user, the other for the experienced computer user.

Comments: Mince is unusual, because it is a full screen editor which operates via continuous user interaction with the text. The command characters have been selected for maximum convenience. Even the number of keystrokes necessary to invoke a command has been considered, and the most frequently used commands require the fewest keystrokes.

Add-on or compatible programs: Scribble is the text-formatting companion to Mince. It allows you to specify the logical structure of a document rather than the specific formatting details.

Price: Suggested retail prices are Mince—$175.00, Scribble—$175.00, and both programs ordered together—$275.00.

Newscript™

Publisher: Prosoft, Box 839, North Hollywood, CA 91603.

Computer system requirements: TRS-80 Model I or III, 48K, disk drive. Lowercase adapter required for Model I.

Description: In addition to the standard group of word-processing program features, Newscript offers some that are unusual in its price range. Headers, footers, indexing, table of contents references, and extremely flexible print formatting (including provisions for subscripts, superscripts, double width characters, and proportional spacing are standard. Also included are form letter and mailing list merging capabilities.

Add-on or compatible programs: Mailing Labels is a program that allows the user to print labels from Newscript lists. Dvorak Keyboard Support alters the keyboard through software to support the alternate key arrangement. A new module of daisy wheel printers, which creates true proportional spacing with right justification, should be on the market by the time you read this.

Price: Suggested retail price is $125.00.

Northword™

Publisher: North Star, 14440 Catalina Street, San Leandro, CA 94577.

Computer system requirements: North Star Horizon or Advantage computers, 56K, two disks, ASP operating system.

Description: Northword features a unique keyboard labeling system that all but eliminates the need to memorize control keys. The program is menu driven, except for the editing functions provided by the keyboard overlay.

Northwood is compatible with other North Star applications software and will produce checks, statements, reports, and personalized documents. A self-teaching manual and sample diskettes are included.

Price: Suggested retail price ranges from $399 to $499, depending on configuration.

Palantir™ Word Processing

Publisher: Designer Software, 3400 Montrose Boulevard, Suite 718, Houston, TX 77006.

Computer system requirements: CP/M system, at least 56K memory.

Description: The Palantir system is a sophisticated word-processing program. In addition to those features you would normally expect in this class of program, automatic hyphenation, automatic accenting, keyed recall of standard phrases, password encryption of files, framing of printed text, and full proportional spacing are included.

Price: Suggested retail price is $425.00.

Perfect Writer™

Publisher: Computer Services Corporation of America, 71 Murray Street, New York, NY 10007.

Computer system requirements: Apple II, Heath/Zenith, TRS-80 Model II, North Star, Osborne 1, Superbrain, Micropolis/Vector or 8-inch CP/M system.

Description: Perfect Writer features automatic formatting of letters or other documents, virtual memory architecture, and a split screen configuration for editing. Other features included are automatic generation of tables of contents and indexes, search and replace capability which locates near misses, microspacing during print, mail-merging capability, and a full range of the normal word-processing commands.

Add-on or compatible programs: Perfect Speller uses a 20,000-word dictionary to locate spelling errors. Perfect Mailer can organize and sort correspondence, develop sophisticated mailing systems, and keep track of your correspondence. Perfect Sort is a sort/merge/extract program that operates on a variety of data.

Price: Suggested retail price is $289.00.

PIE Writer™

Publisher: Hayden Publishing Co., Software Division, 50 Essex Street, Rochelle Park, NJ 07662.

Computer system requirements: Apple II or II Plus, 32K minimum (48K recommended), Disk II, lowercase adapter, or 80-column display board.

Description: PIE Writer is actually divided into two programs, the editor and the formatter. This allows the use of longer text files, since less memory is used for program overhead. Both are written in machine language for fast execution and feature a full range of word-processing capabilities. An optional proportional spacing formatter program is available, making PIE Writer one of the few low priced programs that supports this feature.

Several versions of the program are available. The standard version requires a lowercase adapter. Special versions for each of the commonly available 80-column display boards are also offered.

Price: Suggested retail price is $149.95.

PIE 1.5™

Publisher: The Software Toolworks, 14778 Glorietta Drive, Sherman Oaks, CA 91423.

Computer system requirements: Heath Zenith H89/Z89 and Z90, 8-inch CP/M systems with the H19/Z19 terminal. 32K minimum, 48K recommended.

Description: A full-featured word-processing system for the Heath/Zenith systems can be assembled using PIE 1.5 and Text Formatter. PIE 1.5 features cursor motion keys that allow changes to be typed anywhere on the screen. Function keys perform character and line insert and delete, string search, move and copy single and multiple lines, and scrolling text in the window. Macro capability provides many additional features.

Text Formatter performs fill and justification, page numbering, headers and footers, indents, centering, and underlining. Insertion of other files into a document and multiple disk documents are supported by this program.

Price: Suggested retail prices are PIE 1.5—$29.95 and Text Formatter—$34.95.

Report Writer™

Distributor: Monument Computer Service, Village Data Center, P.O. Box 603, Joshua Tree, CA 92252.

Computer system requirements: Apple II or II Plus, Applesoft ROM, 48K, Disk II (one or two drives). Also available for the Apple II and Apple II Plus with a Corvus Systems Hard Disk. An Apple III version is also offered.

Description: Report Writer is a complete word-processing system which includes built-in mailing list element and form letter preparation system.

Mixed text formats can be printed, and text automatically floats to fit print specifications.

Price: Suggested retail prices are Report Writer—$200.00, Corvus Hard Disk version—$249.95, and Apple III version—$249.95. The operating manual can be ordered separately for $20.00.

Screenwriter II™

Publisher: On-Line Systems, 36575 Mudge Ranch Road, Coarsegold, CA 93614.

Computer system requirements: Apple II or Apple II Plus, 48K, one or more Disk II (DOS 3.3), printer, and interface.

Description: Screenwriter II is one of the word-processing programs for the Apple II that effectively negates the need for additional lowercase and 80-column display hardware. Upper- and lowercase letters in lines of up to 70 characters are generated in software. In supporting multiple disk drives, proportional spacing, multiple headers and footers independent of the text on a page, and alternate character sets, Screenwriter II sets itself apart from many other programs available. Hyphenation, print spooling, editing of text files and BASIC programs, a MACRO function, form letter capability, indexing, virtual memory, and numerous other features are standard.

Comments: The list of features included in this program is even more impressive when you look at the price.

Price: Suggested retail price is $129.95.

Scripsit II™

Publisher: Radio Shack, a division of Tandy Corp., 1300 One Tandy Center, Fort Worth, TX 76102.

Computer system requirements: TRS-80 Model II, 48K minimum (64K recommended), one disk drive (two recommended).

Description: This word-processing-package for the Model II offers some very sophisticated features, such as interactive search and replace, horizontal scrolling, word and character swapping, and suppression of single-word lines at the end of a page. In addition to relatively complete documentation in the form of a user's manual, this program is supplied with an audio training course on cassette tape.

A limited version of Scripsit is available for the TRS-80 Model I and Model III.

Price: Suggested retail price is $199.00. Scriptsit for the Models I and III is $99.95

Select™

Publisher: Select Information Systems, Inc., 919 Sir Francis Drake Boulevard., Kentfield, CA 94904.

Computer system requirements: 48K Apple II or II Plus, two Disk II drives, CP/M card, and 80-column video display board. Versions are also available for IBM, North Star, Cromemco, Vector, Superbrain, NEC, Xerox, and Televideo systems.

Description: Select compares favorably with other CP/M-based word-processing systems in its list of standard features. This is a very capable word-processing system by any measure, but the built-in user friendliness sets it apart from many of the others. In addition to on-screen help functions, a full tutorial system called Teach helps the inexperienced user learn the system.

The command structure is set up in a system of single key mnemonics which can be displayed on the screen at all times. A program development mode is included, along with the capability to run other programs without leaving Select.

Superspell, a proofreading program that leads you step-by-step through its operations, is included.

Comments: Select is one of the most logical and easy to use word-processing systems I have seen for quite some time. The command structure, because of its simplicity, belies the extraordinary capabilities of the program. In addition to the Teach module, the program documentation is organized so relatively experienced word-processing users can rapidly learn most of the command structure.

Price: Suggested retail prices are Select With Superspell—$595.00, Apple Select—$345.00, and Apple Select With Superspell—$595.00. Documentation is available separately for $50.00.

Spellbinder™

Publisher: Lexisoft, Inc., Box 267, Davis, CA 95616.

Computer system requirements: Disk formats and

versions are available for TRS-80 Model II, Pickles & Trout, North Star Horizon and Advantage, Hewlett Packard HP125, Apple, Exidy Sorcerer, Lifeboat, Cromemco, Micropolis, AVL Eagle, Zenith, Superbrain, Vector Graphic, GNAT, Micropolis, Televideo, and Toshiba.

Description: This program is described by the publisher as the "Spellbinder Word-Processing and Office Management System" for good reason. Word-processing capabilities are numerous and diverse. In addition to those one would expect in a program of this price class, Spellbinder includes an on-line hyphenation check, dynamic help system, user-definable space and letter tables, proportional justification, dynamic character spacing, absolute horizontal tabbing, and a full range of mathematical operations. Spellcheck is operated as a system overlay from the Spellbinder command line. Creation and storage of forms templates with automatic tabbing to fields is possible.

The office management functions are provided within the program and by a system of programs called macros. Cuesorting, alphabetizing by name, zip code sorting, mail list merging, two-column printing, line numbering, pattern printing, and batch printing are some of the capabilities included.

Price: Suggested retail price is $495.00

Super-Text 40/80™

Publisher and descriptive information may be found in Chapter 6.

Add-on or compatible programs: Form Letter Module adds form letter and personalized correspondence capabilities to Super-Text 40/80. The Address Book mailing list management program is used to supply the data for form letters.

Text-Master II™

Publisher: Data Access Management Services, 3320 Rivers Avenue, Charleston, SC 29405.
Computer system requirements: MA/COM OSI Challenger series. Operates under OS-65U Version 1.2 or 1.3.
Description: Text Master II is an extended word-processing system with data base interfaces, work sheet capabilities, and expanded printer controls.

Math functions are included, along with the full range of word-processing capabilities found in the original Text-Master.

Volkswriter™

Publisher: Lifetree Software, 177 Webster Street/Suite 342, Monterey, CA 93940.
Computer system requirements: IBM Personal Computer, 64K, one disk drive, and IBM-DOS
Description: Designed for the typist as much as the writer and programmer, Volkswriter handles large or elaborate manuscripts with ease. You can insert a file into your text or create a new one from a portion of your text and define the sequence in which files are to be printed.
Price: Suggested retail price is $195.00.

Word III™

Publisher: Westico, 25 Van Zant Street, Norwalk, CT 06855.
Computer system requirements: Apple III.
Description: Word III is a full screen text-editing and word-processing program for the Apple III. A full range of word-processing capabilities are offered, including use of the special editing keys on the Apple III keyboard.
Price: Suggested retail price is $195.00.

The Word Handler™

For complete information regarding The Word Handler, see Chapter 5.

WordStar™

Publisher: MicroPro International Corporation, 1299 Fourth Street, San Rafael, CA 94901.
Computer system requirements: 48K CP/M and terminal with addressable cursor. Versions are available to run on almost every available microcomputer except the PET, SWTP, Apple I, and III.
Description: WordStar is one of the most sophisticated microcomputer word-processing programs around. The program is entirely screen oriented, user friendly, and has more capabilities than most users will ever need. This is, quite literally, one of the programs that set the standard for many of the most sophisticated programs now being introduced.

The most recent additions to WordStar include easier to understand help menus, horizontal scrolling, and column move features. Print spooling, dynamic page display, print enhancements, decimal point tabulation, and flexible formatting were incorporated into earlier versions.

Add-on or compatible programs: Two optional programs are available; MailMerge, a multiple-purpose mailing-list program, and SpellStar, which locates spelling and typographical errors.

Wordnet86™

Publisher: Monoson Microsystems, Inc., 51 Main Street, P.O. Box 97, Watertown, MA 02172.

Computer system requirements: IBM Personal Computer.

Description: Wordnet86 includes training aids, powerful screen-editing features (including horizontal scrolling), full use of all function keys, user-definable screen forms, and text/data merge. Check with the publisher for more detailed information.

Price: Suggested retail price is $395.00.

WordPro 4 Plus™

Publisher: Professional Software, 166 Crescent Road, Needham, MA 02194.

Computer system requirements: Commodore CBM 8032, 4040, or 8050 disk drives, and CBM printer or ASCII letter-quality printer with special ROM chip.

Description: Offers full columnar mathematics mode, several global functions which operate on an entire disk instead of only one file, simultaneous input-output, and the full range of word-processing features one would expect in a program of this price class. The manual is the form of a tutorial.

Price: Suggested Retail price is $450.00.

Write-On!™

For complete publisher and detailed examination information, see Chapter 4.

Write-On! IBM™

Publisher: Datamost, 9748 Cozycroft Avenue, Chatsworth, CA 91311.

Computer system requirements: IBM Personal Computer, MS-DOS.

Description: In addition to the features found in Write-On! (described in Chapter 4), the IBM version offers an 80-character screen display, a new line edit mode command, automatic dating in several formats, screen preview of printed documents, footers, and an out of paper error message from the printer. A new version supports underlined and boldface printing on Epson and Epsonlike printers.

Price: Suggested retail price is $129.95.

Write-On! III™

Publisher: Datamost, 9748 Cozycroft Avenue, Chatsworth, CA 91311.

Computer system requirements: Apple III, standard DOS operating system.

Description: In addition to the features found in Write-On! (Chapter 4), the Apple III version has been designed to take advantage of many of the special features found in the Apple III. No lowercase, shift key, or 80-column adapters are required for full 24-by-80 text display. Screen preview of printed documents and other features have been incorporated into this version.

Price: Suggested retail price is $129.95.

Zardax™

U.S. Distributor: Action-Research Northwest, 11442 Marine View Drive S.W., Seattle, WA 98146.

Computer system requirements: Apple II Plus or Apple II with autostart, 48 or 64K RAM, one or more Disk II (DOS 3.3). Connectors furnished for wiring of shift and control keys.

Description: Some of the features, as described by the distributor, are quite sophisticated. The program has full upper- and lowercase capability (controlled by shift and control keys) with audible feedback for lock and unlock. For unmodified 40-column Apples, no lowercase adapter is required and on-screen underlining is featured. The program supports use of the Vision-80, Doublevision, Smartterm, or Videx 80-column display boards. Zardax uses standard DOS 3.3 text files and can access text files written by other programs. The program also includes a glossary feature, the ability to define abbreviations for frequently used phrases or control sequences, easy formatting to a variety of printers, and full mail-merge facilities for form letters.

Comments: Zardax is one of the most sophisticated of the new generation of Apple II word-processing programs. Every attempt has been made to hold additional hardware requirements to a bare minimum while providing very sophisticated program capabilities.

Price: Suggested retail price is $295.00.

SPELLING CHECK PROGRAMS

One of the most valuable additions to a word-processing program is some method of checking text for spelling and typographical errors. As you probably noticed in the preceding program listings, several word-processing programs include this feature.

For those who have, or may be considering, a word-processing program without spelling check capabilities, there are several programs that offer this feature as examples of the types of capabilities offered, only two programs are described here.

The Apple Speller™

Publisher: Sensible Software, 6619 Perham Drive, West Bloomfield, MI 48033.

Computer system requirements: Apple II or Apple II Plus, 48K, Disk II (two drives recommended), DOS 3.3.

Description: The Apple Speller can analyze the output of any word-processing program that writes a standard Apple binary or text file to a diskette. The publisher states that the program is compatible with Applewriter, The Executive Secretary, Letter Perfect, Magic Window, Screenwriter II, Super-Text II, and numerous others. An Apple CP/M version is also available.

A 30,000-word dictionary is supplied to which the user may add another 8000 words. Capabilities for creating modified or new dictionaries for special applications are included. Numerous options are provided to control all the activities of the program.

A verification mode, which allows you to examine and dispense with misspelled words in context, is included. The publisher states that the program will proofread a 10-page document in 1 minute if there are no spelling errors and 2 minutes, 15 seconds for an unlimited number of spelling errors.

Spellguard 2.0™

Publisher: Innovative Software Applications, 260 Sheridan/Suite 300, Palo Alto CA 94306.

Computer system requirements: CP/M, 32K, 8080/8085/Z80-based microcomputer and word-processing program such as WordStar, Magic Wand, Electric Pencil, etc. An Apple CP/M version is available.

Description: Spellguard is genearlly regarded as the most popular spelling check program for CP/M-based systems. As supplied, the program includes a 20,000-word dictionary and is entirely menu driven. Also included is a special 19,000-word legal dictionary. Words may be added or deleted from the dictionary with a single keystroke command.

During the process of proofreading, words may be marked in context for later correction, added to the dictionary, ignored, or listed. The process of proofreading is amazingly rapid; the publisher notes that proofreading rates have been benchmarked at 15,000 words in under one minute.

Although it has many features, one of the most noticeable is the user friendliness of this program. Menus are clear and concise, help is readily available, and the documentation is extremely well written. Beginner and expert modes can be selected in the program. The expert mode is faster and has fewer messages.

Comments: This is a fine example of a program designed to do a specific task and do it well. It works so efficiently that you may forget just how sophisticated it really is. If you are using a CP/M-based word processor, Spellguard is one add-on program that deserves your careful consideration.

Price: Suggested retail price is $295.00.

Glossary

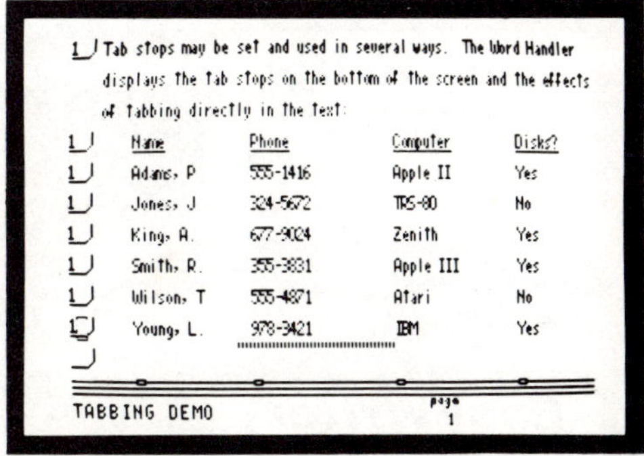

Glossary

access—The process of retrieving data from or placing it into storage. Also used to identify the process of gaining the use of another computer or program via remote linkage.

accuracy—Refers to the ability of a computer, peripheral, or program to maintain a desired degree of precision.

acoustic coupler—*See* modem.

adaptability—The degree to which a program or system can be readily modified to suit differing user requirements. This can refer to either self-modifications included within a program or the ease with which the actual program lines can be changed.

alpha—Term used to designate alphabetic characters. Alphanumeric expands the meaning to include both numeric and alphabetic characters.

alternating margins—Margin settings which adjust the position of printed text on alternate pages. Most often used to set up printed pages for binding where margins on the inside of pages must be wider than those on the outside.

applicability—The extent to which a program or system actually does what it is intended to do.

application software—Programs designed to fulfill a certain function in a specific application. Word-processing programs, mailing list management programs, and accounting systems are examples of application software.

archival storage—The saving of documents or files on storage media for the purpose of providing protection from theft, destruction, or loss of the original or working copies. Archival storage implies that the second set of files be kept separate and secure at all times. See also backup.

ASCII—American Standard Code for Information Interchange. A standardized system of assigning specific bit patterns for numbers, letters, symbols, signs, and operations.

aspect ratio—The ratio of the width to the height of a character.

backspace—The ability to move the cursor or printing mechanism backward for the purpose of

backup. Most word-processing program packages include duplicate, or back-up, copy so operations can continue if the original program disk is damaged.

making a correction or overprinting another character.

backup—Another (and more frequently used) term for archival storage. Often used as a verb to describe the process, backing up files on a regular basis is the only way to insure against loss of valuable data or text. In addition to data files, back-up copies of program disks are frequently made (or provided by program suppliers) so operations can continue despite a damaged or lost original program disk.

BASIC—Beginner's All-purpose Symbolic Instruction Code, a programming language developed at Dartmouth College in 1963. As the acronym suggests, BASIC is relatively easy to learn and use. This language has become the mainstay of the microcomputer world and is available for virtually every small computer on the market.

bidirectional printer—A device which is capable of printing characters while the print head is traveling in both the normal (left to right) and the return (right to left) directions. This capability reduces wasted motion of the printing mechanism and increases the efficiency of the printer. Often combined with logic-seeking capabilities.

block—In word-processing context, block refers to a specific portion of text which is marked and subject to the block operation commands. Used also to describe input/output or working areas in the main memory of a computer (memory block) and a group of consecutive characters considered or transferred as a unit (data block).

boilerplate—Short text files that are used repeatedly as parts of larger documents. Most often, there is little or no modification between uses. The actual document created by the use of boilerplate files is also referred to as a boilerplate.

bold—The ability to overprint a word or phrase to make it stand out from the rest of the text. May also be accomplished through the use of boldface type, which has a heavier outline than most type fonts.

bomb—The complete failure of a program or system.

block. The text enclosed by parentheses has been marked as a block and may be copied, saved, deleted, or unmarked, as noted on the bottom of the screen.

boot—The loading and execution of a few instructions that permit other computer operations to be done. Most often used in the context of booting a disk, which refers to loading the disk operating system into the computer.

bootleg—Refers to the unauthorized copy of a commercial program obtained under less than honorable circumstances. Also known as software piracy, or more colloquially, stealing.

buffer—A section of memory or an external device used to hold data temporarily until it can be processed or transmitted to another device.

bug—A mistake in the design or coding of a program which prevents proper operation.

camera ready copy—Text which is ready to be photographed and used, without further modifications, for offset printing.

cancel—To stop, or abort, a process or program function in progress.

capability—The operational potential of a computer system. Measured in terms of memory size, speed of execution, peripherals attached, display modes available, and so on. Word-processing capability, for instance, means that a computer system has sufficient hardware and software to execute word-processing programs.

card—A term referring to a plug-in circuit board which gives additional capacity to a microcomputer. Also refers to the command reference card included in most word-processing (and other types of) programs.

carriage return—See RETURN.

carrier—A tone used to convey information in telecomputing applications. Carrier tones are transmitted and received by modems. See also modem.

cassette tape—Magnetic tape contained in a plastic carrier which may be used for data storage purposes. Some small computers can use standard audio tape cassettes, while others require special data units.

CATALOG—In disk-based computer systems, this command is used to display the names of files contained on a specific disk. In some com-

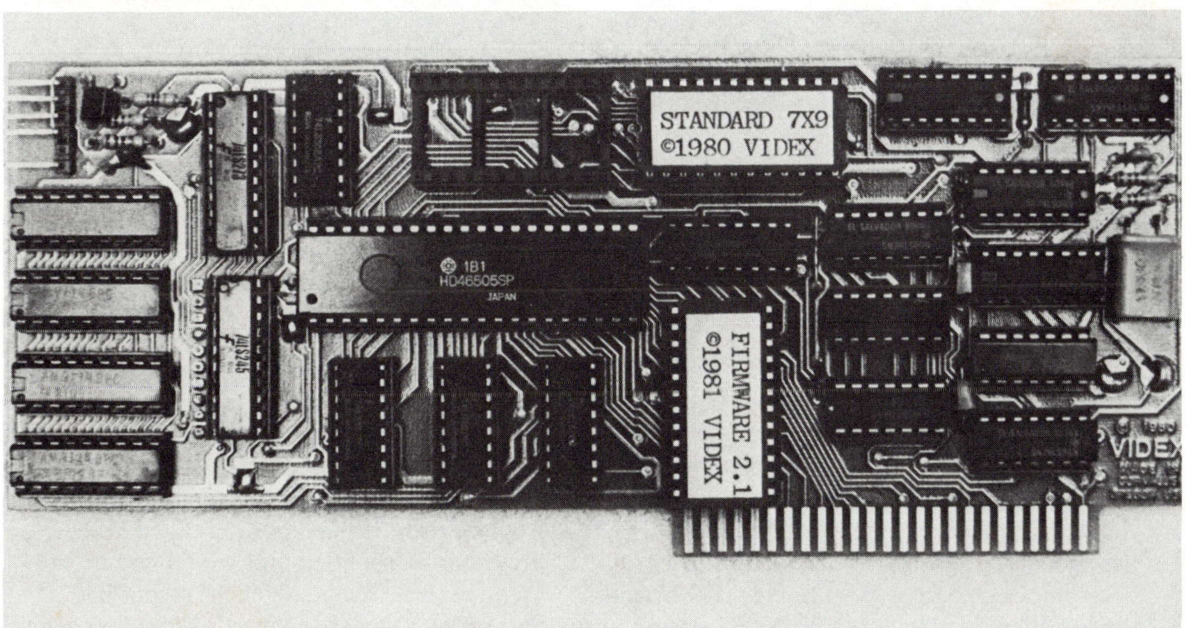

card. This Videx plug-in card adds 80-column display capabilities to the Apple II computer.

```
*A  051   EDITOR
*B  002   KEYIN
*B  003   MACHSUBS
*A  004   DATA FILE CONVERTER
*T  006   REARRANGEMENT SAMPLE
*T  005   TABS EXAMPLE 1
*T  005   TABS EXAMPLE 2
*T  003   KBD INPUT EXAMPLE
*T  004   TEMP MARGIN EXAMPLE 1
*T  006   TEMP MARGIN EXAMPLE 2
*T  005   FORM LETTER EXAMPLE
*T  002   MAILING LABEL EXAMPLE
*T  003   D.DATA FILE EXAMPLE
*T  003   SCRIPT EXAMPLE
 T  004   DEMO
 T  004   P.DEMOPRINT

WHAT DISK FILE DO YOU WANT ?

TYPE 'CATALOG' TO SEE FILES ON THIS DISK


    ==> REARRANGEMENT SAMPLE
```

CATALOG. This command causes the names and information regarding the files contained on a disk to be displayed.

puter systems and programs, this function may be known as a directory. Also used in some word processing programs to designate the list of available commands.

center—To position a group of characters equidistant from the margins on a printed sheet. Most word-processing programs will center lines on command from the user.

central processing unit (CPU)—The principle and most basic operating unit of a computer. Actual manipulation of data occurs in the CPU, which may be one or a combination of chips. Most microcomputers identify the CPU by the type of chip used, such as 6502, Z80, etc.

character—A single digit, letter, punctuation mark, or other symbol which the computer can read or write.

chip—A term frequently used to designate the semiconductor integrated circuits used in computers and related equipment. Often used with a qualifier to indicate the function of the integrated circuit, such as memory chip or processing chip.

clock/calendar card—A printed circuit card which may be installed in a computer for the purpose of obtaining real time information. Data from the card is used in some word-processing programs to label text files with time and date of creation, last change, or most recent use.

command—A signal or set of instructions which control specific computer operations.

communication—The process of exchanging data between two computers or terminal(s) and a host computer. Communication circuits may be hardwired (connected permanently on site) or temporarily established through the use of telephone lines or radio circuits.

continuous form paper—Paper which is supplied in cartons, fanfolded to the size of each sheet. Perforations at the page boundaries, and often along each edge allow the individual sheets to be separated. Fanfold, as it is popularly known, allows lengthy documents to be produced without loading single sheets into the printer at each page break.

contrast—The measure of relative brightness between the bright and dark areas on a video display. Also used to describe the intensity of printed characters relative to the background paper color.

control character—A nonprinting character inserted into a document to transmit specific information to the word-processing program or printer. Control characters are often indicated by inverse video on the CRT display.

conversational processing—See interactive.

conversion—The process of changing data from one processing format, display mode, or storage medium to another. For instance, text files may be converted from all capital letters to upper- and lowercase display.

copy—Most frequently used in computer applications to describe the making of a duplicate data diskette or tape cassette. Copy can also refer to basic material from which documents are prepared (rough copy) or text printed on paper (hard copy).

correct—In word processing, this term refers to the process of replacing unwanted copy. This can take the form of a typing correction, in which case the user can usually backspace the cursor to remove the unwanted character and type in the correct one.

CPI—Abbreviation for characters per inch, a standard measure of the size of printed characters. Most printers used in word-processing applications feature standard Pica (10 CPI) and Elite (12 CPI), in addition to any other print size options.

CP/M—Control Program/for Microprocessors, a popular disk operating system for small computers. Originally developed by Digital Research, Inc.

CPS—Abbreviation for characters per second, a popular measure of printer speed.

crash—Used to describe the dynamic failure of a computer system, peripheral, or program. There are a great many more colorful (but far less socially acceptable) words that can be used to describe the same situation.

create—The term used by most word-processing programs to designate the process of initializing a new document or text file.

CRT—Abbreviation for cathode ray tube, the television-type screen used in computer applications to create a video display.

CTRL—Refers to the control key found on most computer keyboards. This key is used in conjunction with other keys to generate distinctive ASCII codes for specific functions. Often, word-processing programs use CTRL-(key) combinations to produce characters and operations not normally available on the computer keyboard.

cursor—A block, line, or other character on a video display which is used to designate the current screen position being addressed.

daisy wheel—A print element, shaped like a flattened daisy, which is used in many correspondence-quality printers. The characters are contained on arms that extend from the center of the element. In operation, the wheel rotates to the correct position, and the desired character is struck by a small hammer. The hammer forces the character and the ribbon to leave an impression on the paper. Many character fonts are available on daisy wheels. The wheel itself is made of metal or plastic.

dangling line—A single line of a paragraph that appears on a different page from the rest of the paragraph. Dangling lines are classified as either "widows" or "orphans," depending on which part of the paragraph the single line is from. Some word-processing programs are geared to warn the operator or automatically reformat the output to avoid either type of dangling line.

data base—Information stored as data items, usually in the form of records in a file.

data base management—A systematic approach to the updating, retrieval, and storage of information stored in a data base. In larger computer systems, many on-site or remote users may share the same data base and management programs. Most microcomputer data base management systems are designed for single users.

debug—The process of locating and correcting operational errors in a program, operating system, or computer hardware.

decimal alignment—Also known as decimal tabulation or decimal justification. A common word-processing feature which provides for the automatic vertical alignment of decimal points at a predetermined location.

dedicated—Commonly refers to a machine or system reserved for a specific application. For instance, a dedicated word-processing system is one designed for only that capability.

default—Usually refers to default settings, or values established for printer type, page size, margin settings, paragraph indentation, and other parameters when a word-processing system is

delete. The material shown in inverse video will be removed from the text if the delete command is verified.

installed in a particular computer. Most often, the program will use the default settings unless they are changed for a specific file by the user. All microcomputer-based word-processing programs allow the user to change default settings relatively easily.

delete—Removing a character, word, line, or series of lines from a text file. Also used to remove entire text files from a data disk.

dictionary—A file of words (and sometimes hyphenation information) available on the word-processing program itself or separately. Dictionaries are intended to assist the user by providing spelling correction and hyphenation information for text files created by the word-processing program. Due to storage limitations, most microcomputer "spelling check" programs have fairly limited dictionary capacity.

directory file—A specific type of file that describes the layout of other records within a file or on a disk.

disk—A storage device on which information is recorded on the revolving surface of a magnetized disk. Most personal computers use "mini-floppy" disk storage. Floppy disks are thin, magnetized circles enclosed in a sheath which can be readily inserted or removed from a disk drive. Common usage defines floppy disks as being eight inches in diameter, mini-floppies five and a quarter. Storage systems using rigid disks, or disk packs, are becoming increasingly available for small computer systems.

disk drive—A piece of hardware that contains the motor, read/write head, and associated components for the use of disk-based storage. Once a disk is inserted into the drive, all other operations are controlled by the computer's disk operating system (DOS).

display—A common term used to designate the CRT, television receiver, or video monitor used with a microcomputer.

document—In word-processing usage, document

disk drive. Two Apple Disk II drives.

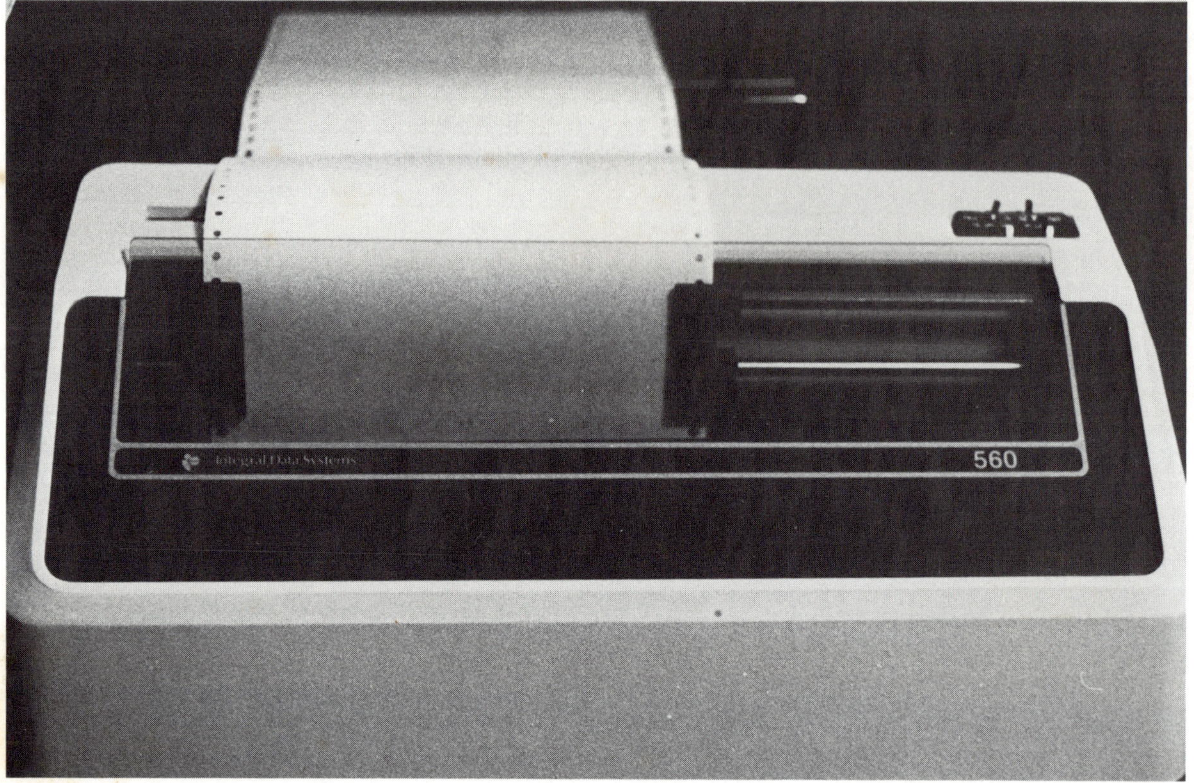

dot-matrix printer. A dot-matrix Paper Tiger 560 printer meets the printing requirements of many word-processing users.

refers to an entity produced by a combination of characters, words, lines, and paragraphs. Also referred to as text files.

documentation—In computer usage, documentation refers to the information accompanying a program. Commercial programs commonly supply documentation in the form of a user's manual containing instructions, description of operations, possible modifications, and so on.

DOS—Abbreviation for disk operating system. A group of programs designed to handle input and output functions, keep track of files, and manage all other operations associated with the use of a disk-based storage system. Some DOS routines are built in to the computer; others must be loaded from a disk before any other programs can be used.

dot leader—A capability contained in some word-processing programs which automatically places a series of dots between two designated items of copy.

dot-matrix printer—An electrostatic, photographic, or wire printer in which characters are formed from individual dots arranged in a matrix pattern. Most matrices are described in terms of the number of dots they contain, such as 5-by-7 or 7-by-9.

double space—Printing text on every other line of a page, leaving a blank line after every printed line. Generally accepted as three printed or typed lines per inch.

draft—A rough, unedited copy of a document. Sometimes preceded by a number of descriptor to indicate progress toward a final, or finished, copy. For instance, you could have a first draft, rough draft, working draft, and so on.

dual-pitch printer—A printing unit capable of producing both the standard 10- and 12-character-per-inch text. Although many printers used for microcomputer word-processing applications are capable of producing several sizes and types of characters, the 10- and 12-per-inch characters are accepted standards for business correspondence.

dump—A term generally associated with the transfer, printing, or display of the contents of a file. Also used colloquially to describe loss of power or program function in the middle of an operation.

editing—The process of correcting or revising the text of a draft prior to its production as a final document. Word-processing programs typically contain a set of commands intended to make the editing process as efficient as possible.

editor—In computer usage, refers to a program that permits the computer user to modify other program or text files. See also text editor.

efficiency—The degree to which a program utilizes the full operational and memory capacity of a computer. Also refers to the savings in time or increased productivity provided by the use of a particular program or system.

electronic mail—The transmission of correspondence by electronic, as opposed to written, means. Corporate computers operated by a network of remote terminals are routinely used in this fashion. Personal computer users may take advantage of electronic mail capabilities through telecomputing systems; messages may be addressed to other users and received by specific request of the addressee. See also telecomputing.

electrostatic printer—A unit which uses an electric charge in the printhead to make characters on specially sensitized paper. Speed and quiet operation are the primary advantages of this type of printer. Although paper quality and print permanence are not suitable for most word-processing applications, electrostatic printers can be used for draft or in-house correspondence applications.

element—In word-processing usage, element refers to the part of a letter-quality printer that actually contains the character set. Elements are commonly available in the form of daisy wheels, print thimbles, or IBM type golfballs.

elite—In the past, this term referred only to the smaller of the two commonly available typewriter print sizes. Recent usage has expanded the term to include all type sizes that contain 12 characters to the inch. Also known as "12 pitch."

embedded command—A word-processing program instruction which can be inserted into text as it is entered. This type of command affects the final format of the printed text but is not itself printed.

emphasized printing—A method of printing whereby characters are enlarged or expanded for emphasis. This is done by printing a shadow image of the original character, overprinting several times, or using a different character font.

ERROR—The message displayed by a computer when it encounters an unacceptable condition in program or peripheral operation. Most personal computers include provisions for informing the user as to the nature of the ERROR indicated.

error trapping—The process of examining, by means of decision routines, the input to and operation of a program with the intention of allowing the user to correct error conditions before they result in the loss of data or program operation. Short subroutines, called error-handling routines, provide messages and outline procedures to resolve problems. Effective error trapping is one of the prerequisites to creating a user friendly program. See also reenter.

ESC—The ESCape key found on computer keyboards. Although it generates a nonprinting ASCII character, ESC is frequently used for control of specific program functions. For example, on computer without functional shift keys, ESC can be used to provide upper- and lowercase selection.

execute—A command which instructs a computer program to initiate a specified operation. The time required to complete the operation is referred to as execution time.

expression—In computer usage, expression refers to a series of constants, variables, or functions connected by operational symbols and punctuation which cause a desired operation to take place. Word-processing programs often allow the user to define a text expression which will be printed by pressing one or two keys.

fabric ribbon—A typewriter or printer ribbon made of cotton, nylon, or silk. Most fabric ribbons last a long time and are relatively inexpensive. Print quality is fairly good with the first pass through the printer but deteriorates markedly with each successive use. To combat this problem and extend ribbon life, some printing units incorporate a method of reinking the ribbon as it is used. Fabric ribbons are frequently used to produce rough draft copies of documents, although many dot-matrix printers use them exclusively.

file—A collection of related information which is treated as a unit for the purposes of manipulation and storage. Text files contain data used during the execution of a program; program files contain the statements necessary to direct the computer to operate in a particular fashion.

film ribbon—A typewriter or printer ribbon made of polyethylene or Mylar. Most film ribbons are for single pass printing. They deposit all their colored matter onto the paper, leaving only the base material at the spot where a character has struck. The ribbon is exhausted when all the available character locations have been used once. Print quality with film ribbons is considerably better than with fabric ribbons, although they are much more expensive to use.

final copy—The highest quality end product capable of being produced by a word-processing system. Final copies are printed only after all editing is completed and revisions made. Print clarity, paper quality, and finished appearance are contributors to the overall professional impression conveyed by a final copy.

firmware—A computer program, or set of programs, permanently contained in a semiconductor chip. The instructions contained in the chip are nonvolatile; they remain intact despite power failure or computer problems. Many of the monitor and operating routines for microcomputers are contained in firmware. Some frequently used utility programs are also offered in this configuration.

flag—An indicator used to determine whether or not a specific action has occurred during the execution of a program. Usually described in terms of the type of action, such as error flag to indicate an error.

flash—A display mode in which the character(s) alternate between normal (white on black) and inverse (black on white) video.

floppy disk—A flexible plastic disk, resembling a phonograph record, coated with magnetic material, and enclosed in a sheath. Used in drives designed to spin the disk inside its sheath and read or write information via a "head" held in close proximity to the disk surface through an opening provided in the sheath. Floppy disk is also used to designate 8-inch diameter diskettes, while mini-floppy refers to the 5-and-¼ inch variety.

flowchart—Graphic representation of a sequence of operations using symbols to represent specific operations. Flowcharts are used in computer program construction and are occasionally included in the documentation for word-processing programs.

flush—In word-processing applications, flush means even with. Flush left means even with the left margin, and flush right even with the right margin. See also justification, ragged left, and ragged right.

font—In the past, font referred to an assortment of type characters in one size and style. It is now generally accepted to mean a complete character set in one particular size and style contained on a print element or in a printer's firmware.

foot—The bottom of a page.

footer—A specific line that appears at the bottom of each page of a document. Most word-processing programs allow you to designate a line or series of lines to be printed automatically as footers.

footnote—Text that appears at the bottom of a page and describes or defines some portion of the text contained on that page. Some word-processing programs provide for automatic management of footnotes; others allow manual placement by indicating the amount of space remaining on the page.

foreground/background processing—The ability of a computer to process a high priority foreground program, switching to a subsidiary background program during the times the primary program is not using the CPU. An example of foreground/background processing is print spooling, a process that allows the computer to direct output to the printer concurrently with other word-processing operations. To be truly effective, operation of the background program should not significantly deteriorate the performance of the foreground program.

form—A preprinted document used for a specific purpose. Checks, purchase orders, and invoices are a few of the more commonly used forms. Use of forms with word-processing programs may be limited if the program does not contain capabilities for precise alignment of printing within predefined areas.

form feed—Refers to the capbility of some printers to handle paper produced in continuous fan-folded strips or rolls. Form feed is also a printer control command which causes the paper to advance to the top of the next sheet.

form letter—In some applications, form letters are preprinted documents to which are added the name and address desired. Word-processing programs have expanded this to mean standardized letters which can be personalized by changing a small number of words or phrases. Most word-processing form letters are individually produced, eliminating the characteristic form letter look.

format—A predetermined arrangement of characters, lines, fields, etc. Refers to both the capabilities of a video display and the arrangement of printed information on a page. When used in the context of a video display, format usually refers to the number of lines vertically and the number of characters per horizontal line that can be displayed simultaneously, such as 24-by-80. Some video display terminals have a feature known as format mode which allows construction and use of a predefined video screen for multiple item input sequences. Printing formats are defined in terms of margins, indentation, page length, print size, and so on. Most word-processing programs allow you to predefine several standard formats for use with specific types of text files. Some programs also allow you to change output format parameters during the process of text input.

formed character—Characters which are raised from the surface of a daisy wheel, print thimble, golf ball element, or key bar. Formed characters offer the best print quality but usually are not as rapidly imprinted on a page as dot-matrix characters.

friction feed—In printing applications, refers to the movement of paper controlled by the action of a rolling cylinder to which the paper is held by smaller friction rollers. Most typewriters use friction feed. This method of paper handling is generally used with individual sheets and is less precise than tractor feed or pin feed.

full page display—The capability to display an entire printed page on the video screen. This feature is found in some dedicated word-

```
PRINTER ADDRESS IN HEX            : 0001
HIBIT OFF OR ON                   : ON
CARRIAGE RETURN DELAY (0-255)     : 0
FORM FEED OR SHEET FEED           : FORM
LEFT MARGIN                       : 1
RIGHT MARGIN                      : 120
PARAGRAPH INDENTATION             : 4
TOP MARGIN                        : 5
TEXT LENGTH                       : 56
BOTTOM MARGIN                     : 5
```

```
AUTO PAGE NUMBERING               : OFF
PAGE NUMBER TOP OR BOTTOM         : TOP
MARGIN LINE FOR PAGE NUMBER       : 3
PAGE NUMBER TAB POSITION          : 39
BACKSPACE CHARACTER (HEX)         : 88
UNDERLINE CHARACTER (HEX)         : 0F

PRESS <RETURN> TO FINISH OR
PRESS <ESC> TO START OVER
```

format. Default values for the formatting of printed documents are often set during the initial configuration of a word-processing program. Most programs allow you to alter format parameters during the process of text input or editing.

processing systems but has not yet been widely adopted in microcomputer-based programs.

function—Special purpose or characteristic actions within a program, such as editing functions. Also refers to a type or sequence of calculations contained in an arithmetic statement in other types of programs. Most computer languages include several predefined mathematical functions.

function keys—In many dedicated word-processing systems, extra keys are provided to control special functions. Since most microcomputer keyboards contain only the necessary number of keys, this function is sometimes emulated by providing access to special functions through a combination of two or more keystrokes. Often the escape or control key is used in conjunction with another key for this purpose.

galley proof—A preliminary print-out of text in columnar form. Used for checking prior to the final version of document being typeset or printed.

GIGO—An abbreviation widely used in computer circles to mean garbage in, garbage out. Word processing, like all other computer applications, is capable of outputting data only as good as that initially entered.

global change—The ability of a word-processing program to change a specified word or portion of text wherever it appears in a document by using a single instruction. This feature is also known as global replace or repetitive correction.

global search—The ability of a word-processing program to locate every occurrence of a specified word or portion of text in a document. Closely related to global change, both features are found in most word-processing programs.

graphics—Sophisticated pictures that show the results of computations in a form that is easily interpreted and remembered. Also refers to the ability of a computer to display data in the form of pictures or graphs. Simple graphic displays are within the capability of all computers, but an increasing number are being offered with sophisticated graphics features. Some word-processing programs allow you to mix graphics and text on a printed page.

handshaking—A status communication process between two devices. This process insures the receiving device is ready to accept data before the transmitting device begins to send it. The most obvious uses for handshaking or situations where the speed of transmission must be adjusted to meet the needs of a considerably slower receiving device. A good example of this can be seen in printers attached to your computer. Most printers are not capable of accepting data at anywhere near the normal transmission rate of the computer. Handshaking is also used to report receiving device errors (like printer out of paper) and halt transmission of further data until the error condition has been resolved.

hard copy—A document which has been printed on paper.

hard disk—A type of mass storage device that uses either a single disk or a stack of several solid disks (hence, the term hard disk) in a drive designed for their use. Hard disk storage systems offer considerably faster data access and greater storage capacity than their floppy-disk counterparts. Prices of hard disk units are steadily declining to the point where their use with microcomputers is becoming practical. See also Winchester disk.

hardware—A general term used to designate all the electronic and mechanical components of a computer system.

hardwired—Refers to peripherals permanently connected to a computer by some form of cable.

head—Usually refers to the electromagnetic device contained in a cassette tape or disk drive unit. The head reads, records, and erases data on the magnetic media used.

header—Opposite of footer. A specific line that appears at the top of each page of a document. Most word-processing programs allow you to designate a line or series of lines that can automatically be printed as headers.

help file—A direct self-teaching facility, provided on a program disk, designed to help you learn program operations. Help files usually explain the nature of the program, special commands used, and techniques necessary to insure proper operation of the program. Many word-processing programs provide some type of help file, although it is often a short refresher of concepts presented in the program manual.

highlight—A means of displaying a character or series of characters that stand out from the surrounding text. Inverse video or flashing from normal to inverse video are standard ways of highlighting on a video display. Overstriking, underlining, italics, or different print sizes are some of the ways text may be highlighted when printing.

home—Usually refers to the starting position of the cursor on a video display. Nearly all microcomputers designate the home position as the top character position.

horizontal scroll—Providing the capability to view a selected portion of a document that is too wide to be viewed in its entirety on a video display. The effect of horizontal scrolling is that of a limited width "window" that can be opened to any designated portion of the document in memory.

horizontal tab—The ability to move the cursor (or print head) horizontally across the screen (or paper) to any preselected position. Most word-processing programs provide for multiple horizontal tabs to be defined across the document width selected.

hot zone—In word-processing applications, this is defined as the maximum number of blank spaces allowable between the end of a line and the right margin. Used primarily with hyphenation capabilities; the operator is expected to supply a hyphenation decision if a word is too long for a line but will exceed the predefined hot zone if moved to the next.

housekeeping—Necessary overhead or administrative functions contained within a program. Most often, housekeeping operations are done automatically when needed. Some common housekeeping operations include rearranging data on a disk, clearing specific areas of memory, and reading default parameters. Some programs suspend operations for a few seconds to handle housekeeping chores; others do them in a foreground/background manner.

hyphenation—Dividing a word between syllables at the end of a line of text. This is used to make the length of printed lines more consistent. Some programs offer hyphenation dictionaries which handle this chore automatically, but such features are very rare in microcomputer-based programs.

IC—An abbreviation for integrated circuit. See chip.

I/O—An abbreviation used in computer circles to designate input/output.

impact printer—A type of printer in which the character element directly strikes the paper (and usually a ribbon) to produce an impression.

indentation—To start a line or lines of type a specified number of spaces from the margin. The first line of a paragraph is often indented five spaces from the left margin.

index—The list of key words and phrases (and associated page numbers) found in a book or manual. Some of the word-processing systems available for microcomputers include an indexing function which automatically prints an index after the final formatting of a document. Also sometimes used to refer to the catalog or directory of files on a mass storage disk.

initialize—To start up or set the basic conditions for an operation. Initializing a program involves setting the basic routines and data necessary for operation. In most word-processing programs, you set the operating specifications the first time you use the program. Thereafter, initializing is done automatically each time the program is booted. Initializing a disk means formatting the disk to accept the data that will be stored later.

ink jet—A method of printing in which characters are formed by actually squirting ink onto the paper. Ink jet printers are more commonly used in large data-processing installations than in small word-processing systems.

input—The process of adding information to the computer's memory or files. When used as a BASIC command, INPUT prompts and accepts data. In most word-processing applications, input refers to typing information from the keyboard or retrieving text from a disk file.

insert—Word-processing programs universally allow insertion of new material into previously stored text. The command itself is usually a variation of the word "insert" and is thought of as an editing function.

integrated system—In a hardware context, this refers to a computer and peripherals that work together without the need for additional devices. Programs that share data with each other are also referred to as integrated systems.

intelligent terminal—A printing or video display terminal that has both memory and processing capacity. Microcomputers are sometimes used as intelligent terminals in time-sharing systems.

interactive—Refers to programs which accept user input and act immediately as a result of that input. The course of action followed by the program is entirely dependent upon input from the user. Also known as conversational processing, since the user is in a sense directly conversing with the computer.

interface—A common boundary between pieces of equipment in a data processing system. For example, an interface must be provided between a computer and printer.

interrupt—A break in the normal flow of program operation such that processing can be resumed from that point. Interrupts are usually the result of signals from an external device which diverts the attention of the processor from the primary operation being handled. An example of an inter-rupt would be a word-processing program temporarily halting the printing of a document due to an out of paper signal generated by the printer.

inverse—Refers to the printing of characters in a mode opposite to that normally used. On a video display, normal operation prints white on a black background, and inverse prints black on white. Some printers are also capable of printing inverse characters. These are white on a solid black background.

italics—A type font in which the letters usually slope to the right, used for emphasis or to set a particular portion of a document apart from the rest of the text.

justification—The process of adjusting printed lines to exactly fit predetermined margins. The method used by most word-processing programs is to place the first printed character on the left margin, the last one on the right, and add spaces between words to make the line fit exactly (this is called word spacing). Some printers are capable of varying the spaces between characters and can use a combination of character and word spacing for justification. Although justification is usually interpreted as filling complete lines, some programs have commands to justify left, right, center, or about a decimal point. See also flush.

K—Commonly used abbreviation for kilo, a prefix meaning one thousand. In computer usage, K means 1024. For instance, 4K memory capacity means 4096 bytes.

keyboard—The portion of a terminal or computer equipped with a typewriter arrangement of switches. The keyboard is the primary input and control device for most microcomputers. Most microcomputer keyboards follow the standard QWERTY arrangement and closely resemble those of office typewriters. See also QWERTY keyboard.

keystroke—A single depression of a key on a computer keyboard. Some programs use multi-

keyboard. The Apple II keyboard closely resembles that of a standard office typewriter.

ple keystrokes for specific control and utility functions.

KSR—Abbreviation for keyboard send and receive unit, a printer device equipped with a keyboard and capable of being used as a terminal.

language—A system of vocabulary and rules of syntax used to enter instructions. Computer languages are either low level, such as machine language, or high level, such as BASIC or FORTRAN. Word processing has a language of its own in which many terms and operation descriptions have become standardized.

letterhead—Bond paper on which a name and address are printed. Often a company name, identifying logo, or other extras are added. Most businesses, and many individuals, consider their letterhead extremely important in conveying a positive impression to the recipient of their correspondence.

letter-quality printer—Traditionally refers to a printer which uses fully formed characters and produces very high quality print. Also known as

formed character printer or correspondence-quality printer. Letter-quality printers are more often known by the type of character element used for printing, such as a daisy wheel printer. Some dot-matrix printers are capable of producing letter-quality print using overstriking or dense matrix techniques.

license—An agreement required by some program suppliers that grants you permission to use a program on a specific computer for a designated purpose. The purpose of licensing arrangements is to prevent unauthorized copying or dissemination of a program. In return for agreeing to the nondisclosure terms, you are often granted the right to make back-up copies of the program for protection of your data and operational continuity.

light pen—A high speed photosensitive computer peripheral which can be used as a direct input device. The name is quite descriptive, because most light pens resemble a ball-point pen with a lens at one end and a cord attached to the computer at the other. In practical use, the light pen may be touched to a particular area of a video display screen for purposes such as selecting menu options or directing cursor movements.

line—A single, printed line of text.

line number—In computer applications, refers to an integer preceding a program line which determines the order of storage and execution of the lines. Some word-processing programs use line numbers to order and manipulate the text. Line-oriented word-processing programs are much less common than those which are character oriented.

Line printer—A high speed printer that produces a full line of text at a time, rather than printing character by character. Usually the characters are contained on a continuous band or chain, although some line printers use lasers, ink jets, or other advanced technology. Line printers are rarely used in microcomputer-based word-processing systems because of their prohibitive cost.

line spacing—Usually refers to the center-to-center space between lines on a printed page. More often described in terms of the number of lines per inch. An accepted standard has been six lines per inch, but some printers used in word-processing applications are capable of printing eight. Also used to refer to the number of blank lines between each printed line: single spacing leaves no blank line, double spacing one, triple spacing two, and so on.

link—A pointer contained in some data structures which identifies the next item in that structure. As implemented in microcomputer word-processing systems, links are used at the beginning or end of a text file to join files for printing or editing purposes. Links may also be used separately to specify several files for printing or editing.

LOAD—The command used by some computers to read a program or file from disk or tape into the computer's memory. A similar command is used by some word-processing programs to retrieve files from disk storage.

lock—Usually refers to unique features incorporated into a program to prevent unauthorized copying or listing of the actual program lines (program lock). LOCK, as a computer command, is used to prevent accidental overwriting or deletion of a disk file.

logic seeking—A method of increasing printer throughout by printing only the portion of a line which actually contains characters. Blank spaces are ignored and the next line of printed characters is initiated immediately after the last character on a line is printed. This eliminates the need for a printhead or carriage to travel the entire length of a line to print only a few characters.

loop—In computer usage, loop refers to a series of instructions which are executed many times for a set number of times. Accidental continuous loops will repeat indefinitely.

lowercase—Refers to small letters, as opposed to capitals (uppercase).

LPM—Abbreviation for lines per minute, a measure of the speed of a printer.

machine language—The operating language of a computer. Machine-language instructions are recorded in a form which is directly usable by the computer, as opposed to higher level language instructions which must be translated by the computer prior to actually being executed. Programs written in machine language are usually more memory efficient and operate faster than those in other languages.

mailing list—In computer terms, refers to a data base management system that incorporates name, address, and other pertinent information regarding several individuals. Mailing list management programs are often included as a part of word-processing systems or may be purchased separately. The format for data contained in a mailing list management system is fairly rigidly defined.

mainframe—In a traditional sense, refers to the main part of a computer. More commonly used to

mailing list. Mailing list information management capabilities are included in many word-processing programs. The format shown here has been designed using the Electronic Card File system found in The Executive Secretary.

describe larger computer systems which support the use of multiple peripherals and remote terminals.

margin—The area on a page which is left unprinted. Commonly defined in terms of location: top, bottom, left, and right. The effect of margins is that of creating a plain border around the printed text.

mass storage—Any means of storing data outside the main memory of a computer. In microcomputing applications, refers to tape or disk storage systems.

matrix—A tabular arrangement of elements. Number matrices are used for mathematical operations. Wires in a printhead may also be arranged in a matrix, commonly referred to as a dot-matrix configuration.

medium—In computer terms, refers to a specific material on which data can be stored. Magnetic tapes or disks are common storage mediums.

memory—Any device into which information can be copied, held, and retrieved at a later time. Common computer usage defines memory as that which is contained in the computer itself, as opposed to storage which is external. Computer memory can be divided into two broad categories: RAM (Random Access Memory) which can be read from or written to by the user and ROM (Read Only Memory) which can only be read from and cannot be changed by the user during ordinary computer operations.

menu—The display of a number of options from

menu. The title page and main selection menu of Super-Text allows the user to designate the operation desired.

which the user selects the one desired. Program menus are often constructed on several levels, each more specific than the last.

merge—To combine two or more parts into a new entity. In word-processing applications, usually refers to the capability to copy text from one document file to another.

microcomputer—In a broad sense, a computer which uses a microprocessor chip in its CPU. More commonly, used to describe any small computer.

microprocessor—An integrated circuit central processing unit (CPU) which is limited, by design, to handling significantly smaller words (bytes) than a full sized CPU. Microprocessors are designed to handle 8 (and are being introduced for 16) bytes, whereas full sized computers are capable of using up to 64-byte words.

mini-floppy disk—Commonly refers to a flexible storage disk which is 5-and-¼ inches in diameter. See also floppy disk.

modem—Abbreviation for modulator/demodulator, a device which converts data from a form compatible with computers to a form usable with transmission facilities and vice versa. Primarily used in telecomputing applications. Usually described in terms of the method of coupling to a telephone line, either acoustic or direct coupled.

module—An add-on capability or interchangeable element which is offered for a particular program or system. Word-processing programs may offer mailing list or form letter modules as separate entities which may be added later.

monitor—Most commonly refers to a specially designed type of CRT (cathode ray tube) display unit capable of accepting and displaying composite video output from a computer. Also refers to a supervisory program used primarily to control the operation of other programs or the computer itself.

move—The ability of a word-processing program to shift characters or groups of characters from one position in a document to another.

multistrike ribbon—A type of film ribbon designed for more than a single printing pass. Usually yields both high quality printing and longer life than single strike film ribbons.

nonembedded command—A program instruction which is acted upon immediately. Some examples of nonembedded commands include insert, delete, and move.

nonimpact printer—A type of printer that uses heat, electrostatic charge, laser light, or ink jets to create marks on paper. Some types of nonimpact printers require the use of a specially coated paper.

nonvolatile storage—Storage medium on which data is not lost due to power failure. Cassette tapes and disk are forms of nonvolatile storage.

normal—In one sense, refers to the usual video display mode of white characters on a black background.

off-line—A mode of operation in which peripheral equipment is used independently of the central processing unit (CPU).

on-line—A mode of operation which is directly involved with the CPU.

operating system—A collection of utility routines for supervising the operation of a computer or peripheral. Disk operating systems, for instance, manage the operations of disk-based storage.

operator—In one sense, a symbol which designates what operation is to be performed. Mathematical operators, for instance, direct operation of the five basic mathematical functions (add, subtract, multiply, divide, raise to a power). In some word-processing contexts, refers to a person specially trained to operate word-processing equipment.

optical character recognition—A special hardware unit designed to convert typed material into a form directly usable by a computer. The application potential of optical character recognition to word processing but has not been widely developed.

options—In a computer program, options provide you with flexibility to personalize the program to your particular application and system capabilities. Options are usually selected through the use of a program menu.

orphan—See dangling line.

output—Data received from the computer as a result of program manipulation of input data. Also refers to the final documents or other information produced by the action of a word-processing system.

overstrike—Printing over a character with the same or a different character for the purpose of making the combination stand out from the surrounding text or producing a character not normally available on a given printer. Often the second printing is done at a position slightly offset from the first to create a fuller or more completely formed character. This technique is used to produce letter-quality print from some dot-matrix units.

page—In computer usage, a unit used to allocate memory or partition programs. Usually refers to the amount of data that can be displayed on the video screen at one time. Word-processing usage refers to a page as the amount of printed material that fits on a single sheet of paper.

pagination—The process of dividing a text file into printed pages. Most word-processing systems automatically handle pagination chores according to page size parameters set by the operator. Some method of overriding automatic pagination is provided, usually by commands embedded in the text.

paging—Movement of text on a video display by complete pages through the use of the "next page" and "previous page" command incorporated into the word-processing program.

paragraph—A collection of words and lines that comprises a complete thought. The beginning of each paragraph in a text file is signaled by a return or special paragraph command. Many word-processing systems feature a paragraph command which automatically inserts a designated number of spaces prior to accepting text input (paragraph indentation).

parallel—Usually refers to a method of interfacing a printer which transmits or receives data character by character rather than bit by bit. Computer usage of the term refers to the simultaneous storage or transmission of all bits comprising a character or word in storage location.

parameter—A definable characteristic of a system, item, or device.

Pascal—A computer programming language that stresses a structured approach. Named after Blaise Pascal, this language is rapidly gaining acceptance in microcomputing circles. Several word-processing programs are written in Pascal.

peripheral—A device, intended to serve a specific function, that is attached to a computer. Common microcomputer peripherals include disk drives, printers, modems, and video display units.

personal computer—A computer devoted primarily to personal use. The term is widely used to refer to microcomputers, although the largest mainframe could qualify, if it were dedicated to personal use.

personalization—Used to denote hardware or program capabilities that meet the user's operational requirements. Also, some programs are personalized by entering data unique to the user.

phototypesetting—A process of preparing text for reproduction by actually photographing the original. The resulting negative is used to prepare a reproduction master. Any character fonts or figures that can be photographed can be used in the production process.

pica—In the past, this term referred only to the larger of the two commonly available typewriter print sizes. More recent usage has expanded the term to include all type sizes that contain ten characters to the inch. Also known as "10 pitch."

pin feed—A method of paper handling that uses sprocketlike pins to move paper which has holes punched on either side. The paper used is fanfold sheets or continuous rolls. Most types of paper are designed for easy removal of the pin feed holes after printing is completed. Pin feed (also known as tractor feed) systems are generally acknowledged to be more precise than the commonly used methods of friction feeding paper.

platen—A rubber coated cylinder against which the paper is placed in a typewriter or printer. In addition to helping move the paper through the printer, the platen provides a suitable surface for creating character impressions through the action of a printhead or typing element.

point—A standardized measure used in printing applications to specify type sizes and spacing. There are 72 points to the inch.

pointer—See link.

preview—A capability included in some word-processing programs which allows you to visualize what the printed text will look like by seeing it on the video display. Printed page parameters are used in this mode, although the screen may not be capable of showing all the characters included. Most preview modes allow you to specify a movable "window" with which to examine portions of the printed text.

PRINT—A computer command which causes characters to be displayed on the video screen or printed. Also used by some word-processing programs to initiate printing operations.

print format—See format.

print image file—A text file containing text already formatted and ready for final printing.

print intensity—Refers to the amount of force with which a character strikes the paper. Some printers allow you to adjust the print intensity to compensate for the number of copies contained in multiple part forms.

print quality—A measure, often subjective, of the clarity and readability of characters generated by a printer. Although there is no universal standard for print quality, characters are often compared to perfectly formed characters such as those found in some typewriter fonts.

printer—A peripheral device which produces hard copies of a computer's output. In some cases, the printer is combined with a keyboard to form a terminal. The variety of printers available to microcomputer uses ranges from inexpensive, draft-quality to sophisticated letter-quality graphic reproduction units.

printhead—Usually refers to the part of a printer which contains a dot-matrix arrangement of wires, holes, or screen and is actually involved in the production of characters. Sometimes used in a broader sense to include the character-producing part of a printer or typewriter.

printwheel—A common term for the daisy wheel, thimble, or other character element used in certain printers.

program—A set of instructions which direct a computer's operations. Can also be used as a verb, meaning the actual process of assembling the necessary instructions. In word-processing applications, program can also refer to the ability of some programs to respond to a long series of sequential instructions from the operator.

program package—Refers to the documentation, disks, reference materials, and other information received when purchasing a particular program.

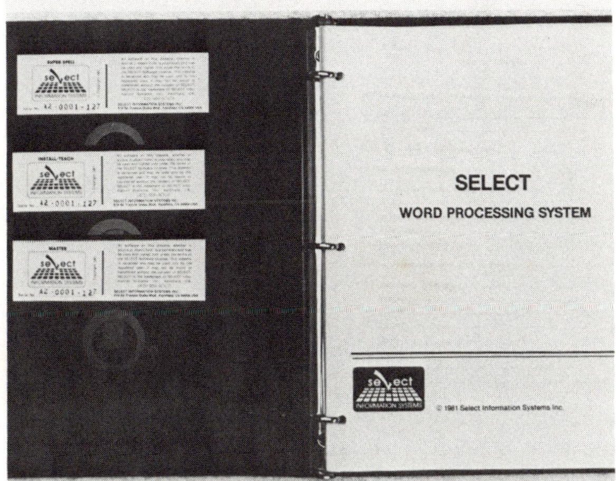

program package. The Select word-processing program package includes three disks, user's manual, reference materials, and other pertinent information.

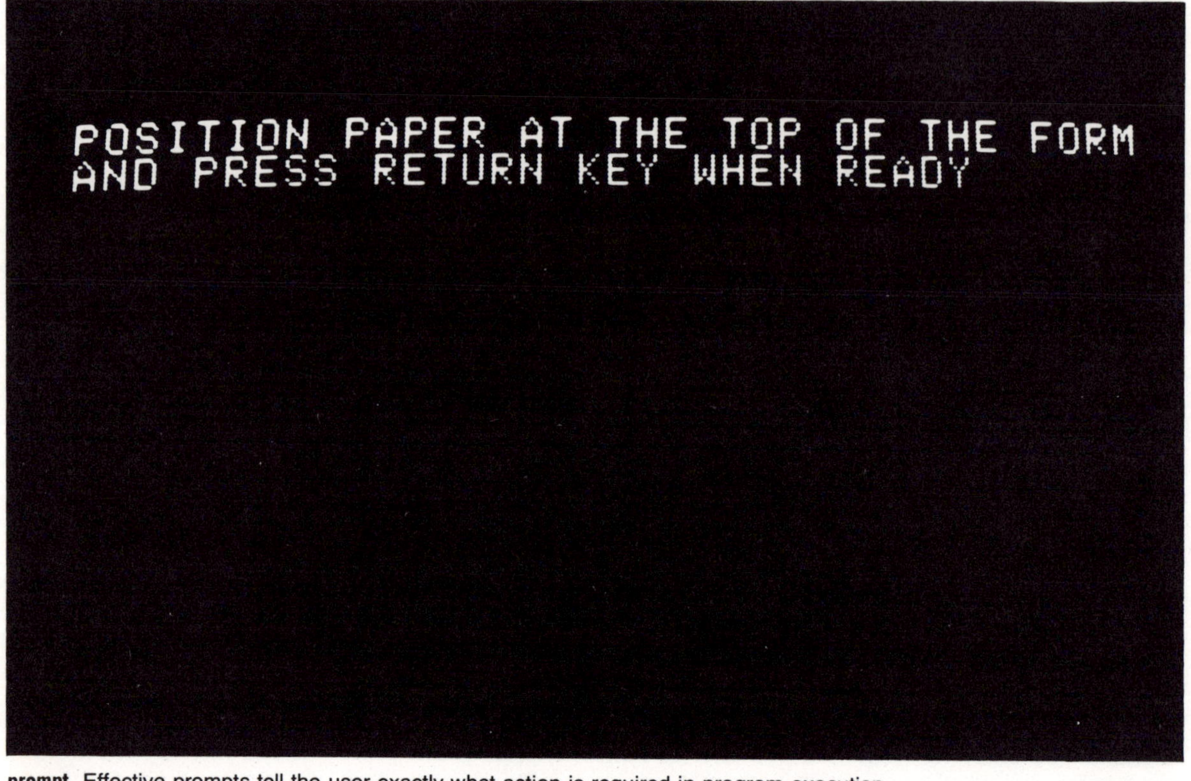

prompt. Effective prompts tell the user exactly what action is required in program execution.

prompt—A statement printed by the computer to inform the operator that some action is now required. Effective prompts inform the operator exactly what type of response is expected, for instance, "FILE NAME?" or "NUMBER OF COPIES?" One of the best measures of the user friendliness of a program is the quality and clarity of its prompts.

proofreading—Comparing a draft copy against a document for the purpose of correcting errors in spelling, punctuation, capitalization, etc.

proportional spacing—A feature found in some printers which varies the spacing between characters according to the size of the adjacent characters. Many proportional spacing printers are also capable of infinitely varying intercharacter spaces, a definite advantage in achieving nicely justified text. A few of the presently available word-processing programs are capable of using infinitely proportional spacing features.

protected field—An area on a video display that cannot be altered by the operator, usually used for input prompts or descriptive information needed for the operation in progress. The capability of creating and using protected fields is referred to as Format mode. See also format.

queue—A series of items waiting for a particular operation in a word-processing program. A printing queue, for instance, contains the names of files or items to be printed in sequence.

Qume—The trade name for a printing mechanism using a high speed, interchangeable print wheel. Often used generically to describe all printers having a similar mechanism.

QWERTY keyboard—A term used to designate

the standard typewriter keyboard. The name comes from the arrangement of some of the keys. Most microcomputers use this type of keyboard arrangement.

ragged left—A type of print formatting in which the lines are aligned with the right margin. See ragged right.

ragged right—A type of print formatting in which the lines are aligned with the left margin, leaving the line ends "ragged" on the right side of the page. Unless justification is selected, most word-processing systems will automatically produce printed output in this format.

RAM—See memory.

random access file—A type of file containing a number of records of equal size. Primarily used in applications requiring ready access to specific parts of the file. Text files used in word processing are not usually of the random access variety, although mailing list items often are.

read—The process of retrieving data from an external storage medium. Reading a disk, for instance, places a copy of the material on the disk into the computer's memory.

real time clock—A computer circuit or peripheral that provides periodic signals allowing the computer to measure actual time between events. A few word-processing systems use real time information, but this capability is rare in microcomputer-based systems.

record—In computer usage, a record is a group of related facts or data. Groups of records are assembled into a file. There are many other uses of this word, depending on the context.

reenter—A prompt used by a program to allow you the opportunity of correcting input that was judged to result in an error condition. See also error trapping.

reformat—Modification of document lines to fit within specified page parameters. Some word-processing programs will automatically reformat documents, while others require the user to verify changes.

refresh—The process of rewriting characters on a video display. This is done automatically by the computer and takes place 60 times per second. Due to extreme rapidity of refreshing, the screen appears to display the characters continuously.

relative—This term is used in word-processing programs to denote one condition that is dependent on another. For instance, some of the programs mentioned in this book feature chapter-relative page numbering and paragraph indentation relative to the left margin.

reliability—The ability of a computer system or program to function without failure over an extended period of time.

remark—A descriptive statement that can be added to file names in some word-processing programs. Remarks are also used in computer programming to insert nonoperational text into program lines.

rename—Most computer operating systems and word-processing programs allow the user to change the name of a file or document with a rename command.

renumber—Word-processing programs that use line numbers usually include a provision for the user to change line numbers with this command. Computer programs are also altered through the use of a similar command found in most programming languages.

replace—A capability found in most word-processing systems that replaces a specified group of characters with another. Where this feature is found, the user is allowed to designate which occurrences of the specified group are to be replaced. See also global change.

required character—One which must be present for a specific operation to take place in a word-processing program, such as a RETURN signaling the first line of a paragraph.

RESET—A key found on most computers which, when pressed, causes immediate and unconditional termination of any program or process in progress.

resolution—In graphics applications, refers to the number of points per square inch that can be displayed or plotted. Printers capable of reproducing graphics are rated in terms of the number of points per square inch they print and their smallest increment of paper movement.

response time—In time-sharing systems, the length of time required for the computer to react to a user command. Also used to measure the amount of time required for a computer to initiate an operation once the proper instructions have been given.

RETURN—Used to designate the RETURN or ENTER key found on most computer keyboards. On typewriters, RETURN causes the carriage to return to the left margin of the paper.

reverse printing—In a strict sense, refers to the printing of characters from right to left on a page. More often used to describe a bidirectional printer.

reverse video—See inverse.

revision—The process of changing the text in a stored document. Revision may be minimal (changing a character or two) or major (changing significant portions of the document). One of the measures of the effectiveness of a word-processing program is the ease with which revisions can be made.

RF converter—Also known as an RF modulator, this is a device which takes the composite video output of the computer and converts it to a modulated radio frequency (RF) signal that can be received by a standard television set tuned to the proper channel. The television set then functions as a video display device for the computer. This method of display is used by many of the popular personal computers.

ribbon—An inked cloth or carbon film spool or cartridge used on impact printers to transfer the image of a character to paper.

ROM—See memory.

rough copy—See draft.

RUN—A computer command used to initiate the execution of a program.

SAVE—In computer usage, used to store a program or data file on tape or disk. Most word-processing programs use a variation of the SAVE command to initiate the storage of a text file on disk.

scale—A series of measurement marks used to aid in the determination of page parameters or values represented by data. Some word-processing programs include a scale to assist the user in obtaining the desired final results from printing operations and aligning printed characters to predefined spaces on forms.

scan—The process of searching through memory or external storage for a specific item.

scrolling—The process by which new lines are displayed on a video screen. Most video displays feature vertical scrolling which adds new lines at the bottom and deletes one line at the top for each new line added. Some systems also allow for horizontal scrolling, allowing characters to move from right to left across the screen.

search—The ability of a word-processing program to locate a specific character or group of characters. Most programs allow for search operations in the forward (from the present point toward the end of the file) and reverse direction. This capability is usually combined with replace. See also global change and global search.

sector—The smallest addressable portion of a track on a floppy disk. Allocation and management of sectors on a disk is automatically handled by the computer's disk operating system (DOS).

security—Refers to the measures taken to prevent unauthorized access to data or computer programs. Also used to describe the relative safety of data once it has been stored in text files on a mass storage device.

serial—A method of printer operation in which one character is printed at a time. Also refers to a method of data transmission where information is transferred one bit at a time.

serial access file—A file in which data must be read or written from the beginning to the end.

Data is arranged so that each item of information is stored immediately after the preceding item. Most text files contained in word-processing documents are of the serial access type. Also known as sequential access files.

shadow printing—A technique used to overprint characters for the purpose of generating boldface type. The printing position for the second pass is offset very slightly from the first to make the lines comprising the characters appear thicker. Sometimes the characters resulting from this method of printing are referred to as emphasized characters.

shift—A key found on computer and typewriter keyboards which is used to change from lower- to uppercase letters. Special modifications are sometimes needed to make a computer's shift key operational for word-processing purposes.

single space—Generally accepted as six printed or typed lines per inch. In a broader sense, text in which every available line is printed. The latter definition would be more appropriate for use with word-processing printers, since some are capable of printing eight or more lines per inch.

single strike ribbon—See film ribbon.

software—A general term which encompasses all the programs used to operate a computer. The opposite term, hardware, refers to the actual electrical or mechanical components of a computer system. See also program.

sort—The ability to assemble information in a specified order. For example, information can be sorted by zip code, state, last name, and so on.

space and a half—Generally refers to printed or typed text containing four lines per inch.

spelling check program—A program designed to examine the contents of a text file for spelling or typographical errors. Words in the file are compared against a dictionary contained in the spelling check system. Those that do not match are flagged for correction, addition to the dictionary, or other disposition. Grammatical usage is not evaluated by most spelling check programs.

Some programs contain specialized dictionaries for various professions, and almost all offer the opportunity to expand and modify the dictionary to suit specific purposes.

split-screen—An editing feature found in some word-processing programs. The text being edited is displayed on half of the screen, the original text on the other. This capability is useful in situations where any changes must be carefully compared to the original text.

stand-alone system—A computer or word-processing system capable of functioning independently of other systems or system compo-

spelling check program. Spellguard is one of the best known spelling check programs for CP /M-based word-processing systems."

nents. A microcomputer word-processing system is usually thought of as a stand-alone system because it does not share peripherals, even though they may be external to the computer itself.

STOP—A command used in BASIC (and some other programming languages) which causes a program to cease execution and display the line number containing the command. Program execution may be resumed from that point with a CONTINUE command. Many word-processing programs use similar capabilities to allow the operator to change print elements, adjust paper, or make other changes. When used in this fashion, the command is usually called STOP, or PAUSE.

store—See SAVE.

subscript—In word-processing applications, refers to a numeral or symbol printed slightly below the normal line of text. Also refers to a number (or numbers) enclosed in parentheses following a variable name describing a specific location in a data array.

superscript—A numeral or symbol which is printed slightly above the normal line of text.

syntax—A system of vocabulary and punctuation rules governing the structure of a computer program. Word-processing programs may also develop their own syntax for operations once the program has been loaded into the computer.

system—In a broad sense, refers to the hardware, software, personnel, and procedures necessary to accomplish a desired operation. A word-processing system for microcomputers may not require much more than just the program, since the computer and associated necessary hardware will probably be used for several different applications.

tab—The ability to move the cursor (or printhead) to any preselected position on the screen. In a traditional sense, tab refers only to horizontal movements. Some word-processing programs also allow for the designation and use of vertical tabs. See also horizontal tab.

tape drive—A mass storage device which uses tape cassettes or reels as the medium for storage and retrieval of text and data files. Most microcomputer tape drives are of the inexpensive, home use variety.

telecomputing—A technique whereby numerous terminal devices can utilize a central computer concurrently for input, processing, and output operations. The most common way of accessing the central computer is through the telephone lines, hence the term telecomputing. You can equip your microcomputer with a modem and the software necessary for this purpose.

ten pitch—See pica.

terminal—Refers to an input-output device capable of transmitting data to and receiving data from the computer system of which it is a part. Most personal computers can serve as either intelligent (memory and processing capability) or dumb (input-output only) terminals.

text—In a broad sense, refers to all the output from a word-processing system. Also used to denote the main body of a document, separate from illustrations or attachments. Computer users refer to the alphanumeric information contained on a video display as text, the opposite of which is graphics.

text editor—A system used for revising computer programs. Often the term is interchanged with word processing, although there are very distinct differences between the two types of systems.

text file—Also known as a data file. Used to store nonprogram information in a mass storage medium. Text files are created, retrieved, and used through appropriate program commands. In word processing, a text file is often used to designate a complete document stored on tape or disk.

text string—A sequence of characters and spaces used for a specific purpose, usually find and re-

```
]Most word processing programs have
some method of allowing the user to set
tab stops and indentation.  Super-Text,
in this example, uses a tab control
line for this purpose.  For instance:

]5,10,15,20
]
]sets tabs at five character intervals
from the left margin.  To use the tab
settings, one can specify CTRL-L (L)
which left justifies, or CTRL-R (R)
which right justifies on the tab stop.

]In addition to the tab stops, a
standard paragraph indentation may be
specified in a format line.  Each time
CTRL-P is encountered, the next line
starts the specified number of spaces
from the left margin and the first
character of the new line is
automatically capitalized.
PSee?
```

tab. Horizontal tabbing capabilities are included in virtually every word-processing program.

place operations within a word-processing program.

thermal printer—A type of printer that makes impressions on specially coated paper through the use of heat. Most thermal printers use a dot-matrix arrangement of wires which apply an instantaneous burst of heat to form characters, as opposed to the ribbon used by most other impact printers.

thimble—A type of printing element used by some formed character printers. The thimble itself resembles a tulip with characters on the petals. Operation of thimble printers is quite similar to those which use daisy wheel print elements.

time sharing—In microcomputing applications, the term is used interchangeably with telecomputing. Also refers to the use of any computer or peripheral device by several users concurrently, Few microcomputers are capable of performing as hosts for time-sharing operations, but almost all can be configured to be users of such a system. See also telecomputing, terminal.

touch—Refers to the mechanical feel and use comfort of a keyboard. Computer keyboards are frequently compared to the touch of a quality typewriter and described in those terms.

touch control—An adjustment found on many typewriters permitting the operator to alter the sensitivity of the keyboard to suit individual taste. Such controls are rarely, if ever, found on computer keyboards.

touch sensitive—A type of video display capable of sensing pressure anywhere on the screen, making it easy for the operator to select menu options. Although not yet readily available for microcomputers, such features are likely to be forthcoming in the near future.

track—On a disk used for mass storage, a number of concentric circles are defined by the DOS. Each circle is called a track and is divided into smaller units known as sectors.

tractor feed—See pin feed.

triple space—Commonly refers to two typed or printed lines per inch.

tutorial—In a broad sense, refers to an individualized instructional program about a specific topic. Commonly refers to a program of interactive instruction contained on a program or data disk. Many word-processing programs include tutorial files to familiarize the operator with all facets of program operation. See also help file.

twelve pitch—See elite.

typebar—The traditional method of producing characters from a typewriter, where each key presses an individual arm containing both the upper- and lowercase character. Also known as a "basket."

typeface—See font.

typing height—A measure of the distance from floor to the top of a stand or desk used for keyboard applications. This is commonly about three inches lower than the top of a desk.

underscoring—The automatic underlining of designated groups of characters by a word-processing system. Commonly referred to as underlining.

UNLOCK—In disk operating systems, this command allows the user to remove previously imposed restrictions against writing to or deleting a specific file. The capability of setting disk file restrictions is not commonly included in word-processing programs, although the actual program is probably in a locked file on the disk.

update—Refers to the procedures used to modify a file for the purpose of incorporating current information. Frequently used as a verb to describe the actual process used. Text files are routinely updated by word-processing programs. Some programs automatically keep track of the most recent date and time the file was revised.

uppercase—The capital letters of a character font, as opposed to the small (lowercase) letters.

user—The person who actually operates a program or system. In most microcomputing applications, the computer owner and operator are one and the same.

user friendliness—The degree to which a program or system provides for the capabilities and limitations of the operator. Easy to understand menus, helpful prompts and concise operational terms are but a few of the components of user friendliness.

users' group—An organization comprised of individuals who share a common interest either through owning similar computer systems or using their computers in similar applications. Most groups are formed for the purpose of exchanging information. Microcomputer user groups are generally very beneficial to the novice user of a system. Your local dealer may be able to provide some information on groups in your area. Larger groups frequently publish newsletters as a method of exchanging information.

user's manual—A book supplied with a word-processing program that outlines the operational details of the program. Often, the manual includes tutorial material designed to help the user take advantage of all the features included in the program. Comprehensive manuals should also include error recovery techniques, operational limitations, and other information that may be needed during the course of program use. See also documentation, help file, tutorial.

utility—A program or function within a program that provides for operations outside the normal course of system operation. Computer utilities include disk management routines, number base conversions, and sorting routines. Word-processing programs include utility routines for adjusting default parameters, system maintenance, and peripheral functions.

utility typing—A term used to designate typing not routinely done by word processing, such as addressing an envelope, typing a short response to a letter, or filling in a form.

variable—In computer applications, this is a data item that assumes different values during the execution of a program. Form letter programs frequently allow the user to designate variables for specific items contained in a mailing list or data file.

VDT—Abbreviation for video display terminal, another way of designating a unit which contains at least a CRT (cathode ray tube) and keyboard.

VERIFY—A command available in some versions of BASIC that allows the user to check the accuracy of information contained in mass storage files. Also a prompt used by some programs to double-check before initiating a potentially disastrous operation, such as deleting a file.

vertical scrolling—See scrolling.

vertical tab—See tab.

video display—The display of the output from a computer on the face of a cathode ray tube (CRT). This may be accomplished through the use of a specially constructed terminal, composite video output displayed on a monitor, or RF modulated signals shown on a standard television receiver.

voice grade line—Refers to a telephone circuit which has been judged to meet the specifications for standard voice grade communication. In most instances, voice grade lines are used for relatively low speed data communications with good reliability.

voice input—The control of specific computer functions by the spoken word.

voice synthesis—Digital generation of approximations of the sounds of human speech. This is an area undergoing rapid development. Conceivably, conversational output from the computer will be used in place of printed messages on the screen.

volatile storage—Memory in which data becomes lost when power is removed. RAM, unless protected by a back-up battery or power system, is usually volatile.

volume—Usually refers to a single item of mass storage media that contains documents. Each volume contains a directory identifying its contents.

WAIT—A command allowing the computer programmer to insert a conditional pause into a program. For word-processing users, this wait may be for the purpose of changing disks, print elements, or adjusting paper. See also STOP.

widow—See dangling line.

"wild card" character—A nonspecific character used in search operations. Any printable character will match with that designated as a "wild card" character.

Winchester disk—A type of hard disk storage system in which the sensitive mechanical components and disks are totally sealed to prevent the entry of contaminants. Since the actual storage elements are not removable, Winchester disk units usually include a provision to create back-up files on floppy disks or cassette tapes.

window—Usually refers to a text window, the area on a video screen that is used to display and scroll text. Some microcomputers and word-processing programs allow you to modify the size and location of the window for the purpose of viewing selected portions of the text contained in the computer's memory.

word—What we are talking about processing.

word processing—A computerized approach to putting words on paper in a more efficient and accurate fashion.

word-processing center—Any place where you put your computer, printer, and all the necessary paraphernalia necessary to do the job.

wraparound—The ability of word-processing system to automatically move a word to the next line if it will cause the line to exceed the preselected right margin.

x-y plotter—A hard copy device capable of plotting points along either or both of two axes. Used in conjunction with a computer, the x-y plotter may be used to plot coordinate points in the form of a graph or line drawing. Some of the newest printers will essentially duplicate the action of an x-y plotter, permitting graphic displays to be intermingled with text in a document file.

xerographic printer—A type of computer printer that operates on the same principle as a xerographic copier. Speed and quality of copy are characteristic of this type of printer, although the cost is prohibitive for most microcomputer applications at this time.

zap—The colloquial term used to describe the removal of data from the memory of a computer.

zone—See hot zone.

Sources of Information

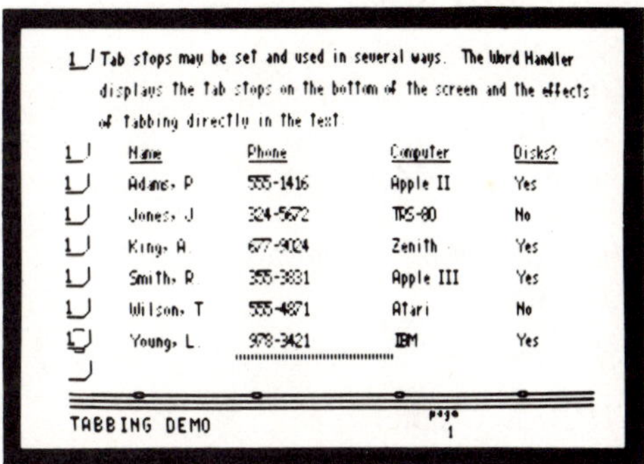

Sources of Information

The following publications provide information about computers and word-processing systems.

PERIODICALS

Many computer-oriented periodicals feature reviews, new product announcements, and articles regarding word-processing programs. Although many periodicals are published, the following may be of some interest to you. After each periodical name is given the publications specific computer emphasis (if any).

BUSS: Independent Newsletters of Heath Co. Computers (Heath/Zenith)
716 East Street, S.E.
Washington, DC 20003

BYTE (General)
P.O. Box 590
Martinsville, NJ 08836

Call -A.P.P.L.E. (Apple)
304 Main Avenue South, Suite 300
Renton, WA 98055

CLOAD Magazine, Inc.   (TRS-80)
P.O. Box 1267
Goleta, CA 93017

COMPUTE (6502-based computers)
P.O. Box 5406
Greensboro, NC 27403

Creative Computing (General)
P.O. Box 789-M
Morristown, NJ 07960

Cursor (PET, CBM)
Box 550
Goleta, CA 93017

Desktop Computing (General)
P.O. Box 917
Farmingdale, NY 11737

InfoWorld (General, published weekly)
375 Cochituate Road
Box 880
Framingham, MA 01701

Interface Age (General)
16704 Marquardt Avenue
Cerritos, CA 90701

MICRO (6502-based computers)
P.O. Box 6502
Chelmsford, MA 01824

Microcomputing (General)
P.O. Box 997
Farmingdale, NY 11737

NIBBLE (Apple)
Micro-Sparc, Inc.
P.O. Box 325
Lincoln, MA 01773

PEEK (65) (OSI)
62 Southgate Avenue
Annapolis, MD 21401

Personal Computing (General)
1050 Commonwealth Avenue
Boston, MA 02215

SoftSide (Apple, Atari, TRS-80)
515 Abbot Drive
Broomall, PA 19008

SOFTALK (Apple)
11021 Magnolia Boulevard
North Hollywood, CA 91601

Word Processing News: A Writer's POV on Word Processing.
1765 N. Highland Avenue
Hollywood, CA 90028

BOOKS

New books on microcomputers and word processing are appearing at a rapid rate. Check your local computer store, or contact some of the publishers listed below:

dilithium Press
11000 S.W. 11th Street #E
Beaverton, OR 97005

Hayden Book Company, Inc.
50 Essex Street
Rochelle Park, NJ 07662

Howard W. Sams & Co., Inc.
2310 West 62nd Street
Indianapolis, IN 46206

Microcomputer Applications
P.O. Box E
Suisun City, CA 94585

Prentice-Hall, Inc.
Englewood Cliffs, NJ 07632

QUE Corporation
6515 East 82nd Street
Suite 110
Indianapolis, IN 46250

TAB Books, Inc.
Blue Ridge Summit, PA 17214

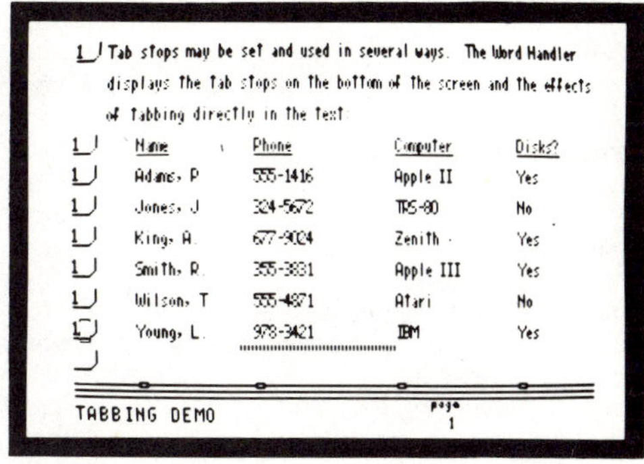

Tab stops may be set and used in several ways. The Word Handler
displays the tab stops on the bottom of the screen and the effects
of tabbing directly in the text.
Name   Phone   Computer   Disks?
Adams, P   555-1416   Apple II   Yes
Jones, J   324-5672   TRS-80   No
King, A.   677-9004   Zenith   Yes
Smith, R.   555-3831   Apple III   Yes
Wilson, T   555-4871   Atari   No
Young, L.   978-3421   IBM   Yes
TABBING DEMO   page
                                        1

Index

NOTICES

Apple DOS 3.2, Apple DOS 3.3, Applesoft, Apple II, Apple II Plus, Apple III, and Apple Writer are registered trademarks of Apple Computer Corp.

Apple Speller is a registered trademark of Sensible Software

Benchmark Mail List and Benchmark Word Processor are registered trademarks of Metasoft Corp.

CP/M is a registered trademark of Digital Research, Inc.

Dot Plot Graphics is a registered trademark of Integral Data Systems, Inc.

EasyMailer Professional System, EasyMover, EasyWriter Professional System, and EasyWriter II are registered trademarks of Information Unlimited Software, Inc.

Editrix 1.0 and Graphtrix 1.3 are registered trademarks of Data Transforms

Electric Pencil is a registered trademark of IJG Computer Services

The Executive Secretary is a registered trademark of Sof/Sys, Inc.

The Final Word, Mince, and Scribble are registered trademarks of Mark of the Unicorn

GrafixPLUS is a registered trademark of Anadex, Inc.

Letter Master, LetteRite, and Report Writer are distributed by Monument Computer Service

Letter Perfect and Data Perfect are registered trademarks of LJK Enterprises

Magic Wand, Magic Spell, Magic Messenger, and Magic Address are registered trademarks of Peachtree Software Incorporated

Magic Window, Magic Words, and Magic Mailer are registered trademarks of ARTSCI, Inc.

Maxi Pros is a registered trademark of Aardvark Technical Services

Memorite III is a registered trademark of Vector Graphic

Newscript, Dvorak Keyboard Support, and Mailing Labels are registered trademarks of Prosoft

Northword is a registered trademark of North Star

Palantir Word Processing is a registered trademark of Designer Software

Perfect Writer, Perfect Speller, Perfect Mailer, and Perfect Sort are registered trademarks of Computer Services Corporation of America

PIE 1.5 is a registered trademark of the Software Toolworks

PIE Writer is a registered trademark of Hayden Publishing Co.

Screen Writer II is a registered trademark of On-Line Systems

Scripsit II, TRS-80 Model I, Model II, and Model III are registered trademarks of Radio Shack, a division of Tandy Corp.

Select and Superspell are registered trademarks of Select Information Systems, Inc.

Spellbinder and Spellcheck are registered trademarks Lexisoft, Inc.

Spellguard 2.0 is a registered trademark of Innovative Software Applications

Spinwriter is a registered trademark of NEC Information Systems, Inc.

Super-Text 40/80, The Address Book, Autolink, and Form Letter Module are registered trademarks of Muse Software

Text Master II is a registered trademark of Data Access Management Services

Visicalc is a registered trademark of Personal Software

Volkswriter is a registered trademark of Lifetree Software

The Word Handler is a registered trademark of Silicon Valley Systems

Wordnet 86 is a registered trademark of Monoson Microsystems, Inc.

WordPro 4 Plus is a registered trademark of Professional Software

WordStar, SpellStar, and MailMerge are registered trademarks of MicroPro International Corporation

Word III is a registered trademark of Westico

Write-On!, Write-On! IBM, and Write-On! III are registered trademarks of Datamost

Zardax is distributed in the U.S. by Action-Research Northwest